ספר תהלים קורן

The Koren Illustrated Tehillim

The Magerman Edition

Koren Publishers Jerusalem

The Koren Illustrated Tehillim
The Magerman Edition
First Hebrew/English Edition, 2020

Koren Publishers Jerusalem Ltd.
POB 4044, Jerusalem 91040, ISRAEL
POB 8531, New Milford, CT 06776, USA

www.korenpub.com

Koren Tanakh Font © 1962, 2022 Koren Publishers Jerusalem Ltd.
Koren Siddur Font and text design © 1981, 2022 Koren Publishers Jerusalem Ltd.
Translation of Psalms text © The Magerman Edition of the Koren Tanakh,
2020 Koren Publishers Jerusalem Ltd.
Illustrations © Baruch Nachshon

Tehillim, Hebrew/English, hardcover, ISBN 978-965-7767-77-1

Second printing, 2022

ספר תהלים קורן

THE KOREN ILLUSTRATED TEHILLIM

TRANSLATION BY

Rabbi Jonathan Sacks זצ״ל and Sara Daniel

INTRODUCTIONS BY

Rabbi Dr. Tzvi Hersh Weinreb

KOREN PUBLISHERS JERUSALEM

PUBLISHER'S PREFACE

Of all the books of the Tanakh, no book has brought more comfort to those in emotional pain, more joy to those celebrating, more praise and thanks to God, than *Sefer Tehillim*, the book of Psalms. It is with great pride that we present this new edition of *The Koren Tehillim*. There is something unique about a book that carries within it the words to express the gamut of human experience; our joy, gratitude, reverence, fear, sorrow and anguish; words that seem to continually speak to us in whatever time and place we find ourselves. The age-old poetry of *Tehillim* has comforted our people throughout the generations, marked our celebrations, and given voice to our ongoing conversation with God.

As always, we have incorporated the textual accuracy and aesthetic design for which Koren is renowned, but there are two significant innovations to this edition.

First, the translation by Rabbi Lord Jonathan Sacks and Mrs. Sara Daniel, collaboratively. Rabbi Sacks is perhaps the most eloquent writer of the present age on the crucial importance of religion in our lives, both personally and societally. Their collaboration brings a new, eloquent, and clear translation of the beauty of the Psalms.

Secondly, we are privileged to present the commentary of Rabbi Dr. Tzvi Hersh Weinreb. A former community rabbi, leader of the Jewish Orthodox Union for over a decade, as well as a trained and practicing psychologist, Rabbi Weinreb brings together a deeply rooted knowledge of traditional texts with a compassionate understanding of the human condition, to provide an insightful commentary that explores the specific meaning of each psalm. Why do we turn to the psalms in particular situations? What can we learn from the circumstances under which a psalm was composed? Rabbi Weinreb has created a unique analysis which aims to guide the reader in his or her search for meaning and a more profound understanding of Psalms.

In addition, an illustration by renowned artist Baruch Nachson precedes each chapter. Each of these illustrations relates to the following chapter and may serve as a visual interpretation of that chapter. The merging of beautiful typography with inspirational art has always been a signature of Koren Publishers Jerusalem and we are pleased to continue this tradition by publishing this edition of *The Koren Tehillim*.

But finally: while we recognize the universality of need of all peoples to take comfort in the Psalms of King David, we never forget that they were composed right here, in Jerusalem, three thousand years ago. We who live here today have the profound honor in walking amidst those same valleys he walked, to see the same beautiful nature he saw. We never forget the centrality of the Land of Israel, and of Judea and Jerusalem, when reading these verses.

If we have brought some comfort to the troubled, or an even greater appreciation of the beauty and depths of some of the most sublime poetry ever composed, we will be satisfied.

Matthew Miller, Publisher
Koren Jerusalem, 5781 (2020/21)

Happy is the one who does not walk in the counsel of the wicked

I face a difficult choice. Good versus Evil. How can I choose?
Will I not regret my choice of the former,
when the latter has such obvious advantages?

PSALM 1

1 Happy is the one
who does not walk in the counsel
of the wicked,
who does not stand on the path
of sinners,
who does not sit among
the jeering cynics –

אַשְׁרֵי־הָאִישׁ
אֲשֶׁר ׀ לֹא הָלַךְ בַּעֲצַת
רְשָׁעִים
וּבְדֶרֶךְ חַטָּאִים לֹא עָמָד
וּבְמוֹשַׁב לֵצִים לֹא יָשָׁב׃

2 instead, the Lord's teaching
is all his desire,
and he contemplates that teaching
day and night.

כִּי אִם בְּתוֹרַת יהוה חֶפְצוֹ
וּבְתוֹרָתוֹ יֶהְגֶּה יוֹמָם וָלָיְלָה׃

3 He is like a tree planted
on streams of water
yielding fruit in its season,
its leaves never withering –
all it produces thrives.

וְהָיָה כְּעֵץ שָׁתוּל עַל־פַּלְגֵי
מָיִם
אֲשֶׁר פִּרְיוֹ ׀ יִתֵּן בְּעִתּוֹ
וְעָלֵהוּ לֹא־יִבּוֹל
וְכֹל אֲשֶׁר־יַעֲשֶׂה יַצְלִיחַ׃

4 Not so the wicked –
they are like chaff blown away
by the wind.

לֹא־כֵן הָרְשָׁעִים
כִּי אִם־כַּמֹּץ אֲשֶׁר־תִּדְּפֶנּוּ
רוּחַ׃

5 Therefore,
the wicked will not endure judgment,
nor the sinners
among the righteous crowd.

עַל־כֵּן ׀
לֹא־יָקֻמוּ רְשָׁעִים בַּמִּשְׁפָּט
וְחַטָּאִים בַּעֲדַת צַדִּיקִים׃

6 For the Lord cares for the way
of the righteous,
while the way of the wicked
will be lost forever.

כִּי־יוֹדֵעַ יהוה דֶּרֶךְ צַדִּיקִים
וְדֶרֶךְ רְשָׁעִים תֹּאבֵד׃

I tell now of the Lord's decree: He told me, "You are My child;

this very day I fathered you

I am frightened. Powerful nations abound.
They threaten harm, particularly to Israel.
They are serious, fanatically serious.
They defy all that we hold holy. I tremble.

PSALM 2

לָמָּה רָגְשׁוּ גוֹיִם
וּלְאֻמִּים יֶהְגּוּ־רִיק׃

1 Why do the nations clamor;
why do the peoples plot futilities?

יִתְיַצְּבוּ ׀ מַלְכֵי־אֶרֶץ
וְרוֹזְנִים נוֹסְדוּ־יָחַד
עַל־יהוה וְעַל־מְשִׁיחוֹ׃

2 Kings of the earth stand ready;
leaders have bonded together
against the Lord and His anointed –

נְנַתְּקָה אֶת־מוֹסְרוֹתֵימוֹ
וְנַשְׁלִיכָה מִמֶּנּוּ עֲבֹתֵימוֹ׃

3 "Let us sever their bonds
and cast away their cords."

יוֹשֵׁב בַּשָּׁמַיִם יִשְׂחָק
אֲדֹנָי יִלְעַג־לָמוֹ׃

4 The One who dwells in heaven
shall laugh;
the Lord will mock them,

אָז יְדַבֵּר אֵלֵימוֹ בְאַפּוֹ
וּבַחֲרוֹנוֹ יְבַהֲלֵמוֹ׃

5 then He will speak to them in His fury;
He will fill them with terror
in His rage:

וַאֲנִי נָסַכְתִּי מַלְכִּי
עַל־צִיּוֹן הַר־קׇדְשִׁי׃

6 "I have set My king over Zion
My holy mountain."

אֲסַפְּרָה אֶל חֹק
יהוה אָמַר אֵלַי בְּנִי־אַתָּה
אֲנִי הַיּוֹם יְלִדְתִּיךָ׃

7 I tell now of the Lord's decree:
He told me, "You are My child;
this very day I fathered you.

שְׁאַל מִמֶּנִּי
וְאֶתְּנָה גוֹיִם נַחֲלָתֶךָ
וַאֲחֻזָּתְךָ אַפְסֵי־אָרֶץ׃

8 Just ask of Me –
I shall give you nations
for your inheritance,
estate to the ends of the earth.

תְּרֹעֵם בְּשֵׁבֶט בַּרְזֶל
כִּכְלִי יוֹצֵר תְּנַפְּצֵם׃

9 You will crush them with an iron rod;
You will shatter them like pottery."

וְעַתָּה מְלָכִים הַשְׂכִּילוּ
הִוָּסְרוּ שֹׁפְטֵי אָרֶץ׃

10 And now, kings, be wise;
be warned, judges of the earth:

עִבְדוּ אֶת־יהוה בְּיִרְאָה
וְגִילוּ בִּרְעָדָה׃

11 Serve the Lord with reverence
and tremble as you exalt.

נַשְּׁקוּ־בַֿר

פֶּן־יֶאֱנַף ׀ וְתֹאבְדוּ דֶרֶךְ

כִּי־יִבְעַר כִּמְעַט אַפֹּו

אַשְׁרֵי כָּל־חֹוסֵי בֹו:

12 Pay homage sincerely

lest He grow angry

and you lose your way,

for His fury flares up in a moment.

Happy are all who seek refuge in Him.

I tell now of the Lord's decree: He told me,
"You are My child; this very day I fathered you"

There can be nothing worse.
I must flee from my own son, my flesh and blood.
Those closest to me have betrayed me.
This is worse than facing enemy armies.
I am overwhelmed, helpless. I am driven into hiding.

PSALM 3

מִזְמוֹר לְדָוִד
בְּבָרְחוֹ מִפְּנֵי ׀ אַבְשָׁלוֹם בְּנוֹ:

1 A psalm of David,
when he fled from his son Avshalom

יהוה מָה־רַבּוּ צָרָי
רַבִּים קָמִים עָלָי:

2 Lord, my foes are so many –
so many rise up against me;

רַבִּים אֹמְרִים לְנַפְשִׁי
אֵין יְשׁוּעָתָה לּוֹ בֵאלֹהִים
סֶלָה:

3 so many say of me,
"He has no salvation in God" –
Selah –

וְאַתָּה יהוה מָגֵן בַּעֲדִי
כְּבוֹדִי וּמֵרִים רֹאשִׁי:

4 but You, Lord,
are the shield that protects me,
my honor;
the One who raises my head.

קוֹלִי אֶל־יהוה אֶקְרָא
וַיַּעֲנֵנִי מֵהַר קָדְשׁוֹ סֶלָה:

5 My voice cries out to the Lord;
He answers me
from His holy mountain – Selah.

אֲנִי שָׁכַבְתִּי וָאִישָׁנָה
הֱקִיצוֹתִי
כִּי יהוה יִסְמְכֵנִי:

6 I lie down to sleep;
I wake again,
for the Lord sustains me.

לֹא־אִירָא מֵרִבְבוֹת עָם
אֲשֶׁר סָבִיב שָׁתוּ עָלָי:

7 I do not fear the myriads of men,
those encamped all around me.

קוּמָה יהוה ׀ הוֹשִׁיעֵנִי אֱלֹהַי
כִּי־הִכִּיתָ אֶת־כָּל־אֹיְבַי לֶחִי
שִׁנֵּי רְשָׁעִים שִׁבַּרְתָּ:

8 Rise up, Lord;
save me, my God!
You have smashed all my foes
across the jaw;
You have broken the teeth of the wicked.

לַיהוה הַיְשׁוּעָה
עַל־עַמְּךָ בִרְכָתֶךָ
סֶלָה:

9 Salvation is the Lord's –
Your blessing rests on Your people –
Selah.

You have filled my heart with more joy than others feel in their abundance of grain and wine

I am eager to dialogue with those who have betrayed me, because I am confident that the Lord will hear my prayers. I don't want to fight with them. I wish they were sufficiently open-minded to hear my side of the story. My God is their God. Why can they not understand that? Why not forgive each other? We would accomplish so much if we could just work together.

PSALM 4

לַמְנַצֵּחַ בִּנְגִינוֹת
מִזְמוֹר לְדָוִד:

1 To the lead singer,
accompanied by music –
a psalm of David

בְּקָרְאִי עֲנֵנִי ׀
אֱלֹהֵי צִדְקִי בַּצָּר הִרְחַבְתָּ לִּי
חׇנֵּנִי וּשְׁמַע תְּפִלָּתִי:

2 When I call out, answer me,
O God of my vindication;
in my distress You set me free –
show me grace and hear my prayer.

בְּנֵי־אִישׁ
עַד־מֶה כְבוֹדִי לִכְלִמָּה
תֶּאֱהָבוּן רִיק
תְּבַקְשׁוּ כָזָב סֶלָה:

3 All you people –
how long will my honor be disgraced;
how long will you love emptiness;
how long will you seek illusions? –Selah.

וּדְעוּ כִּי־הִפְלָה יהוה חָסִיד לוֹ
יהוה יִשְׁמַע בְּקָרְאִי אֵלָיו:

4 Know that the Lord singles out
those who are faithful to Him;
when I cry out to the Lord, He will
hear.

רִגְזוּ וְאַל־תֶּחֱטָאוּ
אִמְרוּ בִלְבַבְכֶם עַל־מִשְׁכַּבְכֶם
וְדֹמּוּ סֶלָה:

5 Tremble and do not sin;
contemplate as you lie awake;
stay silent – Selah.

זִבְחוּ זִבְחֵי־צֶדֶק
וּבִטְחוּ אֶל־יהוה:

6 Offer sincere offerings,
and place Your trust in the Lord.

רַבִּים אֹמְרִים
מִי־יַרְאֵנוּ טוֹב
נְסָה־עָלֵינוּ אוֹר פָּנֶיךָ יהוה:

7 So many say,
"Who will show us goodness?"
Direct the light of Your face upon us,
Lord.

נָתַתָּה שִׂמְחָה בְלִבִּי
מֵעֵת דְּגָנָם וְתִירוֹשָׁם רָבּוּ:

8 You have filled my heart with more joy
than others feel in their abundance of
grain and wine.

בְּשָׁלוֹם יַחְדָּו אֶשְׁכְּבָה וְאִישָׁן
כִּי־אַתָּה יהוה לְבָדָד
לָבֶטַח תּוֹשִׁיבֵנִי:

9 In peace I shall lie down
and sleep soundly,
for You alone, Lord, keep me safe.

Listen to the sound of my plea, my King and God, for to You I pray

Words cannot express my thoughts and emotions.
My thoughts are numerous and chaotic.
My emotions are frightening and overwhelming.
Thus, I pray that God not only hears my words,
but reads my mind.

PSALM 5

לַמְנַצֵּחַ אֶל־הַנְּחִילוֹת
מִזְמוֹר לְדָוִד:

1 To the lead singer, on the *neḥilot* – a psalm of David

אִמְרַי הַאֲזִינָה ׀ יהוה
בִּינָה הֲגִיגִי:

2 Give ear to my words, LORD;
understand my reflections;

הַקְשִׁיבָה ׀ לְקוֹל שַׁוְעִי
מַלְכִּי וֵאלֹהָי
כִּי־אֵלֶיךָ אֶתְפַּלָּל:

3 listen to the sound of my plea,
my King and God,
for to You I pray.

יהוה בֹּקֶר תִּשְׁמַע קוֹלִי
בֹּקֶר אֶעֱרָךְ־לְךָ וַאֲצַפֶּה:

4 LORD, hear my voice in the morning;
in the morning I plead before You
in expectation,

כִּי ׀ לֹא אֵל־חָפֵץ רֶשַׁע ׀ אָתָּה
לֹא יְגֻרְךָ רָע:

5 for You are not a God who desires wickedness;
evil cannot abide with You.

לֹא־יִתְיַצְּבוּ הוֹלְלִים
לְנֶגֶד עֵינֶיךָ
שָׂנֵאתָ כָּל־פֹּעֲלֵי אָוֶן:

6. The brazen will not stand
before Your eyes;
You hate all evildoers.

תְּאַבֵּד דֹּבְרֵי כָזָב
אִישׁ־דָּמִים וּמִרְמָה
יְתָעֵב ׀ יהוה:

7 You destroy those who speak lies;
men of blood and deceit
the LORD despises.

וַאֲנִי בְּרֹב חַסְדְּךָ אָבוֹא בֵיתֶךָ
אֶשְׁתַּחֲוֶה אֶל־הֵיכַל־קָדְשְׁךָ
בְּיִרְאָתֶךָ:

8 But I, with Your great loving-kindness,
will come to Your House;
I will worship at Your holy Sanctuary
in reverence of You.

הושר

יהוה ׀ נְחֵנִי בְצִדְקָתֶךָ
לְמַעַן שׁוֹרְרָי
הַיְשַׁר לְפָנַי דַּרְכֶּךָ:

9 LORD, lead me in Your righteousness
because of my oppressors.
Make Your path straight before me,

כִּי אֵין בְּפִיהוּ נְכוֹנָה
קִרְבָּם הַוּוֹת
קֶבֶר־פָּתוּחַ גְּרֹנָם
לְשׁוֹנָם יַחֲלִיקוּן:

10 for there is not a true word on their lips;
their insides churn with malice;
their slippery tongues lead
to the open grave of their throats.

הַאֲשִׁימֵם ׀ אֱלֹהִים

11 Condemn them, God;

יִפְּלוּ מִמֹּעֲצוֹתֵיהֶם

let them fall by their own counsel.

בְּרֹב פִּשְׁעֵיהֶם הַדִּיחֵמוֹ

Drive them away for their many crimes,

כִּי מָרוּ בָךְ:

for they have rebelled against You.

וְיִשְׂמְחוּ כָל־חוֹסֵי בָךְ

12 Let all those who take refuge in You
rejoice;

לְעוֹלָם יְרַנֵּנוּ וְתָסֵךְ עָלֵימוֹ

let them ever sing for joy
as You shelter them;

וְיַעְלְצוּ בְךָ אֹהֲבֵי שְׁמֶךָ:

let those who love Your name
exult in You,

כִּי־אַתָּה תְּבָרֵךְ צַדִּיק יהוה

13 for You bless the righteous, O LORD,

כַּצִּנָּה רָצוֹן תַּעְטְרֶנּוּ:

sheathing them with favor like a shield.

The LORD has heard my pleas; the LORD will accept my prayer

I am sick. I mean sick! I have never felt this bad in my entire life.
It hurts. It really hurts. I cannot stand the pain.
I am scared. Really scared. Can no one help me?
I never felt this close to death. I do not want to die.

PSALM 6

לַמְנַצֵּחַ בִּנְגִינוֹת עַל־ 1
הַשְּׁמִינִית מִזְמוֹר לְדָוִד:

יהוה אַל־בְּאַפְּךָ תוֹכִיחֵנִי 2
וְאַל־בַּחֲמָתְךָ תְיַסְּרֵנִי:

חָנֵּנִי יהוה 3
כִּי אֻמְלַל אָנִי
רְפָאֵנִי יהוה
כִּי נִבְהֲלוּ עֲצָמָי:

וְנַפְשִׁי נִבְהֲלָה מְאֹד 4
וְאַתָּ יהוה עַד־מָתָי:

שׁוּבָה יהוה 5
חַלְּצָה נַפְשִׁי
הוֹשִׁיעֵנִי לְמַעַן חַסְדֶּךָ:

כִּי אֵין בַּמָּוֶת זִכְרֶךָ 6
בִּשְׁאוֹל מִי יוֹדֶה־לָּךְ:

יָגַעְתִּי ׀ בְּאַנְחָתִי 7
אַשְׂחֶה בְכָל־לַיְלָה מִטָּתִי
בְּדִמְעָתִי עַרְשִׂי אַמְסֶה:

עָשְׁשָׁה מִכַּעַס עֵינִי 8
עָתְקָה בְּכָל־צוֹרְרָי:

סוּרוּ מִמֶּנִּי כָּל־פֹּעֲלֵי אָוֶן 9
כִּי־שָׁמַע יהוה קוֹל בִּכְיִי:

שָׁמַע יהוה תְּחִנָּתִי 10
יהוה תְּפִלָּתִי יִקָּח:

יֵבֹשׁוּ ׀ וְיִבָּהֲלוּ מְאֹד כָּל־אֹיְבָי 11
יָשֻׁבוּ יֵבֹשׁוּ רָגַע:

1 To the lead singer,
  accompanied by music on the *sheminit* –
  a psalm of David

2 Lord, do not reproach me in Your anger;
  do not punish me in Your fury.

3 Be gracious to me, LORD,
  for I am wretched;
  heal me, LORD,
  for my bones shake with agony.

4 My soul is in grave agony –
  and You, O LORD – oh, how long?

5 Come back, LORD –
  rescue my soul;
  save me for the sake of Your love,

6 for there is no mention of You in death;
  who can praise You from the grave?

7 I am weary with sighing –
  each night I flood my bed with weeping;
  I drench my couch in tears.

8 My eye grows dim from grief,
  worn out from all my foes.

9 Leave me, all you evildoers,
  for the LORD has heard
  the sound of my weeping;

10 The LORD has heard my pleas;
   the LORD will accept my prayer.

11 Shame and agony will seize all my foes;
   they will turn back in sudden shame.

He has dug a pit and hollowed it out, and he himself will fall into that hole

It would be much easier if I knew exactly
who my enemies were. But it is so hard to tell.
What's worse, some of my enemies are not all bad;
they have positive aspects to them.
It is hard to fight someone when you feel sorry for him.

PSALM 7

שִׁגָּיֹ֗ון לְדָ֫וִ֥ד אֲשֶׁר־שָׁ֥ר לַיהוָ֑ה עַל־דִּבְרֵי־כ֝֗וּשׁ בֶּן־יְמִינִֽי׃	1	A *shiggayon* of David, which he sang to the LORD concerning Kush, a Binyaminite
יהוה אֱלֹהַי בְּךָ֣ חָסִ֑יתִי הוֹשִׁיעֵ֥נִי מִכָּל־רֹ֝דְפַ֗י וְהַצִּילֵֽנִי׃	2	O LORD my God, in You I take refuge. Save me and deliver me from all my foes
פֶּן־יִטְרֹ֣ף כְּאַרְיֵ֣ה נַפְשִׁ֑י פֹּ֝רֵ֗ק וְאֵ֣ין מַצִּֽיל׃	3	lest they ravage me like a lion, tearing me apart, with no one to save me.
יהוה אֱלֹהַי אִם־עָשִׂ֣יתִי זֹ֑את אִם־יֶשׁ־עָ֥וֶל בְּכַפָּֽי׃	4	O LORD, my God, if I have done this, if there is guilt on my hands,
אִם־גָּ֭מַלְתִּי שֽׁוֹלְמִ֥י רָ֑ע וָאֲחַלְּצָ֖ה צוֹרְרִ֣י רֵיקָֽם׃	5	if I have repaid my allies with harm or plundered my rivals without cause,
יִֽרַדֹּ֥ף אוֹיֵ֨ב ׀ נַפְשִׁ֡י וְיַשֵּׂ֗ג וְיִרְמֹ֣ס לָאָ֣רֶץ חַיָּ֑י וּכְבוֹדִ֓י ׀ לֶעָפָ֖ר יַשְׁכֵּ֣ן סֶֽלָה׃	6	then let my enemies pursue and overtake me; let them trample me into the ground and lay my body in the dust – Selah.
ק֘וּמָ֤ה יהוה ׀ בְּאַפֶּ֗ךָ הִ֭נָּשֵׂא בְּעַבְר֣וֹת צוֹרְרָ֑י וְע֥וּרָה אֵ֝לַ֗י מִשְׁפָּ֥ט צִוִּֽיתָ׃	7	Arise, O LORD, in Your anger; rear up in wrath against my enemies and rouse, for my sake, the judgment You decreed.
וַעֲדַ֣ת לְ֭אֻמִּים תְּסוֹבְבֶ֑ךָּ וְ֝עָלֶ֗יהָ לַמָּר֥וֹם שֽׁוּבָה׃	8	The assembly of peoples will surround You; take Your seat over them on high.
יהוה יָדִ֪ין עַ֫מִּ֥ים שָׁפְטֵ֥נִי יהוה כְּצִדְקִ֖י וּכְתֻמִּ֣י עָלָֽי׃	9	The LORD will judge nations; vindicate me, O LORD, according to my righteousness and integrity.
יִגְמָר־נָ֬א רַ֨ע ׀ רְשָׁעִים֮ וּתְכוֹנֵ֪ן צַ֫דִּ֥יק וּבֹחֵ֣ן לִ֭בּוֹת וּכְלָי֑וֹת אֱלֹהִ֥ים צַדִּֽיק׃	10	Let the evil of the wicked come to an end, and let the righteous stand firm – You who search hearts and minds, O Righteous God.

מָגִנִּי עַל־אֱלֹהִים
מוֹשִׁיעַ יִשְׁרֵי־לֵב:

11 My shield is God,
who saves the upright of heart.

אֱלֹהִים שׁוֹפֵט צַדִּיק
וְאֵל זֹעֵם בְּכָל־יוֹם:

12 God vindicates the righteous,
growing livid every day.

אִם־לֹא יָשׁוּב חַרְבּוֹ יִלְטוֹשׁ
קַשְׁתּוֹ דָרַךְ וַיְכוֹנְנֶהָ:

13 If someone fails to repent
and sharpens his sword
and draws his bow and aims,

וְלוֹ הֵכִין כְּלֵי־מָוֶת
חִצָּיו לְדֹלְקִים יִפְעָל:

14 then he has prepared the instruments
of his own death;
he has poisoned his arrows for himself,

הִנֵּה יְחַבֶּל־אָוֶן
וְהָרָה עָמָל וְיָלַד שָׁקֶר:

15 for he has spawned evil,
he is pregnant with treachery,
and he breeds falsehood.

בּוֹר כָּרָה וַיַּחְפְּרֵהוּ
וַיִּפֹּל בְּשַׁחַת יִפְעָל:

16 He has dug a pit and hollowed it out,
and he himself will fall into that hole.

יָשׁוּב עֲמָלוֹ בְרֹאשׁוֹ
וְעַל קָדְקֳדוֹ חֲמָסוֹ יֵרֵד:

17 His treachery will come back
on his own head;
his violence will crash down
on his own skull.

אוֹדֶה יהוה כְּצִדְקוֹ
וַאֲזַמְּרָה שֵׁם־יהוה עֶלְיוֹן:

18 I will praise the LORD for His
righteousness;
I will sing to the name of the LORD
Most High.

Birds of the skies, and fish of the sea – whatever travels the paths of the seas

What a wonderful world.
I look up at the heavens on a cloudless night.
I gaze at the moon and stars. Amazing!
Here on earth, I observe the baby nursing at its mother's breast.
Astounding! At moments like these I am in awe of God.
I feel like a mere speck in His infinite universe.

PSALM 8

לַמְנַצֵּחַ עַל־הַגִּתִּית
מִזְמוֹר לְדָוִד:

1 To the lead singer, on the *gittit*–
a psalm of David

יְהוָה אֲדֹנֵינוּ
מָה־אַדִּיר שִׁמְךָ בְּכָל־הָאָרֶץ
אֲשֶׁר־תְּנָה הוֹדְךָ עַל־הַשָּׁמָיִם:

2 O Lord our Master,
How mighty is Your name
throughout the earth;
Your majesty extends across the heavens!

מִפִּי עוֹלְלִים ׀ וְיֹנְקִים יִסַּדְתָּ עֹז
לְמַעַן צוֹרְרֶיךָ
לְהַשְׁבִּית אוֹיֵב וּמִתְנַקֵּם:

3 From the coos of little ones and babies
You founded power against Your foes,
silencing enemies and avengers.

כִּי־אֶרְאֶה שָׁמֶיךָ
מַעֲשֵׂה אֶצְבְּעֹתֶיךָ
יָרֵחַ וְכוֹכָבִים אֲשֶׁר כּוֹנָנְתָּה:

4 When I behold Your heavens,
the work of Your fingertips,
the moon and stars that You designed,

מָה־אֱנוֹשׁ כִּי־תִזְכְּרֶנּוּ
וּבֶן־אָדָם כִּי תִפְקְדֶנּוּ:

5 what are mortals,
that You should be mindful of them;
human beings,
that You should take note of them?

וַתְּחַסְּרֵהוּ מְּעַט מֵאֱלֹהִים
וְכָבוֹד וְהָדָר תְּעַטְּרֵהוּ:

6 Yet You have set them just below God
and crowned them with glory
and splendor.

תַּמְשִׁילֵהוּ בְּמַעֲשֵׂי יָדֶיךָ
כֹּל שַׁתָּה תַחַת־רַגְלָיו:

7 You made them rulers over Your
handiwork;
You set it all beneath their feet –

צֹנֶה וַאֲלָפִים כֻּלָּם
וְגַם בַּהֲמוֹת שָׂדָי:

8 all flocks and herds,
beasts of the field,

צִפּוֹר שָׁמַיִם וּדְגֵי הַיָּם
עֹבֵר אָרְחוֹת יַמִּים:

9 birds of the skies, and fish of the sea –
whatever travels the paths of the seas.

יְהוָה אֲדֹנֵינוּ
מָה־אַדִּיר שִׁמְךָ בְּכָל־הָאָרֶץ:

10 O Lord our Master,
how mighty is Your name
throughout the earth!

But the LORD abides forever; He has established His throne for judgment

I am just one person, an insignificant part of the crowd.
I celebrate the achievements of my community.
But I ask God, "What about me? Where are my triumphs?"
I feel neglected, lost in the larger picture.
Yes, God helps the mighty and the many.
But will He help poor little me?

PSALM 9

לַמְנַצֵּחַ עַל־מוּת לַבֵּן
מִזְמוֹר לְדָוִד:

1 To the lead singer, *Al Mot Labben* –
a psalm of David

אוֹדֶה יהוה בְּכָל־לִבִּי
אֲסַפְּרָה כָּל־נִפְלְאוֹתֶיךָ:

2 I thank You, Lord, with all my heart;
let me tell of all Your wonders.

אֶשְׂמְחָה וְאֶעֶלְצָה בָךְ
אֲזַמְּרָה שִׁמְךָ עֶלְיוֹן:

3 I rejoice and exult in You;
let me sing praise to Your name,
Most High.

בְּשׁוּב־אוֹיְבַי אָחוֹר
יִכָּשְׁלוּ וְיֹאבְדוּ מִפָּנֶיךָ:

4 My enemies retreat;
they stumble and perish before You,

כִּי־עָשִׂיתָ מִשְׁפָּטִי וְדִינִי
יָשַׁבְתָּ לְכִסֵּא שׁוֹפֵט צֶדֶק:

5 for You have upheld my case
and my cause;
You have sat enthroned
as righteous Judge;

גָּעַרְתָּ גוֹיִם אִבַּדְתָּ רָשָׁע
שְׁמָם מָחִיתָ לְעוֹלָם וָעֶד:

6 You have blasted nations
and destroyed the wicked,
blotting out their names
for ever and all time.

הָאוֹיֵב ׀ תַּמּוּ חֳרָבוֹת לָנֶצַח
וְעָרִים נָתַשְׁתָּ
אָבַד זִכְרָם הֵמָּה:

7 The enemies are finished,
ruined forever;
You have overthrown their cities –
every trace of them is lost.

וַיהוה לְעוֹלָם יֵשֵׁב
כּוֹנֵן לַמִּשְׁפָּט כִּסְאוֹ:

8 But the Lord abides forever;
He has established His throne
for judgment.

וְהוּא יִשְׁפֹּט־תֵּבֵל בְּצֶדֶק
יָדִין לְאֻמִּים בְּמֵישָׁרִים:

9 He will judge the world with justice
and try the cause of peoples fairly.

וִיהִי יהוה מִשְׂגָּב לַדָּךְ
מִשְׂגָּב לְעִתּוֹת בַּצָּרָה:

10 The Lord is a stronghold
for the downtrodden,
a stronghold in times of trouble.

וְיִבְטְחוּ בְךָ יוֹדְעֵי שְׁמֶךָ
כִּי לֹא־עָזַבְתָּ דֹרְשֶׁיךָ יהוה:

11 Those who know Your name
trust in You,
for You never forsake those
who seek You, LORD.

זַמְּרוּ לַיהוה יֹשֵׁב צִיּוֹן
הַגִּידוּ בָעַמִּים עֲלִילוֹתָיו:

12 Sing praise to the LORD
who dwells in Zion;
tell of His deeds among the peoples.

עניים

כִּי־דֹרֵשׁ דָּמִים אוֹתָם זָכָר
לֹא־שָׁכַח צַעֲקַת עֲנָוִים:

13 For the Avenger of blood remembers;
He does not forget the cry
of the suffering.

חָנְנֵנִי יהוה
רְאֵה עָנְיִי מִשֹּׂנְאָי
מְרוֹמְמִי מִשַּׁעֲרֵי־מָוֶת:

14 Show me grace, LORD –
see how my enemies make me suffer,
You who lift me up from the gates
of death,

לְמַעַן אֲסַפְּרָה כָּל־תְּהִלָּתֶיךָ
בְּשַׁעֲרֵי בַת־צִיּוֹן
אָגִילָה בִּישׁוּעָתֶךָ:

15 so that I may sing all Your praises
at the gates of the daughter of Zion
and rejoice in Your deliverance.

טָבְעוּ גוֹיִם בְּשַׁחַת עָשׂוּ
בְּרֶשֶׁת־זוּ טָמָנוּ נִלְכְּדָה
רַגְלָם:

16 The nations have fallen into their own pit;
their feet are tangled in their own
hidden net.

נוֹדַע יהוה מִשְׁפָּט עָשָׂה
בְּפֹעַל כַּפָּיו נוֹקֵשׁ רָשָׁע הִגָּיוֹן
סֶלָה:

17 The LORD is famed for His justice
while the wicked are ensnared
by the work of their own hands –
higgayon – Selah.

יָשׁוּבוּ רְשָׁעִים לִשְׁאוֹלָה
כָּל־גּוֹיִם שְׁכֵחֵי אֱלֹהִים:

18 The wicked return to Sheol,
all nations that forget God,

עָנִוִים

כִּי לֹא לָנֶצַח יִשָּׁכַח אֶבְיוֹן
תִּקְוַת עֲנָוִים תֹּאבַד לָעַד:

19 but the needy will not be forgotten
for long;
the hope of the suffering
will never be lost.

קוּמָה יהוה אַל־יָעֹז אֱנוֹשׁ
יִשָּׁפְטוּ גוֹיִם עַל־פָּנֶיךָ׃

20 Arise, LORD; do not let mortals prevail –
let the nations be judged before You.

שִׁיתָה יהוה ׀ מוֹרָה לָהֶם
יֵדְעוּ גוֹיִם אֱנוֹשׁ הֵמָּה סֶּלָה׃

21 Strike them with fear, LORD;
let the nations know
they are but mortal – Selah.

You have heard what the lowly desire, LORD; strengthen their hearts and lend Your ear

I feel alienated, frustrated, abandoned by God.
My enemy comes at me out of nowhere.
He is arrogant, deceitful, and vicious.
Worse, he does not seem to be accountable to God.
Is there no justice?

PSALM 10

לָמָה יְהוה תַּעֲמֹד בְּרָחוֹק
תַּעְלִים לְעִתּוֹת בַּצָּרָה:

1 Why, Lord, do You stand far off,
hiding Yourself in times of trouble?

בְּגַאֲוַת רָשָׁע יִדְלַק עָנִי
יִתָּפְשׂוּ ׀ בִּמְזִמּוֹת זוּ חָשָׁבוּ:

2 The proud wicked persecute the poor –
let them be trapped
by their own devious schemes! –

כִּי־הִלֵּל רָשָׁע עַל־תַּאֲוַת נַפְשׁוֹ
וּבֹצֵעַ בֵּרֵךְ נִאֵץ ׀ יְהוה:

3 for the wicked boast of their lust;
the avaricious curse and revile the
Lord.

רָשָׁע כְּגֹבַהּ אַפּוֹ בַּל־יִדְרֹשׁ
אֵין אֱלֹהִים כָּל־מְזִמּוֹתָיו:

4 In their sheer arrogance, the wicked say,
"He will never call us to account";
in all their scheming, they say,
"There is no God."

יָחִילוּ דְרָכָו ׀ בְּכָל־עֵת
מָרוֹם מִשְׁפָּטֶיךָ מִנֶּגְדּוֹ
כָּל־צוֹרְרָיו יָפִיחַ בָּהֶם:

5 Their ways always prosper –
Your justice is far above them.
As for their foes, they snort at them.

אָמַר בְּלִבּוֹ בַּל־אֶמּוֹט
לְדֹר וָדֹר אֲשֶׁר לֹא־בְרָע:

6 They say to themselves,
"I will not be shaken;
I will never encounter trouble."

אָלָה ׀ פִּיהוּ מָלֵא וּמִרְמוֹת וָתֹךְ
תַּחַת לְשׁוֹנוֹ עָמָל וָאָוֶן:

7 Curses fill their mouths,
deceit and malice;
treachery and cruelty lie beneath their
tongues.

יֵשֵׁב ׀ בְּמַאְרַב חֲצֵרִים
בַּמִּסְתָּרִים יַהֲרֹג נָקִי
עֵינָיו לְחֵלְכָה יִצְפֹּנוּ:

8 They lurk in backwater places,
murdering innocents where no one sees;
their eyes stalk the helpless.

יֶאֱרֹב בַּמִּסְתָּר ׀ כְּאַרְיֵה בְסֻכֹּה
יֶאֱרֹב לַחֲטוֹף עָנִי
יַחְטֹף עָנִי בְּמָשְׁכוֹ בְרִשְׁתּוֹ:

9 They lurk, hidden like a lion in its lair,
lurk to snatch away the poor;
they snatch away the poor
and drag them off in their net.

וְדָכָה יָשֹׁחַ
חֶלְכָּאִים וְנָפַל בַּעֲצוּמָיו חֵל כָּאִים:

10 They stoop, they crouch,
and the helpless fall prey to their clutches.

אָמַ֣ר בְּ֭לִבּוֹ
שָׁ֣כַֽח אֵ֑ל
הִסְתִּ֥יר פָּ֝נָ֗יו בַּל־רָאָ֥ה לָנֶֽצַח׃

11 They say to themselves,
"God has forgotten –
He has hidden His face
and averted His gaze forever."

קוּמָ֤ה יְהֹוָ֗ה
אֵ֭ל נְשָׂ֣א יָדֶ֑ךָ
אַל־תִּשְׁכַּ֥ח עֲנָוִֽים׃

עניים

12 Rise up, Lord;
God, raise Your hand –
do not forget the poor!

עַל־מֶ֤ה ׀ נִאֵ֖ץ רָשָׁ֥ע ׀ אֱלֹהִ֑ים
אָמַ֥ר בְּ֝לִבּ֗וֹ לֹ֣א תִדְרֹֽשׁ׃

13 Why do the wicked revile God,
thinking,
"You will never call us to account"?

רָאִ֡תָה
כִּֽי־אַתָּ֤ה ׀ עָ֘מָ֤ל וָכַ֨עַס ׀ תַּבִּיט֮
לָתֵ֪ת בְּיָ֫דֶ֥ךָ
עָלֶ֗יךָ יַעֲזֹ֥ב חֵלֶ֑כָה
יָ֝ת֗וֹם אַתָּ֤ה ׀ הָיִ֬יתָ עוֹזֵֽר׃

14 You do see!
You do note treachery and torment
and take them into Your hands;
the helpless commit themselves to You;
You have always helped the orphan.

שְׁ֭בֹר זְר֣וֹעַ רָשָׁ֑ע
וָ֝רָ֗ע תִּֽדְרוֹשׁ־רִשְׁע֥וֹ
בַל־תִּמְצָֽא׃

15 Break the arms of the wicked;
call the evil to account
for their wickedness
until it is gone.

יְהֹוָ֣ה מֶ֭לֶךְ עוֹלָ֣ם וָעֶ֑ד
אָבְד֥וּ ג֝וֹיִ֗ם מֵֽאַרְצֽוֹ׃

16 The Lord is King forever and ever;
the nations shall perish from His land.

תַּאֲוַ֬ת עֲנָוִ֣ים שָׁמַ֣עְתָּ יְהֹוָ֑ה
תָּכִ֥ין לִ֝בָּ֗ם תַּקְשִׁ֥יב אָזְנֶֽךָ׃

17 You have heard what the lowly desire,
Lord;
strengthen their hearts and lend Your ear

לִשְׁפֹּ֥ט יָת֗וֹם וָ֫דָ֥ךְ
בַּל־יוֹסִ֥יף ע֑וֹד לַעֲרֹ֥ץ אֱנ֗וֹשׁ
מִן־הָאָֽרֶץ׃

18 to bring justice to the orphan
and the downtrodden
so that mere earthly mortals
will never spread terror again.

The Lord is in His holy sanctuary; the Lord is on His heavenly throne

I once felt secure. But now I feel like a little bird,
driven from place to place, never allowed to rest.
My problems are vicious, unrelenting. The earth is shaking;
its firm foundations withdraw from underneath me.
God promised me His protection.
I cling desperately to His assurance.

PSALM 11

לַמְנַצֵּחַ לְדָוִד
בַּיהוה ׀ חָסִיתִי
אֵיךְ תֹּאמְרוּ לְנַפְשִׁי
נוּדִי הַרְכֶם צִפּוֹר:

נוֹדוּ

1 To the lead singer, of David
In the LORD I take shelter –
how can you say to me,
"Flee your mountain like a bird –

כִּי הִנֵּה הָרְשָׁעִים יִדְרְכוּן קֶשֶׁת
כּוֹנְנוּ חִצָּם עַל־יֶתֶר
לִירוֹת בְּמוֹ־אֹפֶל לְיִשְׁרֵי־לֵב:

2 for look, the wicked,
they draw their bows taut,
set their arrows on the string
to shoot from the shadows
at the upright –

כִּי הַשָּׁתוֹת יֵהָרֵסוּן
צַדִּיק מַה־פָּעָל:

3 for the foundations will soon
be destroyed."
What are the righteous to do?

יהוה ׀ בְּהֵיכַל קָדְשׁוֹ
יהוה בַּשָּׁמַיִם כִּסְאוֹ
עֵינָיו יֶחֱזוּ
עַפְעַפָּיו יִבְחֲנוּ בְּנֵי אָדָם:

4 The LORD is in His holy sanctuary;
the LORD is on His heavenly throne;
His eyes gaze down;
He examines humanity;

יהוה צַדִּיק יִבְחָן
וְרָשָׁע וְאֹהֵב חָמָס
שָׂנְאָה נַפְשׁוֹ:

5 the LORD examines righteous and
wicked.
He despises the lover of violence;

יַמְטֵר עַל־רְשָׁעִים פַּחִים
אֵשׁ וְגָפְרִית וְרוּחַ זִלְעָפוֹת
מְנָת כּוֹסָם:

6 He will rain down soot and fire
and sulfur on the wicked;
scorching winds are their portion.

כִּי־צַדִּיק יהוה צְדָקוֹת אָהֵב
יָשָׁר יֶחֱזוּ פָנֵימוֹ:

7 For the LORD is righteous;
He loves what is right.
The upright will gaze upon His face.

To the lead singer, on the *sheminit* – a psalm of David

It is a world of lies. Deceit and hypocrisy prevail.
Falseness is used as a weapon to manipulate the naïve
and the gullible. I would love to encounter pure truth.
But would I recognize pure truth if I saw it?

PSALM 12

לַמְנַצֵּחַ עַל־הַשְּׁמִינִית
מִזְמוֹר לְדָוִד:

1 To the lead singer, on the *sheminit* –
a psalm of David

הוֹשִׁיעָה יהוה כִּי־גָמַר חָסִיד
כִּי־פַסּוּ אֱמוּנִים מִבְּנֵי אָדָם:

2 Help, LORD, for the godly are no more,
for the faithful have faded from humanity.

שָׁוְא ׀ יְדַבְּרוּ אִישׁ אֶת־רֵעֵהוּ
שְׂפַת חֲלָקוֹת בְּלֵב וָלֵב יְדַבֵּרוּ:

3 People tell each other lies;
they are smooth-talking and two-faced.

יַכְרֵת יהוה כָּל־שִׂפְתֵי חֲלָקוֹת
לָשׁוֹן מְדַבֶּרֶת גְּדֹלוֹת:

4 May the LORD cut off
all these smooth lips,
these arrogant wagging tongues

אֲשֶׁר אָמְרוּ ׀ לִלְשֹׁנֵנוּ נַגְבִּיר
שְׂפָתֵינוּ אִתָּנוּ
מִי אָדוֹן לָנוּ:

5 that declare, "Our tongues shall prevail;
our lips are our own –
who is our master?"

מִשֹּׁד עֲנִיִּים מֵאַנְקַת אֶבְיוֹנִים
עַתָּה אָקוּם יֹאמַר יהוה
אָשִׁית בְּיֵשַׁע יָפִיחַ לוֹ:

6 "Because of the oppression of the poor,
the groans of the needy,
I will now rise up," declares the LORD;
"I will grant them the safety they sigh for."

אִמֲרוֹת יהוה אֲמָרוֹת טְהֹרוֹת
כֶּסֶף צָרוּף בַּעֲלִיל לָאָרֶץ
מְזֻקָּק שִׁבְעָתָיִם:

7 The LORD's words are pure words,
like silver refined in an earthen furnace,
purified seven times over.

אַתָּה־יהוה תִּשְׁמְרֵם
תִּצְּרֶנּוּ ׀ מִן־הַדּוֹר זוּ לְעוֹלָם:

8 You, LORD, will watch over them
and protect them from this generation
forever –

סָבִיב רְשָׁעִים יִתְהַלָּכוּן
כְּרֻם זֻלּוּת לִבְנֵי אָדָם:

9 as the wicked strut around,
and obscenity is prized among humanity.

But I have placed my trust in Your loyalty; my heart will delight in Your salvation

I will sing to the LORD, for He has been good to me

Why am I suffering? How long will I suffer?
Will it get worse? It can't possibly get worse!
It is hard to believe in God when there is no hope.

PSALM 13

לַמְנַצֵּחַ מִזְמוֹר לְדָוִד: 1

To the lead singer – a psalm of David

עַד־אָנָה יהוה תִּשְׁכָּחֵנִי נֶצַח 2
עַד־אָנָה ׀ תַּסְתִּיר אֶת־פָּנֶיךָ
מִמֶּנִּי:

For how long, LORD, will You forget
me? Forever?
For how long will You hide Your face
from me?

עַד־אָנָה אָשִׁית עֵצוֹת בְּנַפְשִׁי 3
יָגוֹן בִּלְבָבִי יוֹמָם
עַד־אָנָה ׀ יָרוּם אֹיְבִי עָלָי:

For how long will I have worries
in my mind
and sorrow in my heart each day?
For how long will my enemy triumph
over me?

הַבִּיטָה עֲנֵנִי יהוה אֱלֹהָי 4
הָאִירָה עֵינַי פֶּן־אִישַׁן הַמָּוֶת:

Look at me; answer me,
O LORD my God.
Light up my eyes
lest I fall into a death-sleep,

פֶּן־יֹאמַר אֹיְבִי יְכָלְתִּיו 5
צָרַי יָגִילוּ כִּי אֶמּוֹט:

lest my enemy declare,
"I have bested him!" –
lest my foes delight at my collapse.

וַאֲנִי ׀ בְּחַסְדְּךָ בָטַחְתִּי 6
יָגֵל לִבִּי בִּישׁוּעָתֶךָ
אָשִׁירָה לַיהוה כִּי גָמַל עָלָי:

But I have placed my trust in Your loyalty;
my heart will delight in Your salvation.
I will sing to the LORD,
for He has been good to me.

Oh, that Israel's salvation might come from Zion! When the LORD restores

His people's fortune, Yaakov will rejoice; Israel will be glad

Our entire society is corrupt.
There is not a single good person out there.
Spirituality? Forget about it!
Everyone derides and mocks whatever smacks of religion.
This must change. It can't go on this way.

PSALM 14

לַמְנַצֵּחַ לְדָוִד
אָמַר נָבָל בְּלִבּוֹ אֵין אֱלֹהִים
הִשְׁחִיתוּ הִתְעִיבוּ עֲלִילָה
אֵין עֹשֵׂה־טוֹב׃

1 To the lead singer, of David
The brute says in his heart,
"There is no God."
They are corrupt;
they wreak vile schemes;
there is no one who does good.

יְהוָה מִשָּׁמַיִם הִשְׁקִיף
עַל־בְּנֵי־אָדָם
לִרְאוֹת הֲיֵשׁ מַשְׂכִּיל
דֹּרֵשׁ אֶת־אֱלֹהִים׃

2 The Lord looks down from heaven
at humanity
to see if someone has the sense
to seek out God,

הַכֹּל סָר יַחְדָּו נֶאֱלָחוּ
אֵין עֹשֵׂה־טוֹב
אֵין גַּם־אֶחָד׃

3 but all have turned away,
altogether tainted;
there is no one who does good,
not even one.

הֲלֹא יָדְעוּ כָּל־פֹּעֲלֵי אָוֶן
אֹכְלֵי עַמִּי אָכְלוּ לֶחֶם
יְהוָה לֹא קָרָאוּ׃

4 Have they no knowledge,
all those evildoers,
who devour My people
as if devouring bread,
who do not call out to the Lord?

שָׁם ׀ פָּחֲדוּ פָחַד
כִּי־אֱלֹהִים בְּדוֹר צַדִּיק׃

5 There they will be struck with terror,
for God is among the abodes of the
righteous.

עֲצַת־עָנִי תָבִישׁוּ
כִּי יְהוָה מַחְסֵהוּ׃

6 You would rebuff the counsel of the poor,
but the Lord is their shelter.

מִי יִתֵּן מִצִּיּוֹן יְשׁוּעַת יִשְׂרָאֵל
בְּשׁוּב יְהוָה שְׁבוּת עַמּוֹ
יָגֵל יַעֲקֹב יִשְׂמַח יִשְׂרָאֵל׃

7 Oh, that Israel's salvation might come
from Zion!
When the Lord restores
His people's fortune,
Yaakov will rejoice; Israel will be glad.

The one whose ways are blameless, who does what is right, who speaks truth from the heart

He gets no attention. He receives no public acclaim, and shuns worldly recognition. Nobody notices this decent but quiet person who lives down the street. But he's my idea of a holy man.

PSALM 15

מִזְמוֹר לְדָוִד
יהוה מִי־יָגוּר בְּאָהֳלֶךָ
מִי־יִשְׁכֹּן בְּהַר קָדְשֶׁךָ:

1 A psalm of David
LORD, who may dwell in Your tent?
Who may live on Your holy mountain?

הוֹלֵךְ תָּמִים וּפֹעֵל צֶדֶק
וְדֹבֵר אֱמֶת בִּלְבָבוֹ:

2 The one whose ways are blameless,
who does what is right,
who speaks truth from the heart;

לֹא־רָגַל ׀ עַל־לְשֹׁנוֹ
לֹא־עָשָׂה לְרֵעֵהוּ רָעָה
וְחֶרְפָּה לֹא־נָשָׂא עַל־קְרֹבוֹ:

3 the one who has no malice on his tongue,
who does no wrong to his fellow,
who does not cast a slur
against his neighbor;

נִבְזֶה ׀ בְּעֵינָיו נִמְאָס
וְאֶת־יִרְאֵי יהוה יְכַבֵּד
נִשְׁבַּע לְהָרַע וְלֹא יָמִר:

4 the one who scorns those who are vile,
who honors those who fear the LORD,
who keeps an oath even when it hurts;

כַּסְפּוֹ ׀ לֹא־נָתַן בְּנֶשֶׁךְ
וְשֹׁחַד עַל־נָקִי לֹא־לָקָח
עֹשֵׂה אֵלֶּה לֹא יִמּוֹט לְעוֹלָם:

5 the one who does not loan money
for interest,
who does not take a bribe
against the innocent –
anyone who acts thus
will never be shaken.

As for the holy ones in the land, the mighty who were all my delight

I am on a spiritual "high." I feel God close to me.
I glimpse the possibility of getting even closer to Him.
There are so many blessings in my life. I appreciate them.
But I want more.

PSALM 16

מִכְתָּם לְדָוִד
שָׁמְרֵנִי אֵל כִּי־חָסִיתִי בָךְ:

אָמַרְתְּ לַיהוה אֲדֹנָי אָתָּה
טוֹבָתִי בַּל־עָלֶיךָ:

לִקְדוֹשִׁים אֲשֶׁר־בָּאָרֶץ הֵמָּה
וְאַדִּירֵי כָּל־חֶפְצִי־בָם:

יִרְבּוּ עַצְּבוֹתָם אַחֵר מָהָרוּ
בַּל־אַסִּיךְ נִסְכֵּיהֶם מִדָּם
וּבַל־אֶשָּׂא אֶת־שְׁמוֹתָם
עַל־שְׂפָתָי:

יהוה מְנָת־חֶלְקִי וְכוֹסִי
אַתָּה תּוֹמִיךְ גּוֹרָלִי:

חֲבָלִים נָפְלוּ־לִי בַּנְּעִמִים
אַף־נַחֲלָת שָׁפְרָה עָלָי:

אֲבָרֵךְ אֶת־יהוה אֲשֶׁר יְעָצָנִי
אַף־לֵילוֹת יִסְּרוּנִי כִלְיוֹתָי:

שִׁוִּיתִי יהוה לְנֶגְדִּי תָמִיד
כִּי מִימִינִי בַּל־אֶמּוֹט:

לָכֵן ׀ שָׂמַח לִבִּי וַיָּגֶל כְּבוֹדִי
אַף־בְּשָׂרִי יִשְׁכֹּן לָבֶטַח:

כִּי ׀ לֹא־תַעֲזֹב נַפְשִׁי לִשְׁאוֹל
חֲסִידֶךָ   לֹא־תִתֵּן חֲסִידְךָ
לִרְאוֹת שָׁחַת:

תּוֹדִיעֵנִי אֹרַח חַיִּים
שֹׂבַע שְׂמָחוֹת אֶת־פָּנֶיךָ
נְעִמוֹת בִּימִינְךָ נֶצַח:

1 A *mikhtam* of David
Protect me, God, for in You I take refuge.

2 I said to the LORD, "You are my LORD;
My favor comes from none but You."

3 As for the holy ones in the land,
the mighty who were all my delight,

4 may those who court other gods
suffer many sorrows –
I will not pour out their libations
of blood;
I will not bear their names on my lips.

5 The LORD is my chosen portion
and my cup.
You direct my fate.

6 A sweet heritage has fallen to my lot;
my share is delightful to me.

7 I will bless the Lord who has guided me;
even at night, my conscience stirs me.

8 I have set the LORD before me always;
He is at my right hand;
I shall not be shaken.

9 Therefore my heart is glad,
my spirit rejoices,
and my body rests secure,

10 for You will not abandon me to Sheol
nor let Your devoted one see the Pit.

11 You will teach me the path of life.
In Your presence is fullness of joy;
at Your right hand, bliss for evermore.

As for me, in justice I will gaze upon Your face; wide awake, I am sated with Your image

I pray, but will He hear my prayers?
After all, I am sure that I am far from perfect in His eyes.
I have such ferocious problems.
I need His mercy. What can I possibly do to earn His mercy?

PSALM 17

תְּפִלָּה לְדָוִד
שִׁמְעָה יהוה ׀ צֶדֶק
הַקְשִׁיבָה רִנָּתִי הַאֲזִינָה תְפִלָּתִי
בְּלֹא שִׂפְתֵי מִרְמָה׃

מִלְּפָנֶיךָ מִשְׁפָּטִי יֵצֵא
עֵינֶיךָ תֶּחֱזֶינָה מֵישָׁרִים׃

בָּחַנְתָּ לִבִּי ׀ פָּקַדְתָּ לַּיְלָה
צְרַפְתַּנִי בַל־תִּמְצָא
זַמֹּתִי בַּל־יַעֲבָר־פִּי׃

לִפְעֻלּוֹת אָדָם בִּדְבַר שְׂפָתֶיךָ
אֲנִי שָׁמַרְתִּי אָרְחוֹת פָּרִיץ׃

תָּמֹךְ אֲשֻׁרַי בְּמַעְגְּלוֹתֶיךָ
בַּל־נָמוֹטּוּ פְעָמָי׃

אֲנִי־קְרָאתִיךָ כִי־תַעֲנֵנִי אֵל
הַט־אָזְנְךָ לִי שְׁמַע אִמְרָתִי׃

הַפְלֵה חֲסָדֶיךָ מוֹשִׁיעַ חוֹסִים
מִמִּתְקוֹמְמִים בִּימִינֶךָ׃

שָׁמְרֵנִי כְּאִישׁוֹן בַּת־עָיִן
בְּצֵל כְּנָפֶיךָ תַּסְתִּירֵנִי׃

מִפְּנֵי רְשָׁעִים זוּ שַׁדּוּנִי
אֹיְבַי בְּנֶפֶשׁ יַקִּיפוּ עָלָי׃

חֶלְבָּמוֹ סָגְרוּ
פִּימוֹ דִּבְּרוּ בְגֵאוּת׃

אַשֻּׁרֵינוּ עַתָּה סְבָבוּנוּ   סבבוני
עֵינֵיהֶם יָשִׁיתוּ לִנְטוֹת בָּאָרֶץ׃

1 A prayer of David
   Hear, LORD, what is just;
     listen to my plea;
   give ear to my prayer,
     mouthed without deceit.

2 May I be vindicated before You –
   Your eyes will behold what is right.

3 You have searched my heart,
   visited me by night,
   tried me, and found nothing amiss.
   I shut my mouth tight against offense.

4 As for what others do,
   by the words of Your lips
   I myself keep away
   from the paths of the violent.

5 My steps have adhered to Your pathways;
   my feet have never faltered.

6 I call on You for You will answer me, God;
   lend Your ear to me; listen to my words.

7 Show Your wondrous loyalty,
   You who save with Your right hand
   those who seek refuge from adversaries.

8 Guard me like the apple of Your eye;
   hide me in the shade of Your wings

9 from the wicked who assault me,
   my deadly enemies who encircle me.

10 Their hearts are callous;
   their mouths flaunt and gloat.

11 Now they close in around our steps,
   combing the ground with their gaze

דְּמְיֹנוֹ כְּאַרְיֵה יִכְסוֹף לִטְרֹף
וְכִכְפִיר יֹשֵׁב בְּמִסְתָּרִים:

12 like a lion hungering for prey,
   like a young lion crouching in ambush.

קוּמָה יהוה
קַדְּמָה פָנָיו הַכְרִיעֵהוּ
פַּלְּטָה נַפְשִׁי מֵרָשָׁע חַרְבֶּךָ:

13 Rise up, Lord;
   confront them; bring them down.
   Rescue me from the wicked
   with Your sword,

מִמְתִים יָדְךָ ׀ יהוה
מִמְתִים מֵחֶלֶד
חֶלְקָם בַּחַיִּים וּצְפוּנְךָ
תְּמַלֵּא בִטְנָם יִשְׂבְּעוּ בָנִים
וְהִנִּיחוּ יִתְרָם לְעוֹלְלֵיהֶם:

וצפינך

14 from people, O Lord, by Your hand,
   from people whose share in life is fleeting.
   As for those You treasure, fill their bellies;
   their children, too, will be sated
   and leave what remains
   for their own little ones.

אֲנִי בְּצֶדֶק אֶחֱזֶה פָנֶיךָ
אֶשְׂבְּעָה בְהָקִיץ תְּמוּנָתֶךָ:

15 As for me,
   in justice I will gaze upon Your face;
   wide awake, I am sated with Your image.

...so I praise You among the nations, Lord, and sing to Your name

It has been such a long time,
with so many different kinds of problems.
My enemies are gone, my difficulties are resolved,
and my pain is relieved. How thankful I am to the One Above.
He was always my only hope, and He came through.

PSALM 18

לַמְנַצֵּחַ לְעֶבֶד יהוה לְדָוִד 1
אֲשֶׁר דִּבֶּר ׀ לַיהוה אֶת־דִּבְרֵי
הַשִּׁירָה הַזֹּאת
בְּיוֹם ׀ הִצִּיל־יהוה אוֹתוֹ מִכַּף
כָּל־אֹיְבָיו וּמִיַּד שָׁאוּל:

וַיֹּאמַר אֶרְחָמְךָ יהוה חִזְקִי: 2

יהוה ׀ סַלְעִי וּמְצוּדָתִי וּמְפַלְטִי 3
אֵלִי צוּרִי אֶחֱסֶה־בּוֹ
מָגִנִּי וְקֶרֶן־יִשְׁעִי מִשְׂגַּבִּי:

מְהֻלָּל אֶקְרָא יהוה 4
וּמִן־אֹיְבַי אִוָּשֵׁעַ:

אֲפָפוּנִי חֶבְלֵי־מָוֶת 5
וְנַחֲלֵי בְלִיַּעַל יְבַעֲתוּנִי:

חֶבְלֵי שְׁאוֹל סְבָבוּנִי 6
קִדְּמוּנִי מוֹקְשֵׁי מָוֶת:

בַּצַּר־לִי ׀ אֶקְרָא יהוה 7
וְאֶל־אֱלֹהַי אֲשַׁוֵּעַ
יִשְׁמַע מֵהֵיכָלוֹ קוֹלִי
וְשַׁוְעָתִי לְפָנָיו ׀ תָּבוֹא בְאָזְנָיו:

וַתִּגְעַשׁ וַתִּרְעַשׁ ׀ הָאָרֶץ 8
וּמוֹסְדֵי הָרִים יִרְגָּזוּ
וַיִּתְגָּעֲשׁוּ כִּי־חָרָה לוֹ:

עָלָה עָשָׁן ׀ בְּאַפּוֹ 9
וְאֵשׁ־מִפִּיו תֹּאכֵל
גֶּחָלִים בָּעֲרוּ מִמֶּנּוּ:

1 To the lead singer –
of the Lord's servant, of David,
who uttered these words of song
to the Lord;
on the day that the Lord saved him
from the hands of all his enemies
and from the hands of Sha'ul,

2 he said, I love You, O Lord, my
strength.

3 The Lord is my rock, my fortress,
my rescuer;
my God is the rock of my refuge,
my shield, the horn of my salvation,
my haven.

4 Praise! When I call on the Lord,
I am saved from my enemies.

5 The cords of death assailed me;
deadly torrents engulfed me;

6 the cords of Sheol entangled me;
snares of death confronted me.

7 In my distress I called on the Lord;
I cried out to my God;
He heard my voice from His temple,
and my cry rang in His ears.

8 Then the earth shook and shuddered;
the very mountain beds trembled;
they shuddered from His wrath.

9 Smoke issued from His nostrils;
devouring flames flared from His mouth;
from Him gleaming coals blazed forth.

וַיֵּ֣ט שָׁ֭מַיִם וַיֵּרַ֑ד וַ֝עֲרָפֶ֗ל תַּ֣חַת רַגְלָֽיו׃	10 He bent the heavens and descended, dense cloud beneath His feet;
וַיִּרְכַּ֣ב עַל־כְּ֭רוּב וַיָּעֹ֑ף וַ֝יֵּ֗דֶא עַל־כַּנְפֵי־רֽוּחַ׃	11 He mounted a cherub and flew, soaring on wings of wind.
יָ֤שֶׁת חֹ֨שֶׁךְ ׀ סִתְר֗וֹ סְבִֽיבוֹתָ֥יו סֻכָּת֑וֹ חֶשְׁכַת־מַ֝֗יִם עָבֵ֥י שְׁחָקִֽים׃	12 He enveloped Himself in darkness, a shelter all around Him of heavy storm clouds dark with rain.
מִנֹּ֗גַהּ נֶ֥גְדּ֫וֹ עָבָ֥יו עָבְר֑וּ בָּ֝רָ֗ד וְגַחֲלֵי־אֵֽשׁ׃	13 The brilliant glow of His presence pierced His clouds with hail and fiery coals.
וַיַּרְעֵ֬ם בַּשָּׁמַ֨יִם ׀ יְֽהֹוָ֗ה וְ֭עֶלְיוֹן יִתֵּ֣ן קֹל֑וֹ בָּ֝רָ֗ד וְגַחֲלֵי־אֵֽשׁ׃	14 The Lord thundered from the heavens; the Most High raised His voice with hail and fiery coals.
וַיִּשְׁלַ֣ח חִ֭צָּיו וַיְפִיצֵ֑ם וּבְרָקִ֥ים רָ֝֗ב וַיְהֻמֵּֽם׃	15 He shot His arrows and scattered them; He hurled lightning bolts and routed them.
וַיֵּ֤רָא֨וּ ׀ אֲפִ֬יקֵי מַ֗יִם וַיִּגָּלוּ֮ מוֹסְד֢וֹת תֵּ֫בֵ֥ל מִגַּעֲרָתְךָ֥ יְהֹוָ֑ה מִ֝נִּשְׁמַ֗ת ר֣וּחַ אַפֶּֽךָ׃	16 The ocean bed was exposed, the foundations of the world laid bare by Your onslaught, Lord, from the blast of Your breath.
יִשְׁלַ֣ח מִ֭מָּרוֹם יִקָּחֵ֑נִי יַֽ֝מְשֵׁ֗נִי מִמַּ֥יִם רַבִּֽים׃	17 From on high He reached down and took me; He drew me out of the mighty waters.
יַצִּילֵ֗נִי מֵאֹיְבִ֥י עָ֑ז וּ֝מִשֹּׂנְאַ֗י כִּֽי־אָמְצ֥וּ מִמֶּֽנִּי׃	18 He saved me from my fierce enemy, from foes too strong for me.
יְקַדְּמ֥וּנִי בְיוֹם־אֵידִ֑י וַֽיְהִי־יְהֹוָ֖ה לְמִשְׁעָ֣ן לִֽי׃	19 They confronted me on my direst day, but the Lord was my support.
וַיּוֹצִיאֵ֥נִי לַמֶּרְחָ֑ב יְ֝חַלְּצֵ֗נִי כִּ֘י חָ֥פֵֽץ בִּֽי׃	20 He brought me out to freedom; He rescued me because He delighted in me.

<table>
<tr><td>

יִגְמְלֵנִי יְהוָה כְּצִדְקִי
כְּבֹר יָדַי יָשִׁיב לִי:

</td><td>

21 The Lord rewarded me as I deserved;
as my hands were clean, He repaid me,

</td></tr>
<tr><td>

כִּי־שָׁמַרְתִּי דַּרְכֵי יְהוָה
וְלֹא־רָשַׁעְתִּי מֵאֱלֹהָי:

</td><td>

22 for I kept the ways of the Lord
and did not betray my God,

</td></tr>
<tr><td>

כִּי כָל־מִשְׁפָּטָיו לְנֶגְדִּי
וְחֻקֹּתָיו לֹא־אָסִיר מֶנִּי:

</td><td>

23 for all His laws are before me;
I will not cast aside His statutes.

</td></tr>
<tr><td>

וָאֱהִי תָמִים עִמּוֹ
וָאֶשְׁתַּמֵּר מֵעֲוֹנִי:

</td><td>

24 I am blameless to Him
and keep myself from sin,

</td></tr>
<tr><td>

וַיָּשֶׁב־יְהוָה לִי כְצִדְקִי
כְּבֹר יָדַי לְנֶגֶד עֵינָיו:

</td><td>

25 so the Lord repaid me as I deserved,
as my hands were clean in His sight.

</td></tr>
<tr><td>

עִם־חָסִיד תִּתְחַסָּד
עִם־גְּבַר תָּמִים תִּתַּמָּם:

</td><td>

26 You deal loyally with those who are loyal;
to the blameless You show Yourself
blameless;

</td></tr>
<tr><td>

עִם־נָבָר תִּתְבָּרָר
וְעִם־עִקֵּשׁ תִּתְפַּתָּל:

</td><td>

27 You are pure with those who are pure,
but with the crooked, You twist and turn,

</td></tr>
<tr><td>

כִּי־אַתָּה עַם־עָנִי תוֹשִׁיעַ
וְעֵינַיִם רָמוֹת תַּשְׁפִּיל:

</td><td>

28 for it is You who bring salvation
to a humble people
but humiliate haughty eyes,

</td></tr>
<tr><td>

כִּי־אַתָּה תָּאִיר נֵרִי
יְהוָה אֱלֹהַי יַגִּיהַּ חָשְׁכִּי:

</td><td>

29 for it is You who lights my lamp.
The Lord my God lights up my
darkness;

</td></tr>
<tr><td>

כִּי־בְךָ אָרֻץ גְּדוּד
וּבֵאלֹהַי אֲדַלֶּג־שׁוּר:

</td><td>

30 with You I can rush a ridge;
with my God I can leap over a wall.

</td></tr>
<tr><td>

הָאֵל תָּמִים דַּרְכּוֹ
אִמְרַת־יְהוָה צְרוּפָה
מָגֵן הוּא לְכֹל ׀ הַחֹסִים בּוֹ:

</td><td>

31 God's ways are blameless,
the Lord's words are pure;
He is a shield to all who take refuge
in Him.

</td></tr>
</table>

כִּי מִי אֱלוֹהַ מִבַּלְעֲדֵי יהוה 32 For who is a god besides the Lᴏʀᴅ;
וּמִי צוּר זוּלָתִי אֱלֹהֵינוּ:   who is a rock besides our God?

הָאֵל הַמְאַזְּרֵנִי חָיִל   33 God is the one who girds me with power;
וַיִּתֵּן תָּמִים דַּרְכִּי: He makes my way sound.

מְשַׁוֶּה רַגְלַי כָּאַיָּלוֹת   34 He makes my legs like a deer's
וְעַל בָּמֹתַי יַעֲמִידֵנִי: and stands me on the heights;

מְלַמֵּד יָדַי לַמִּלְחָמָה   35 He trains my hands for battle
וְנִחֲתָה קֶשֶׁת־נְחוּשָׁה זְרוֹעֹתָי: so that my arms can bend a bow
                                    of bronze.

וַתִּתֶּן־לִי מָגֵן יִשְׁעֶךָ   36 You gave me the shield of Your victory;
וִימִינְךָ תִסְעָדֵנִי   Your right hand sustained me;
וְעַנְוַתְךָ תַרְבֵּנִי: Your gentleness made me great.

תַּרְחִיב צַעֲדִי תַחְתָּי   37 You made my steps broad and firm;
וְלֹא מָעֲדוּ קַרְסֻלָּי: my feet never faltered.

אֶרְדּוֹף אוֹיְבַי וְאַשִּׂיגֵם   38 I pursued my enemies
וְלֹא־אָשׁוּב עַד־כַּלּוֹתָם: and overtook them,
                                    never turning back until they perished.

אֶמְחָצֵם וְלֹא־יֻכְלוּ קוּם   39 I crushed them
יִפְּלוּ תַּחַת רַגְלָי: until they could rise no more;
                                    they fell beneath my feet.

וַתְּאַזְּרֵנִי חַיִל לַמִּלְחָמָה   40 You girded me with power for battle
תַּכְרִיעַ קָמַי תַּחְתָּי: and sunk my adversaries far beneath me;

וְאֹיְבַי נָתַתָּה לִּי עֹרֶף   41 You made my enemies turn tail
וּמְשַׂנְאַי אַצְמִיתֵם: before me;
                                    my foes, too, I destroyed.

יְשַׁוְּעוּ וְאֵין־מוֹשִׁיעַ   42 They cried out, but there was no savior –
עַל־יהוה וְלֹא עָנָם: out to the Lᴏʀᴅ,
                                    but He did not answer them –

וָאֶשְׁחָקֵם כְּעָפָר עַל־פְּנֵי־רֻוּחַ
כְּטִיט חוּצְוֹת אֲרִיקֵם׃

43   while I ground them up
     like dust in the wind;
     I poured them out like street-mud.

תְּפַלְּטֵנִי מֵרִיבֵי עָם
תְּשִׂימֵנִי לְרֹאשׁ גּוֹיִם
עַם לֹא־יָדַעְתִּי יַעַבְדֽוּנִי׃

44   You rescued me from civil strife;
     You have set me as the head of nations;
     peoples I never knew of serve me.

לְשֵׁמַע אֹזֶן יִשָּׁמְעוּ לִי
בְּנֵי־נֵכָר יְכַחֲשׁוּ־לִֽי׃

45   They merely hear of me and obey;
     foreign peoples come cringing before me.

בְּנֵי־נֵכָר יִבֹּלוּ
וְיַחְרְגוּ מִמִּסְגְּרוֹתֵיהֶֽם׃

46   Foreign peoples lose heart
     and come trembling out of their forts.

חַי־יְהֹוָה וּבָרוּךְ צוּרִי
וְיָרוּם אֱלוֹהֵי יִשְׁעִֽי׃

47   The LORD lives! Blessed is my rock;
     exalted is the God of my rescue! –

הָאֵל הַנּוֹתֵן נְקָמוֹת לִי
וַיַּדְבֵּר עַמִּים תַּחְתָּֽי׃

48   the God who grants vengeance to me,
     who subjugates people under me.

מְפַלְּטִי מֵאֹיְבָי
אַף מִן־קָמַי תְּרוֹמְמֵנִי
מֵאִישׁ חָמָס תַּצִּילֵֽנִי׃

49   My rescuer from my enemies,
     You raise me above those
     who rise against me;
     You save me from violent men,

עַל־כֵּן ׀ אוֹדְךָ בַגּוֹיִם ׀ יְהֹוָה
וּלְשִׁמְךָ אֲזַמֵּֽרָה׃

50   so I praise You among the nations, Lord,
     and sing to Your name.

מִגְדֹּל יְשׁוּעוֹת מַלְכּוֹ
וְעֹשֶׂה חֶסֶד ׀ לִמְשִׁיחוֹ
לְדָוִד וּלְזַרְעוֹ עַד־עוֹלָֽם׃

51   He grants great victories to His king
     and shows loyalty to His anointed,
     to David and his seed forever.

The Lord's teaching is perfect, reviving the spirit; the Lord's decree is steadfast, making the simple wise

Days like today make it all worthwhile. Everything fits.
The wonders of nature thrill me.
I am fascinated by God's wisdom.
Why can't every day be like today?

PSALM 19

לַמְנַצֵּחַ מִזְמוֹר לְדָוִד:	1	To the lead singer – a psalm of David
הַשָּׁמַיִם מְסַפְּרִים כְּבוֹד־אֵל וּמַעֲשֵׂה יָדָיו מַגִּיד הָרָקִיעַ:	2	The heavens tell of God's glory; the skies proclaim His handiwork.
יוֹם לְיוֹם יַבִּיעַ אֹמֶר וְלַיְלָה לְּלַיְלָה יְחַוֶּה־דָּעַת:	3	Day to day pours forth speech; night to night expresses knowledge.
אֵין־אֹמֶר וְאֵין דְּבָרִים בְּלִי נִשְׁמָע קוֹלָם:	4	There is no speech; there are no words; their voice is not heard,
בְּכָל־הָאָרֶץ ׀ יָצָא קַוָּם וּבִקְצֵה תֵבֵל מִלֵּיהֶם לַשֶּׁמֶשׁ שָׂם־אֹהֶל בָּהֶם:	5	yet their music carries across the land, their words to the end of the earth. In them He has set a tent for the sun,
וְהוּא כְּחָתָן יֹצֵא מֵחֻפָּתוֹ יָשִׂישׂ כְּגִבּוֹר לָרוּץ אֹרַח:	6	which emerges like a groom from his marriage chamber, glowing like a champion about to run his course.
מִקְצֵה הַשָּׁמַיִם ׀ מוֹצָאוֹ וּתְקוּפָתוֹ עַל־קְצוֹתָם וְאֵין נִסְתָּר מֵחַמָּתוֹ:	7	It rises at one end of the heaven and circuits to the other; nothing can hide from its heat.
תּוֹרַת יהוה תְּמִימָה מְשִׁיבַת נָפֶשׁ עֵדוּת יהוה נֶאֱמָנָה מַחְכִּימַת פֶּתִי:	8	The Lord's teaching is perfect, reviving the spirit; the Lord's decree is steadfast, making the simple wise.
פִּקּוּדֵי יהוה יְשָׁרִים מְשַׂמְּחֵי־לֵב מִצְוַת יהוה בָּרָה מְאִירַת עֵינָיִם:	9	The Lord's precepts are just, cheering the heart; the Lord's commandment is radiant, lighting up the eyes.
יִרְאַת יהוה ׀ טְהוֹרָה עוֹמֶדֶת לָעַד מִשְׁפְּטֵי־יהוה אֱמֶת צָדְקוּ יַחְדָּו:	10	Fear of the Lord is pure, enduring forever; the Lord's judgments are true and righteous without exception –

הַנֶּחֱמָדִים מִזָּהָב וּמִפַּז רָב 11 more precious than gold,
וּמְתוּקִים מִדְּבַשׁ than boundless fine gold,
וְנֹפֶת צוּפִים: sweeter than honey,
than nectar from the honeycomb.

גַּם־עַבְדְּךָ נִזְהָר בָּהֶם 12 Your servant, too, is careful of them;
בְּשָׁמְרָם עֵקֶב רָב: in keeping them there is great reward.

שְׁגִיאוֹת מִי־יָבִין 13 Yet who can discern his errors?
מִנִּסְתָּרוֹת נַקֵּנִי: Cleanse me of hidden faults.

גַּם מִזֵּדִים ׀ חֲשֹׂךְ עַבְדֶּךָ 14 Spare Your servant from the insolent;
אַל־יִמְשְׁלוּ־בִי אָז אֵיתָם let them rule me not.
וְנִקֵּיתִי מִפֶּשַׁע רָב: Then shall I be blameless,
cleansed of grave sin.

יִהְיוּ לְרָצוֹן ׀ אִמְרֵי־פִי 15 May the words of my mouth
וְהֶגְיוֹן לִבִּי לְפָנֶיךָ and my heart's reflections
יהוה צוּרִי וְגֹאֲלִי: please You, Lord,
my rock and redeemer.

Some trust in chariots, others in horses, but we call on the name of the LORD our God

I am safe, but my friend is in trouble.
I feel helpless. I wish there were something I could do for him.
But there *is* something I can do for him. I can pray.

PSALM 20

לַמְנַצֵּחַ מִזְמוֹר לְדָוִד׃ 1 To the lead singer – a psalm of David

יַעַנְךָ יהוה בְּיוֹם צָרָה 2 May the LORD answer you
יְשַׂגֶּבְךָ שֵׁם ׀ אֱלֹהֵי יַעֲקֹב׃ in times of trouble;
may the name of Yaakov's God
protect you.

יִשְׁלַח־עֶזְרְךָ מִקֹּדֶשׁ 3 May He send you help
וּמִצִּיּוֹן יִסְעָדֶךָּ׃ from the Sanctuary
and support you from Zion.

יִזְכֹּר כָּל־מִנְחֹתֶךָ 4 May He recall all your grain offerings
וְעוֹלָתְךָ יְדַשְּׁנֶה סֶלָה׃ and accept your burnt offerings – Selah.

יִתֶּן־לְךָ כִלְבָבֶךָ 5 May He give you your heart's desire
וְכָל־עֲצָתְךָ יְמַלֵּא׃ and ensure that all your plans succeed.

נְרַנְּנָה ׀ בִּישׁוּעָתֶךָ 6 We will shout for joy at Your salvation
וּבְשֵׁם־אֱלֹהֵינוּ נִדְגֹּל and raise a banner in our God's name.
יְמַלֵּא יהוה כָּל־מִשְׁאֲלוֹתֶיךָ׃ May the LORD grant all your requests.

עַתָּה יָדַעְתִּי 7 Now I know
כִּי הוֹשִׁיעַ ׀ יהוה מְשִׁיחוֹ that the LORD saves His anointed,
יַעֲנֵהוּ מִשְּׁמֵי קָדְשׁוֹ that He answers him
בִּגְבֻרוֹת יֵשַׁע יְמִינוֹ׃ from His holy heaven
with the saving power of His right hand.

אֵלֶּה בָרֶכֶב וְאֵלֶּה בַסּוּסִים 8 Some trust in chariots, others in horses,
וַאֲנַחְנוּ ׀ בְּשֵׁם־יהוה אֱלֹהֵינוּ but we call on the name of the LORD
נַזְכִּיר׃ our God.

הֵמָּה כָּרְעוּ וְנָפָלוּ 9 They crumple and fall,
וַאֲנַחְנוּ קַּמְנוּ וַנִּתְעוֹדָד׃ but we rise up and stand firm.

יהוה הוֹשִׁיעָה 10 LORD, grant victory!
הַמֶּלֶךְ יַעֲנֵנוּ בְיוֹם־קָרְאֵנוּ׃ May the King answer us when we call.

His glory is great through Your victory; You lavish majesty and splendor upon him

I always knew he could do it. He fought so many enemies.
He overcame so many obstacles. Now he has achieved it all.
But so many others are jealous of him. Success is never secure.

PSALM 21

לַמְנַצֵּחַ מִזְמוֹר לְדָוִד׃ 1   To the lead singer – a psalm of David

יְהוָה בְּעָזְּךָ יִשְׂמַח־מֶלֶךְ 2   Lᴏʀᴅ, the king rejoices in Your might;
וּבִישׁוּעָתְךָ מַה־יָּגֶל מְאֹד׃   how he delights in Your victory!

יָגִיל

תַּאֲוַת לִבּוֹ נָתַתָּה לּוֹ 3   You have granted him his heart's desire
וַאֲרֶשֶׁת שְׂפָתָיו בַּל־מָנַעְתָּ   and not denied the requests of his lips –
סֶּלָה׃   Selah.

כִּי־תְקַדְּמֶנּוּ בִּרְכוֹת טוֹב 4   You have welcomed him
תָּשִׁית לְרֹאשׁוֹ עֲטֶרֶת פָּז׃   with rich blessing
  and set a golden crown upon his head.

חַיִּים ׀ שָׁאַל מִמְּךָ נָתַתָּה לּוֹ 5   He asked You for life,
אֹרֶךְ יָמִים עוֹלָם וָעֶד׃   and You have granted it –
  long life for evermore.

גָּדוֹל כְּבוֹדוֹ בִּישׁוּעָתֶךָ 6   His glory is great through Your victory;
הוֹד וְהָדָר תְּשַׁוֶּה עָלָיו׃   You lavish majesty and splendor
  upon him,

כִּי־תְשִׁיתֵהוּ בְרָכוֹת לָעַד 7   bestowing upon him eternal blessing,
תְּחַדֵּהוּ בְשִׂמְחָה אֶת־פָּנֶיךָ׃   cheering him with the joy of
  Your presence,

כִּי־הַמֶּלֶךְ בֹּטֵחַ בַּיהוָה 8   for the king trusts in the Lᴏʀᴅ;
וּבְחֶסֶד עֶלְיוֹן בַּל־יִמּוֹט׃   with the loyalty of the Most High
  he will never be shaken.

תִּמְצָא יָדְךָ לְכָל־אֹיְבֶיךָ 9   Your hand reaches all Your enemies;
יְמִינְךָ תִּמְצָא שֹׂנְאֶיךָ׃   Your right hand reaches those
  who hate You.

תְּשִׁיתֵמוֹ ׀ כְּתַנּוּר אֵשׁ 10   You set them ablaze like a furnace
לְעֵת פָּנֶיךָ   when You appear;
יְהוָה בְּאַפּוֹ יְבַלְּעֵם   in His wrath, the Lᴏʀᴅ will engulf them,
וְתֹאכְלֵם אֵשׁ׃   and fire will consume them.

פִּרְיָמוֹ מֵאֶרֶץ תְּאַבֵּד 11   You wipe their offspring from the earth,
וְזַרְעָם מִבְּנֵי אָדָם׃   their seed from among men,

כִּי־נָטוּ עָלֶיךָ רָעָה
חָשְׁבוּ מְזִמָּה
בַּל־יוּכָלוּ:

12 for they plotted evil toward You;
they devised schemes
but could not succeed.

כִּי תְּשִׁיתֵמוֹ שֶׁכֶם
בְּמֵיתָרֶיךָ תְּכוֹנֵן עַל־פְּנֵיהֶם:

13 You will put them to flight,
aiming Your bow at their faces.

רוּמָה יהוה בְעֻזֶּךָ
נָשִׁירָה וּנְזַמְּרָה גְבוּרָתֶךָ:

14 Rise up, LORD, in Your might;
we will sing and praise Your power.

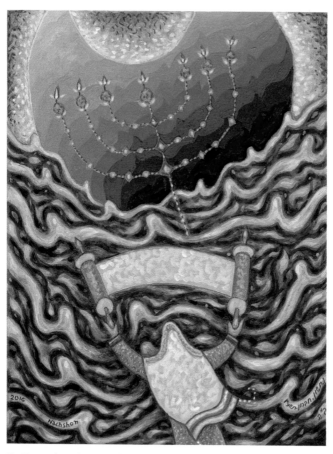

But You are the Holy One, enthroned on Israel's praises

I am worthless. Prayers work for others; for me they are futile.
The odds are against me. I am helpless.
I must become more hopeful, more optimistic.
I will change the way I think of myself. I have great potential.

PSALM 22

לַמְנַצֵּחַ עַל־אַיֶּלֶת הַשַּׁחַר
מִזְמוֹר לְדָוִד:

1 To the lead singer, a dawn song–
   a psalm of David

אֵלִי אֵלִי לָמָה עֲזַבְתָּנִי
רָחוֹק מִישׁוּעָתִי
דִּבְרֵי שַׁאֲגָתִי:

2 O God, my God –
   why have You forsaken me?
   So far from my salvation
   are the words that I roar.

אֱלֹהַי אֶקְרָא יוֹמָם וְלֹא תַעֲנֶה
וְלַיְלָה וְלֹא־דוּמִיָּה לִי:

3 My God, I cry out to You by day,
   but You do not answer,
   and by night – without relief.

וְאַתָּה קָדוֹשׁ
יוֹשֵׁב תְּהִלּוֹת יִשְׂרָאֵל:

4 But You are the Holy One,
   enthroned on Israel's praises.

בְּךָ בָּטְחוּ אֲבֹתֵינוּ
בָּטְחוּ וַתְּפַלְּטֵמוֹ:

5 In You our ancestors placed their trust;
   they trusted, and You delivered them.

אֵלֶיךָ זָעֲקוּ וְנִמְלָטוּ
בְּךָ בָטְחוּ וְלֹא־בוֹשׁוּ:

6 To You they cried out and were saved;
   in You they trusted
   and were not let down.

וְאָנֹכִי תוֹלַעַת וְלֹא־אִישׁ
חֶרְפַּת אָדָם וּבְזוּי עָם:

7 But I am a worm, not human –
   scorned by men,
   disgraced among people.

כָּל־רֹאַי יַלְעִגוּ לִי
יַפְטִירוּ בְשָׂפָה יָנִיעוּ רֹאשׁ:

8 Whoever sees me mocks me;
   they curl their lips and shake their heads.

גֹּל אֶל־יהוה יְפַלְּטֵהוּ
יַצִּילֵהוּ כִּי חָפֵץ בּוֹ:

9 "Look to the LORD – let Him deliver;
   let Him save him, if He delights in him,"

כִּי־אַתָּה גֹחִי מִבָּטֶן
מַבְטִיחִי עַל־שְׁדֵי אִמִּי:

10 for it is You who drew me out
    from the womb,
    You who kept me safe
    at my mother's breast.

עָלֶיךָ הָשְׁלַכְתִּי מֵרָחֶם
מִבֶּטֶן אִמִּי אֵלִי אָתָּה:

11 I have been in Your care since birth;
    from my mother's womb,
    You have been my God.

אַל־תִּרְחַק מִמֶּנִּי
כִּי־צָרָה קְרוֹבָה
כִּי־אֵין עוֹזֵר:

12 Do not stray far from me
for trouble is near,
with no one to help.

סְבָבוּנִי פָּרִים רַבִּים
אַבִּירֵי בָשָׁן כִּתְּרוּנִי:

13 Many bulls surround me;
fierce beasts of the Bashan close in on me.

פָּצוּ עָלַי פִּיהֶם
אַרְיֵה טֹרֵף וְשֹׁאֵג:

14 Their jaws open wide against me
like ravenous roaring lions.

כַּמַּיִם נִשְׁפַּכְתִּי
וְהִתְפָּרְדוּ כָּל־עַצְמוֹתָי
הָיָה לִבִּי כַּדּוֹנָג
נָמֵס בְּתוֹךְ מֵעָי:

15 I dissolve like water,
all my limbs falling to pieces,
my heart melting like wax within me.

יָבֵשׁ כַּחֶרֶשׂ ׀ כֹּחִי
וּלְשׁוֹנִי מֻדְבָּק מַלְקוֹחָי
וְלַעֲפַר־מָוֶת תִּשְׁפְּתֵנִי:

16 My strength is dried up like clay shards;
my tongue sticks to my palate;
You lay me down in the dust of death,

כִּי סְבָבוּנִי כְּלָבִים
עֲדַת מְרֵעִים הִקִּיפוּנִי
כָּאֲרִי יָדַי וְרַגְלָי:

17 for hounds are all around me;
a vicious pack encircles me,
at my hands and feet like a lion.

אֲסַפֵּר כָּל־עַצְמוֹתָי
הֵמָּה יַבִּיטוּ יִרְאוּ־בִי:

18 I count all my bones
as they look on and gloat.

יְחַלְּקוּ בְגָדַי לָהֶם
וְעַל־לְבוּשִׁי יַפִּילוּ גוֹרָל:

19 They divide up my garments
among themselves
and cast lots for my clothing.

וְאַתָּה יהוה אַל־תִּרְחַק
אֱיָלוּתִי לְעֶזְרָתִי חוּשָׁה:

20 But You, LORD – do not be distant,
O my Help; rush to my aid;

הַצִּילָה מֵחֶרֶב נַפְשִׁי
מִיַּד־כֶּלֶב יְחִידָתִי:

21 save my life from the sword,
my precious soul from those hounds;

הוֹשִׁיעֵנִי מִפִּי אַרְיֵה
וּמִקַּרְנֵי רֵמִים עֲנִיתָנִי:

22 rescue me from the lions' jaws;
deliver me from the horns of wild bulls.

אֲסַפְּרָה שִׁמְךָ לְאֶחָי
בְּתוֹךְ קָהָל אֲהַלְלֶךָּ:

23 I will tell of Your name to my kin;
I will praise You
in the midst of the assembly.

יִרְאֵי יהוה ׀ הַלְלוּהוּ
כָּל־זֶרַע יַעֲקֹב כַּבְּדוּהוּ
וְגוּרוּ מִמֶּנּוּ כָּל־זֶרַע יִשְׂרָאֵל:

24 You who fear the LORD, praise Him;
honor Him, all you seed of Yaakov;
revere Him, all you seed of Israel,

כִּי לֹא־בָזָה וְלֹא שִׁקַּץ
עֱנוּת עָנִי
וְלֹא־הִסְתִּיר פָּנָיו מִמֶּנּוּ
וּבְשַׁוְּעוֹ אֵלָיו שָׁמֵעַ:

25 for He has not spurned or scorned
the suffering of the lowly;
He has not hidden His face from them;
when they cried out to Him, He listened.

מֵאִתְּךָ תְּהִלָּתִי
בְּקָהָל רָב נְדָרַי אֲשַׁלֵּם
נֶגֶד יְרֵאָיו:

26 You inspire my praise
before the great assembly;
I will pay my vows
before those who revere Him.

יֹאכְלוּ עֲנָוִים ׀ וְיִשְׂבָּעוּ יְהַלְלוּ
יהוה דֹּרְשָׁיו
יְחִי לְבַבְכֶם לָעַד:

27 The lowly will eat and be satisfied;
those who seek the LORD
will praise Him –
may your hearts rejoice forever!

יִזְכְּרוּ ׀ וְיָשֻׁבוּ אֶל־יהוה
כָּל־אַפְסֵי־אָרֶץ
וְיִשְׁתַּחֲווּ לְפָנֶיךָ
כָּל־מִשְׁפְּחוֹת גּוֹיִם:

28 Let all the ends of the earth remember
and turn to the LORD;
let all families of the nations
bow before You

כִּי לַיהוה הַמְּלוּכָה
וּמֹשֵׁל בַּגּוֹיִם:

29 for the kingship is the LORD's;
He rules over the nations.

אָכְלוּ וַיִּשְׁתַּחֲווּ ׀
כָּל־דִּשְׁנֵי־אָרֶץ
לְפָנָיו יִכְרְעוּ כָּל־יוֹרְדֵי עָפָר
וְנַפְשׁוֹ לֹא חִיָּה:

30 All those who thrive on the land
will feast and worship;
all those who descend to the dust
shall kneel before Him –
those who cannot endure.

31 Posterity will serve Him;
   future generations will be told
   about the LORD,

זֶרַע יַעַבְדֶנּוּ
יְסֻפַּר לַאדֹנָי לַדּוֹר:

32 and they, in turn,
   will tell of His righteousness,
   of His deeds, to the people yet unborn.

יָבֹאוּ וְיַגִּידוּ צִדְקָתוֹ
לְעַם נוֹלָד כִּי עָשָׂה:

He lets me lie down in green pastures; He leads me beside still waters

A strange calm has come over me.
It is not that my troubles are gone.
But I have given them over to a "Higher Power."
That relieves me from a lot of pressure.
I have more freedom to solve my problems by myself.

PSALM 23

מִזְמוֹר לְדָוִד
יהוה רֹעִי לֹא אֶחְסָר:

בִּנְאוֹת דֶּשֶׁא יַרְבִּיצֵנִי
עַל־מֵי מְנֻחוֹת יְנַהֲלֵנִי:

נַפְשִׁי יְשׁוֹבֵב
יַנְחֵנִי בְמַעְגְּלֵי־צֶדֶק
לְמַעַן שְׁמוֹ:

גַּם כִּי־אֵלֵךְ בְּגֵיא צַלְמָוֶת
לֹא־אִירָא רָע כִּי־אַתָּה עִמָּדִי
שִׁבְטְךָ וּמִשְׁעַנְתֶּךָ
הֵמָּה יְנַחֲמֻנִי:

תַּעֲרֹךְ לְפָנַי ׀ שֻׁלְחָן נֶגֶד צֹרְרָי
דִּשַּׁנְתָּ בַשֶּׁמֶן רֹאשִׁי
כּוֹסִי רְוָיָה:

אַךְ ׀ טוֹב וָחֶסֶד יִרְדְּפוּנִי
כָּל־יְמֵי חַיָּי
וְשַׁבְתִּי בְּבֵית־יהוה
לְאֹרֶךְ יָמִים:

1 A psalm of David
The LORD is my Shepherd;
I lack nothing.

2 He lets me lie down in green pastures;
He leads me beside still waters.

3 He refreshes my soul,
guiding me along the right paths
for the sake of His name.

4 Though I walk through the valley
of the shadow of death,
I fear no evil, for You are with me;
Your rod and Your staff encourage me.

5 You set a table before me
in the face of my foes;
You anoint my head with oil;
my cup brims over.

6 May only goodness and kindness
follow me
all the days of my life;
let me live in the LORD's House
forevermore.

Lift up your heads, O gates; rise up, eternal doors, so that the King of glory may enter

I definitely believe in God and I am in awe of him.
Why should my trivial affairs matter to Him?
Maybe He cares about some prominent person's good deeds.
But mine? No way.

PSALM 24

לְדָוִד מִזְמוֹר
לַיהוה הָאָרֶץ וּמְלוֹאָהּ
תֵּבֵל וְיֹשְׁבֵי בָהּ:

1 Of David – a psalm
The Lord owns the earth
and all it contains,
the world and all who live in it,

כִּי־הוּא עַל־יַמִּים יְסָדָהּ
וְעַל־נְהָרוֹת יְכוֹנְנֶהָ:

2 for He founded it on the seas,
set it on the streams.

מִי־יַעֲלֶה בְהַר־יהוה
וּמִי־יָקוּם בִּמְקוֹם קָדְשׁוֹ:

3 Who may ascend the Lord's mountain?
Who may stand in His holy place?

נְקִי כַפַּיִם וּבַר־לֵבָב
אֲשֶׁר לֹא־נָשָׂא לַשָּׁוְא נַפְשִׁי   נפשו
וְלֹא נִשְׁבַּע לְמִרְמָה:

4 Those who have clean hands
and pure hearts,
who do not take false oaths by My life,
who have not sworn deceitfully,

יִשָּׂא בְרָכָה מֵאֵת יהוה
וּצְדָקָה מֵאֱלֹהֵי יִשְׁעוֹ:

5 they shall receive blessing from the Lord,
due reward from the God of their
salvation.

זֶה דּוֹר דֹּרְשָׁו
מְבַקְשֵׁי פָנֶיךָ יַעֲקֹב סֶלָה:

6 Such is the generation who seek Him –
Yaakov who seek Your presence, Selah.

שְׂאוּ שְׁעָרִים ׀ רָאשֵׁיכֶם
וְהִנָּשְׂאוּ פִּתְחֵי עוֹלָם
וְיָבוֹא מֶלֶךְ הַכָּבוֹד:

7 Lift up your heads, O gates;
rise up, eternal doors,
so that the King of glory may enter.

מִי זֶה מֶלֶךְ הַכָּבוֹד
יהוה עִזּוּז וְגִבּוֹר
יהוה גִּבּוֹר מִלְחָמָה:

8 Who is the King of glory?
It is the Lord, strong and mighty,
the Lord mighty in battle.

שְׂאוּ שְׁעָרִים ׀ רָאשֵׁיכֶם וּשְׂאוּ
פִּתְחֵי עוֹלָם
וְיָבֹא מֶלֶךְ הַכָּבוֹד:

9 Lift up your heads, O gates;
lift them up, eternal doors,
so that the King of glory may enter.

מִי הוּא זֶה מֶלֶךְ הַכָּבוֹד
יהוה צְבָאוֹת
הוּא מֶלֶךְ הַכָּבוֹד סֶלָה:

10 Who is this King of glory?
The Lord of hosts –
He is the King of glory – Selah.

The Lord confides in those who fear Him; to them He reveals His covenant

I never asked for all of these responsibilities.
I am stuck with them.
I am in way over my head. Who can help me handle it all?
Can God be my guide? There is no one else for me to rely on.

PSALM 25

לְדָוִד
אֵלֶיךָ יְהוֹה נַפְשִׁי אֶשָּׂא׃

1 Of David
To You, O LORD, I lift up my soul;

אֱלֹהַי
בְּךָ בָטַחְתִּי אַל־אֵבוֹשָׁה
אַל־יַעַלְצוּ אוֹיְבַי לִי׃

2 in You, my God, I place my trust.
Do not let me be put to shame;
do not let my enemies gloat over me.

גַּם כָּל־קֹוֶיךָ לֹא יֵבֹשׁוּ
יֵבֹשׁוּ הַבּוֹגְדִים רֵיקָם׃

3 Let none who hope for You
be put to shame,
but let traitors, empty-handed,
be ashamed.

דְּרָכֶיךָ יְהוֹה הוֹדִיעֵנִי
אֹרְחוֹתֶיךָ לַמְּדֵנִי׃

4 Show me Your ways, LORD;
teach me Your paths.

הַדְרִיכֵנִי בַאֲמִתֶּךָ ׀ וְלַמְּדֵנִי
כִּי־אַתָּה אֱלֹהֵי יִשְׁעִי
אוֹתְךָ קִוִּיתִי כָּל־הַיּוֹם׃

5 Guide me in Your truth; teach me,
for You are the God of my salvation;
I constantly look to You in hope.

זְכֹר־רַחֲמֶיךָ יְהוֹה וַחֲסָדֶיךָ
כִּי מֵעוֹלָם הֵמָּה׃

6 Remember Your compassion, LORD,
Your loyalty,
for they have always been.

חַטֹּאות נְעוּרַי ׀
וּפְשָׁעַי אַל־תִּזְכֹּר
כְּחַסְדְּךָ זְכָר־לִי־אַתָּה
לְמַעַן טוּבְךָ יְהוֹה׃

7 Do not remember the sins of my youth
or my offenses,
but remember me in keeping with
Your loyalty,
in keeping with Your goodness, LORD.

טוֹב־וְיָשָׁר יְהוֹה
עַל־כֵּן יוֹרֶה חַטָּאִים בַּדָּרֶךְ׃

8 Good and upright is the LORD;
therefore He shows sinners the way;

יַדְרֵךְ עֲנָוִים בַּמִּשְׁפָּט
וִילַמֵּד עֲנָוִים דַּרְכּוֹ׃

9 He guides the lowly along the right path
and teaches the lowly His way.

כָּל־אָרְחוֹת יְהוֹה חֶסֶד וֶאֱמֶת
לְנֹצְרֵי בְרִיתוֹ וְעֵדֹתָיו׃

10 All the ways of the Lord are loyal and true
to those who keep His covenant,
His rules.

לְמַעַן־שִׁמְךָ יהוה
וְסָלַחְתָּ לַעֲוֺנִי כִּי רַב־הוּא:

11 For the sake of Your name, LORD,
forgive my sin though it is great.

מִי־זֶה הָאִישׁ יְרֵא יהוה
יוֹרֶנּוּ בְּדֶרֶךְ יִבְחָר:

12 Who, then, is one who fears the LORD?
He will show them which path to choose.

נַפְשׁוֹ בְּטוֹב תָּלִין
וְזַרְעוֹ יִירַשׁ אָרֶץ:

13 They will live good lives,
and their children will inherit the earth.

סוֹד יהוה לִירֵאָיו
וּבְרִיתוֹ לְהוֹדִיעָם:

14 The LORD confides
in those who fear Him;
to them He reveals His covenant.

עֵינַי תָּמִיד אֶל־יהוה
כִּי הוּא־יוֹצִיא מֵרֶשֶׁת רַגְלָי:

15 My eyes are ever on the LORD,
for only He can free my feet from the net.

פְּנֵה־אֵלַי וְחָנֵּנִי
כִּי־יָחִיד וְעָנִי אָנִי:

16 Turn to me and show me favor,
for I am lonely and suffering;

צָרוֹת לְבָבִי הִרְחִיבוּ
מִמְּצוּקוֹתַי הוֹצִיאֵנִי:

17 my heart swells with grief;
relieve me from my agony;

רְאֵה עָנְיִי וַעֲמָלִי
וְשָׂא לְכָל־חַטֹּאותָי:

18 see my suffering and my pain,
and forgive all my sins.

רְאֵה־אוֹיְבַי כִּי־רָבּוּ
וְשִׂנְאַת חָמָס שְׂנֵאוּנִי:

19 See how many enemies I have
and their violent hatred toward me.

שָׁמְרָה נַפְשִׁי וְהַצִּילֵנִי
אַל־אֵבוֹשׁ כִּי־חָסִיתִי בָךְ:

20 Protect me and save me;
let me not be put to shame,
for in You I take refuge.

תֹּם־וָיֹשֶׁר יִצְּרוּנִי
כִּי קִוִּיתִיךָ:

21 Let integrity and decency keep me,
for I look to You in hope.

פְּדֵה אֱלֹהִים אֶת־יִשְׂרָאֵל
מִכֹּל צָרוֹתָיו:

22 May God free Israel
from all its grief.

O LORD, I love the abode of Your House, the dwelling place of Your glory!

I can't tolerate disingenuous people. I may not be perfect, but at least I am sincere. I don't preach one thing and then do another. I dislike hypocrites. I avoid them when I can.

PSALM 26

לְדָוִד ׀ שָׁפְטֵנִי יהוה
כִּי־אֲנִי בְּתֻמִּי הָלַכְתִּי
וּבַיהוָה בָּטַחְתִּי לֹא אֶמְעָד׃

1 Of David. Judge me, LORD,
for I have walked blamelessly;
I place my trust in the LORD;
I do not waver.

בְּחָנֵנִי יהוה וְנַסֵּנִי
צרופה
צָרְפָה כִלְיוֹתַי וְלִבִּי׃

2 Test me, LORD; try me;
probe my heart and mind,

כִּי־חַסְדְּךָ לְנֶגֶד עֵינָי
וְהִתְהַלַּכְתִּי בַּאֲמִתֶּךָ׃

3 for Your loyalty is before my eyes,
and I walk in Your truth.

לֹא־יָשַׁבְתִּי עִם־מְתֵי־שָׁוְא
וְעִם נַעֲלָמִים לֹא אָבוֹא׃

4 I do not sit with corrupt people
or associate with hypocrites;

שָׂנֵאתִי קְהַל מְרֵעִים
וְעִם־רְשָׁעִים לֹא אֵשֵׁב׃

5 I despise the company of evildoers
and will not tolerate the wicked.

אֶרְחַץ בְּנִקָּיוֹן כַּפָּי
וַאֲסֹבְבָה אֶת־מִזְבַּחֲךָ יהוה׃

6 I wash my hands in innocence
and walk around Your altar, LORD,

לַשְׁמִעַ בְּקוֹל תּוֹדָה
וּלְסַפֵּר כָּל־נִפְלְאוֹתֶיךָ׃

7 raising my voice in thanksgiving
and telling of all Your wonders.

יהוה אָהַבְתִּי מְעוֹן בֵּיתֶךָ
וּמְקוֹם מִשְׁכַּן כְּבוֹדֶךָ׃

8 O Lord, I love the abode of Your House,
the dwelling place of Your glory!

אַל־תֶּאֱסֹף עִם־חַטָּאִים נַפְשִׁי
וְעִם־אַנְשֵׁי דָמִים חַיָּי׃

9 Do not sweep me away with sinners,
my life with the men of blood

אֲשֶׁר־בִּידֵיהֶם זִמָּה
וִימִינָם מָלְאָה שֹּׁחַד׃

10 in whose hands are evil schemes,
their right hands full of bribes,

וַאֲנִי בְּתֻמִּי אֵלֵךְ
פְּדֵנִי וְחָנֵּנִי׃

11 for I will walk on blamelessly;
redeem me and show me grace.

רַגְלִי עָמְדָה בְמִישׁוֹר
בְּמַקְהֵלִים אֲבָרֵךְ יהוה׃

12 My feet stand on even ground;
among the crowd, I bless the LORD.

Of David. The LORD is my light and my salvation – whom need I fear?

Externally my life is full. But my inner life is empty.
A voice inside of me is calling. I strain to hear it.
What is it saying?

PSALM 27

לְדָוִד ׀ יהוה ׀ אוֹרִי וְיִשְׁעִי
מִמִּי אִירָא
יהוה מָעוֹז־חַיַּי מִמִּי אֶפְחָד:

1 Of David
The Lord is my light and my salvation –
whom need I fear?
The Lord is the stronghold of my life –
whom need I dread?

בִּקְרֹב עָלַי ׀ מְרֵעִים
לֶאֱכֹל אֶת־בְּשָׂרִי
צָרַי וְאֹיְבַי לִי
הֵמָּה כָשְׁלוּ וְנָפָלוּ:

2 When evildoers close in on me
to devour my flesh,
it is they, my enemies and foes,
who stumble and fall.

אִם־תַּחֲנֶה עָלַי ׀ מַחֲנֶה
לֹא־יִירָא לִבִּי
אִם־תָּקוּם עָלַי מִלְחָמָה
בְּזֹאת אֲנִי בוֹטֵחַ:

3 Should an army besiege me,
my heart would not fear.
Should war break out against me,
I would still be confident.

אַחַת ׀ שָׁאַלְתִּי מֵאֵת־יהוה
אוֹתָהּ אֲבַקֵּשׁ
שִׁבְתִּי בְּבֵית־יהוה
כָּל־יְמֵי חַיַּי
לַחֲזוֹת בְּנֹעַם־יהוה
וּלְבַקֵּר בְּהֵיכָלוֹ:

4 One thing I ask of the Lord;
this alone I seek:
to live in the Lord's House
all the days of my life,
to gaze on the beauty of the Lord,
and to worship in His Temple,

כִּי יִצְפְּנֵנִי ׀ בְּסֻכֹּה בְּיוֹם רָעָה
יַסְתִּרֵנִי בְּסֵתֶר אָהֳלוֹ
בְּצוּר יְרוֹמְמֵנִי:

5 for He will keep me safe in His shelter
in times of terror;
He will hide me
under the cover of His tent;
He will set me high upon a rock.

וְעַתָּה יָרוּם רֹאשִׁי עַל אֹיְבַי
סְבִיבוֹתַי
וְאֶזְבְּחָה בְאָהֳלוֹ זִבְחֵי תְרוּעָה
אָשִׁירָה וַאֲזַמְּרָה לַיהוה:

6 Now my head is high above the enemies
around me –
I will sacrifice in His tent
with shouts of joy;
I will sing and chant praises to the Lord.

שְׁמַע־יהוה קוֹלִי אֶקְרָא
וְחָנֵּנִי וַעֲנֵנִי:

7 Hear my voice, Lord, when I call;
show me grace and answer me.

לְךָ ׀ אָמַר לִבִּי בַּקְּשׁוּ פָנָי
אֶת־פָּנֶיךָ יהוה אֲבַקֵּשׁ:

8 Of You my heart whispers,
"Seek My presence" –
Your presence, LORD, I will seek.

אַל־תַּסְתֵּר פָּנֶיךָ ׀ מִמֶּנִּי אַל
תַּט־בְּאַף עַבְדֶּךָ
עֶזְרָתִי הָיִיתָ
אַל־תִּטְּשֵׁנִי וְאַל־תַּעַזְבֵנִי
אֱלֹהֵי יִשְׁעִי:

9 Do not hide Your face from me;
do not turn Your servant away in anger.
You have been my help –
do not reject or forsake me,
God, my Savior.

כִּי־אָבִי וְאִמִּי עֲזָבוּנִי
וַיהוה יַאַסְפֵנִי:

10 Were my father and my mother
to forsake me,
the LORD would take me in.

הוֹרֵנִי יהוה דַּרְכֶּךָ
וּנְחֵנִי בְּאֹרַח מִישׁוֹר
לְמַעַן שׁוֹרְרָי:

11 Teach me Your way, LORD;
lead me on a level path
because of my oppressors.

אַל־תִּתְּנֵנִי בְּנֶפֶשׁ צָרָי
כִּי קָמוּ־בִי עֵדֵי־שֶׁקֶר
וִיפֵחַ חָמָס:

12 Do not abandon me to the will
of my foes,
for false witnesses have risen against me,
breathing violence.

לוּלֵא הֶאֱמַנְתִּי
לִרְאוֹת בְּטוּב־יהוה
בְּאֶרֶץ חַיִּים:

13 Were it not for my faith
that I will see the LORD's goodness
in the land of the living…

קַוֵּה אֶל־יהוה
חֲזַק וְיַאֲמֵץ לִבֶּךָ
וְקַוֵּה אֶל־יהוה:

14 Hope in the LORD;
be strong and brave of heart,
and hope in the LORD.

Save Your people; bless Your heritage; tend them and sustain them forever

I couldn't survive without friends.
But some of them have disappointed me in a significant way.
How can I learn to choose the right friends?
I can pray to God to help me. I can celebrate when He steers me in the right direction.

PSALM 28

לְדָוִ֡ד אֵלֶ֤יךָ יְהֹוָ֨ה ׀ אֶקְרָא֮	1 Of David. To You, O Lᴏʀᴅ, I call;
צוּרִי֮ אַֽל־תֶּחֱרַ֢שׁ מִ֫מֶּ֥נִּי	O my rock, be not deaf to my cry,
פֶּן־תֶּחֱשֶׁ֥ה מִמֶּ֑נִּי	for if You remain silent,
וְ֝נִמְשַׁ֗לְתִּי עִם־י֥וֹרְדֵי בֽוֹר׃	I shall be like those who plummet
	to the Pit.
שְׁמַ֤ע ק֣וֹל תַּ֭חֲנוּנַי בְּשַׁוְּעִ֣י אֵלֶ֑יךָ	2 Hear the sound of my plea
בְּנׇשְׂאִ֥י יָ֝דַ֗י אֶל־דְּבִ֥יר קׇדְשֶֽׁךָ׃	when I cry out to You,
	when I lift my hands
	toward Your holiest sanctuary.
אַל־תִּמְשְׁכֵ֣נִי עִם־רְשָׁעִים֮	3 Do not pull me away with the wicked,
וְעִם־פֹּ֢עֲלֵ֫י אָ֥וֶן	with evildoers
דֹּבְרֵ֣י שָׁ֭לוֹם עִם־רֵעֵיהֶ֑ם	who feign peace with one another
וְ֝רָעָ֗ה בִּלְבָבָֽם׃	but harbor malice in their hearts.
תֶּן־לָהֶ֣ם כְּפׇעֳלָם֮ וּכְרֹ֢עַ	4 Pay them back for their actions,
מַעַלְלֵ֫יהֶ֥ם	for their malicious acts;
כְּמַעֲשֵׂ֣ה יְ֭דֵיהֶם תֵּ֣ן לָהֶ֑ם	pay them back for their deeds –
הָשֵׁ֖ב גְּמוּלָ֣ם לָהֶֽם׃	treat them as they deserve,
כִּ֤י לֹ֤א יָבִ֡ינוּ אֶל־פְּעֻלֹּ֣ת יְהֹוָה֮	5 for they do not recognize the Lᴏʀᴅ's acts
וְאֶל־מַ֘עֲשֵׂ֢ה יָדָ֥יו	or His handiwork.
יֶ֝הֶרְסֵ֗ם וְלֹ֣א יִבְנֵֽם׃	May He break them down,
	not build them up.
בָּר֥וּךְ יְהֹוָ֑ה	6 Blessed is the Lᴏʀᴅ,
כִּי־שָׁ֝מַ֗ע ק֣וֹל תַּחֲנוּנָֽי׃	who has heard the sound of my plea;
יְהֹוָ֤ה ׀ עֻזִּ֥י וּמָגִנִּי֮	7 the Lᴏʀᴅ is my might and my protector;
בּ֤וֹ בָטַ֥ח לִבִּ֗י וְֽנֶ֫עֱזָ֥רְתִּי	my heart trusted Him,
וַיַּעֲלֹ֥ז לִבִּ֑י וּֽמִשִּׁירִ֥י אֲהוֹדֶֽנּוּ׃	and I received help.
	My heart exults,
	and I praise Him with my song.
יְהֹוָ֥ה עֹֽז־לָ֑מוֹ	8 The Lᴏʀᴅ is their strength,
וּמָ֘ע֤וֹז יְשׁוּע֖וֹת מְשִׁיח֣וֹ הֽוּא׃	the saving stronghold of His anointed.

9 Save Your people;
bless Your heritage;
tend them and sustain them forever.

הוֹשִׁיעָה ׀ אֶת־עַמֶּךָ וּבָרֵךְ
אֶת־נַחֲלָתֶךָ
וּרְעֵם וְנַשְּׂאֵם עַד־הָעוֹלָם׃

The LORD's voice rings with power; the LORD's voice rings with splendor!

Have you ever really felt God?
I never did until that camping trip.
We were outdoors in a hurricane, for three days and three nights.
Trees were falling, streams were overflowing,
thunder was roaring. That's when I first felt God.

PSALM 29

מִזְמוֹר לְדָוִד
הָבוּ לַיהוה בְּנֵי אֵלִים
הָבוּ לַיהוה כָּבוֹד וָעֹז׃

הָבוּ לַיהוה כְּבוֹד שְׁמוֹ
הִשְׁתַּחֲווּ לַיהוה
בְּהַדְרַת־קֹדֶשׁ׃

קוֹל יהוה עַל־הַמָּיִם
אֵל־הַכָּבוֹד הִרְעִים
יְהוָה עַל־מַיִם רַבִּים׃

קוֹל־יְהוָה בַּכֹּחַ
קוֹל יְהוָה בֶּהָדָר׃

קוֹל יהוה שֹׁבֵר אֲרָזִים
וַיְשַׁבֵּר יְהוָה אֶת־אַרְזֵי הַלְּבָנוֹן׃

וַיַּרְקִידֵם כְּמוֹ־עֵגֶל
לְבָנוֹן וְשִׂרְיוֹן כְּמוֹ בֶן־רְאֵמִים׃

קוֹל־יְהוָה חֹצֵב לַהֲבוֹת אֵשׁ׃

קוֹל יהוה יָחִיל מִדְבָּר
יָחִיל יְהוָה מִדְבַּר קָדֵשׁ׃

קוֹל יהוה ׀ יְחוֹלֵל אַיָּלוֹת
וַיֶּחֱשֹׂף יְעָרוֹת
וּבְהֵיכָלוֹ כֻּלּוֹ אֹמֵר כָּבוֹד׃

יהוה לַמַּבּוּל יָשָׁב
וַיֵּשֶׁב יְהוָה מֶלֶךְ לְעוֹלָם׃

יְהוָה עֹז לְעַמּוֹ יִתֵּן
יְהוָה ׀ יְבָרֵךְ אֶת־עַמּוֹ בַשָּׁלוֹם׃

1 A psalm of David
Render to the Lord, you angelic beings –
render to the Lord glory and might.

2 Render to the Lord
the glory due His name;
bow to the Lord
in the splendor of holiness.

3 The Lord's voice echoes over the waters;
the God of glory thunders;
the Lord thunders over
the mighty waters.

4 The Lord's voice rings with power;
the Lord's voice rings with splendor!

5 The Lord's voice breaks cedars;
the Lord shatters the cedars of Lebanon –

6 He makes them skip like a calf,
Lebanon and Siryon like a young wild ox.

7 The Lord's voice sparks fiery flames!

8 The Lord's voice shakes the desert;
the Lord shakes the desert of Kadesh.

9 The Lord's voice terrifies the deer
and strips the forests bare,
and in His Temple all say, "Glory!"

10 The Lord sat enthroned at the flood;
the Lord sits enthroned as King forever.

11 May the Lord give might to His people;
may the Lord bless His people with peace.

A psalm of David – a song for the dedication of the House

I was complacent. I thought I had it made.
Everything changed in the blink of an eye.
Joyous dance turned into heartbreak.
Another blink of an eye, and again everything changed.
I danced once more.

PSALM 30

מִזְמוֹר שִׁיר־חֲנֻכַּת הַבַּיִת
לְדָוִד׃

1 A psalm of David –
a song for the dedication of the House

אֲרוֹמִמְךָ יהוה כִּי דִלִּיתָנִי
וְלֹא־שִׂמַּחְתָּ אֹיְבַי לִי׃

2 I will exalt You, LORD,
for You have lifted me up;
You have not let my enemies
gloat over me.

יהוה אֱלֹהָי
שִׁוַּעְתִּי אֵלֶיךָ וַתִּרְפָּאֵנִי׃

3 LORD, my God,
I cried out to You, and You healed me;

יהוה הֶעֱלִיתָ מִן־שְׁאוֹל נַפְשִׁי
חִיִּיתַנִי מִיָּרְדִי־בוֹר׃

מיורדי

4 LORD, You lifted me from Sheol;
You saved me from plummeting
to the Pit.

זַמְּרוּ לַיהוה חֲסִידָיו
וְהוֹדוּ לְזֵכֶר קָדְשׁוֹ׃

5 Sing to the LORD, you His devoted;
give thanks to His holy name,

כִּי רֶגַע ׀ בְּאַפּוֹ חַיִּים בִּרְצוֹנוֹ
בָּעֶרֶב יָלִין בֶּכִי וְלַבֹּקֶר רִנָּה׃

6 for His wrath lasts but a moment,
but His favor a lifetime;
at night there may be weeping,
but the morning brings joy.

וַאֲנִי אָמַרְתִּי בְשַׁלְוִי
בַּל־אֶמּוֹט לְעוֹלָם׃

7 In my serenity I said,
"I shall never be shaken."

יהוה בִּרְצוֹנְךָ הֶעֱמַדְתָּה
לְהַרְרִי עֹז
הִסְתַּרְתָּ פָנֶיךָ הָיִיתִי נִבְהָל׃

8 In Your favor, LORD,
You made me stand firm as a mountain,
but when You hid Your face,
I was terrified.

אֵלֶיךָ יהוה אֶקְרָא
וְאֶל־אֲדֹנָי אֶתְחַנָּן׃

9 To You, LORD, I called;
to my LORD I pleaded,

מַה־בֶּצַע בְּדָמִי
בְּרִדְתִּי אֶל שָׁחַת
הֲיוֹדְךָ עָפָר הֲיַגִּיד אֲמִתֶּךָ׃

10 "What gain would there be in my death
if I went down to the grave?
Can dust praise You?
Can it declare Your truth?

שְׁמַע־יְהוָה וְחָנֵּנִי
יְהוָֹה הֱיֵה־עֹזֵר לִי:

11 Hear, LORD, and show me grace;
LORD, be my help."

הָפַכְתָּ מִסְפְּדִי לְמָחוֹל לִי
פִּתַּחְתָּ שַׂקִּי וַתְּאַזְּרֵנִי שִׂמְחָה:

12 You have turned my mourning
into dancing;
You have untied my sackcloth
and clothed me with joy

לְמַעַן ׀ יְזַמֶּרְךָ כָבוֹד וְלֹא יִדֹּם
יְהוָה אֱלֹהַי לְעוֹלָם אוֹדֶךָּ:

13 so that my soul may sing to You
and not be silent.
LORD my God, I will praise You forever.

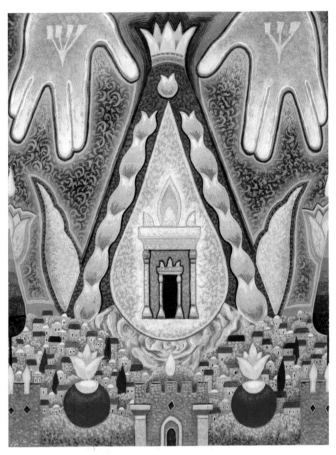

Be strong and of determined hearts, all you who wait for the LORD

I struggle in two ways. I struggle to escape a sly and determined enemy. I struggle to trust God. It came to me in a flash. There is but one struggle.

PSALM 31

לַמְנַצֵּחַ מִזְמוֹר לְדָוִד: 1   To the lead singer – a psalm of David

בְּךָ־יהוה חָסִיתִי 2   In You, Lord, I take refuge;
אַל־אֵבוֹשָׁה לְעוֹלָם   may I never be put to shame;
בְּצִדְקָתְךָ פַלְּטֵנִי: rescue me in Your righteousness.

הַטֵּה אֵלַי ׀ אָזְנְךָ 3   Lend Your ear to me;
מְהֵרָה הַצִּילֵנִי   swiftly save me;
הֱיֵה לִי ׀ לְצוּר־מָעוֹז   be my rock of refuge,
לְבֵית מְצוּדוֹת לְהוֹשִׁיעֵנִי: a stronghold of salvation,

כִּי־סַלְעִי וּמְצוּדָתִי אָתָּה 4   for You are my rock and my fortress.
וּלְמַעַן שִׁמְךָ תַּנְחֵנִי וּתְנַהֲלֵנִי: Lead me and guide me
  for the sake of Your name.

תּוֹצִיאֵנִי מֵרֶשֶׁת זוּ טָמְנוּ לִי 5   Free me from this net they laid for me,
כִּי־אַתָּה מָעוּזִּי: for You are my stronghold.

בְּיָדְךָ אַפְקִיד רוּחִי 6   I place my spirit in Your hand –
פָּדִיתָה אוֹתִי יהוה אֵל אֱמֶת: You set me free, Lord, God of truth.

שָׂנֵאתִי הַשֹּׁמְרִים הַבְלֵי־שָׁוְא 7   I despise those who rely on futilities –
וַאֲנִי אֶל־יהוה בָּטָחְתִּי: as for me, I trust in the Lord.

אָגִילָה וְאֶשְׂמְחָה בְּחַסְדֶּךָ 8   I will delight and rejoice in Your loyalty:
אֲשֶׁר רָאִיתָ אֶת־עָנְיִי   You saw my suffering;
יָדַעְתָּ בְּצָרוֹת נַפְשִׁי: You knew of my grave danger;

וְלֹא הִסְגַּרְתַּנִי בְּיַד־אוֹיֵב 9   You did not disclose me to enemy hands;
הֶעֱמַדְתָּ בַמֶּרְחָב רַגְלָי: You let me go free.

חָנֵּנִי יהוה כִּי צַר לִי 10   Show me grace, Lord, for I am in danger;
עָשְׁשָׁה בְכַעַס עֵינִי   torment wastes my eyes,
נַפְשִׁי וּבִטְנִי: my being, my insides.

כִּי כָלוּ בְיָגוֹן חַיַּי 11   My life is spent with sorrow;
וּשְׁנוֹתַי בַּאֲנָחָה   my years seep away in sighs;
כָּשַׁל בַּעֲוֹנִי כֹחִי וַעֲצָמַי   my strength fades because of my sin;
עָשֵׁשׁוּ:   my bones waste away.

מִכָּל־צֹרְרַי הָיִיתִי חֶרְפָּה
וְלִשְׁכֵנַי ׀ מְאֹד
וּפַחַד לִמְיֻדָּעָי
רֹאַי בַּחוּץ נָדְדוּ מִמֶּנִּי:

12 I am the scorn of all my foes,
even more so to my neighbors;
I am a horror to my friends;
whoever sees me on the streets
shrinks away from me.

נִשְׁכַּחְתִּי כְּמֵת מִלֵּב
הָיִיתִי כִּכְלִי אֹבֵד:

13 I have been forgotten like the dead,
like a long-discarded vessel,

כִּי שָׁמַעְתִּי ׀ דִּבַּת רַבִּים
מָגוֹר מִסָּבִיב
בְּהִוָּסְדָם יַחַד עָלַי
לָקַחַת נַפְשִׁי זָמָמוּ:

14 for I have heard the whispers of many–
terror on every side! –
as they all conspire against me,
scheming to take my life.

וַאֲנִי ׀ עָלֶיךָ בָטַחְתִּי יהוה
אָמַרְתִּי אֱלֹהַי אָתָּה:

15 But I place my trust in You, O Lord;
I say, "You are my God."

בְּיָדְךָ עִתֹּתָי
הַצִּילֵנִי מִיַּד־אוֹיְבַי וּמֵרֹדְפָי:

16 My fate is in Your hands;
save me from the hands of my enemies
and pursuers.

הָאִירָה פָנֶיךָ עַל־עַבְדֶּךָ
הוֹשִׁיעֵנִי בְחַסְדֶּךָ:

17 Shine Your face on Your servant;
save me in Your loyalty.

יהוה אַל־אֵבוֹשָׁה כִּי קְרָאתִיךָ
יֵבֹשׁוּ רְשָׁעִים יִדְּמוּ לִשְׁאוֹל:

18 Let me not be put to shame, Lord,
for I call upon You;
let the wicked be shamed
and silenced to Sheol.

תֵּאָלַמְנָה שִׂפְתֵי שָׁקֶר
הַדֹּבְרוֹת עַל־צַדִּיק עָתָק
בְּגַאֲוָה וָבוּז:

19 Let deceitful lips be stilled
that speak brashly against the righteous
with arrogance and contempt.

מָה רַב טוּבְךָ
אֲשֶׁר־צָפַנְתָּ לִּירֵאֶיךָ
פָּעַלְתָּ לַחֹסִים בָּךְ
נֶגֶד בְּנֵי אָדָם:

20 How great is the goodness
You keep in store for those who fear You;
You act for those who take refuge in You
in the full view of all.

תַּסְתִּירֵם ׀ בְּסֵתֶר פָּנֶיךָ
מֵרֻכְסֵי אִישׁ
תִּצְפְּנֵם בְּסֻכָּה מֵרִיב לְשֹׁנֽוֹת:

21 Shelter them in Your safe presence
from human guile;
shield them within Your cover
from scathing tongues.

בָּרוּךְ יְהוָה
כִּי הִפְלִיא חַסְדּוֹ לִי
בְּעִיר מָצֽוֹר:

22 Blessed is the LORD
who has shown me His wondrous loyalty
in a city under siege.

וַאֲנִי ׀ אָמַרְתִּי בְחָפְזִי
נִגְרַזְתִּי מִנֶּגֶד עֵינֶיךָ
אָכֵן שָׁמַעְתָּ קוֹל תַּחֲנוּנַי
בְּשַׁוְּעִי אֵלֶֽיךָ:

23 Even when I said rashly,
"I am cut off from Your sight,"
You still heard the sound of my plea
when I cried out to You.

אֶהֱבוּ אֶת־יְהוָה כָּל־חֲסִידָיו
אֱמוּנִים נֹצֵר יְהוָה
וּמְשַׁלֵּם עַל־יֶתֶר עֹשֵׂה גַאֲוָֽה:

24 Love the LORD, all you His devoted ones;
the LORD protects the faithful
and amply punishes
those who act in arrogance.

חִזְקוּ וְיַאֲמֵץ לְבַבְכֶם
כָּל־הַמְיַחֲלִים לַיהוָֽה:

25 Be strong and of determined hearts,
all you who wait for the LORD.

Rejoice in the LORD; delight, righteous ones; sing out loud, all you upright of heart!

People talk about guilt as if it is a bad thing.
To some extent, they are correct. I know. I've been there.
I've sinned and been shamed. I've suffered the pain of remorse.
I discovered that God forgives. He even brought me closer to Him.

PSALM 32

לְדָוִד מַשְׂכִּיל
אַשְׁרֵי נְשׂוּי־פֶּשַׁע כְּסוּי חֲטָאָה:

1 Of David – a *maskil*
Happy is the one whose offense
has been forgiven,
whose sin has been covered over.

אַשְׁרֵי אָדָם לֹא יַחְשֹׁב יהוה
לוֹ עָוֹן
וְאֵין בְּרוּחוֹ רְמִיָּה:

2 Happy is the one whom the Lord
does not hold guilty,
whose spirit is devoid of deceit.

כִּי־הֶחֱרַשְׁתִּי בָּלוּ עֲצָמָי
בְּשַׁאֲגָתִי כָּל־הַיּוֹם:

3 When I remained silent,
my body wasted away
from my howling all day long,

כִּי ׀ יוֹמָם וָלַיְלָה
תִּכְבַּד עָלַי יָדֶךָ
נֶהְפַּךְ לְשַׁדִּי בְּחַרְבֹנֵי קַיִץ
סֶלָה:

4 for day and night,
Your hand weighed down upon me;
my vitality dried up as if scorched
by summer heat –
Selah.

חַטָּאתִי אוֹדִיעֲךָ
וַעֲוֹנִי לֹא־כִסִּיתִי
אָמַרְתִּי
אוֹדֶה עֲלֵי פְשָׁעַי לַיהוה
וְאַתָּה נָשָׂאתָ עֲוֹן חַטָּאתִי
סֶלָה:

5 I admitted my sin to You
and did not cover up my guilt;
I said,
"I confess my offenses to the Lord,"
and You forgave the guilt of my sin –
Selah.

עַל־זֹאת יִתְפַּלֵּל כָּל־חָסִיד ׀
אֵלֶיךָ לְעֵת מְצֹא
רַק לְשֵׁטֶף מַיִם רַבִּים
אֵלָיו לֹא יַגִּיעוּ:

6 Thus let all those pray to You
at the moment of discovery
so that the rush of mighty waters
will not reach them.

אַתָּה ׀ סֵתֶר לִי מִצַּר תִּצְּרֵנִי
רָנֵּי פַלֵּט תְּסוֹבְבֵנִי סֶלָה:

7 You are my shelter;
You keep me from danger;
You surround me
with glad shouts of rescue – Selah.

אַשְׂכִּילְךָ ׀ וְאֽוֹרְךָ
בְּדֶֽרֶךְ־זֶ֣ו תֵלֵ֑ךְ
אִיעֲצָ֖ה עָלֶ֣יךָ עֵינִֽי׃

8 I will instruct you and guide you
along the path you should follow;
I will counsel you
and keep My eye on you.

אַל־תִּהְי֤וּ ׀ כְּס֣וּס כְּפֶ֗רֶד
אֵ֣ין הָבִ֑ין
בְּמֶֽתֶג־וָרֶ֣סֶן עֶדְי֣וֹ לִבְל֑וֹם
בַּ֝֗ל קְרֹ֣ב אֵלֶֽיךָ׃

9 Do not be senseless like a horse or mule
that must be curbed by bit and bridle –
far be it from you!

רַבִּ֥ים מַכְאוֹבִ֗ים לָרָ֫שָׁ֥ע
וְהַבּוֹטֵ֥חַ בַּיהוָ֑ה חֶ֝֗סֶד
יְסוֹבְבֶֽנּוּ׃

10 Many are the torments of the wicked,
while those who trust in the Lord
are surrounded by loving-kindness.

שִׂמְח֬וּ בַֽיהוָ֣ה וְ֭גִילוּ צַדִּיקִ֑ים
וְ֝הַרְנִ֗ינוּ כָּל־יִשְׁרֵי־לֵֽב׃

11 Rejoice in the Lord;
delight, righteous ones;
sing out loud, all you upright of heart!

Give thanks to the Lord with the harp; sing praise to Him with the ten-stringed lute

They deride me behind my back. They spread lies about me.
They scheme to rid the world of me.
For what should I possibly apologize?
I must trust God to frustrate their plans. I have no other recourse.

PSALM 33

רַנְּנוּ צַדִּיקִים בַּיהוָה
לַיְשָׁרִים נָאוָה תְהִלָּה:

1 Sing joyfully to the LORD,
 you righteous ones;
 praise from the upright is beautiful.

הוֹדוּ לַיהוָה בְּכִנּוֹר
בְּנֵבֶל עָשׂוֹר זַמְּרוּ־לוֹ:

2 Give thanks to the LORD with the harp;
 sing praise to Him
 with the ten-stringed lute.

שִׁירוּ־לוֹ שִׁיר חָדָשׁ
הֵיטִיבוּ נַגֵּן בִּתְרוּעָה:

3 Sing Him a new song;
 play your best with joyous shout,

כִּי־יָשָׁר דְּבַר־יְהוָה
וְכָל־מַעֲשֵׂהוּ בֶּאֱמוּנָה:

4 for the LORD's word is right,
 and all His deeds are faithful.

אֹהֵב צְדָקָה וּמִשְׁפָּט
חֶסֶד יְהוָה מָלְאָה הָאָרֶץ:

5 He loves righteousness and justice;
 the earth is full of the LORD's
 loving-kindness.

בִּדְבַר יְהוָה שָׁמַיִם נַעֲשׂוּ
וּבְרוּחַ פִּיו כָּל־צְבָאָם:

6 By the LORD's word
 the heavens were made,
 by His breath all their starry host.

כֹּנֵס כַּנֵּד מֵי הַיָּם
נֹתֵן בְּאֹצָרוֹת תְּהוֹמוֹת:

7 He gathers the sea waters as if in a heap
 and stores the depths in treasuries.

יִירְאוּ מֵיהוָה כָּל־הָאָרֶץ
מִמֶּנּוּ יָגוּרוּ כָּל־יֹשְׁבֵי תֵבֵל:

8 Let all the earth fear the LORD;
 let all inhabitants of the world
 revere Him,

כִּי הוּא אָמַר וַיֶּהִי
הוּא־צִוָּה וַיַּעֲמֹד:

9 for He spoke and it came to be
 at His command; it stood firm.

יְהוָה הֵפִיר עֲצַת־גּוֹיִם
הֵנִיא מַחְשְׁבוֹת עַמִּים:

10 The LORD foils the plans of nations;
 He thwarts the intentions of peoples.

עֲצַת יְהוָה לְעוֹלָם תַּעֲמֹד
מַחְשְׁבוֹת לִבּוֹ לְדֹר וָדֹר:

11 The LORD's plans endure forever,
 His heart's intents for all generations.

אַשְׁרֵי הַגּוֹי אֲשֶׁר־יְהוָה אֱלֹהָיו
הָעָם בָּחַר לְנַחֲלָה לוֹ:

12 Happy is the nation
 whose God is the LORD,
 the people He has chosen as His own.

מִשָּׁמַיִם הִבִּיט יְהֹוָה
רָאָה אֶת־כָּל־בְּנֵי הָאָדָם:

מִמְּכוֹן־שִׁבְתּוֹ הִשְׁגִּיחַ
אֶל כָּל־יֹשְׁבֵי הָאָרֶץ:

הַיֹּצֵר יַחַד לִבָּם
הַמֵּבִין אֶל־כָּל־מַעֲשֵׂיהֶם:

אֵין־הַמֶּלֶךְ נוֹשָׁע בְּרָב־חָיִל
גִּבּוֹר לֹא־יִנָּצֵל בְּרָב־כֹּחַ:

שֶׁקֶר הַסּוּס לִתְשׁוּעָה
וּבְרֹב חֵילוֹ לֹא יְמַלֵּט:

הִנֵּה עֵין יְהֹוָה אֶל־יְרֵאָיו
לַמְיַחֲלִים לְחַסְדּוֹ:

לְהַצִּיל מִמָּוֶת נַפְשָׁם
וּלְחַיּוֹתָם בָּרָעָב:

נַפְשֵׁנוּ חִכְּתָה לַיהֹוָה
עֶזְרֵנוּ וּמָגִנֵּנוּ הוּא:

כִּי־בוֹ יִשְׂמַח לִבֵּנוּ
כִּי בְשֵׁם קָדְשׁוֹ בָטָחְנוּ:

יְהִי־חַסְדְּךָ יְהֹוָה עָלֵינוּ
כַּאֲשֶׁר יִחַלְנוּ לָךְ:

13 The Lord looks down from heaven
and sees all of humanity;

14 from His dwelling place He watches
over all inhabitants of the earth.

15 He forms the hearts of all
and discerns all their deeds.

16 A king is not saved by a vast force;
a warrior is not delivered
by great strength.

17 A horse is a vain hope for victory;
despite its great strength,
it cannot bring salvation.

18 Yes, the eye of the Lord is on those
who fear Him,
on those who place their hopes
in His kindness,

19 rescuing them from death,
keeping them alive in famine.

20 We await the Lord;
He is our help and shield.

21 In Him our hearts rejoice,
for we trust in His holy name.

22 May Your loving-kindness
be upon us, Lord,
for we place our hope in You.

Glorify the Lord with me; let us exalt His name together

My tongue is not visible and symbolizes my inner self:
I keep my tongue from evil.
My lips are visible externally
and they symbolize my outer self: Everyday concerns.
I keep my lips from uttering deceit.
I long for many days to enjoy prosperity.

PSALM 34

לְדָוִד
בְּשַׁנּוֹתוֹ אֶת־טַעְמוֹ
לִפְנֵי אֲבִימֶלֶךְ
וַיְגָרְשֵׁהוּ וַיֵּלַךְ׃

1 Of David,
when he feigned insanity
before Avimelekh,
who drove him away, and he left

אֲבָרְכָה אֶת־יהוה בְּכָל־עֵת
תָּמִיד תְּהִלָּתוֹ בְּפִי׃

2 I will bless the LORD at all times;
His praise will be always on my lips.

בַּיהוה תִּתְהַלֵּל נַפְשִׁי
יִשְׁמְעוּ עֲנָוִים וְיִשְׂמָחוּ׃

3 My soul will glory in the LORD;
let the lowly hear this and rejoice.

גַּדְּלוּ לַיהוה אִתִּי
וּנְרוֹמְמָה שְׁמוֹ יַחְדָּו׃

4 Glorify the LORD with me;
let us exalt His name together.

דָּרַשְׁתִּי אֶת־יהוה וְעָנָנִי
וּמִכָּל־מְגוּרוֹתַי הִצִּילָנִי׃

5 I sought the Lord, and He answered me;
He saved me from all my fears.

הִבִּיטוּ אֵלָיו וְנָהָרוּ
וּפְנֵיהֶם אַל־יֶחְפָּרוּ׃

6 Those who look to Him are radiant;
let their faces not be downcast.

זֶה עָנִי קָרָא וַיהוה שָׁמֵעַ
וּמִכָּל־צָרוֹתָיו הוֹשִׁיעוֹ׃

7 This poor person called,
and the LORD heard;
He saved him from all his troubles.

חֹנֶה מַלְאַךְ־יהוה סָבִיב לִירֵאָיו
וַיְחַלְּצֵם׃

8 The LORD's angel encamps
around those who fear Him
and comes to their rescue.

טַעֲמוּ וּרְאוּ כִּי־טוֹב יהוה
אַשְׁרֵי הַגֶּבֶר יֶחֱסֶה־בּוֹ׃

9 Taste for yourselves;
see that the LORD is good;
happy are those who take refuge in Him.

יְראוּ אֶת־יהוה קְדֹשָׁיו
כִּי־אֵין מַחְסוֹר לִירֵאָיו׃

10 Fear the LORD, you His holy ones,
for those who fear Him lack nothing.

כְּפִירִים רָשׁוּ וְרָעֵבוּ
וְדֹרְשֵׁי יהוה
לֹא־יַחְסְרוּ כָל־טוֹב׃

11 Lions may grow weak and hungry,
but those who seek the LORD
will never lack any good.

לְכוּ־בָנִים שִׁמְעוּ־לִי
12 Come, my children, listen to me;
יִרְאַת יהוה אֲלַמֶּדְכֶם:
I will teach you the fear of the LORD.

מִי־הָאִישׁ הֶחָפֵץ חַיִּים
13 Who among you desires life;
אֹהֵב יָמִים לִרְאוֹת טוֹב:
who longs to see many good years?

נְצֹר לְשׁוֹנְךָ מֵרָע
14 Then keep your tongue from evil,
וּשְׂפָתֶיךָ מִדַּבֵּר מִרְמָה:
your lips from speaking deceit.

סוּר מֵרָע וַעֲשֵׂה־טוֹב
15 Turn away from evil and do good;
בַּקֵּשׁ שָׁלוֹם וְרָדְפֵהוּ:
strive for peace and pursue it.

עֵינֵי יהוה אֶל־צַדִּיקִים
16 The eyes of the Lord are on the righteous;
וְאָזְנָיו אֶל־שַׁוְעָתָם:
His ears are attuned to their cry.

פְּנֵי יהוה בְּעֹשֵׂי רָע
17 The LORD's face is set
לְהַכְרִית מֵאֶרֶץ זִכְרָם:
against those who do evil,
to erase their memory from the earth.

צָעֲקוּ וַיהוה שָׁמֵעַ
18 The LORD hears when they cry out;
וּמִכָּל־צָרוֹתָם הִצִּילָם:
He delivers them from all their troubles.

קָרוֹב יהוה לְנִשְׁבְּרֵי־לֵב
19 The LORD is close to the brokenhearted;
וְאֶת־דַּכְּאֵי־רוּחַ יוֹשִׁיעַ:
He saves those who are crushed in spirit.

רַבּוֹת רָעוֹת צַדִּיק
20 Many troubles may befall the righteous,
וּמִכֻּלָּם יַצִּילֶנּוּ יהוה:
but the LORD delivers him
from all of them;

שֹׁמֵר כָּל־עַצְמוֹתָיו
21 He protects every one of his bones
אַחַת מֵהֵנָּה לֹא נִשְׁבָּרָה:
so that none of them will be broken.

תְּמוֹתֵת רָשָׁע רָעָה
22 Evil will slay the wicked;
וְשֹׂנְאֵי צַדִּיק יֶאְשָׁמוּ:
the enemies of the righteous
will be condemned.

פּוֹדֶה יהוה נֶפֶשׁ עֲבָדָיו
23 The LORD redeems the lives
וְלֹא יֶאְשְׁמוּ כָּל־הַחֹסִים בּוֹ:
of His servants;
none who take refuge in Him
will be condemned.

Then will my tongue express Your justice, Your praises all day long

When I pray, I do not stand still. I sway. My entire body prays.
I fell ill. Every limb was vulnerable. I engaged in battle.
Each muscle was endangered. I recovered from my disease.
I vanquished my foe. Every limb now prays,
and every muscle sways.

PSALM 35

לְדָוִד ׀ רִיבָה יהוה אֶת־יְרִיבַי
לְחַם אֶת־לֹחֲמָי:

הַחֲזֵק מָגֵן וְצִנָּה
וְקוּמָה בְּעֶזְרָתִי:

וְהָרֵק חֲנִית וּסְגֹר
לִקְרַאת רֹדְפָי
אֱמֹר לְנַפְשִׁי יְשֻׁעָתֵךְ אָנִי:

יֵבֹשׁוּ וְיִכָּלְמוּ מְבַקְשֵׁי נַפְשִׁי
יִסֹּגוּ אָחוֹר וְיַחְפְּרוּ
חֹשְׁבֵי רָעָתִי:

יִהְיוּ כְּמֹץ לִפְנֵי־רוּחַ
וּמַלְאַךְ יהוה דּוֹחֶה:

יְהִי־דַרְכָּם חֹשֶׁךְ וַחֲלַקְלַקֹּת
וּמַלְאַךְ יהוה רֹדְפָם:

כִּי־חִנָּם טָמְנוּ־לִי שַׁחַת רִשְׁתָּם
חִנָּם חָפְרוּ לְנַפְשִׁי:

תְּבוֹאֵהוּ שׁוֹאָה לֹא־יֵדָע
וְרִשְׁתּוֹ אֲשֶׁר־טָמַן תִּלְכְּדוֹ
בְּשׁוֹאָה יִפָּל־בָּהּ:

וְנַפְשִׁי תָּגִיל בַּיהוה
תָּשִׂישׂ בִּישׁוּעָתוֹ:

כָּל עַצְמוֹתַי ׀ תֹּאמַרְנָה
יהוה מִי כָמוֹךָ
מַצִּיל עָנִי מֵחָזָק מִמֶּנּוּ
וְעָנִי וְאֶבְיוֹן מִגֹּזְלוֹ:

1 Of David. Contend with those
who contend with me, Lord;
fight those who fight me;

2 take up shield and armor
and rise up to help me;

3 unsheathe spear and javelin
against my pursuers.
Tell me, "I am your salvation."

4 Let those who seek my life
be shamed and humiliated;
let those who plot my ruin
retreat in disgrace.

5 Let them be like chaff in the wind,
driven by the Lord's angel;

6 let their way be dark and slippery,
with the Lord's angel in pursuit,

7 for they laid a trap for me without cause;
without cause they dug a pit for me;

8 let ruin ravage them suddenly;
let them be caught in their own trap
and fall into it to their utter ruin,

9 but my soul will delight in the Lord,
rejoicing in His salvation.

10 Every inch of my being declares,
"O Lord, who is like You?
You save the poor
from those too strong for them,
the poor and needy
from those who exploit them."

יָקוּמוּן עֵדֵי חָמָס
אֲשֶׁר לֹא־יָדַעְתִּי יִשְׁאָלוּנִי:

11 False witnesses suddenly come forward,
   interrogating me
   about things I know not;

יְשַׁלְּמוּנִי רָעָה תַּחַת טוֹבָה
שְׁכוֹל לְנַפְשִׁי:

12 they repay good with evil–
   I am left bereaved,

וַאֲנִי ׀ בַּחֲלוֹתָם לְבוּשִׁי שָׂק
עִנֵּיתִי בַצּוֹם נַפְשִׁי
וּתְפִלָּתִי עַל־חֵיקִי תָשׁוּב:

13 for when they were ill I donned sackcloth,
   made myself suffer with fasting,
   prayer surging in my chest;

כְּרֵעַ־כְּאָח לִי הִתְהַלָּכְתִּי
כַּאֲבֶל־אֵם קֹדֵר שַׁחוֹתִי:

14 I went about as if it were my own friend,
   my own brother,
   bowed in gloom
   as if mourning for my mother,

וּבְצַלְעִי שָׂמְחוּ וְנֶאֱסָפוּ
נֶאֶסְפוּ עָלַי נֵכִים וְלֹא יָדַעְתִּי
קָרְעוּ וְלֹא־דָמּוּ:

15 but when I stumbled,
   they swarmed in glee;
   wretches suddenly swarmed about me,
   tearing at me without cease.

בְּחַנְפֵי לַעֲגֵי מָעוֹג
חָרֹק עָלַי שִׁנֵּימוֹ:

16 With a vile, mocking leer,
   they gnash their teeth at me.

אֲדֹנָי כַּמָּה תִּרְאֶה
הָשִׁיבָה נַפְשִׁי מִשֹּׁאֵיהֶם
מִכְּפִירִים יְחִידָתִי:

17 How long, LORD, will You look on?
   Save me from their onslaught,
   my precious life from lions.

אוֹדְךָ בְּקָהָל רָב
בְּעַם עָצוּם אֲהַלְלֶךָּ:

18 I will thank You before a great assembly;
   I will praise You before a mighty throng.

אַל־יִשְׂמְחוּ־לִי אֹיְבַי שֶׁקֶר
שֹׂנְאַי חִנָּם יִקְרְצוּ־עָיִן:

19 Do not let my treacherous enemies
   gloat over me
   or those who hate me without cause
   narrow their eyes,

כִּי לֹא שָׁלוֹם יְדַבֵּרוּ
וְעַל רִגְעֵי־אֶרֶץ
דִּבְרֵי מִרְמוֹת יַחֲשֹׁבוּן:

20 for they do not speak words of peace;
   they devise treacherous schemes
   against the harmless of the land.

וַיַּרְחִיבוּ עָלַי פִּיהֶם
אָמְרוּ הֶאָח ׀ הֶאָח
רָאֲתָה עֵינֵינוּ:

21 Their mouths open wide against me,
calling "Aha! Aha! Our eyes have seen it!"

רָאִיתָה יְהוָה אַל־תֶּחֱרַשׁ
אֲדֹנָי אַל־תִּרְחַק מִמֶּנִּי:

22 You have seen it, Lord;
do not remain silent;
O Lord, do not be far from me.

הָעִירָה וְהָקִיצָה לְמִשְׁפָּטִי
אֱלֹהַי וַאדֹנָי לְרִיבִי:

23 Awake and rise to my defense;
contend for me, my God, my Lord.

שָׁפְטֵנִי כְצִדְקְךָ יְהוָה אֱלֹהָי
וְאַל־יִשְׂמְחוּ־לִי:

24 Vindicate me in Your justice,
Lord my God;
do not let them gloat over me;

אַל־יֹאמְרוּ בְלִבָּם הֶאָח נַפְשֵׁנוּ
אַל־יֹאמְרוּ בִּלַּעֲנוּהוּ:

25 do not let them tell themselves,
"Aha! As we wished!"
Do not let them say,
"We have swallowed him up!"

יֵבֹשׁוּ וְיַחְפְּרוּ ׀ יַחְדָּו
שְׂמֵחֵי רָעָתִי
יִלְבְּשׁוּ־בֹשֶׁת וּכְלִמָּה
הַמַּגְדִּילִים עָלָי:

26 Let those who gloat at my misfortune
be altogether shamed and disgraced;
let those who boast over me
don shame and humiliation.

יָרֹנּוּ וְיִשְׂמְחוּ חֲפֵצֵי צִדְקִי
וְיֹאמְרוּ תָמִיד יִגְדַּל יְהוָה
הֶחָפֵץ שְׁלוֹם עַבְדּוֹ:

27 May those who delight in my vindication
sing and rejoice;
may they always say,
"Great be the Lord who delights in His
servants' success."

וּלְשׁוֹנִי תֶּהְגֶּה צִדְקֶךָ
כָּל־הַיּוֹם תְּהִלָּתֶךָ:

28 Then will my tongue express Your justice,
Your praises all day long.

Extend Your loyalty to those who know You, Your justice to the upright of heart

I had a free day and went down to the sea.
I saw a bird swoop down from the sky and scoop up a fish.
I exclaimed: Your judgments are like the great deep.
I had a free day and strolled in the woods.
I saw an anthill, protruding but an inch from the ground.
I exclaimed: Your righteousness is like the high mountains.

PSALM 36

לַמְנַצֵּחַ ׀ לְעֶבֶד־יְהֹוָה לְדָוִד׃	1	To the lead singer – of the Lord's servant, of David
נְאֻם־פֶּשַׁע לָרָשָׁע בְּקֶרֶב לִבִּי אֵין־פַּחַד אֱלֹהִים לְנֶגֶד עֵינָיו׃	2	Well do I know what vice whispers to the wicked; there is no fear of God before their eyes.
כִּי־הֶחֱלִיק אֵלָיו בְּעֵינָיו לִמְצֹא עֲוֺנוֹ לִשְׂנֹא׃	3	They flatter themselves in their own eyes that their sin will not be discovered and hated.
דִּבְרֵי־פִיו אָוֶן וּמִרְמָה חָדַל לְהַשְׂכִּיל לְהֵיטִיב׃	4	The words they mouth are treacherous and deceitful; they cannot contemplate doing good;
אָוֶן ׀ יַחְשֹׁב עַל־מִשְׁכָּבוֹ יִתְיַצֵּב עַל־דֶּרֶךְ לֹא־טוֹב רָע לֹא יִמְאָס׃	5	in bed they plot treachery; they are set on a path of no good, never spurning evil.
יְהֹוָה בְּהַשָּׁמַיִם חַסְדֶּךָ אֱמוּנָתְךָ עַד־שְׁחָקִים׃	6	O Lord, Your loyalty reaches the heavens, Your faithfulness the skies;
צִדְקָתְךָ ׀ כְּהַרְרֵי־אֵל מִשְׁפָּטֶיךָ תְּהוֹם רַבָּה אָדָם וּבְהֵמָה תוֹשִׁיעַ ׀ יְהֹוָה׃	7	Your justice is like the mighty mountains, Your judgment like the great deep; O Lord, You save both human and beast.
מַה־יָּקָר חַסְדְּךָ אֱלֹהִים וּבְנֵי אָדָם בְּצֵל כְּנָפֶיךָ יֶחֱסָיוּן׃	8	How precious is Your loyalty, God; people find refuge in the shade of Your wings;
יִרְוְיֻן מִדֶּשֶׁן בֵּיתֶךָ וְנַחַל עֲדָנֶיךָ תַשְׁקֵם׃	9	they feast on the rich plenty of Your House; You quench their thirst with Your river of delights,
כִּי־עִמְּךָ מְקוֹר חַיִּים בְּאוֹרְךָ נִרְאֶה־אוֹר׃	10	for the fountain of life is with You; by Your light we see light.

מְשֹׁךְ חַסְדְּךָ לְיֹדְעֶיךָ
וְצִדְקָתְךָ לְיִשְׁרֵי־לֵב:

11 Extend Your loyalty
to those who know You,
Your justice to the upright of heart.

אַל־תְּבוֹאֵנִי רֶגֶל גַּאֲוָה
וְיַד־רְשָׁעִים אַל־תְּנִדֵנִי:

12 Let no arrogant foot trample me;
let no wicked hand drive me away –

שָׁם נָפְלוּ פֹּעֲלֵי אָוֶן
דֹּחוּ וְלֹא־יָכְלוּ קוּם:

13 there evildoers lie fallen,
forced down, unable to rise.

The righteous will inherit the earth and be settled upon it forever

Anger is harmful.
But I cannot resist expressing my wrath.
I must learn to be satisfied with what I have.
Then my soul will be whole. And my body revived.
Those are the benefits of trusting in God.

PSALM 37

לְדָוִד ׀ 1 Of David

אַל־תִּתְחַר בַּמְּרֵעִים   Do not be incensed at the wicked
אַל־תְּקַנֵּא בְּעֹשֵׂי עַוְלָה: or let your envy be kindled by evildoers,

כִּי כֶחָצִיר מְהֵרָה יִמָּלוּ 2 for they will soon wither like grass
וּכְיֶרֶק דֶּשֶׁא יִבּוֹלוּן: and fade away like greenery.

בְּטַח בַּיהוה וַעֲשֵׂה־טוֹב 3 Trust in the LORD and do good –
שְׁכָן־אֶרֶץ וּרְעֵה אֱמוּנָה: you will be settled in the land,
    secure in your pasture.

וְהִתְעַנַּג עַל־יהוה 4 Delight in the LORD,
וְיִתֶּן־לְךָ מִשְׁאֲלֹת לִבֶּךָ:   and He will grant you your heart's desire.

גּוֹל עַל־יהוה דַּרְכֶּךָ 5 Commit your way to the LORD;
וּבְטַח עָלָיו וְהוּא יַעֲשֶׂה: trust in Him, and He will act:

וְהוֹצִיא כָאוֹר צִדְקֶךָ 6 He will bring out your vindication
וּמִשְׁפָּטֶךָ כַּצָּהֳרָיִם: to light,
    the justice of your cause
    like the noonday sun.

דּוֹם ׀ לַיהוה וְהִתְחוֹלֵל לוֹ 7 Wait for the LORD silently, patiently;
אַל־תִּתְחַר בְּמַצְלִיחַ דַּרְכּוֹ   do not be incensed
בְּאִישׁ עֹשֶׂה מְזִמּוֹת: at those who succeed
    through devious plots.

הֶרֶף מֵאַף וַעֲזֹב חֵמָה 8 Release your anger;
אַל־תִּתְחַר אַךְ־לְהָרֵעַ:   abandon your wrath;
    do not be incensed –
    it leads only to harm,

כִּי־מְרֵעִים יִכָּרֵתוּן 9 for the wicked will be cut off,
וְקֹוֵי יהוה הֵמָּה יִירְשׁוּ־אָרֶץ: while those who hope for the LORD
    shall inherit the earth.

וְעוֹד מְעַט וְאֵין רָשָׁע 10 Very soon, the wicked will be no more;
וְהִתְבּוֹנַנְתָּ עַל־מְקוֹמוֹ   you will look at their place
וְאֵינֶנּוּ:   to find them gone,

וַעֲנָוִים יִירְשׁוּ־אָרֶץ
וְהִתְעַנְּגוּ עַל־רֹב שָׁלוֹם:

11 but the lowly shall inherit the earth;
they will delight in the wealth of peace.

זֹמֵם רָשָׁע לַצַּדִּיק
וְחֹרֵק עָלָיו שִׁנָּיו:

12 The wicked scheme against the righteous,
gnashing their teeth at them,

אֲדֹנָי יִשְׂחַק־לוֹ
כִּי־רָאָה כִּי־יָבֹא יוֹמוֹ:

13 but the LORD laughs at them;
He knows their day will come.

חֶרֶב ׀ פָּתְחוּ רְשָׁעִים
וְדָרְכוּ קַשְׁתָּם
לְהַפִּיל עָנִי וְאֶבְיוֹן
לִטְבוֹחַ יִשְׁרֵי־דָרֶךְ:

14 The wicked unsheathe their swords
and draw their bows
to bring down the poor and the needy,
to slaughter those whose path is straight.

חַרְבָּם תָּבוֹא בְלִבָּם
וְקַשְּׁתוֹתָם תִּשָּׁבַרְנָה:

15 Their swords will pierce their own hearts;
their bows will be shattered.

טוֹב־מְעַט לַצַּדִּיק
מֵהֲמוֹן רְשָׁעִים רַבִּים:

16 The righteous person's precious little
is better
than the vast wealth of the many wicked,

כִּי זְרוֹעוֹת רְשָׁעִים תִּשָּׁבַרְנָה
וְסוֹמֵךְ צַדִּיקִים יְהוָה:

17 for the arms of the wicked will be broken,
while the LORD supports the righteous.

יוֹדֵעַ יְהוָה יְמֵי תְמִימִם
וְנַחֲלָתָם לְעוֹלָם תִּהְיֶה:

18 The LORD cares for the days
of the blameless;
their heritage will last forever.

לֹא־יֵבֹשׁוּ בְּעֵת רָעָה
וּבִימֵי רְעָבוֹן יִשְׂבָּעוּ:

19 They will not suffer shame
when times are hard;
in famine they will still be sated,

כִּי רְשָׁעִים ׀ יֹאבֵדוּ
וְאֹיְבֵי יְהוָה כִּיקַר כָּרִים
כָּלוּ בֶעָשָׁן כָּלוּ:

20 but the wicked will perish;
the Lord's enemies are like meadow grass:
they vanish away like vanishing smoke.

לֹוֶה רָשָׁע וְלֹא יְשַׁלֵּם
וְצַדִּיק חוֹנֵן וְנוֹתֵן:

21 The wicked borrows and does not repay;
the righteous are generous;
they give and give,

כִּי מְבֹרָכָיו יִירְשׁוּ אָרֶץ
וּמְקֻלָּלָיו יִכָּרֵתוּ׃

22 for His blessed ones
shall inherit the earth,
while those cursed by Him
will be cut off.

מֵיהוה מִצְעֲדֵי־גֶבֶר כּוֹנָנוּ
וְדַרְכּוֹ יֶחְפָּץ׃

23 It is the LORD
who makes people's footsteps firm
when He delights in their way;

כִּי־יִפֹּל לֹא־יוּטָל
כִּי־יהוה סוֹמֵךְ יָדוֹ׃

24 when they stumble, they will not fall,
for the LORD holds their hand.

נַעַר ׀ הָיִיתִי גַּם־זָקַנְתִּי
וְלֹא־רָאִיתִי צַדִּיק נֶעֱזָב
וְזַרְעוֹ מְבַקֶּשׁ־לָחֶם׃

25 I was once young; now I am old,
yet I have never seen
the righteous forsaken,
with their children begging for bread.

כָּל־הַיּוֹם חוֹנֵן וּמַלְוֶה
וְזַרְעוֹ לִבְרָכָה׃

26 They are always generous, lending freely,
and their children become a blessing.

סוּר מֵרָע וַעֲשֵׂה־טוֹב
וּשְׁכֹן לְעוֹלָם׃

27 Turn away from evil and do good,
and you will always dwell secure,

כִּי יהוה ׀ אֹהֵב מִשְׁפָּט
וְלֹא־יַעֲזֹב אֶת־חֲסִידָיו
לְעוֹלָם נִשְׁמָרוּ
וְזֶרַע רְשָׁעִים נִכְרָת׃

28 for the LORD loves justice;
He will never abandon His devoted ones.
They will always be kept safe,
while the children of the wicked
will be cut off.

צַדִּיקִים יִירְשׁוּ־אָרֶץ
וְיִשְׁכְּנוּ לָעַד עָלֶיהָ׃

29 The righteous will inherit the earth
and be settled upon it forever.

פִּי־צַדִּיק יֶהְגֶּה חָכְמָה
וּלְשׁוֹנוֹ תְּדַבֵּר מִשְׁפָּט׃

30 Righteous mouths
speak words of wisdom;
their tongues express justice.

תּוֹרַת אֱלֹהָיו בְּלִבּוֹ
לֹא תִמְעַד אֲשֻׁרָיו׃

31 Their God's teaching is in their hearts;
their steps will never falter.

צוֹפֶה רָשָׁע לַצַּדִּיק
וּמְבַקֵּשׁ לַהֲמִיתוֹ:

32 The wicked lie in wait for the righteous,
seeking their death;

יְהוה לֹא־יַעַזְבֶנּוּ בְיָדוֹ
וְלֹא יַרְשִׁיעֶנּוּ בְּהִשָּׁפְטוֹ:

33 the LORD will not abandon them
to their hands
or condemn them when they are judged.

קַוֵּה אֶל־יהוה ׀ וּשְׁמֹר דַּרְכּוֹ
וִירוֹמִמְךָ לָרֶשֶׁת אָרֶץ
בְּהִכָּרֵת רְשָׁעִים תִּרְאֶה:

34 Place your hope in the LORD
and keep His way –
He will raise you up to inherit the earth
as you will see
when the wicked are cut off.

רָאִיתִי רָשָׁע עָרִיץ
וּמִתְעָרֶה כְּאֶזְרָח רַעֲנָן:

35 I have seen a tyrant in his prime,
well-rooted like a verdant native tree,

וַיַּעֲבֹר וְהִנֵּה אֵינֶנּוּ
וָאֲבַקְשֵׁהוּ וְלֹא נִמְצָא:

36 yet suddenly he passes on
and is no more;
I looked for him,
but he was nowhere to be found.

שְׁמָר־תָּם וּרְאֵה יָשָׁר
כִּי־אַחֲרִית לְאִישׁ שָׁלוֹם:

37 Watch and see,
you blameless and upright,
that a future awaits the peaceful person

וּפֹשְׁעִים נִשְׁמְדוּ יַחְדָּו
אַחֲרִית רְשָׁעִים נִכְרָתָה:

38 while sinners will be utterly destroyed;
the future of the wicked will be cut off.

וּתְשׁוּעַת צַדִּיקִים מֵיהוה
מָעוּזָּם בְּעֵת צָרָה:

39 The righteous' deliverance
is from the LORD;
He is their refuge in times of trouble.

וַיַּעְזְרֵם יהוה וַיְפַלְּטֵם
יְפַלְּטֵם מֵרְשָׁעִים וְיוֹשִׁיעֵם
כִּי־חָסוּ בוֹ:

40 The LORD will help them
and rescue them –
rescue them from the wicked
and deliver them,
for they seek refuge in Him.

Do not abandon me, LORD; My God, do not stray far from me

I wish I could forget the pain, the shame,
and the unspeakable horror. *Lehazkir:* To remind myself.
I suffered in silence. I never talk about it.
Lehazkir: To record for eternity. I was desperate, hopeless, alone
and abandoned. Lehazkir: To have Him remember me.

PSALM 38

מִזְמוֹר לְדָוִד לְהַזְכִּיר׃ 1 A psalm of David, *lehazkir* [to remind]

יְהוֹה אַל־בְּקֶצְפְּךָ תוֹכִיחֵנִי 2 LORD, do not reproach me in Your rage
וּבַחֲמָתְךָ תְיַסְּרֵנִי׃ or punish me in Your fury,

כִּי־חִצֶּיךָ נִחֲתוּ בִי 3 for Your arrows strike me;
וַתִּנְחַת עָלַי יָדֶךָ׃ Your hand strikes me!

אֵין־מְתֹם בִּבְשָׂרִי מִפְּנֵי זַעְמֶךָ 4 My body is not sound
אֵין־שָׁלוֹם בַּעֲצָמַי because of Your wrath;
מִפְּנֵי חַטָּאתִי׃ my bones are not well because of my sin.

כִּי עֲוֺנֹתַי עָבְרוּ רֹאשִׁי 5 My offenses have piled up above my head
כְּמַשָּׂא כָבֵד יִכְבְּדוּ מִמֶּנִּי׃ like a heavy burden, too heavy to bear.

הִבְאִישׁוּ נָמַקּוּ חַבּוּרֹתָי 6 My wounds reek and fester
מִפְּנֵי אִוַּלְתִּי׃ because of my foolishness.

נַעֲוֵיתִי שַׁחֹתִי עַד־מְאֹד 7 I am utterly stooped over, hunched up,
כָּל־הַיּוֹם קֹדֵר הִלָּכְתִּי׃ my gait gloomy all day long,

כִּי־כְסָלַי מָלְאוּ נִקְלֶה 8 for my insides burn fiercely;
וְאֵין מְתֹם בִּבְשָׂרִי׃ my body is not sound.

נְפוּגוֹתִי וְנִדְכֵּיתִי עַד־מְאֹד 9 I have grown so weak, so broken;
שָׁאַגְתִּי מִנַּהֲמַת לִבִּי׃ I roar out from the uproar in my mind,

אֲדֹנָי נֶגְדְּךָ כָל־תַּאֲוָתִי 10 "LORD, all I ache for is known to You;
וְאַנְחָתִי מִמְּךָ לֹא־נִסְתָּרָה׃ My groans are not hidden from You."

לִבִּי סְחַרְחַר עֲזָבַנִי כֹחִי 11 My heart is throbbing;
וְאוֹר־עֵינַי גַּם־הֵם אֵין אִתִּי׃ my strength has left me;
the light is long gone from my eyes.

אֹהֲבַי ׀ וְרֵעַי מִנֶּגֶד נִגְעִי יַעֲמֹדוּ 12 My loved ones, my friends –
וּקְרוֹבַי מֵרָחֹק עָמָדוּ׃ they shrink away at my suffering;
those I was close to keep their distance

וַיְנַקְשׁוּ ׀ מְבַקְשֵׁי נַפְשִׁי וְדֹרְשֵׁי רָעָתִי דִּבְּרוּ הַוּוֹת וּמִרְמוֹת כָּל־הַיּוֹם יֶהְגּוּ:	13 while those who seek my life lay their snares; those who seek my harm scheme viciously, plotting their treacherous plots all day,
וַאֲנִי כְחֵרֵשׁ לֹא אֶשְׁמָע וּכְאִלֵּם לֹא יִפְתַּח־פִּיו:	14 but I am like a deaf person who cannot hear, like a dumb person who cannot speak;
וָאֱהִי כְּאִישׁ אֲשֶׁר לֹא־שֹׁמֵעַ וְאֵין בְּפִיו תּוֹכָחוֹת:	15 I am like one who cannot hear and cannot answer back,
כִּי־לְךָ יְהוָה הוֹחָלְתִּי אַתָּה תַעֲנֶה אֲדֹנָי אֱלֹהָי:	16 yet for You, LORD, I wait in hope; You will answer me, LORD my God,
כִּי־אָמַרְתִּי פֶּן־יִשְׂמְחוּ־לִי בְּמוֹט רַגְלִי עָלַי הִגְדִּילוּ:	17 for I fear they will gloat over me and, when my foot slips, swagger over me–
כִּי־אֲנִי לְצֶלַע נָכוֹן וּמַכְאוֹבִי נֶגְדִּי תָמִיד:	18 for I am on the verge of collapse and constantly in pain.
כִּי־עֲוֹנִי אַגִּיד אֶדְאַג מֵחַטָּאתִי:	19 I admit my guilt; I regret my sin.
וְאֹיְבַי חַיִּים עָצֵמוּ וְרַבּוּ שֹׂנְאַי שָׁקֶר:	20 My mortal enemies are fierce; so many hate me without cause.
וּמְשַׁלְּמֵי רָעָה תַּחַת טוֹבָה יִשְׂטְנוּנִי תַּחַת רָדְפִי־טוֹב: רדופי	21 Those who repay good with evil oppose me for pursuing good.
אַל־תַּעַזְבֵנִי יְהוָה אֱלֹהַי אַל־תִּרְחַק מִמֶּנִּי:	22 Do not abandon me, LORD; My God, do not stray far from me.
חוּשָׁה לְעֶזְרָתִי אֲדֹנָי תְּשׁוּעָתִי:	23 Rush to my help, O LORD, my salvation.

My heart burned within me, my thoughts blazed

How does one get close to God? Some seek Him in nature's wonders. Some find Him in His words. Some embrace Him, grateful for His blessings. I come closest to Him. I need Him.

PSALM 39

לֵידִיתוּן

לַמְנַצֵּחַ לִידיּתוּן
מִזְמוֹר לְדָוִד׃

1 For the lead singer, for *Yedutun* –
a psalm of David

אָמַרְתִּי אֶשְׁמְרָה דְרָכַי
מֵחֲטוֹא בִלְשׁוֹנִי
אֶשְׁמְרָה־לְפִי מַחְסוֹם
בְּעֹד רָשָׁע לְנֶגְדִּי׃

2 I was determined to watch my ways
and not to sin with my tongue;
I would keep my mouth shut tight
so long as the wicked
were in my presence.

נֶאֱלַמְתִּי דוּמִיָּה
הֶחֱשֵׁיתִי מִטּוֹב
וּכְאֵבִי נֶעְכָּר׃

3 I remained silent;
I kept perfectly still,
but my pain grew intense –

חַם־לִבִּי ׀ בְּקִרְבִּי
בַּהֲגִיגִי תִבְעַר־אֵשׁ
דִּבַּרְתִּי בִּלְשׁוֹנִי׃

4 my heart burned within me,
my thoughts blazed,
and I spoke up:

הוֹדִיעֵנִי יהוה ׀ קִצִּי
וּמִדַּת יָמַי מַה־הִיא
אֵדְעָה מֶה־חָדֵל אָנִי׃

5 "Tell me when it will end, LORD,
the number of my days–
that I may know how fleeting I am."

הִנֵּה טְפָחוֹת ׀ נָתַתָּה יָמַי
וְחֶלְדִּי כְאַיִן נֶגְדֶּךָ
אַךְ־כָּל־הֶבֶל כָּל־אָדָם נִצָּב
סֶלָה׃

6 You have measured out my days
in handbreadths,
and my lifespan is as nothing before You.
Alas, all humanity, however firm it stands,
is but a mere breath – Selah.

אַךְ־בְּצֶלֶם ׀ יִתְהַלֶּךְ־אִישׁ
אַךְ־הֶבֶל יֶהֱמָיוּן
יִצְבֹּר וְלֹא־יֵדַע מִי־אֹסְפָם׃

7 Alas, people are but walking shadows,
their restless bustle but mere breath;
they hoard without knowing
who will gather in.

וְעַתָּה מַה־קִּוִּיתִי אֲדֹנָי
תּוֹחַלְתִּי לְךָ הִיא׃

8 And now, what can I wait for, LORD?
My only hope is You.

מִכָּל־פְּשָׁעַי הַצִּילֵנִי
חֶרְפַּת נָבָל אַל־תְּשִׂימֵנִי׃

9 Save me from all my sins;
do not let me be scorned by fools.

נֶאֱלַמְתִּי לֹא אֶפְתַּח־פִּי
כִּי אַתָּה עָשִׂיתָ:

10 I will keep silent;
I will not open my mouth,
for it is Your doing.

הָסֵר מֵעָלַי נִגְעֶךָ
מִתִּגְרַת יָדְךָ אֲנִי כָלִיתִי:

11 Remove Your scourge from me;
I waste away from the blows
of Your hand.

בְּתוֹכָחוֹת עַל־עָוֹן ׀ יִסַּרְתָּ אִישׁ
וַתֶּמֶס כָּעָשׁ חֲמוּדוֹ
אַךְ הֶבֶל כָּל־אָדָם סֶלָה:

12 Punishing offense, You bring suffering,
crumbling people's treasures like a moth.
Alas, all humanity is but fleeting breath.
Selah.

שִׁמְעָה תְפִלָּתִי ׀ יהוה
וְשַׁוְעָתִי ׀ הַאֲזִינָה
אֶל־דִּמְעָתִי אַל־תֶּחֱרַשׁ
כִּי גֵר אָנֹכִי עִמָּךְ
תּוֹשָׁב כְּכָל־אֲבוֹתָי:

13 Hear my prayer, LORD;
give ear to my cry;
do not remain silent at my tears,
for to You, I am but a passerby,
a mere transient like all my ancestors.

הָשַׁע מִמֶּנִּי וְאַבְלִיגָה
בְּטֶרֶם אֵלֵךְ וְאֵינֶנִּי:

14 Let me be, so I may smile again
before I pass away and am no more.

He placed a new song on my lips, a song of praise for our God

Is it blasphemous to say to God, "Keep up the good work"?
Usually, I pray to God when I am really hurting.
But this time, things are going well. I am singing a new song.
Sing along with me. I am praying a new prayer. Join me.
Together we can make the good times last.

PSALM 40

לַמְנַצֵּחַ לְדָוִד מִזְמֽוֹר: 1

קַוֺּה קִוִּיתִי יהוה 2
וַיֵּט אֵלַי וַיִּשְׁמַע שַׁוְעָתִֽי:

וַיַּעֲלֵנִי ׀ מִבּוֹר שָׁאוֹן מִטִּיט הַיָּוֵן 3
וַיָּקֶם עַל־סֶלַע רַגְלַי
כּוֹנֵן אֲשֻׁרָֽי:

וַיִּתֵּן בְּפִי ׀ שִׁיר חָדָשׁ 4
תְּהִלָּה לֵאלֹהֵינוּ
יִרְאוּ רַבִּים וְיִירָאוּ
וְיִבְטְחוּ בַּיהוָֽה:

אַשְׁרֵי־הַגֶּבֶר 5
אֲשֶׁר־שָׂם יהוה מִבְטַחוֹ
וְלֹא־פָנָה אֶל־רְהָבִים
וְשָׂטֵי כָזָֽב:

רַבּוֹת עָשִׂיתָ ׀ אַתָּה ׀ 6
יהוה אֱלֹהַי
נִפְלְאֹתֶיךָ וּמַחְשְׁבֹתֶיךָ אֵלֵינוּ
אֵין ׀ עֲרֹךְ אֵלֶיךָ אַגִּידָה
וַאֲדַבֵּרָה
עָצְמוּ מִסַּפֵּֽר:

זֶבַח וּמִנְחָה ׀ לֹא־חָפַצְתָּ 7
אָזְנַיִם כָּרִיתָ לִּי
עוֹלָה וַחֲטָאָה לֹא שָׁאָֽלְתָּ:

אָז אָמַרְתִּי הִנֵּה־בָאתִי 8
בִּמְגִלַּת־סֵפֶר כָּתוּב עָלָֽי:

1 To the lead singer – of David, a psalm

2 I put all my hope in the Lord;
He bent down to me;
He heard my cry.

3 He raised me out of the pit of despair
from the oozing mud;
He set my feet on solid stone
and steadied my footsteps.

4 He placed a new song on my lips,
a song of praise for our God;
the crowds will see
and be struck with awe
and place their trust in the Lord.

5 Happy are those
who make the Lord their trust
instead of turning to the pompous,
to followers of falsehood,

6 for You have done great things,
O Lord my God;
You have devised such wonders for us;
none can compare to You –
were I to tell of them, to speak of them,
there would be far too many to count.

7 For sacrifice or gift You have no desire –
that You have made clear.
You never asked for burnt offering
or sin offering,

8 so I decided,
"Here – I come with the scroll that was
written for me."

לַעֲשׂוֹת־רְצוֹנְךָ אֱלֹהַי חָפָצְתִּי
וְתוֹרָתְךָ בְּתוֹךְ מֵעָי:

9 To do Your will, God, is my desire;
Your teachings course
through my insides.

בִּשַּׂרְתִּי צֶדֶק ׀ בְּקָהָל רָב
הִנֵּה שְׂפָתַי לֹא אֶכְלָא
יהוה אַתָּה יָדָעְתָּ:

10 I proclaimed Your righteousness
before the great assembly;
see – I have not sealed my lips, Lord,
as You know.

צִדְקָתְךָ לֹא־כִסִּיתִי ׀ בְּתוֹךְ לִבִּי
אֱמוּנָתְךָ וּתְשׁוּעָתְךָ אָמָרְתִּי
לֹא־כִחַדְתִּי חַסְדְּךָ וַאֲמִתְּךָ
לְקָהָל רָב:

11 I have not kept Your justice secret
in my heart;
I proclaim Your devotion and salvation;
I have not denied Your loyalty and truth
before the great assembly.

אַתָּה יהוה
לֹא־תִכְלָא רַחֲמֶיךָ מִמֶּנִּי
חַסְדְּךָ וַאֲמִתְּךָ תָּמִיד יִצְּרוּנִי:

12 As for You, Lord,
do not withhold Your compassion
from me;
let Your loyalty and truth keep me always,

כִּי אָפְפוּ־עָלַי ׀ רָעוֹת
עַד־אֵין מִסְפָּר
הִשִּׂיגוּנִי עֲוֺנֹתַי
וְלֹא־יָכֹלְתִּי לִרְאוֹת
עָצְמוּ מִשַּׂעֲרוֹת רֹאשִׁי
וְלִבִּי עֲזָבָנִי:

13 for endless evil has beset me;
my offenses have caught up with me,
blurring my vision;
they far outnumber the hairs on my head,
and my heart fails within me.

רְצֵה יהוה לְהַצִּילֵנִי
יהוה לְעֶזְרָתִי חוּשָׁה:

14 Show me favor, Lord, and save me;
rush to my help, Lord!

יֵבֹשׁוּ וְיַחְפְּרוּ ׀ יַחַד
מְבַקְשֵׁי נַפְשִׁי לִסְפּוֹתָהּ
יִסֹּגוּ אָחוֹר וְיִכָּלְמוּ
חֲפֵצֵי רָעָתִי:

15 Let those who seek
to snatch away my life
be shamed and disgraced;
let those who wish me harm
retreat in humiliation;

יָשֹׁמּוּ עַל־עֵקֶב בָּשְׁתָּם
הָאֹמְרִים לִי הֶאָח ׀ הֶאָח:

16 let those who leer at me – "Aha! Aha!" –
wallow in their shame.

יָשִׂישׂוּ וְיִשְׂמְחוּ ׀ בְּךָ
כָּל־מְבַקְשֶׁיךָ
יֹאמְרוּ תָמִיד יִגְדַּל יהוה
אֹהֲבֵי תְּשׁוּעָתֶךָ:

17 May all those who seek You
rejoice and delight in You.
May those who long for Your salvation
always proclaim, "The LORD is great!"

וַאֲנִי ׀ עָנִי וְאֶבְיוֹן
אֲדֹנָי יַחֲשָׁב לִי
עֶזְרָתִי וּמְפַלְטִי אַתָּה
אֱלֹהַי אַל־תְּאַחַר:

18 As for me, I am poor and needy;
may the LORD call me to mind.
You are my help and my rescuer –
my God, do not delay.

By this I shall know that You delight in me; my enemies will not crow over me

It is good to visit a sick person. That's sympathy.
It is admirable to understand what he is feeling.
That's empathy. It is wonderful when he knows that you
understand. That's compassion.
That's "Love your neighbor as you love yourself."

PSALM 41

לַמְנַצֵּחַ מִזְמוֹר לְדָוִד׃

1   To the lead singer – a psalm of David

אַשְׁרֵי מַשְׂכִּיל אֶל־דָּל
בְּיוֹם רָעָה יְמַלְּטֵהוּ יהוה׃

2   Happy are those
    who give thought to the weak;
    may the Lord spare them
    in times of misery.

יהוה ׀ יִשְׁמְרֵהוּ וִיחַיֵּהוּ
אשר   וְאֻשַּׁר בָּאָרֶץ
וְאַל־תִּתְּנֵהוּ בְּנֶפֶשׁ אֹיְבָיו׃

3   May the Lord keep them
    and give them life
    so that they will be happy in the land,
    rather than give them up
    to the will of their enemies.

יהוה יִסְעָדֶנּוּ עַל־עֶרֶשׂ דְּוָי
כָּל־מִשְׁכָּבוֹ הָפַכְתָּ בְחָלְיוֹ׃

4   May the Lord sustain them
    on their sickbeds;
    You completely turned back
    their suffering.

אֲנִי־אָמַרְתִּי יהוה חָנֵּנִי
רְפָאָה נַפְשִׁי כִּי־חָטָאתִי לָךְ׃

5   I prayed, "O Lord, show me mercy;
    heal me, for I sinned against You."

אוֹיְבַי יֹאמְרוּ רַע לִי
מָתַי יָמוּת וְאָבַד שְׁמוֹ׃

6   My enemies speak of me with spite:
    "When will he die and his name perish?"

וְאִם־בָּא לִרְאוֹת ׀ שָׁוְא יְדַבֵּר
לִבּוֹ יִקְבָּץ־אָוֶן לוֹ
יֵצֵא לַחוּץ יְדַבֵּר׃

7   If they visit, they babble insincerely
    while malice swells in their heart –
    as soon as they leave, they speak out.

יַחַד עָלַי יִתְלַחֲשׁוּ כָּל־שֹׂנְאָי
עָלַי ׀ יַחְשְׁבוּ רָעָה לִי׃

8   All those who hate me whisper about me,
    imagining the worst for me:

דְּבַר־בְּלִיַּעַל יָצוּק בּוֹ
וַאֲשֶׁר שָׁכַב לֹא־יוֹסִיף לָקוּם׃

9   "Something deadly courses through him;
    he will never rise from his bed again."

גַּם־אִישׁ שְׁלוֹמִי ׀
אֲשֶׁר־בָּטַחְתִּי בוֹ
אוֹכֵל לַחְמִי
הִגְדִּיל עָלַי עָקֵב׃

10   Even my trusted friend –
    who ate of my bread! –
    has treated me with cruel deceit.

וְאַתָּה יהוה חׇנֵּנִי וַהֲקִימֵנִי
וַאֲשַׁלְּמָה לָהֶם:

11 But You, Lord, show me grace;
raise me up
so that I may pay them back –

בְּזֹאת יָדַעְתִּי כִּי־חָפַצְתָּ בִּי
כִּי לֹא־יָרִיעַ אֹיְבִי עָלָי:

12 by this I shall know that You delight
in me;
my enemies will not crow over me.

וַאֲנִי בְּתֻמִּי תָּמַכְתָּ בִּי
וַתַּצִּיבֵנִי לְפָנֶיךָ לְעוֹלָם:

13 As for me, because I am blameless
You support me;
You let me stand firm before You forever.

בָּרוּךְ יהוה ׀ אֱלֹהֵי יִשְׂרָאֵל
מֵהָעוֹלָם וְעַד־הָעוֹלָם
אָמֵן ׀ וְאָמֵן:

14 Blessed is the Lord, God of Israel,
forever and ever,
Amen and Amen.

As a deer pines for flowing streams, my soul pines for You, God

I obey God's will. I'm religious. I pray to God and sing to Him.
I'm spiritual. I thirst for God. I yearn for Him.
I miss Him. I am a mystic.

PSALM 42

לַמְנַצֵּחַ מַשְׂכִּיל לִבְנֵי־קֹרַח׃

1 To the lead singer –
of the sons of Koraḥ, a *maskil*

כְּאַיָּל תַּעֲרֹג עַל־אֲפִיקֵי־מָיִם
כֵּן נַפְשִׁי תַעֲרֹג אֵלֶיךָ אֱלֹהִים׃

2 As a deer pines for flowing streams,
my soul pines for You, God;

צָמְאָה נַפְשִׁי ׀ לֵאלֹהִים
לְאֵל חָי
מָתַי אָבוֹא
וְאֵרָאֶה פְּנֵי אֱלֹהִים׃

3 my soul thirsts for God,
the living God –
oh, when will I come
and appear before God?

הָיְתָה־לִּי דִמְעָתִי לֶחֶם
יוֹמָם וָלָיְלָה
בֶּאֱמֹר אֵלַי כָּל־הַיּוֹם
אַיֵּה אֱלֹהֶיךָ׃

4 My tears have been my fare
day and night
as people ever taunt me,
"Where is your God?"

אֵלֶּה אֶזְכְּרָה ׀
וְאֶשְׁפְּכָה עָלַי ׀ נַפְשִׁי
כִּי אֶעֱבֹר ׀ בַּסָּךְ אֶדַּדֵּם
עַד־בֵּית אֱלֹהִים
בְּקוֹל־רִנָּה וְתוֹדָה
הָמוֹן חוֹגֵג׃

5 Oh, the things I remember
as I pour out my soul:
how I would join the crowd
and march along to the House of God
with elated song and the hum of praise
from the reveling throngs.

מַה־תִּשְׁתּוֹחֲחִי ׀ נַפְשִׁי
וַתֶּהֱמִי עָלָי
הוֹחִלִי לֵאלֹהִים
כִּי־עוֹד אוֹדֶנּוּ יְשׁוּעוֹת פָּנָיו׃

6 Why are you miserable, my soul?
Why do you grieve so within me?
Hope for God –
that I will yet praise Him
in the salvation of His presence.

אֱלֹהַי
עָלַי נַפְשִׁי תִשְׁתּוֹחָח
עַל־כֵּן אֶזְכָּרְךָ מֵאֶרֶץ יַרְדֵּן
וְחֶרְמוֹנִים מֵהַר מִצְעָר׃

7 My God –
my soul is miserable within me;
therefore I think of You
in the land of Jordan,
in the Ḥermon range,
from the Humble Mountain,

תְּהוֹם־אֶל־תְּהוֹם קוֹרֵא
לְקוֹל צִנּוֹרֶיךָ
כָּל־מִשְׁבָּרֶיךָ וְגַלֶּיךָ
עָלַי עָבָרוּ:

8 where deep calls to deep
in the roar of Your waterfalls;
all Your torrents and storm waves
crashed over me.

יוֹמָם ׀ יְצַוֶּה יהוה ׀ חַסְדּוֹ
וּבַלַּיְלָה שִׁירֹה עִמִּי
תְּפִלָּה לְאֵל חַיָּי:

9 By day, the Lord commands His loyalty;
by night, His song is with me –
a prayer to the God of my life.

אוֹמְרָה ׀ לְאֵל סַלְעִי
לָמָה שְׁכַחְתָּנִי
לָמָה־קֹדֵר אֵלֵךְ בְּלַחַץ אוֹיֵב:

10 Let me say to God, my rock,
"Why have You forgotten me?
Why must I walk bent in gloom,
oppressed by my enemies?"

בְּרֶצַח ׀ בְּעַצְמוֹתַי
חֵרְפוּנִי צוֹרְרָי
בְּאָמְרָם אֵלַי כָּל־הַיּוֹם
אַיֵּה אֱלֹהֶיךָ:

11 My enemies' scorn pierces my bones
as they ever taunt me,
"Where is your God?"

מַה־תִּשְׁתּוֹחֲחִי ׀ נַפְשִׁי
וּמַה־תֶּהֱמִי עָלָי
הוֹחִילִי לֵאלֹהִים
כִּי־עוֹד אוֹדֶנּוּ
יְשׁוּעֹת פָּנַי וֵאלֹהָי:

12 Why are you miserable, my soul?
Why do you grieve so within me?
Hope for God –
that I will yet praise Him,
my salvation and my God.

I will praise You with the lyre, God, O my God!

I firmly believe that my cause is just. My opponent believes,
just as firmly, that his cause is just. There are those who say
that we are both right. We just have different "narratives."
Why can't we just negotiate a compromise?
We could if he was trustworthy, honest, and fair.
But he is fraudulent, deceitful, and unjust.

PSALM 43

שָׁפְטֵ֫נִי אֱלֹהִ֥ים ׀
וְרִ֘יבָ֤ה רִיבִ֗י מִגּ֥וֹי לֹא־חָסִ֑יד
מֵאִ֥ישׁ־מִרְמָ֖ה וְעַוְלָ֣ה
תְפַלְּטֵֽנִי׃

1 Vindicate me, God;
contend on my behalf
against an ungodly nation;
from treacherous, corrupt people
rescue me,

כִּֽי־אַתָּ֤ה ׀ אֱלֹהֵ֣י מָֽעוּזִּי֮
לָמָ֪ה זְנַ֫חְתָּ֥נִי
לָֽמָּה־קֹדֵ֥ר אֶתְהַלֵּ֗ךְ
בְּלַ֣חַץ אוֹיֵֽב׃

2 for You are the God of my refuge.
Why do You forsake me?
Why must I walk about bent in gloom,
oppressed by my enemies?

שְׁלַח־אוֹרְךָ֣ וַ֭אֲמִתְּךָ
הֵ֣מָּה יַנְח֑וּנִי
יְבִיא֥וּנִי אֶל־הַר־קׇ֝דְשְׁךָ֗
וְאֶל־מִשְׁכְּנוֹתֶֽיךָ׃

3 Send forth Your light and Your truth –
they will guide me;
they will bring me to
Your holy mountain,
to Your dwelling place,

וְאָב֤וֹאָה ׀ אֶל־מִזְבַּ֬ח אֱלֹהִ֗ים
אֶל־אֵל֮ שִׂמְחַ֢ת גִּ֫ילִ֥י
וְאוֹדְךָ֥ בְכִנּ֗וֹר אֱלֹהִ֥ים אֱלֹהָֽי׃

4 and I will come to the altar of God –
to God, my joy, my delight.
I will praise You with the lyre,
God, O my God!

מַה־תִּשְׁתּ֬וֹחֲחִ֨י ׀ נַפְשִׁי֮
וּמַה־תֶּֽהֱמִ֪י עָ֫לָ֥י
הוֹחִ֣ילִי לֵֽ֭אלֹהִים כִּי־ע֣וֹד אוֹדֶ֑נּוּ
יְשׁוּעֹ֥ת פָּ֝נַ֗י וֵֽאלֹהָֽי׃

5 Why are you miserable, my soul?
Why do you grieve so within me?
Hope for God –
that I will yet praise Him,
my salvation and my God.

In God we glory all day long, and we will ever praise Your name – Selah

When we see the hand of God, we praise Him.
Then, our enemy is speechless.
At times God's hand cannot be seen. Then, our enemy taunts us.
He asks, "Where is your God?" Then, we are speechless.
But we have not forgotten Him.

PSALM 44

לַמְנַצֵּחַ לִבְנֵי־קֹרַח מַשְׂכִּיל׃ 1 To the lead singer –
of the sons of Koraḥ, a *maskil*

אֱלֹהִים ׀ בְּאָזְנֵינוּ שָׁמַעְנוּ 2 God, we heard with our own ears;
אֲבוֹתֵינוּ סִפְּרוּ־לָנוּ our ancestors told us
פֹּעַל־פָּעַלְתָּ בִימֵיהֶם of the deeds You did in their days,
בִּימֵי קֶדֶם׃ in days of old.

אַתָּה ׀ יָדְךָ גּוֹיִם הוֹרַשְׁתָּ 3 By Your hand You planted them,
וַתִּטָּעֵם dispossessing nations;
תָּרַע לְאֻמִּים וַתְּשַׁלְּחֵם׃ You brought evil upon peoples
and drove them out.

כִּי לֹא בְחַרְבָּם יָרְשׁוּ אָרֶץ 4 Not by their swords
וּזְרוֹעָם לֹא־הוֹשִׁיעָה לָּמוֹ did they win the land,
כִּי־יְמִינְךָ וּזְרוֹעֲךָ וְאוֹר פָּנֶיךָ nor did their arms bring them victory.
כִּי רְצִיתָם׃ It was Your right hand, Your arm,
the light of Your face,
for You showed them favor.

אַתָּה־הוּא מַלְכִּי אֱלֹהִים 5 You are my King, God –
צַוֵּה יְשׁוּעוֹת יַעֲקֹב׃ command victory for Yaakov.

בְּךָ צָרֵינוּ נְנַגֵּחַ 6 Through You we will gore our foes,
בְּשִׁמְךָ נָבוּס קָמֵינוּ׃ in Your name trample our adversaries,

כִּי לֹא בְקַשְׁתִּי אֶבְטָח 7 for I do not place my trust in my bow;
וְחַרְבִּי לֹא תוֹשִׁיעֵנִי׃ it is not my sword that will bring
me victory.

כִּי הוֹשַׁעְתָּנוּ מִצָּרֵינוּ 8 It is You who bring us victory
וּמְשַׂנְאֵינוּ הֱבִישׁוֹתָ׃ over our foes,
who bring shame to those who hate us.

בֵּאלֹהִים הִלַּלְנוּ כָל־הַיּוֹם 9 In God we glory all day long,
וְשִׁמְךָ ׀ לְעוֹלָם נוֹדֶה and we will ever praise Your name –
סֶלָה׃ Selah.

אַף־זָנַחְתָּ וַתַּכְלִימֵנוּ
וְלֹא־תֵצֵא בְּצִבְאוֹתֵינוּ:

10 Yet You have forsaken us
and disgraced us;
You no longer accompany our armies.

תְּשִׁיבֵנוּ אָחוֹר מִנִּי־צָר
וּמְשַׂנְאֵינוּ שָׁסוּ לָמוֹ:

11 You make us retreat before foes
while those who hate us plunder away.

תִּתְּנֵנוּ כְּצֹאן מַאֲכָל
וּבַגּוֹיִם זֵרִיתָנוּ:

12 You have allowed us to be devoured
like sheep
and scattered us among the nations,

תִּמְכֹּר־עַמְּךָ בְלֹא־הוֹן
וְלֹא־רִבִּיתָ בִּמְחִירֵיהֶם:

13 selling Your people for next to nothing,
making no profit from their sale.

תְּשִׂימֵנוּ חֶרְפָּה לִשְׁכֵנֵינוּ
לַעַג וָקֶלֶס לִסְבִיבוֹתֵינוּ:

14 You have made us the scorn
of our neighbors,
the laughingstock of those around us,

תְּשִׂימֵנוּ מָשָׁל בַּגּוֹיִם
מְנוֹד־רֹאשׁ בַּלְאֻמִּים:

15 a cautionary tale among the nations –
the peoples shake their heads.

כָּל־הַיּוֹם כְּלִמָּתִי נֶגְדִּי
וּבֹשֶׁת פָּנַי כִּסָּתְנִי:

16 All day long my disgrace haunts me;
my face is draped in shame

מִקּוֹל מְחָרֵף וּמְגַדֵּף
מִפְּנֵי אוֹיֵב וּמִתְנַקֵּם:

17 from the shouts of those
who taunt and revile,
from the enemy and avenger.

כָּל־זֹאת בָּאַתְנוּ וְלֹא
שְׁכַחֲנוּךָ
וְלֹא־שִׁקַּרְנוּ בִּבְרִיתֶךָ:

18 All this has befallen us,
but we have not forgotten You;
we have not betrayed Your covenant.

לֹא־נָסוֹג אָחוֹר לִבֵּנוּ
וַתֵּט אֲשֻׁרֵינוּ מִנִּי אָרְחֶךָ:

19 Our hearts have not turned back;
our steps have not strayed
from Your path

כִּי דִכִּיתָנוּ בִּמְקוֹם תַּנִּים
וַתְּכַס עָלֵינוּ בְצַלְמָוֶת:

20 although You have broken us
where jackals prowl
and draped us in death-shadow.

אִם־שָׁכַחְנוּ שֵׁם אֱלֹהֵינוּ
וַנִּפְרֹשׂ כַּפֵּינוּ לְאֵל זָר:

21 Had we forgotten the name of our God
or spread out our hands
toward an alien god,

הֲלֹא אֱלֹהִים יַחֲקָר־זֹאת
כִּי־הוּא יֹדֵעַ תַּעֲלֻמוֹת לֵב:

22 would God fail to discover this? –
for He knows the secrets of the heart.

כִּי־עָלֶיךָ הֹרַגְנוּ כָל־הַיּוֹם
נֶחְשַׁבְנוּ כְּצֹאן טִבְחָה:

23 For Your sake we constantly face death;
we are considered mere sheep for the
slaughter.

עוּרָה ׀ לָמָּה תִישַׁן ׀ אֲדֹנָי
הָקִיצָה אַל־תִּזְנַח לָנֶצַח:

24 Stir – why do You sleep, Lord?
Rouse Yourself!
Do not forsake us forever.

לָמָּה־פָנֶיךָ תַסְתִּיר
תִּשְׁכַּח עָנְיֵנוּ וְלַחֲצֵנוּ:

25 Why do You hide Your face;
why do You forget our suffering
and misery?

כִּי שָׁחָה לֶעָפָר נַפְשֵׁנוּ
דָּבְקָה לָאָרֶץ בִּטְנֵנוּ:

26 We are dragged down to the dust,
our bodies pressed to the earth.

קוּמָה עֶזְרָתָה לָּנוּ
וּפְדֵנוּ לְמַעַן חַסְדֶּךָ:

27 Arise to help us;
redeem us for the sake of Your loyalty.

Led in gladness and joy; they enter the king's palace

In our tradition, study is a form of worship.
Others study in silence and solitude.
We study together, and we study aloud.
Our words are swords, our arguments arrows.
"War" is a harsh metaphor for study.
But it is an apt metaphor for Torah study.

PSALM 45

לַמְנַצֵּחַ עַל־שֹׁשַׁנִּים לִבְנֵי־קֹרַח
מַשְׂכִּיל שִׁיר יְדִידֹת:

1 To the lead singer – of the sons of Korah,
set to *shoshanim* – a *maskil*, a love song

רָחַשׁ לִבִּי ׀ דָּבָר טוֹב
אֹמֵר אָנִי מַעֲשַׂי לְמֶלֶךְ
לְשׁוֹנִי עֵט ׀ סוֹפֵר מָהִיר:

2 My heart is astir with glad words;
I dedicate this work to the king;
my tongue runs like a skilled scribe's pen.

יָפְיָפִיתָ מִבְּנֵי אָדָם
הוּצַק חֵן בְּשִׂפְתוֹתֶיךָ
עַל־כֵּן בֵּרַכְךָ אֱלֹהִים לְעוֹלָם:

3 You are the fairest of mortals;
your lips brim with grace;
for this, God has blessed you forever.

חֲגוֹר־חַרְבְּךָ עַל־יָרֵךְ גִּבּוֹר
הוֹדְךָ וַהֲדָרֶךָ:

4 Fasten your sword on your thigh,
mighty one,
in your majesty and splendor.

וַהֲדָרְךָ ׀ צְלַח רְכַב
עַל־דְּבַר־אֱמֶת וְעַנְוָה־צֶדֶק
וְתוֹרְךָ נוֹרָאוֹת יְמִינֶךָ:

5 In your splendor, ride on triumphant
for the sake of truth, humility,
and justice,
and may your right hand lead you
to wondrous deeds.

חִצֶּיךָ שְׁנוּנִים
עַמִּים תַּחְתֶּיךָ יִפְּלוּ
בְּלֵב אוֹיְבֵי הַמֶּלֶךְ:

6 Your arrows are sharp
in the hearts of the king's enemies;
peoples fall at your feet.

כִּסְאֲךָ אֱלֹהִים עוֹלָם וָעֶד
שֵׁבֶט מִישֹׁר שֵׁבֶט מַלְכוּתֶךָ:

7 Your divine throne is eternal;
your royal scepter is a scepter of equity.

אָהַבְתָּ צֶּדֶק וַתִּשְׂנָא רֶשַׁע
עַל־כֵּן ׀ מְשָׁחֲךָ אֱלֹהִים אֱלֹהֶיךָ
שֶׁמֶן שָׂשׂוֹן מֵחֲבֵרֶךָ:

8 You love justice and despise evil –
for this, God – your God –
has anointed you out of all your fellows
with oil of bliss.

מֹר־וַאֲהָלוֹת קְצִיעוֹת
כָּל־בִּגְדֹתֶיךָ
מִן־הֵיכְלֵי שֵׁן מִנִּי שִׂמְּחוּךָ:

9 Your robes are all fragrant
with myrrh and aloe and cinnamon.
Lutes echo from ivory chambers,
delighting you.

בְּנוֹת מְלָכִים בִּיקְּרוֹתֶיךָ 10 The daughters of kings
נִצְּבָה שֵׁגַל לִימִינְךָ בְּכֶתֶם are among your noble ladies;
אוֹפִיר: on your right stands the queen
in gold of Ofir.

שִׁמְעִי־בַת וּרְאִי וְהַטִּי אָזְנֵךְ 11 Hear me, daughter;
וְשִׁכְחִי עַמֵּךְ וּבֵית אָבִיךְ: look around and listen;
forget your own people
and your father's house,

וְיִתְאָו הַמֶּלֶךְ יָפְיֵךְ 12 and let the king crave your beauty.
כִּי־הוּא אֲדֹנַיִךְ וְהִשְׁתַּחֲוִי־לוֹ: He is your master now; bow to him.

וּבַת־צֹר ו בְּמִנְחָה פָּנַיִךְ יְחַלּוּ 13 Daughter of Tyre,
עֲשִׁירֵי עָם: the richest of peoples will seek your
favor with gifts.

כָּל־כְּבוּדָּה בַת־מֶלֶךְ פְּנִימָה 14 In all her glory, the princess is inside,
מִמִּשְׁבְּצוֹת זָהָב לְבוּשָׁהּ: adorned in golden filigree;

לִרְקָמוֹת תּוּבַל לַמֶּלֶךְ 15 she is led to the king
בְּתוּלוֹת אַחֲרֶיהָ רֵעוֹתֶיהָ in embroidered finery,
מוּבָאוֹת לָךְ: maidens, her friends, in her train;
they are brought to you,

תּוּבַלְנָה בִּשְׂמָחֹת וָגִיל 16 led in gladness and joy;
תְּבֹאֶינָה בְּהֵיכַל מֶלֶךְ: they enter the king's palace.

תַּחַת אֲבֹתֶיךָ יִהְיוּ בָנֶיךָ 17 Your sons will succeed your fathers;
תְּשִׁיתֵמוֹ לְשָׂרִים בְּכָל־ you will make them princes
הָאָרֶץ: throughout the land.

אַזְכִּירָה שִׁמְךָ בְּכָל־דֹּר וָדֹר 18 I have perpetuated your name
עַל־כֵּן עַמִּים יְהוֹדֻךָ for all generations;
לְעֹלָם וָעֶד: therefore peoples shall praise you
forever and for all time.

There is a river whose streams bring joy to the city of God, to the holy dwelling place of the Most High

Trouble is brewing. But I feel protected. My faith gives me hope. I feel secure. Am I hopelessly naïve? Am I foolishly optimistic? No. I am a realist. I believe in miracles.

PSALM 46

לַמְנַצֵּחַ לִבְנֵי־קֹרַח עַל־עֲלָמוֹת שִׁיר:	1 To the lead singer – a song of the sons of Koraḥ, on *alamot*
אֱלֹהִים לָנוּ מַחֲסֶה וָעֹז עֶזְרָה בְצָרוֹת נִמְצָא מְאֹד:	2 God is our refuge and might, ever present to help in times of trouble,
עַל־כֵּן לֹא־נִירָא בְּהָמִיר אָרֶץ וּבְמוֹט הָרִים בְּלֵב יַמִּים:	3 so we need not fear when the world shifts, when mountains crumble into the heart of the sea –
יֶהֱמוּ יֶחְמְרוּ מֵימָיו יִרְעֲשׁוּ־הָרִים בְּגַאֲוָתוֹ סֶלָה:	4 though its waters rage and foam, though the mountains shudder at its surge – Selah.
נָהָר פְּלָגָיו יְשַׂמְּחוּ עִיר־אֱלֹהִים קְדֹשׁ מִשְׁכְּנֵי עֶלְיוֹן:	5 There is a river whose streams bring joy to the city of God, to the holy dwelling place of the Most High.
אֱלֹהִים בְּקִרְבָּהּ בַּל־תִּמּוֹט יַעְזְרֶהָ אֱלֹהִים לִפְנוֹת בֹּקֶר:	6 God is in its midst; it will never crumble; God will come to its aid at the break of day.
הָמוּ גוֹיִם מָטוּ מַמְלָכוֹת נָתַן בְּקוֹלוֹ תָּמוּג אָרֶץ:	7 Nations rage; kingdoms crumble; He sounds His voice, and the earth dissolves.
יהוה צְבָאוֹת עִמָּנוּ מִשְׂגָּב־לָנוּ אֱלֹהֵי יַעֲקֹב סֶלָה:	8 The LORD of hosts is with us; the God of Yaakov is our refuge – Selah.
לְכוּ־חֲזוּ מִפְעֲלוֹת יהוה אֲשֶׁר־שָׂם שַׁמּוֹת בָּאָרֶץ:	9 Come, gaze at the works of the LORD, at the desolation He has wrought upon the earth.
מַשְׁבִּית מִלְחָמוֹת עַד־קְצֵה הָאָרֶץ קֶשֶׁת יְשַׁבֵּר וְקִצֵּץ חֲנִית עֲגָלוֹת יִשְׂרֹף בָּאֵשׁ:	10 He has ended war all over the earth, breaking bow and snapping spear, burning chariots with fire.

הַרְפּוּ וּדְעוּ כִּי־אָנֹכִי אֱלֹהִים   11 Desist and know that I am God,
אָרוּם בַּגּוֹיִם אָרוּם בָּאָרֶץ: exalted among nations,
                                                        exalted over the earth.

יהוה צְבָאוֹת עִמָּנוּ   12 The LORD of hosts is with us;
מִשְׂגָּב־לָנוּ אֱלֹהֵי יַעֲקֹב סֶלָה: the God of Yaakov is our refuge – Selah.

God ascends amid shouts of joy – the LORD – to the blast of the shofar

There are two types of applause: I applaud your performance.
You did a fine job. We all applaud together. We celebrate as one.
On that great day, the nations will applaud us.
Better still, they will join us as we applaud Him.

PSALM 47

לַמְנַצֵּחַ לִבְנֵי־קֹרַח מִזְמוֹר׃ 1

To the lead singer –
a psalm of the sons of Koraḥ

כָּל־הָעַמִּים תִּקְעוּ־כָף
הָרִיעוּ לֵאלֹהִים בְּקוֹל רִנָּה׃ 2

Clap your hands together, all peoples;
shout out joyfully to God,

כִּי־יהוה עֶלְיוֹן נוֹרָא
מֶלֶךְ גָּדוֹל עַל־כָּל־הָאָרֶץ׃ 3

for the Lord, Most High, is fearsome,
the great King over all the earth.

יַדְבֵּר עַמִּים תַּחְתֵּינוּ
וּלְאֻמִּים תַּחַת רַגְלֵינוּ׃ 4

It is He who subjugates peoples under us,
nations beneath our feet.

יִבְחַר־לָנוּ אֶת־נַחֲלָתֵנוּ
אֶת גְּאוֹן יַעֲקֹב אֲשֶׁר־אָהֵב
סֶלָה׃ 5

He chooses our legacy for us:
the pride of Yaakov, whom he loves –
Selah.

עָלָה אֱלֹהִים בִּתְרוּעָה
יהוה בְּקוֹל שׁוֹפָר׃ 6

God ascends amid shouts of joy –
the Lord – to the blast of the shofar.

זַמְּרוּ אֱלֹהִים זַמֵּרוּ
זַמְּרוּ לְמַלְכֵּנוּ זַמֵּרוּ׃ 7

Sing out to God, sing!
Sing out to our King, sing!

כִּי מֶלֶךְ כָּל־הָאָרֶץ אֱלֹהִים
זַמְּרוּ מַשְׂכִּיל׃ 8

For God is King over all the earth –
sing a psalm of praise!

מָלַךְ אֱלֹהִים עַל־גּוֹיִם
אֱלֹהִים יָשַׁב עַל־כִּסֵּא קָדְשׁוֹ׃ 9

God reigns over nations;
God is seated on His holy throne.

נְדִיבֵי עַמִּים נֶאֱסָפוּ עַם
אֱלֹהֵי אַבְרָהָם
כִּי לֵאלֹהִים מָגִנֵּי־אֶרֶץ
מְאֹד נַעֲלָה׃ 10

The rulers of peoples have gathered,
the people of Avraham's God,
for all the earth's protectors are God's;
He is raised high above.

Beautiful in its heights, the delight of all the earth

What makes Jerusalem beautiful? The mountains which surround
her? The ramparts and towers which can be seen from afar?
Eyes don't see what makes her beautiful. Hearts feel her beauty.
Hearts know loving-kindness. Hearts rejoice.
Hearts find solace in His guidance, even unto death.

PSALM 48

שִׁיר מִזְמוֹר לִבְנֵי־קֹרַח׃	1	A song – a psalm of the sons of Koraḥ
גָּדוֹל יהוה וּמְהֻלָּל מְאֹד בְּעִיר אֱלֹהֵינוּ הַר־קָדְשׁוֹ׃	2	Great is the Lord, of highest praise in the city of our God, His holy mountain,
יְפֵה נוֹף מְשׂוֹשׂ כָּל־הָאָרֶץ הַר־צִיּוֹן יַרְכְּתֵי צָפוֹן קִרְיַת מֶלֶךְ רָב׃	3	beautiful in its heights, the delight of all the earth, Mount Zion, the slopes of Tzafon, city of the great King.
אֱלֹהִים בְּאַרְמְנוֹתֶיהָ נוֹדַע לְמִשְׂגָּב׃	4	God is known as the protector of its palaces.
כִּי־הִנֵּה הַמְּלָכִים נוֹעֲדוּ עָבְרוּ יַחְדָּו׃	5	See how the kings joined forces, advancing together.
הֵמָּה רָאוּ כֵּן תָּמָהוּ נִבְהֲלוּ נֶחְפָּזוּ׃	6	Astounded at the sight, they panicked and fled –
רְעָדָה אֲחָזָתַם שָׁם חִיל כַּיּוֹלֵדָה׃	7	there fear seized them, the agony of a woman in childbirth,
בְּרוּחַ קָדִים תְּשַׁבֵּר אֳנִיּוֹת תַּרְשִׁישׁ׃	8	like ships of Tarshish wrecked by eastern winds.
כַּאֲשֶׁר שָׁמַעְנוּ ׀ כֵּן רָאִינוּ בְּעִיר־יהוה צְבָאוֹת בְּעִיר אֱלֹהֵינוּ אֱלֹהִים יְכוֹנְנֶהָ עַד־עוֹלָם סֶלָה׃	9	The tales are all true – we have seen for ourselves – in the city of the Lord of hosts, in the city of our God. May God preserve it forever, Selah.
דִּמִּינוּ אֱלֹהִים חַסְדֶּךָ בְּקֶרֶב הֵיכָלֶךָ׃	10	Within Your Temple, God, we meditate on Your love.
כְּשִׁמְךָ ׀ אֱלֹהִים כֵּן תְּהִלָּתְךָ עַל־קַצְוֵי־אֶרֶץ צֶדֶק מָלְאָה יְמִינֶךָ׃	11	Your name, God, like Your praise, reaches the ends of the earth; Your right hand is filled with righteousness.

יִשְׂמַח ו הַר־צִיּוֹן תָּגֵלְנָה
בְּנוֹת יְהוּדָה
לְמַעַן מִשְׁפָּטֶיךָ:

12 Let Mount Zion rejoice;
let the towns of Yehuda be glad
because of Your judgments.

סֹבּוּ צִיּוֹן וְהַקִּיפוּהָ
סִפְרוּ מִגְדָּלֶיהָ:

13 Walk around Zion and encircle it;
count its towers;

שִׁיתוּ לִבְּכֶם ו לְחֵילָה פַּסְּגוּ
אַרְמְנוֹתֶיהָ
לְמַעַן תְּסַפְּרוּ לְדוֹר אַחֲרוֹן:

14 note its strong walls;
make your way through its citadels
so that you may tell future generations

כִּי זֶה ו אֱלֹהִים אֱלֹהֵינוּ
עוֹלָם וָעֶד
הוּא יְנַהֲגֵנוּ עַל־מוּת:

15 that this is God, our God,
for ever and ever;
He will guide us for evermore.

I expound my theme to the music of the harp

We strolled along the old cemetery's path every sunny Sunday.
We passed unmarked graves and modest headstones.
The newest grave was dug long before I was born.
All the dead there were forgotten, unnoticed;
except on sunny Sundays.

PSALM 49

לַמְנַצֵּחַ לִבְנֵי־קֹרַח מִזְמוֹר׃	1	To the lead singer – a psalm of the sons of Koraḥ
שִׁמְעוּ־זֹאת כָּל־הָעַמִּים הַאֲזִינוּ כָּל־יֹשְׁבֵי חָלֶד׃	2	Hear this, all you peoples; listen, all dwellers of this world,
גַּם־בְּנֵי אָדָם גַּם־בְּנֵי־אִישׁ יַחַד עָשִׁיר וְאֶבְיוֹן׃	3	low and high, rich and poor alike.
פִּי יְדַבֵּר חָכְמוֹת וְהָגוּת לִבִּי תְבוּנוֹת׃	4	My mouth will speak words of wisdom; my heart's utterance, understanding.
אַטֶּה לְמָשָׁל אָזְנִי אֶפְתַּח בְּכִנּוֹר חִידָתִי׃	5	I listen with care to a parable; I expound my theme to the music of the harp.
לָמָּה אִירָא בִּימֵי רָע עֲוֹן עֲקֵבַי יְסוּבֵּנִי׃	6	Why should I fear when evil days come, when wicked deceivers surround me–
הַבֹּטְחִים עַל־חֵילָם וּבְרֹב עָשְׁרָם יִתְהַלָּלוּ׃	7	those who trust in their wealth, who boast of their great riches.
אָח לֹא־פָדֹה יִפְדֶּה אִישׁ לֹא־יִתֵּן לֵאלֹהִים כָּפְרוֹ׃	8	No person can ever redeem another or pay God the price of his release;
וְיֵקַר פִּדְיוֹן נַפְשָׁם וְחָדַל לְעוֹלָם׃	9	the ransom of a life is costly; no payment will ever be enough
וִיחִי־עוֹד לָנֶצַח לֹא יִרְאֶה הַשָּׁחַת׃	10	to let him live forever, never seeing the grave.
כִּי יִרְאֶה ׀ חֲכָמִים יָמוּתוּ יַחַד כְּסִיל וָבַעַר יֹאבֵדוּ וְעָזְבוּ לַאֲחֵרִים חֵילָם׃	11	For all can see that wise men die and that the foolish and senseless all perish, leaving their wealth to others.
קִרְבָּם בָּתֵּימוֹ ׀ לְעוֹלָם מִשְׁכְּנֹתָם לְדֹר וָדֹר קָרְאוּ בִשְׁמוֹתָם עֲלֵי אֲדָמוֹת׃	12	They think their houses will last forever, their dwellings for all generations– they give their names to their estates,

וְאָדָם בִּיקָר בַּל־יָלִין 13 but a person, despite his wealth,
נִמְשַׁל כַּבְּהֵמוֹת נִדְמוּ: cannot linger;
he is like the beasts that perish.

זֶה דַרְכָּם כֵּסֶל לָמוֹ 14 Such is the fate of the foolish,
וְאַחֲרֵיהֶם ׀ בְּפִיהֶם יִרְצוּ the end of those
סֶלָה: pleased with their own words – Selah.

כַּצֹּאן ׀ לִשְׁאוֹל שַׁתּוּ מָוֶת יִרְעֵם 15 They go down to Sheol like sheep;
וַיִּרְדּוּ בָם יְשָׁרִים ׀ לַבֹּקֶר death will be their shepherd.
וְצוּרָם וְצִירָם לְבַלּוֹת שְׁאוֹל מִזְּבֻל לוֹ: The upright will rule over them
in the morning.
Their forms will decay in Sheol,
far from their noble mansions.

אַךְ־אֱלֹהִים יִפְדֶּה נַפְשִׁי 16 But God will redeem my life from Sheol,
מִיַּד שְׁאוֹל for He will take me – Selah.
כִּי יִקָּחֵנִי סֶלָה:

אַל־תִּירָא כִּי־יַעֲשִׁר אִישׁ 17 Fear not when people grow rich,
כִּי־יִרְבֶּה כְּבוֹד בֵּיתוֹ: when their houses rise in esteem,

כִּי לֹא בְמוֹתוֹ יִקַּח הַכֹּל 18 for they will take nothing with them
לֹא־יֵרֵד אַחֲרָיו כְּבוֹדוֹ: in death;
their esteem will not descend with them.

כִּי־נַפְשׁוֹ בְּחַיָּיו יְבָרֵךְ 19 Though they counted themselves
וְיוֹדֻךָ כִּי־תֵיטִיב לָךְ: blessed in life,
for people praise you when you prosper,

תָּבוֹא עַד־דּוֹר אֲבוֹתָיו 20 they too will join the ranks
עַד־נֵצַח לֹא יִרְאוּ־אוֹר: of their ancestors,
who will never see the light again.

אָדָם בִּיקָר וְלֹא יָבִין 21 A person with wealth
נִמְשַׁל כַּבְּהֵמוֹת נִדְמוּ: but without understanding
is like the beasts that perish.

From Zion, pure beauty, God shines forth

"Thank you" is a confession. It is an admission that I need You; that I couldn't have done it myself. Who wants to feel inadequate? It is hard to say "thank you." Yet, all You want from me is my gratitude. You have everything else.

PSALM 50

מִזְמוֹר לְאָסָף	1	A psalm of Asaf
אֵל ׀ אֱלֹהִים יְהֹוה דִּבֶּר		God, the LORD God, speaks
וַיִּקְרָא־אָרֶץ		and summons the earth
מִמִּזְרַח־שֶׁמֶשׁ עַד־מְבֹאוֹ:		from where the sun rises to where it sets.
מִצִּיּוֹן מִכְלַל־יֹפִי	2	From Zion, pure beauty,
אֱלֹהִים הוֹפִיעַ:		God shines forth.
יָבֹא אֱלֹהֵינוּ וְאַל־יֶחֱרַשׁ	3	Let our God come;
אֵשׁ־לְפָנָיו תֹּאכֵל		let Him not hold back –
וּסְבִיבָיו נִשְׂעֲרָה מְאֹד:		a devouring fire flares before Him;
		a wild storm rages around Him.
יִקְרָא אֶל־הַשָּׁמַיִם מֵעָל	4	He calls on the earth
וְאֶל־הָאָרֶץ לָדִין עַמּוֹ:		and the heavens above
		for the judgment of His people:
אִסְפוּ־לִי חֲסִידָי	5	"Gather my devoted ones to Me,
כֹּרְתֵי בְרִיתִי עֲלֵי־זָבַח:		those who forged a covenant with Me
		by sacrifice."
וַיַּגִּידוּ שָׁמַיִם צִדְקוֹ	6	The heavens tell of His justice,
כִּי־אֱלֹהִים ׀ שֹׁפֵט הוּא סֶלָה:		for God Himself is the judge – Selah.
שִׁמְעָה עַמִּי ׀ וַאֲדַבֵּרָה	7	Listen, My people, and I will speak;
יִשְׂרָאֵל וְאָעִידָה בָּךְ		Israel, I will testify against you:
אֱלֹהִים אֱלֹהֶיךָ אָנֹכִי:		I am God, your God.
לֹא עַל־זְבָחֶיךָ אוֹכִיחֶךָ	8	I do not rebuke you for your sacrifices
וְעוֹלֹתֶיךָ לְנֶגְדִּי תָמִיד:		or for your burnt offerings
		ever before Me.
לֹא־אֶקַּח מִבֵּיתְךָ פָר	9	I claim no bulls of your house,
מִמִּכְלְאֹתֶיךָ עַתּוּדִים:		no he-goats from your folds,
כִּי־לִי כָל־חַיְתוֹ־יָעַר	10	for all the forest beasts are Mine,
בְּהֵמוֹת בְּהַרְרֵי־אָלֶף:		the cattle of a thousand hills;
יָדַעְתִּי כָּל־עוֹף הָרִים	11	I know every bird of the mountains;
וְזִיז שָׂדַי עִמָּדִי:		the creatures of the fields belong to Me.

אִם־אֶרְעַב לֹא־אֹמַר לָךְ
כִּי־לִי תֵבֵל וּמְלֹאָהּ:

12 Were I to hunger, I would not tell you,
for Mine is the world and all that fills it.

הַאוֹכַל בְּשַׂר אַבִּירִים
וְדַם עַתּוּדִים אֶשְׁתֶּה:

13 Do I eat the flesh of bulls?
Do I drink the blood of he-goats?

זְבַח לֵאלֹהִים תּוֹדָה
וְשַׁלֵּם לְעֶלְיוֹן נְדָרֶיךָ:

14 Offer to God a thanksgiving sacrifice;
pay your vows to the Most High.

וּקְרָאֵנִי בְּיוֹם צָרָה
אֲחַלֶּצְךָ וּתְכַבְּדֵנִי:

15 When you call Me in times of trouble,
I will rescue you, and you will honor Me.

וְלָרָשָׁע ׀ אָמַר אֱלֹהִים
מַה־לְּךָ לְסַפֵּר חֻקָּי
וַתִּשָּׂא בְרִיתִי עֲלֵי־פִיךָ:

16 But to the wicked, God says,
"How dare you recite My laws
or bear My covenant on your lips –

וְאַתָּה שָׂנֵאתָ מוּסָר
וַתַּשְׁלֵךְ דְּבָרַי אַחֲרֶיךָ:

17 you who despise discipline
and toss My words behind you?

אִם־רָאִיתָ גַנָּב וַתִּרֶץ עִמּוֹ
וְעִם מְנָאֲפִים חֶלְקֶךָ:

18 When you see a thief,
you are drawn to him;
you associate with adulterers;

פִּיךָ שָׁלַחְתָּ בְרָעָה
וּלְשׁוֹנְךָ תַּצְמִיד מִרְמָה:

19 you speak evil freely;
your tongue adheres to deceit;

תֵּשֵׁב בְּאָחִיךָ תְדַבֵּר
בְּבֶן־אִמְּךָ תִּתֶּן־דֹּפִי:

20 you sit and slander your brother,
maligning the child of your own mother.

אֵלֶּה עָשִׂיתָ ׀ וְהֶחֱרַשְׁתִּי
דִּמִּיתָ הֱיוֹת־אֶהְיֶה כָמוֹךָ
אוֹכִיחֲךָ וְאֶעֶרְכָה לְעֵינֶיךָ:

21 If all this you do and I hold back,
You might imagine I am like you,
so I will rebuke you
and charge you outright.

בִּינוּ־נָא זֹאת שֹׁכְחֵי אֱלוֹהַּ
פֶּן־אֶטְרֹף וְאֵין מַצִּיל:

22 Consider this, you who forget God,
lest I tear you apart,
with no one to save you:

זֹבֵחַ תּוֹדָה יְֽכַבְּדָ֥נְנִי
וְשָׂ֥ם דֶּ֑רֶךְ
אַ֭רְאֶ֗נּוּ בְּיֵ֣שַׁע אֱלֹהִֽים׃

23 those who bring Me offerings
of thanksgiving honor Me,
and as for those
who are following My way,
I will show them God's salvation."

Favor Zion with Your goodness; rebuild the walls of Jerusalem

I will not deny my guilt. I am guilty. I am obsessed.
Visions of my sinful act haunt me.
Sin is a part of me. I would make any sacrifice to be able to shed
my sin. God does not want sacrifice. He wants my broken heart.
He has it.

PSALM 51

	לַמְנַצֵּחַ מִזְמוֹר לְדָוִד:	1 To the lead singer – a psalm of David,
	בְּבוֹא־אֵלָיו נָתָן הַנָּבִיא	2 when the prophet Natan came to him
	כַּאֲשֶׁר־בָּא אֶל־בַּת־שָׁבַע:	after he came to Batsheva
	חָנֵּנִי אֱלֹהִים כְּחַסְדֶּךָ	3 Show me grace, God, in Your loyalty;
	כְּרֹב רַחֲמֶיךָ מְחֵה פְשָׁעָי:	in Your great mercy, erase my offense;
הרבה	הֶרֶב כַּבְּסֵנִי מֵעֲוֹנִי	4 wash me well of my guilt;
	וּמֵחַטָּאתִי טַהֲרֵנִי:	purify me of my sin,
	כִּי־פְשָׁעַי אֲנִי אֵדָע	5 for I am aware of my transgression,
	וְחַטָּאתִי נֶגְדִּי תָמִיד:	and my sin is ever before me.
	לְךָ לְבַדְּךָ ׀ חָטָאתִי	6 I sinned against You alone;
	וְהָרַע בְּעֵינֶיךָ עָשִׂיתִי	I committed what is evil in Your eyes,
	לְמַעַן תִּצְדַּק בְּדָבְרֶךָ	so Your sentence is just,
	תִּזְכֶּה בְשָׁפְטֶךָ:	and Your judgment is fair.
	הֵן־בְּעָווֹן חוֹלָלְתִּי	7 Yes, with guilt I came to be;
	וּבְחֵטְא יֶחֱמַתְנִי אִמִּי:	in sin did my mother conceive me.
	הֵן־אֱמֶת חָפַצְתָּ בַטֻּחוֹת	8 Yes, You desire truth to course
	וּבְסָתֻם חָכְמָה תוֹדִיעֵנִי:	deep within me–
		to teach wisdom to my innermost self.
	תְּחַטְּאֵנִי בְאֵזוֹב וְאֶטְהָר	9 Purge me with hyssop,
	תְּכַבְּסֵנִי וּמִשֶּׁלֶג אַלְבִּין:	and I will be pure;
		wash me, and I will be whiter than snow.
	תַּשְׁמִיעֵנִי שָׂשׂוֹן וְשִׂמְחָה	10 Let me hear gladness and joy;
	תָּגֵלְנָה עֲצָמוֹת דִּכִּיתָ:	let the bones You have crushed rejoice.
	הַסְתֵּר פָּנֶיךָ מֵחֲטָאָי	11 Hide Your face from my sins;
	וְכָל־עֲוֹנֹתַי מְחֵה:	erase all my guilt.
	לֵב טָהוֹר בְּרָא־לִי אֱלֹהִים	12 Create a pure heart for me, God;
	וְרוּחַ נָכוֹן חַדֵּשׁ בְּקִרְבִּי:	renew a firm spirit within me.

אַל־תַּשְׁלִיכֵנִי מִלְּפָנֶיךָ
וְרוּחַ קָדְשְׁךָ אַל־תִּקַּח מִמֶּנִּי׃

13 Do not cast me away from Your presence
or take Your holy spirit away from me.

הָשִׁיבָה לִּי שְׂשׂוֹן יִשְׁעֶךָ
וְרוּחַ נְדִיבָה תִסְמְכֵנִי׃

14 Restore your glad salvation to me;
let a willing spirit sustain me.

אֲלַמְּדָה פֹשְׁעִים דְּרָכֶיךָ
וְחַטָּאִים אֵלֶיךָ יָשׁוּבוּ׃

15 I will teach offenders Your ways,
and sinners will come back to You.

הַצִּילֵנִי מִדָּמִים ׀ אֱלֹהִים
אֱלֹהֵי תְּשׁוּעָתִי
תְּרַנֵּן לְשׁוֹנִי צִדְקָתֶךָ׃

16 Save me from bloodshed, God,
God of my salvation;
my tongue will sing of Your justice.

אֲדֹנָי שְׂפָתַי תִּפְתָּח
וּפִי יַגִּיד תְּהִלָּתֶךָ׃

17 O Lord, open my lips,
and my mouth will declare Your praise.

כִּי ׀ לֹא־תַחְפֹּץ זֶבַח וְאֶתֵּנָה
עוֹלָה לֹא תִרְצֶה׃

18 You have no desire for me
to bring sacrifice;
You do not want burnt offerings.

זִבְחֵי אֱלֹהִים רוּחַ נִשְׁבָּרָה
לֵב־נִשְׁבָּר וְנִדְכֶּה
אֱלֹהִים לֹא תִבְזֶה׃

19 To God, a broken spirit is an offering;
a crushed and broken heart, God,
You will not spurn.

הֵיטִיבָה בִרְצוֹנְךָ אֶת־צִיּוֹן
תִּבְנֶה חוֹמוֹת יְרוּשָׁלָ͏ִם׃

20 Favor Zion with Your goodness;
rebuild the walls of Jerusalem.

אָז תַּחְפֹּץ זִבְחֵי־צֶדֶק
עוֹלָה וְכָלִיל
אָז יַעֲלוּ עַל־מִזְבַּחֲךָ פָרִים׃

21 Then You will delight in sincere sacrifices,
burnt offerings and whole offerings;
then bulls will be offered up on Your altar.

But I am like a flourishing olive tree in the House of God

I am stunned, shocked, disillusioned. I thought you were a pious man, an honest man, and a friend. I was vulnerable. You were in a position to help me. But you betrayed me. No punishment is sufficient for your murderous treachery.

PSALM 52

לַמְנַצֵּחַ מַשְׂכִּיל לְדָוִד׃ 1

To the lead singer – of David, a *maskil*,

בְּבוֹא ׀ דּוֹאֵג הָאֲדֹמִי 2
וַיַּגֵּד לְשָׁאוּל וַיֹּאמֶר לוֹ
בָּא דָוִד אֶל־בֵּית אֲחִימֶלֶךְ׃

when Doeg the Edomite came
and informed Sha'ul, telling him,
"David went to the house of Aḥimelekh."

מַה־תִּתְהַלֵּל בְּרָעָה הַגִּבּוֹר 3
חֶסֶד אֵל כָּל־הַיּוֹם׃

Why do you boast of evil, powerful one?
God's loyalty is everlasting.

הַוּוֹת תַּחְשֹׁב לְשׁוֹנֶךָ 4
כְּתַעַר מְלֻטָּשׁ עֹשֵׂה רְמִיָּה׃

Your tongue wreaks malice,
carving mischief like a sharpened razor;

אָהַבְתָּ רָּע מִטּוֹב 5
שֶׁקֶר ׀ מִדַּבֵּר צֶדֶק סֶלָה׃

you love evil more than good,
lying more than speaking truth – Selah.

אָהַבְתָּ כָל־דִּבְרֵי־בָלַע 6
לְשׁוֹן מִרְמָה׃

You love all words of carnage,
all treacherous speech,

גַּם־אֵל יִתָּצְךָ לָנֶצַח 7
יַחְתְּךָ וְיִסָּחֲךָ מֵאֹהֶל
וְשֵׁרֶשְׁךָ מֵאֶרֶץ חַיִּים סֶלָה׃

but God will tear you down
once and for all;
He will snatch you up
and uproot you from your home,
your roots from the land of the living –
Selah.

וְיִרְאוּ צַדִּיקִים וְיִירָאוּ 8
וְעָלָיו יִשְׂחָקוּ׃

Then the righteous will look on in awe,
and they will mock him:

הִנֵּה הַגֶּבֶר לֹא יָשִׂים 9
אֱלֹהִים מָעוּזּוֹ
וַיִּבְטַח בְּרֹב עָשְׁרוֹ
יָעֹז בְּהַוָּתוֹ׃

"Here is someone who would not make
God his refuge
but trusted in his great wealth
and grew powerful through malice."

וַאֲנִי ׀ כְּזַיִת רַעֲנָן בְּבֵית אֱלֹהִים 10
בָּטַחְתִּי בְחֶסֶד־אֱלֹהִים
עוֹלָם וָעֶד׃

But I am like a flourishing olive tree
in the House of God;
I will trust in God's loyalty
forever and for all time.

אֽוֹדְךָ לְעוֹלָם כִּי עָשִׂיתָ
וַאֲקַוֶּה שִׁמְךָ כִי־טוֹב
נֶגֶד חֲסִידֶיךָ:

11 I will praise You forever
for what You have done;
I will proclaim that Your name is good
in the presence of Your devoted ones.

Oh, that Israel's salvation might come from Zion; when God restores His people's fortune, Yaakov will rejoice; Israel will be glad

Once again, look what I'm up against.
My enemy is thoroughly evil; blasphemous, cynical, derisive.
I wish that my salvation would be as complete
as is the hostility I face. I wish I could be happy again.

PSALM 53

לַמְנַצֵּחַ עַל־מָחֲלַת
מַשְׂכִּיל לְדָוִד׃

אָמַר נָבָל בְּלִבּוֹ אֵין אֱלֹהִים
הִשְׁחִיתוּ וְהִתְעִיבוּ עָוֶל
אֵין עֹשֵׂה־טוֹב׃

אֱלֹהִים מִשָּׁמַיִם הִשְׁקִיף
עַל־בְּנֵי־אָדָם
לִרְאוֹת הֲיֵשׁ מַשְׂכִּיל
דֹּרֵשׁ אֶת־אֱלֹהִים׃

כֻּלּוֹ סָג יַחְדָּו נֶאֱלָחוּ
אֵין עֹשֵׂה־טוֹב אֵין גַּם־אֶחָד׃

הֲלֹא יָדְעוּ פֹּעֲלֵי אָוֶן
אֹכְלֵי עַמִּי אָכְלוּ לֶחֶם
אֱלֹהִים לֹא קָרָאוּ׃

שָׁם ׀ פָּחֲדוּ־פַחַד לֹא־הָיָה פָחַד
כִּי־אֱלֹהִים פִּזַּר עַצְמוֹת חֹנָךְ
הֱבִשֹׁתָה כִּי־אֱלֹהִים מְאָסָם׃

מִי יִתֵּן מִצִּיּוֹן יְשֻׁעוֹת יִשְׂרָאֵל
בְּשׁוּב אֱלֹהִים שְׁבוּת עַמּוֹ
יָגֵל יַעֲקֹב יִשְׂמַח יִשְׂרָאֵל׃

1 To the lead singer, on *maḥalat* –
of David, a *maskil*

2 The brute says in his heart,
"There is no God."
They are corrupt;
they wreak vile schemes;
there is no one who does good.

3 God looks down from heaven
at humanity
to see if someone has the sense
to seek out God,

4 but all are treacherous,
altogether tainted;
there is no one who does good,
not even one.

5 Have they no knowledge, those evildoers
who devour my people
as if devouring bread,
who do not call out to God?

6 There they were struck with terror,
such terror as never before,
for God scattered the bones
of your attackers;
You have put them to shame,
for God has rejected them.

7 Oh, that Israel's salvation
might come from Zion;
when God restores His people's fortune,
Yaakov will rejoice;
Israel will be glad.

To You I will offer a freewill sacrifice; I will praise Your name, LORD, for it is good

They are strangers, coming out of nowhere.
Yet they betray me, joining my enemies.
Whom can I trust? I can only trust the Almighty.

PSALM 54

לַמְנַצֵּחַ בִּנְגִינֹת
מַשְׂכִּיל לְדָוִד:

1 To the lead singer,
accompanied by music –
of David, a *maskil*,

בְּבוֹא הַזִּיפִים וַיֹּאמְרוּ לְשָׁאוּל
הֲלֹא דָוִד מִסְתַּתֵּר עִמָּנוּ:

2 when the Zifites came and told Sha'ul,
"David is hiding among us"

אֱלֹהִים בְּשִׁמְךָ הוֹשִׁיעֵנִי
וּבִגְבוּרָתְךָ תְדִינֵנִי:

3 God, save me by Your name;
with Your might, vindicate me.

אֱלֹהִים שְׁמַע תְּפִלָּתִי
הַאֲזִינָה לְאִמְרֵי־פִי:

4 God, hear my prayer;
give ear to the words I mouth,

כִּי זָרִים ׀ קָמוּ עָלַי
וְעָרִיצִים בִּקְשׁוּ נַפְשִׁי
לֹא שָׂמוּ אֱלֹהִים לְנֶגְדָּם
סֶלָה:

5 for strangers have risen up against me;
cruel men seek my life,
men who have no regard for God –
Selah.

הִנֵּה אֱלֹהִים עֹזֵר לִי
אֲדֹנָי בְּסֹמְכֵי נַפְשִׁי:

6 Look – God is my helper;
the Lord is the one who sustains my life.

יָשִׁיב הָרַע לְשֹׁרְרָי
בַּאֲמִתְּךָ הַצְמִיתֵם:

ישוב

7 He will repay my oppressors for their evil.
By Your truth, destroy them.

בִּנְדָבָה אֶזְבְּחָה־לָּךְ
אוֹדֶה שִּׁמְךָ יְהוָה כִּי־טוֹב:

8 To You I will offer a freewill sacrifice;
I will praise Your name, LORD,
for it is good,

כִּי מִכָּל־צָרָה הִצִּילָנִי
וּבְאֹיְבַי רָאֲתָה עֵינִי:

9 for He has saved me from all danger;
my eyes have seen my enemies' downfall.

And I cried, "If only I had wings like a dove, I would fly away and find rest

You taught me all I know. You were my confidant.
We dreamed dreams together. We were so close.
I cannot believe that you betrayed me, slyly and viciously.
I will fight back, and I will win.

PSALM 55

לַמְנַצֵּחַ בִּנְגִינֹת
מַשְׂכִּיל לְדָוִד׃

1 To the lead singer,
accompanied by music –
of David, a *maskil*

הַאֲזִינָה אֱלֹהִים תְּפִלָּתִי
וְאַל־תִּתְעַלַּם מִתְּחִנָּתִי׃

2 Give ear, God, to my prayer;
do not ignore my plea;

הַקְשִׁיבָה לִּי וַעֲנֵנִי
אָרִיד בְּשִׂיחִי וְאָהִימָה׃

3 hear me and answer me.
Restless, I wail and cry out –

מִקּוֹל אוֹיֵב מִפְּנֵי עָקַת רָשָׁע
כִּי־יָמִיטוּ עָלַי אָוֶן
וּבְאַף יִשְׂטְמוּנִי׃

4 at the clamor of the enemy,
at the cruelty of the wicked,
for they bring evil crashing down on me;
they pounce on me with fury.

לִבִּי יָחִיל בְּקִרְבִּי
וְאֵימוֹת מָוֶת נָפְלוּ עָלָי׃

5 My heart trembles within me;
I am gripped with death-terror;

יִרְאָה וָרַעַד יָבֹא בִי
וַתְּכַסֵּנִי פַּלָּצוּת׃

6 fear and shaking seize me;
I am stifled with horror.

וָאֹמַר
מִי־יִתֶּן־לִי אֵבֶר כַּיּוֹנָה
אָעוּפָה וְאֶשְׁכֹּנָה׃

7 And I cried,
"If only I had wings like a dove,
I would fly away and find rest;

הִנֵּה אַרְחִיק נְדֹד
אָלִין בַּמִּדְבָּר סֶלָה׃

8 oh, I would roam far away
and alight in the wilderness – Selah.

אָחִישָׁה מִפְלָט לִי
מֵרוּחַ סֹעָה מִסָּעַר׃

9 I would soon find shelter
from the raging wind and storm."

בַּלַּע אֲדֹנָי פַּלַּג לְשׁוֹנָם
כִּי־רָאִיתִי חָמָס וְרִיב בָּעִיר׃

10 Thwart them, Lord;
confound their speech,
for I see violence and strife in the city.

יוֹמָם וָלַיְלָה
יְסוֹבְבֻהָ עַל־חוֹמֹתֶיהָ
וְאָוֶן וְעָמָל בְּקִרְבָּהּ׃

11 Day and night they patrol its walls;
evil and suffering are in its midst.

הַוּוֹת בְּקִרְבָּהּ	12 In its midst is corruption;
וְלֹא־יָמִישׁ מֵרְחֹבָהּ	treachery and deceit never cease
תֹּךְ וּמִרְמָה:	to haunt its square,

כִּי לֹא־אוֹיֵב יְחָרְפֵנִי וְאֶשָּׂא	13 but it is not an enemy who taunts me –
לֹא־מְשַׂנְאִי עָלַי הִגְדִּיל	that I could bear –
וְאֶסָּתֵר מִמֶּנּוּ:	it is not a foe who looms over me,
	for then I could hide.

וְאַתָּה אֱנוֹשׁ כְּעֶרְכִּי	14 It is you, a person like me –
אַלּוּפִי וּמְיֻדָּעִי:	my companion, my friend.

אֲשֶׁר יַחְדָּו נַמְתִּיק סוֹד	15 We shared sweet closeness
בְּבֵית אֱלֹהִים נְהַלֵּךְ בְּרָגֶשׁ:	as we walked among the crowd
	at the House of God.

ישימות

יַשִּׁיא מָוֶת ׀ עָלֵימוֹ	16 May He set death upon them;
יֵרְדוּ שְׁאוֹל חַיִּים	may they go down to Sheol alive,
כִּי־רָעוֹת בִּמְגוּרָם בְּקִרְבָּם:	for evil has permeated their minds,
	their very being.

אֲנִי אֶל־אֱלֹהִים אֶקְרָא	17 I will call out to God;
וַיהוָה יוֹשִׁיעֵנִי:	the LORD will save me.

עֶרֶב וָבֹקֶר וְצָהֳרַיִם	18 Evening, morning, noon
אָשִׂיחָה וְאֶהֱמֶה	I wail and cry out,
וַיִּשְׁמַע קוֹלִי:	and He hears my voice.

פָּדָה בְשָׁלוֹם נַפְשִׁי מִקְּרָב־לִי	19 He redeems me unharmed
כִּי־בְרַבִּים הָיוּ עִמָּדִי:	from the battle I wage
	as if many are on my side.

יִשְׁמַע ׀ אֵל ׀ וְיַעֲנֵם	20 God, enthroned as of old,
וְיֹשֵׁב קֶדֶם סֶלָה	will hear and humble them – Selah –
אֲשֶׁר אֵין חֲלִיפוֹת לָמוֹ	for they will never change;
וְלֹא יָרְאוּ אֱלֹהִים:	they will never fear God.

שָׁלַח יָדָיו בִּשְׁלֹמָיו	21 That man lashed out at his own allies;
חִלֵּל בְּרִיתוֹ:	he violated his pact.

חָלְקוּ ׀ מַחֲמָאֹת פִּיו וְקָרָב־לִבּוֹ
רַכּוּ דְבָרָיו מִשֶּׁמֶן
וְהֵמָּה פְתִחוֹת:

22 His speech was smooth as butter,
but war was in his heart;
his words seemed soft as oil,
but they were drawn swords.

הַשְׁלֵךְ עַל־יְהוָה ׀ יְהָבְךָ
וְהוּא יְכַלְכְּלֶךָ
לֹא־יִתֵּן לְעוֹלָם מוֹט לַצַּדִּיק:

23 Cast your burden upon the Lord,
and He will sustain you;
He will never let the righteous be shaken,

וְאַתָּה אֱלֹהִים ׀
תּוֹרִדֵם לִבְאֵר שַׁחַת
אַנְשֵׁי דָמִים וּמִרְמָה
לֹא־יֶחֱצוּ יְמֵיהֶם
וַאֲנִי אֶבְטַח־בָּךְ:

24 but You, God,
will plunge them down the deepest pit –
men of blood, deceitful men
will not live out half their days,
while I will trust in You.

That I may walk before God in the light of life

This time things are really bad. There is no exit.
I am scared to death. But God feels near. I can pray to Him.
I can even thank Him. Things will work out.

PSALM 56

לַמְנַצֵּחַ ׀ עַל־יֹ֥ונַת אֵ֣לֶם רְחֹקִים֮
לְדָוִ֪ד מִ֫כְתָּ֥ם
בֶּאֱחֹ֨ז אוֹת֖וֹ פְלִשְׁתִּ֣ים בְּגַֽת׃

1 To the lead singer,
on *yonat elem reḥokim* –
a *mikhtam* of David,
when the Philistines seized him in Gat

חָנֵּ֣נִי אֱ֭לֹהִים כִּֽי־שְׁאָפַ֣נִי אֱנ֑וֹשׁ
כָּל־הַ֝יּ֗וֹם לֹחֵ֥ם יִלְחָצֵֽנִי׃

2 Show me grace, God,
for mortals hound me;
all day long my foes oppress me;

שָׁאֲפ֣וּ שׁ֭וֹרְרַי כָּל־הַיּ֑וֹם
כִּֽי־רַבִּ֨ים לֹחֲמִ֖ים לִ֣י מָרֽוֹם׃

3 all day long my oppressors trample me;
so many attack me, Exalted One!

י֥וֹם אִירָ֑א
אֲ֝נִ֗י אֵלֶ֥יךָ אֶבְטָֽח׃

4 When I fear,
I trust in You –

בֵּֽאלֹהִים֮ אֲהַלֵּ֪ל דְּבָ֫ר֥וֹ
בֵּאלֹהִ֣ים בָּ֭טַחְתִּי לֹ֣א אִירָ֑א
מַה־יַּעֲשֶׂ֖ה בָשָׂ֣ר לִֽי׃

5 in God, whose word I praise,
in God I trust; I do not fear –
what can mere flesh do to me?

כָּל־הַ֭יּוֹם דְּבָרַ֣י יְעַצֵּ֑בוּ
עָלַ֖י כָּל־מַחְשְׁבֹתָ֣ם לָרָֽע׃

6 All day long they move me to grief;
all their plans against me are evil;

יָג֤וּרוּ ׀ יִצְפֹּ֗נוּ הֵ֭מָּה
עֲקֵבַ֣י יִשְׁמֹ֑רוּ
כַּאֲשֶׁ֖ר קִוּ֣וּ נַפְשִֽׁי׃

יצפינו

7 they lie in wait,
tracing my footsteps,
eager to take my life.

עַל־אָ֥וֶן פַּלֶּט־לָ֑מוֹ
בְּאַ֓ף עַמִּ֨ים ׀ הוֹרֵ֬ד אֱלֹהִֽים׃

8 Uproot them for their evil;
cast down such people in Your wrath,
God!

נֹדִ֨י סָפַ֪רְתָּה אָ֥תָּה
שִׂ֣ימָה דִמְעָתִ֣י בְנֹאדֶ֑ךָ
הֲ֝לֹ֗א בְּסִפְרָתֶֽךָ׃

9 You count my wanderings;
You store my tears in Your vial;
are they not in Your records?

אָ֤ז יָ֘שׁ֤וּבוּ אוֹיְבַ֣י אָ֭חוֹר
בְּי֣וֹם אֶקְרָ֑א
זֶה־יָ֝דַ֗עְתִּי כִּֽי־אֱלֹהִ֥ים לִֽי׃

10 Then, on the day that I call,
my enemies will retreat;
this I know, for God is with me.

בֵּאלֹהִים אֲהַלֵּל דָּבָר
בַּיהֹוָה אֲהַלֵּל דָּבָר:

11 In God, whose word I praise,
in the Lᴏʀᴅ, whose word I praise,

בֵּאלֹהִים בָּטַחְתִּי לֹא אִירָא
מַה־יַּעֲשֶׂה אָדָם לִי:

12 in God I trust; I do not fear –
what can man do to me?

עָלַי אֱלֹהִים נְדָרֶיךָ
אֲשַׁלֵּם תּוֹדֹת לָךְ:

13 I must fulfill my vows to You, God;
I will give thank offerings to You,

כִּי הִצַּלְתָּ נַפְשִׁי מִמָּוֶת
הֲלֹא רַגְלַי מִדֶּחִי
לְהִתְהַלֵּךְ לִפְנֵי אֱלֹהִים
בְּאוֹר הַחַיִּים:

14 for You have saved me from death,
my feet from stumbling,
that I may walk before God
in the light of life.

Stir, my soul! Stir, harp and lyre!

I am trapped in a cave.
I am surrounded by lions, spears, arrows, and swords.
I don't know why, but I am confident that I will escape to safety.
Bring me my harp now!
Strange as it may seem, I am ready to sing.

PSALM 57

לַמְנַצֵּחַ אַל־תַּשְׁחֵת
לְדָוִד מִכְתָּם
בְּבָרְחוֹ מִפְּנֵי־שָׁאוּל בַּמְּעָרָה:

1 To the lead singer, *al tashḥet* –
a *mikhtam* of David
in the cave, when he was fleeing
from Sha'ul

חָנֵּנִי אֱלֹהִים ׀ חָנֵּנִי
כִּי בְךָ חָסָיָה נַפְשִׁי
וּבְצֵל־כְּנָפֶיךָ אֶחְסֶה
עַד יַעֲבֹר הַוּוֹת:

2 Show me grace, God; show me grace,
for in You I take refuge.
I will take refuge
in the shade of Your wings
until disaster has passed.

אֶקְרָא לֵאלֹהִים עֶלְיוֹן
לָאֵל גֹּמֵר עָלָי:

3 I will call on God, the Most High,
to the God who grants me fulfillment.

יִשְׁלַח מִשָּׁמַיִם ׀ וְיוֹשִׁיעֵנִי
חֵרֵף שֹׁאֲפִי סֶלָה
יִשְׁלַח אֱלֹהִים חַסְדּוֹ וַאֲמִתּוֹ:

4 He will send from heaven and save me;
He will bring those who crush me to
shame – Selah.
God will send His loyalty and truth.

נַפְשִׁי ׀ בְּתוֹךְ לְבָאִם
אֶשְׁכְּבָה לֹהֲטִים
בְּנֵי־אָדָם שִׁנֵּיהֶם חֲנִית וְחִצִּים
וּלְשׁוֹנָם חֶרֶב חַדָּה:

5 I am bounded by lions,
forced to dwell among ravenous beasts,
men whose teeth are spears and arrows,
their tongues sharpened swords.

רוּמָה עַל־הַשָּׁמַיִם אֱלֹהִים
עַל כָּל־הָאָרֶץ כְּבוֹדֶךָ:

6 Rise up, God, over the heavens;
unleash Your glory over all the earth.

רֶשֶׁת ׀ הֵכִינוּ לִפְעָמַי כָּפַף נַפְשִׁי
כָּרוּ לְפָנַי שִׁיחָה
נָפְלוּ בְתוֹכָהּ סֶלָה:

7 They rigged a net to trip me up,
to entrap me;
they dug a pit in my path
but fell into it themselves – Selah.

נָכוֹן לִבִּי אֱלֹהִים נָכוֹן לִבִּי
אָשִׁירָה וַאֲזַמֵּרָה:

8 My heart is sound, God;
my heart is sound –
I will sing and chant praises.

עוּרָה כְבוֹדִי עוּרָה הַנֵּבֶל וְכִנּוֹר
אָעִירָה שָּׁחַר:

9 Stir, my soul! Stir, harp and lyre!
I will stir the dawn.

אוֹדְךָ בָעַמִּים ׀ אֲדֹנָי
אֲזַמֶּרְךָ בַּלְאֻמִּים:

10 I will praise You
among the peoples, LORD;
I will chant Your praise
among the nations,

כִּי־גָדֹל עַד־שָׁמַיִם חַסְדֶּךָ
וְעַד־שְׁחָקִים אֲמִתֶּךָ:

11 for Your loyalty is as high as the heavens;
Your truth reaches the skies.

רוּמָה עַל־שָׁמַיִם אֱלֹהִים
עַל כָּל־הָאָרֶץ כְּבוֹדֶךָ:

12 Rise up, God, over the heavens;
unleash Your glory over all the earth.

People will say, "The righteous do harvest fruit; there is, after all,
divine justice on earth."

They know that I am right. They see the injustice which has been
perpetrated against me. Yet they remain silent.
Are they malicious? Are they corrupt? Are they cowardly?
Do I not matter to them? I know. They are indifferent.
That's the worst sin of all.

PSALM 58

לַמְנַצֵּחַ אַל־תַּשְׁחֵת
לְדָוִד מִכְתָּם: 1

To the lead singer, *al tashḥet* –
a *mikhtam* of David

הַאֻמְנָם אֵלֶם צֶדֶק תְּדַבֵּרוּן
מֵישָׁרִים תִּשְׁפְּטוּ בְּנֵי אָדָם: 2

Do you truly decree justice,
powerful ones?
Do you judge people with equity?

אַף־בְּלֵב עוֹלֹת תִּפְעָלוּן
בָּאָרֶץ חֲמַס יְדֵיכֶם תְּפַלֵּסוּן: 3

No, your hearts churn out injustice;
your hands mete out violence in the land.

זֹרוּ רְשָׁעִים מֵרָחֶם
תָּעוּ מִבֶּטֶן דֹּבְרֵי כָזָב: 4

The wicked have been wayward
since birth –
those liars, astray from the womb.

חֲמַת־לָמוֹ כִּדְמוּת חֲמַת־נָחָשׁ
כְּמוֹ־פֶתֶן חֵרֵשׁ יַאְטֵם אָזְנוֹ: 5

Their venom is like snake venom;
they are as deaf as the cobra
that stops its ears

אֲשֶׁר לֹא־יִשְׁמַע
לְקוֹל מְלַחֲשִׁים
חוֹבֵר חֲבָרִים מְחֻכָּם: 6

to tune out the whispers of the charmer,
the most skilled of enchanters.

אֱלֹהִים הֲרָס־שִׁנֵּימוֹ בְּפִימוֹ
מַלְתְּעוֹת כְּפִירִים נְתֹץ ׀
יהוה: 7

God, crush the teeth in their mouths;
smash the fangs of these young lions;
Lord,

יִמָּאֲסוּ כְמוֹ־מַיִם
יִתְהַלְּכוּ־לָמוֹ
יִדְרֹךְ חִצּוֹ כְּמוֹ יִתְמֹלָלוּ: 8

may they melt away like water
and vanish;
when they aim their arrows,
let them crumble

כְּמוֹ שַׁבְּלוּל תֶּמֶס יַהֲלֹךְ
נֵפֶל אֵשֶׁת בַּל־חָזוּ שָׁמֶשׁ: 9

like a snail dissolving as it moves,
like a stillborn that never sees the sun.

בְּטֶרֶם יָבִינוּ סִּירֹתֵיכֶם אָטָד
כְּמוֹ־חַי כְּמוֹ־חָרוֹן יִשְׂעָרֶנּוּ: 10

Before your thorns harden to bramble,
He will whirl them away in wild fury.

11 The righteous will rejoice
at the sight of vengeance
and rinse their feet
in the blood of the wicked.

יִשְׂמַח צַדִּיק כִּי־חָזָה נָקָם
פְּעָמָיו יִרְחַץ בְּדַם הָרָשָׁע׃

12 People will say,
"The righteous do harvest fruit;
there is, after all, divine justice on earth."

וְיֹאמַר אָדָם
אַךְ־פְּרִי לַצַּדִּיק
אַךְ יֵשׁ־אֱלֹהִים שֹׁפְטִים
בָּאָרֶץ׃

But I will sing of Your might; each morning I will laud Your loving-kindness

I don't want my enemies punished. Rather, may they reform themselves. I don't want them to disappear. Rather, may they change their ways. I certainly don't want to see them perish. Rather, have them learn the lessons of their misdeeds. Then I'll sing a song, But I won't sing it alone. They'll all join me.

PSALM 59

לַמְנַצֵּחַ אַל־תַּשְׁחֵת
לְדָוִד מִכְתָּם
בִּשְׁלֹחַ שָׁאוּל וַיִּשְׁמְרוּ אֶת־
הַבַּיִת לַהֲמִיתוֹ:

1 To the lead singer, *al tashḥet* –
a *mikhtam* of David
when Shaʾul sent guards to David's
house to kill him

הַצִּילֵנִי מֵאֹיְבַי ׀ אֱלֹהָי
מִמִּתְקוֹמְמַי תְּשַׂגְּבֵנִי:

2 Save me from my enemies, God;
protect me from those
who rise against me.

הַצִּילֵנִי מִפֹּעֲלֵי אָוֶן
וּמֵאַנְשֵׁי דָמִים הוֹשִׁיעֵנִי:

3 Save me from evildoers;
deliver me from men of blood,

כִּי הִנֵּה אָרְבוּ לְנַפְשִׁי
יָגוּרוּ עָלַי עַזִּים
לֹא־פִשְׁעִי וְלֹא־חַטָּאתִי יְהוָה:

4 for look – they lurk in ambush –
fierce men lie in wait for me
for no crime or offense of mine, LORD;

בְּלִי־עָו‍ֹן יְרֻצוּן וְיִכּוֹנָנוּ
עוּרָה לִקְרָאתִי וּרְאֵה:

5 for no fault of mine
they rush at me, ready to attack.
Look – rouse Yourself for my sake.

וְאַתָּה יְהוָה־אֱלֹהִים ׀
צְבָאוֹת אֱלֹהֵי יִשְׂרָאֵל
הָקִיצָה לִפְקֹד כָּל־הַגּוֹיִם
אַל־תָּחֹן כָּל־בֹּגְדֵי אָוֶן סֶלָה:

6 You, LORD God of hosts,
are the God of Israel;
stir and call all the nations to account;
show no mercy to evil traitors – Selah.

יָשׁוּבוּ לָעֶרֶב יֶהֱמוּ כַכָּלֶב
וִיסוֹבְבוּ עִיר:

7 They come out at nightfall,
growling like dogs,
prowling about the city.

הִנֵּה ׀ יַבִּיעוּן בְּפִיהֶם
חֲרָבוֹת בְּשִׂפְתוֹתֵיהֶם
כִּי־מִי שֹׁמֵעַ:

8 See how they rant, their lips like swords,
thinking, "Who can hear us?"

וְאַתָּה יְהוָה תִּשְׂחַק־לָמוֹ
תִּלְעַג לְכָל־גּוֹיִם:

9 But You, LORD, mock them;
You hold all the nations in contempt.

עֻזּוֹ אֵלֶיךָ אֶשְׁמֹרָה
כִּי־אֱלֹהִים מִשְׂגַּבִּי:

10 O Mighty One, I watch for You,
for God is my stronghold.

חסדו

אֱלֹהֵי חַסְדִּי יְקַדְּמֵנִי
אֱלֹהִים יַרְאֵנִי בְשֹׁרְרָי:

11 My loyal God will go out before me;
God will show me my enemies' downfall.

אַל־תַּהַרְגֵם ׀ פֶּן־יִשְׁכְּחוּ עַמִּי
הֲנִיעֵמוֹ בְחֵילְךָ וְהוֹרִידֵמוֹ
מָגִנֵּנוּ אֲדֹנָי:

12 Do not kill them
lest my people forget,
but send them staggering by Your force;
bring them down, LORD, our shield.

חַטַּאת־פִּימוֹ דְּבַר־שְׂפָתֵימוֹ
וְיִלָּכְדוּ בִגְאוֹנָם
וּמֵאָלָה וּמִכַּחַשׁ יְסַפֵּרוּ:

13 For the sins of their mouths,
for the words of their lips,
let them be trapped by their own
arrogance,
by the curses and lies they utter.

כַּלֵּה בְחֵמָה כַּלֵּה וְאֵינֵמוֹ
וְיֵדְעוּ כִּי־אֱלֹהִים מֹשֵׁל בְּיַעֲקֹב
לְאַפְסֵי הָאָרֶץ סֶלָה:

14 Destroy them in Your fury;
destroy them until they are no more.
Then it will be known
to the ends of the earth
that God rules over Yaakov – Selah.

וְיָשֻׁבוּ לָעֶרֶב יֶהֱמוּ כַכָּלֶב
וִיסוֹבְבוּ עִיר:

15 They come out at nightfall,
growling like dogs,
prowling about the city.

ינועון

הֵמָּה יְנִיעוּן לֶאֱכֹל
אִם־לֹא יִשְׂבְּעוּ וַיָּלִינוּ:

16 They stagger about, scavenging,
whining when they are discontent,

וַאֲנִי ׀ אָשִׁיר עֻזֶּךָ
וַאֲרַנֵּן לַבֹּקֶר חַסְדֶּךָ
כִּי־הָיִיתָ מִשְׂגָּב לִי
וּמָנוֹס בְּיוֹם צַר־לִי:

17 but I will sing of Your might;
each morning I will laud
Your loving-kindness,
for You have been my stronghold,
my haven in times of trouble.

עֻזִּי אֵלֶיךָ אֲזַמֵּרָה
כִּי־אֱלֹהִים מִשְׂגַּבִּי
אֱלֹהֵי חַסְדִּי:

18 My Mighty One,
to You I will chant praise,
for God is my stronghold,
the God who shows me loyalty.

With God, we will triumph valiantly, and He will trample our enemies

Life is never perfect. Even when we win, we lose.
In war there are casualties. Successful surgery leaves scars.
Effective medicines have side effects.
We praise God for helping us achieve victory.
Yet we think He has abandoned us.

PSALM 60

לַמְנַצֵּחַ עַל־שׁוּשַׁן עֵדוּת
מִכְתָּם לְדָוִד לְלַמֵּד:

1 To the lead singer, on *shushan edut*,
a *mikhtam* of David, for instruction,

בְּהַצּוֹתוֹ ׀ אֶת אֲרַם נַהֲרַיִם
וְאֶת־אֲרַם צוֹבָה
וַיָּשָׁב יוֹאָב וַיַּךְ אֶת־אֱדוֹם
בְּגֵיא־מֶלַח
שְׁנֵים עָשָׂר אָלֶף:

2 when he fought against Aram Naharaim
and Aram Tzova,
while Yoav returned and defeated
twelve thousand men of Edom
in the Valley of Salt.

אֱלֹהִים זְנַחְתָּנוּ פְרַצְתָּנוּ
אָנַפְתָּ תְּשׁוֹבֵב לָנוּ:

3 God, You have forsaken us, shattered us,
shown Your anger.
Now restore us!

הִרְעַשְׁתָּה אֶרֶץ פְּצַמְתָּהּ
רְפָה שְׁבָרֶיהָ כִי־מָטָה:

4 You have made the land shudder
and split it open;
mend its cracks, for it is falling apart.

הִרְאִיתָ עַמְּךָ קָשָׁה
הִשְׁקִיתָנוּ יַיִן תַּרְעֵלָה:

5 You have made Your people suffer;
You have poured us poisoned wine,

נָתַתָּה לִּירֵאֶיךָ נֵּס לְהִתְנוֹסֵס
מִפְּנֵי קֹשֶׁט סֶלָה:

6 but You have given those who revere You
a waving banner beyond bowshot –
Selah.

לְמַעַן יֵחָלְצוּן יְדִידֶיךָ
הוֹשִׁיעָה יְמִינְךָ וַעֲנֵנִי:

7 That Your dear ones may be rescued,
let Your right hand bring victory –
answer me!

אֱלֹהִים ׀ דִּבֶּר בְּקָדְשׁוֹ אֶעְלֹזָה
אֲחַלְּקָה שְׁכֶם
וְעֵמֶק סֻכּוֹת אֲמַדֵּד:

8 God promised in His sanctuary
that I would triumph.
I will divide up Shekhem
and measure out the Valley of Sukot;

לִי גִלְעָד ׀ וְלִי מְנַשֶּׁה וְאֶפְרַיִם
מָעוֹז רֹאשִׁי
יְהוּדָה מְחֹקְקִי:

9 Gilad and Menashe will be mine;
Efrayim will be my chief stronghold,
Yehuda my scepter.

מוֹאָב ׀ סִיר רַחְצִי
עַל־אֱדוֹם אַשְׁלִיךְ נַעֲלִי
עָלַי פְּלֶשֶׁת הִתְרֹעָעִי:

10 Moav will be my washbasin;
at Edom I will fling my shoe;
Philistia, applaud me!

מִי יֹבִלֵנִי עִיר מָצֹור
מִי נָחַנִי עַד־אֱדֹום:

11 But who will bring me
to the besieged cities?
Who will lead me to Edom?

הֲלֹא־אַתָּה אֱלֹהִים זְנַחְתָּנוּ
וְלֹא־תֵצֵא אֱלֹהִים בְּצִבְאֹותֵינוּ:

12 Have You not forsaken us, God?
God, You no longer march out
with our forces.

הָבָה־לָּנוּ עֶזְרָת מִצָּר
וְשָׁוְא תְּשׁוּעַת אָדָם:

13 Come to our aid against the enemy,
for human help is worthless.

בֵּאלֹהִים נַעֲשֶׂה־חָיִל
וְהוּא יָבוּס צָרֵינוּ:

14 With God, we will triumph valiantly,
and He will trample our enemies.

Add days to the days of the king; may he live on for many generations!

I am here today. I do not want to be gone tomorrow.
You can say that I am selfish. I want both worlds.
I want my words heard, here and now.
I want my lips to murmur forever, even in the grave.

PSALM 61

לַמְנַצֵּחַ ׀ עַל־נְגִינַת לְדָוִד׃	1	To the lead singer, accompanied by music – of David
שִׁמְעָה אֱלֹהִים רִנָּתִי הַקְשִׁיבָה תְּפִלָּתִי׃	2	Hear my plea, God; listen to my prayer.
מִקְצֵה הָאָרֶץ ׀ אֵלֶיךָ אֶקְרָא בַּעֲטֹף לִבִּי בְּצוּר־יָרוּם מִמֶּנִּי תַנְחֵנִי׃	3	From the end of the earth I call to You when my heart is faint; lead me up to a rock far above me,
כִּי־הָיִיתָ מַחְסֶה לִי מִגְדַּל־עֹז מִפְּנֵי אוֹיֵב׃	4	for You have been my refuge, a tower of strength against the enemy.
אָגוּרָה בְאָהׇלְךָ עוֹלָמִים אֶחֱסֶה בְסֵתֶר כְּנָפֶיךָ סֶּלָה׃	5	Let me dwell in Your tent forever and take refuge in the shelter of Your wings – Selah –
כִּי־אַתָּה אֱלֹהִים שָׁמַעְתָּ לִנְדָרָי נָתַתָּ יְרֻשַּׁת יִרְאֵי שְׁמֶךָ׃	6	for You, God, hear my vows. Grant me the legacy of those who revere Your name.
יָמִים עַל־יְמֵי־מֶלֶךְ תּוֹסִיף שְׁנוֹתָיו כְּמוֹ־דֹר וָדֹר׃	7	Add days to the days of the king; may he live on for many generations!
יֵשֵׁב עוֹלָם לִפְנֵי אֱלֹהִים חֶסֶד וֶאֱמֶת מַן יִנְצְרֻהוּ׃	8	May he ever be seated in God's presence; appoint loyalty and truth to keep him,
כֵּן אֲזַמְּרָה שִׁמְךָ לָעַד לְשַׁלְּמִי נְדָרַי ׀ יוֹם ׀ יוֹם׃	9	so I will ever sing praises to Your name, fulfilling my vows day after day.

Trust in Him at all times, O people; pour out your hearts before Him;
God is our refuge – Selah

We all want security. Some find it in status and power.
Others find it in wealth. Those things don't last. I trust God.
I have learned to wait for Him with great patience.
He has never let me down.

PSALM 62

לַמְנַצֵּחַ עַל־יְדוּתוּן 1
מִזְמוֹר לְדָוִד:

To the lead singer, for *Yedutun* –
a psalm of David

אַךְ אֶל־אֱלֹהִים דּוּמִיָּה נַפְשִׁי 2
מִמֶּנּוּ יְשׁוּעָתִי:

For God alone my soul waits silently;
from Him is my salvation.

אַךְ־הוּא צוּרִי וִישׁוּעָתִי 3
מִשְׂגַּבִּי לֹא־אֶמּוֹט רַבָּה:

He alone is my rock and salvation,
my stronghold – I will never be shaken.

עַד־אָנָה ׀ תְּהוֹתְתוּ עַל־אִישׁ 4
תְּרָצְּחוּ כֻלְּכֶם
כְּקִיר נָטוּי גָּדֵר הַדְּחוּיָה:

How long will you come crashing down
on people,
all you murderous men,
like a crooked wall, a tottering fence?

אַךְ מִשְּׂאֵתוֹ ׀ יָעֲצוּ לְהַדִּיחַ 5
יִרְצוּ כָזָב
בְּפִיו יְבָרֵכוּ
וּבְקִרְבָּם יְקַלְלוּ־סֶלָה:

Scheming to topple the people
from their height,
they relish lies;
their mouths bless
while their insides curse – Selah.

אַךְ לֵאלֹהִים דּוֹמִּי נַפְשִׁי 6
כִּי־מִמֶּנּוּ תִּקְוָתִי:

Wait for God in silence, my soul,
for my hope is from Him.

אַךְ־הוּא צוּרִי וִישׁוּעָתִי 7
מִשְׂגַּבִּי לֹא אֶמּוֹט:

He alone is my rock and salvation,
my stronghold – I will not be shaken.

עַל־אֱלֹהִים יִשְׁעִי וּכְבוֹדִי 8
צוּר־עֻזִּי מַחְסִי בֵּאלֹהִים:

My deliverance and honor rest on God,
the rock of my strength;
in God is my refuge.

בִּטְחוּ בוֹ בְכָל־עֵת ׀ עָם 9
שִׁפְכוּ־לְפָנָיו לְבַבְכֶם
אֱלֹהִים מַחֲסֶה־לָּנוּ סֶלָה:

Trust in Him at all times, O people;
pour out your hearts before Him;
God is our refuge – Selah.

אַךְ ׀ הֶבֶל בְּנֵי־אָדָם 10
כָּזָב בְּנֵי אִישׁ
בְּמֹאזְנַיִם לַעֲלוֹת
הֵמָּה מֵהֶבֶל יָחַד:

But people are mere breath;
humans are but an illusion;
placed on a scale all together,
they are lighter than a breath.

אַל־תִּבְטְח֬וּ בְעֹ֨שֶׁק 11 Place not trust in extortion
וּבְגָזֵ֗ל אַל־תֶּ֫הְבָּ֥לוּ or false hopes in robbery;
חַ֤יִל ׀ כִּֽי־יָנ֑וּב אַל־תָּשִׁ֥יתוּ לֵֽב׃ should force pay off, give it no heed.

אַחַ֤ת ׀ דִּבֶּ֬ר אֱלֹהִ֗ים 12 God made one pronouncement,
שְׁתַּֽיִם־ז֥וּ שָׁמָ֑עְתִּי I heard these two:
כִּ֥י עֹ֝֗ז לֵֽאלֹהִֽים׃ That power belongs to God;

וּלְךָֽ־אֲדֹנָ֥י חָ֑סֶד 13 and that loyalty, Lord, is Yours,
כִּֽי־אַתָּ֓ה תְשַׁלֵּ֖ם לְאִ֣ישׁ for You will reward each person
כְּֽמַעֲשֵֽׂהוּ׃ according to his deeds.

So I have visions of You in the Sanctuary of Your might and glory

Sometimes I feel that God is with me,
at my side. I feel such a glow, such warmth, so connected.
It doesn't last long. When it is over I feel dry and empty.
He left me. Suddenly, the feeling returns. He is back.
He decides when to be near me and when to be far away.
I wish He would let me decide.

PSALM 63

מִזְמוֹר לְדָוִד בִּהְיוֹתוֹ
בְּמִדְבַּר יְהוּדָה:

1 A psalm of David, when he was in the
Wilderness of Yehuda

אֱלֹהִים ׀ אֵלִי אַתָּה אֲשַׁחֲרֶךָּ
צָמְאָה לְךָ ׀ נַפְשִׁי
כָּמַהּ לְךָ בְשָׂרִי
בְּאֶרֶץ־צִיָּה וְעָיֵף בְּלִי־מָיִם:

2 O God, You are my God;
I seek You desperately.
My soul thirsts for You;
my flesh longs for You
in a parched and weary land
that has no water,

כֵּן בַּקֹּדֶשׁ חֲזִיתִךָ
לִרְאוֹת עֻזְּךָ וּכְבוֹדֶךָ:

3 so I have visions of You in the Sanctuary
of Your might and glory.

כִּי־טוֹב חַסְדְּךָ מֵחַיִּים
שְׂפָתַי יְשַׁבְּחוּנְךָ:

4 Your loving-kindness is better than life,
so my lips praise You,

כֵּן אֲבָרֶכְךָ בְחַיָּי
בְּשִׁמְךָ אֶשָּׂא כַפָּי:

5 so I will bless You as long as I live
as I lift up my hands in Your name.

כְּמוֹ חֵלֶב וָדֶשֶׁן תִּשְׂבַּע נַפְשִׁי
וְשִׂפְתֵי רְנָנוֹת יְהַלֶּל־פִּי:

6 My soul will be nourished
as with a rich feast;
my mouth will sing praises
with joyful lips.

אִם־זְכַרְתִּיךָ עַל־יְצוּעָי
בְּאַשְׁמֻרוֹת אֶהְגֶּה־בָּךְ:

7 I think of You upon my bed;
I contemplate You in the vigil of night,

כִּי־הָיִיתָ עֶזְרָתָה לִּי
וּבְצֵל כְּנָפֶיךָ אֲרַנֵּן:

8 for You have been my help,
and I revel in the shade of Your wings.

דָּבְקָה נַפְשִׁי אַחֲרֶיךָ
בִּי תָּמְכָה יְמִינֶךָ:

9 My soul clings to You;
Your right hand supports me.

וְהֵמָּה לְשׁוֹאָה יְבַקְשׁוּ נַפְשִׁי
יָבֹאוּ בְּתַחְתִּיּוֹת הָאָרֶץ:

10 As for those who seek to destroy my life,
may they reach the lowest depths
of the earth.

יַגִּירֻהוּ עַל־יְדֵי־חָרֶב
מְנָת שֻׁעָלִים יִהְיוּ:

11 May the sword spill their blood;
may they be the prey of foxes,

וְהַמֶּלֶךְ יִשְׂמַח בֵּאלֹהִים 12
יִתְהַלֵּל כָּל־הַנִּשְׁבָּע בּוֹ
כִּי יִסָּכֵר פִּי דוֹבְרֵי־שָׁקֶר:

12 but the king will rejoice in God;
all who swear by Him will glory,
while the mouths of liars
will be stopped up.

The righteous will rejoice in the LORD and take refuge in Him; all the upright of heart will exult

I am in trouble. I am under attack. I am terrified.
I'm able to fight power and might.
But the terror I feel cripples me. If only I were not so frightened.
Lord, save me from the fear of my enemies.

PSALM 64

לַמְנַצֵּחַ מִזְמוֹר לְדָוִד:	1	To the lead singer – a psalm of David
שְׁמַע־אֱלֹהִים קוֹלִי בְשִׂיחִי מִפַּחַד אוֹיֵב תִּצֹּר חַיָּי:	2	Hear my voice, God, in my lament; keep my life from the terror of the enemy.
תַּסְתִּירֵנִי מִסּוֹד מְרֵעִים מֵרִגְשַׁת פֹּעֲלֵי אָוֶן:	3	Hide me from the band of wicked men, from the riotous mob of evildoers
אֲשֶׁר שָׁנְנוּ כַחֶרֶב לְשׁוֹנָם דָּרְכוּ חִצָּם דָּבָר מָר:	4	who sharpen their tongues like swords, who aim bitter words like arrows
לִירוֹת בַּמִּסְתָּרִים תָּם פִּתְאֹם יֹרֻהוּ וְלֹא יִירָאוּ:	5	and shoot from ambush at the blameless, shooting suddenly, without fear.
יְחַזְּקוּ־לָמוֹ ׀ דָּבָר רָע יְסַפְּרוּ לִטְמוֹן מוֹקְשִׁים אָמְרוּ מִי יִרְאֶה־לָּמוֹ:	6	They arm themselves with evil schemes; they plot to lay secret snares, thinking, "Who can see them?"
יַחְפְּשׂוּ־עוֹלֹת תַּמְנוּ חֵפֶשׂ מְחֻפָּשׂ וְקֶרֶב אִישׁ וְלֵב עָמֹק:	7	They seek out vile crimes, exhausting every possible plan in the depths of the human mind and heart,
וַיֹּרֵם אֱלֹהִים חֵץ פִּתְאוֹם הָיוּ מַכּוֹתָם:	8	but God will shoot them down; with a sudden arrow they will be wounded;
וַיַּכְשִׁילוּהוּ עָלֵימוֹ לְשׁוֹנָם יִתְנֹדֲדוּ כָּל־רֹאֵה בָם:	9	their own tongues will trip them up, and all who see them will shudder.
וַיִּירְאוּ כָּל־אָדָם וַיַּגִּידוּ פֹּעַל אֱלֹהִים וּמַעֲשֵׂהוּ הִשְׂכִּילוּ:	10	Then all people will be struck with fear; they will tell of God's works and contemplate His deeds.
יִשְׂמַח צַדִּיק בַּיהוה וְחָסָה בוֹ וְיִתְהַלְלוּ כָּל־יִשְׁרֵי־לֵב:	11	The righteous will rejoice in the LORD and take refuge in Him; all the upright of heart will exult.

Hearer of prayer, to You all flesh will come

For some, He is to be found in the tempest.
Thunder and lightning are His signs. Others find Him in His Law.
Mercy and Forgiveness are His signs. I find Him when I walk along
a country road. His signs are His wheat fields,
swaying in His wind; His pastures well watered;
grape leaves in His vineyards glistening in His sun.
They make no sound, but they sing a joyous song.

PSALM 65

לַמְנַצֵּחַ מִזְמוֹר לְדָוִד שִׁיר׃ 1 To the lead singer, a psalm –
a song of David

לְךָ דֻמִיָּה תְהִלָּה אֱלֹהִים בְּצִיּוֹן 2 Praise awaits You in Zion, God;
וּלְךָ יְשֻׁלַּם־נֶדֶר׃ to You vows are paid.

שֹׁמֵעַ תְּפִלָּה 3 Hearer of prayer,
עָדֶיךָ כָּל־בָּשָׂר יָבֹאוּ׃ to You all flesh will come.

דִּבְרֵי עֲוֺנֹת גָּבְרוּ מֶנִּי 4 When acts of sin overwhelm me,
פְּשָׁעֵינוּ אַתָּה תְכַפְּרֵם׃ You forgive our transgressions.

אַשְׁרֵי ׀ תִּבְחַר 5 Happy are those whom You choose,
וּתְקָרֵב יִשְׁכֹּן חֲצֵרֶיךָ those You bring close to dwell
נִשְׂבְּעָה בְּטוּב בֵּיתֶךָ in Your courtyards.
קְדֹשׁ הֵיכָלֶךָ׃ May we be sated with the goodness
of Your House,
Your Holy Sanctuary.

נוֹרָאוֹת ׀ בְּצֶדֶק תַּעֲנֵנוּ 6 Answer us with wondrous deeds
אֱלֹהֵי יִשְׁעֵנוּ in Your righteousness,
מִבְטָח כָּל־קַצְוֵי־אֶרֶץ O God, our savior–
וְיָם רְחֹקִים׃ hope of all the ends of the earth
and the distant seas,

מֵכִין הָרִים בְּכֹחוֹ 7 who set down the mountains
נֶאְזָר בִּגְבוּרָה׃ in His power,
so girded in strength is He,

מַשְׁבִּיחַ ׀ שְׁאוֹן יַמִּים 8 who stills the roaring seas,
שְׁאוֹן גַּלֵּיהֶם the roaring of the waves,
וַהֲמוֹן לְאֻמִּים׃ the clamor of the nations.

וַיִּירְאוּ ׀ יֹשְׁבֵי קְצָוֺת מֵאוֹתֹתֶיךָ 9 Those who live at the ends of the earth
מוֹצָאֵי־בֹקֶר וָעֶרֶב תַּרְנִין׃ are awed by Your signs.
The lands of sunrise and sunset
You move to joyful song.

פָּקַ֥דְתָּ הָאָ֨רֶץ ׀ וַתְּשֹׁ֪קְקֶ֡הָ
רַבַּ֬ת תַּעְשְׁרֶ֗נָּה
פֶּ֣לֶג אֱ֭לֹהִים מָ֣לֵא מָ֑יִם
תָּכִ֥ין דְּ֝גָנָ֗ם כִּי־כֵ֥ן תְּכִינֶֽהָ׃

10 You care for the land and water it
and make it very rich,
with God-given streams
brimming with water,
You provide the people's grain –
thus You have arranged it all.

תְּלָמֶ֣יהָ רַ֭וֵּה נַחֵ֣ת גְּדוּדֶ֑הָ
בִּרְבִיבִ֥ים תְּמֹגְגֶ֗נָּה
צִמְחָ֥הּ תְּבָרֵֽךְ׃

11 Water its furrows; level its ridges;
Soften it with showers;
bless its growth.

עִ֭טַּרְתָּ שְׁנַ֣ת טוֹבָתֶ֑ךָ
וּ֝מַעְגָּלֶ֗יךָ יִרְעֲפ֥וּן דָּֽשֶׁן׃

12 You have crowned the year
with Your goodness;
Your pathways overflow with richness.

יִ֭רְעֲפוּ נְא֣וֹת מִדְבָּ֑ר
וְ֝גִ֗יל גְּבָע֥וֹת תַּחְגֹּֽרְנָה׃

13 The wild pasturelands overflow;
the hills are girded with joy.

לָבְשׁ֬וּ כָרִ֨ים ׀ הַצֹּ֗אן
וַעֲמָקִ֥ים יַֽעַטְפוּ־בָ֑ר
יִ֝תְרוֹעֲע֗וּ אַף־יָשִֽׁירוּ׃

14 The meadows are clothed with sheep;
the valleys are decked with grain –
they shout for joy; they burst into song.

He turned sea to dry land; they crossed the river on foot – there we rejoiced in Him

Some ponder, some wonder. I ponder the suffering of our long exile. I wonder at our survival. When I ponder, I pray. When I wonder, I sing. When will we all ponder and wonder? Then we will all pray. Then we will all sing.

PSALM 66

לַמְנַצֵּחַ שִׁיר מִזְמוֹר
הָרִיעוּ לֵאלֹהִים כָּל־הָאָרֶץ:

1 To the lead singer, a song – a psalm
Shout for joy to God, all the earth;

זַמְּרוּ כְבוֹד־שְׁמוֹ
שִׂימוּ כָבוֹד תְּהִלָּתוֹ:

2 sing the glory of His name;
laud Him with glorious praise.

אִמְרוּ לֵאלֹהִים
מַה־נּוֹרָא מַעֲשֶׂיךָ
בְּרֹב עֻזְּךָ יְכַחֲשׁוּ־לְךָ אֹיְבֶיךָ:

3 Proclaim to God,
"How wondrous are Your deeds!
In Your sheer strength,
Your enemies come cringing before You."

כָּל־הָאָרֶץ ׀ יִשְׁתַּחֲווּ לְךָ
וִיזַמְּרוּ־לָךְ
יְזַמְּרוּ שִׁמְךָ סֶלָה:

4 All the earth bows down before You
and sings to You,
singing to Your name – Selah.

לְכוּ וּרְאוּ מִפְעֲלוֹת אֱלֹהִים
נוֹרָא עֲלִילָה עַל־בְּנֵי אָדָם:

5 Come, see the works of God,
the acts that move humanity to awe.

הָפַךְ יָם ׀ לְיַבָּשָׁה
בַּנָּהָר יַעַבְרוּ בְרָגֶל
שָׁם נִשְׂמְחָה־בּוֹ:

6 He turned sea to dry land;
they crossed the river on foot –
there we rejoiced in Him.

מֹשֵׁל בִּגְבוּרָתוֹ ׀ עוֹלָם
עֵינָיו בַּגּוֹיִם תִּצְפֶּינָה
הַסּוֹרְרִים ׀ אַל־יָרוּמוּ לָמוֹ
סֶלָה:

יָרִימוּ

7 He rules over the world in His might,
His eyes keeping watch over the nations
so that the rebellious will not rise up –
Selah.

בָּרְכוּ עַמִּים ׀ אֱלֹהֵינוּ
וְהַשְׁמִיעוּ קוֹל תְּהִלָּתוֹ:

8 Bless our God, O you peoples;
let His praise resound.

הַשָּׂם נַפְשֵׁנוּ בַּחַיִּים
וְלֹא־נָתַן לַמּוֹט רַגְלֵנוּ:

9 He keeps us among the living,
never letting our feet slip.

כִּי־בְחַנְתָּנוּ אֱלֹהִים
צְרַפְתָּנוּ כִּצְרָף־כָּסֶף:

10 For You, God, have tested us,
refining us as silver is refined:

הֲבֵאתָנוּ בַמְּצוּדָה
שַׂמְתָּ מוּעָקָה בְמָתְנֵינוּ:

11 You led us into a trap,
placing shackles around our waists;

הִרְכַּבְתָּ אֱנוֹשׁ לְרֹאשֵׁנוּ
בָּאנוּ־בָאֵשׁ וּבַמַּיִם וַתּוֹצִיאֵנוּ
לָרְוָיָה:

12 You let people ride over us;
    we have been through fire and water,
    but You brought us out to freedom.

אָבוֹא בֵיתְךָ בְעוֹלוֹת
אֲשַׁלֵּם לְךָ נְדָרָי:

13 I will enter Your House
    with burnt offerings;
    to You I will honor my vows –

אֲשֶׁר־פָּצוּ שְׂפָתָי
וְדִבֶּר־פִּי בַּצַּר־לִי:

14 those that crossed my lips,
    that my mouth uttered in my distress.

עֹלוֹת מֵחִים אַעֲלֶה־לָּךְ
עִם־קְטֹרֶת אֵילִים
אֶעֱשֶׂה בָקָר עִם־עַתּוּדִים
סֶלָה:

15 Fat burnt offerings I will offer up to You,
    the rich aroma of roasting rams;
    I will prepare bulls and he-goats –
    Selah.

לְכוּ־שִׁמְעוּ וַאֲסַפְּרָה
כָּל־יִרְאֵי אֱלֹהִים
אֲשֶׁר עָשָׂה לְנַפְשִׁי:

16 Come, listen, all you who fear God;
    I will tell of what He did for me.

אֵלָיו פִּי־קָרָאתִי
וְרוֹמַם תַּחַת לְשׁוֹנִי:

17 My mouth called out to Him,
    high praise upon my tongue;

אָוֶן אִם־רָאִיתִי בְלִבִּי
לֹא יִשְׁמַע אֲדֹנָי:

18 had evil been in my heart,
    the LORD would not have listened,

אָכֵן שָׁמַע אֱלֹהִים
הִקְשִׁיב בְּקוֹל תְּפִלָּתִי:

19 but God did listen –
    He paid heed to my prayer.

בָּרוּךְ אֱלֹהִים
אֲשֶׁר לֹא־הֵסִיר תְּפִלָּתִי
וְחַסְדּוֹ מֵאִתִּי:

20 Blessed is God,
    who has not turned away my prayer,
    nor His loyalty from me.

May God be gracious to us and bless us. May He shine His face upon us – Selah

Have you ever gone to court? I think I'm totally right, and you think you are. The judge decides. We're both disappointed. It won't be long now before all the nations face His court. He, the Judge, will decide.

PSALM 67

לַמְנַצֵּחַ בִּנְגִינֹת
מִזְמוֹר שִׁיר:

1 To the lead singer,
accompanied by stringed instruments –
a psalm, a song

אֱלֹהִים יְחָנֵּנוּ וִיבָרְכֵנוּ
יָאֵר פָּנָיו אִתָּנוּ סֶלָה:

2 May God be gracious to us and bless us.
May He shine His face upon us – Selah.

לָדַעַת בָּאָרֶץ דַּרְכֶּךָ
בְּכָל־גּוֹיִם יְשׁוּעָתֶךָ:

3 Then will Your way be known on earth,
Your salvation among all the nations.

יוֹדוּךָ עַמִּים ׀ אֱלֹהִים
יוֹדוּךָ עַמִּים כֻּלָּם:

4 Let the peoples praise You, God;
let all peoples praise You.

יִשְׂמְחוּ וִירַנְּנוּ לְאֻמִּים
כִּי־תִשְׁפֹּט עַמִּים מִישֹׁר
וּלְאֻמִּים ׀ בָּאָרֶץ תַּנְחֵם
סֶלָה:

5 Let nations rejoice and sing for joy,
for You judge the peoples justly
and guide the nations of the earth –
Selah.

יוֹדוּךָ עַמִּים ׀ אֱלֹהִים
יוֹדוּךָ עַמִּים כֻּלָּם:

6 Let the peoples praise You, God;
let all peoples praise You.

אֶרֶץ נָתְנָה יְבוּלָהּ
יְבָרְכֵנוּ אֱלֹהִים אֱלֹהֵינוּ:

7 The earth has yielded its harvest;
may God, our God, bless us.

יְבָרְכֵנוּ אֱלֹהִים
וְיִירְאוּ אוֹתוֹ כָּל־אַפְסֵי־אָרֶץ:

8 God will bless us,
and all will revere Him
to the ends of the earth.

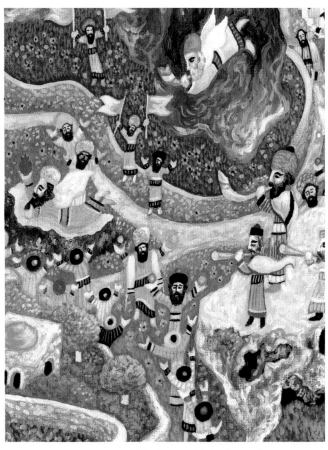

While the righteous rejoice and exult before God, delighted and joyful

There are the mighty, and there is the Mightiest of All.
The mighty are indifferent to the common person.
Why should they care about him?
They have other concerns, bigger things to worry about.
The Mightiest of All cares, especially for the common person.

PSALM 68

לַמְנַצֵּחַ לְדָוִד מִזְמוֹר שִׁיר׃	1	To the lead singer, of David – a psalm, a song
יָקוּם אֱלֹהִים יָפוּצוּ אוֹיְבָיו וְיָנוּסוּ מְשַׂנְאָיו מִפָּנָיו׃	2	Let God arise and His enemies be scattered; let His foes flee before Him.
כְּהִנְדֹּף עָשָׁן תִּנְדֹּף כְּהִמֵּס דּוֹנַג מִפְּנֵי־אֵשׁ יֹאבְדוּ רְשָׁעִים מִפְּנֵי אֱלֹהִים׃	3	As smoke disperses, disperse them; as wax melts before fire, may the wicked perish before God,
וְצַדִּיקִים יִשְׂמְחוּ יַעַלְצוּ לִפְנֵי אֱלֹהִים וְיָשִׂישׂוּ בְשִׂמְחָה׃	4	while the righteous rejoice and exult before God, delighted and joyful.
שִׁירוּ ׀ לֵאלֹהִים זַמְּרוּ שְׁמוֹ סֹלּוּ לָרֹכֵב בָּעֲרָבוֹת בְּיָהּ שְׁמוֹ וְעִלְזוּ לְפָנָיו׃	5	Sing to God; sing praises to His name. Laud Him who rides the clouds – the Lord is His name – and exult before Him.
אֲבִי יְתוֹמִים וְדַיַּן אַלְמָנוֹת אֱלֹהִים בִּמְעוֹן קָדְשׁוֹ׃	6	Father of orphans, judge of widows, God is in His holy abode.
אֱלֹהִים ׀ מוֹשִׁיב יְחִידִים ׀ בַּיְתָה מוֹצִיא אֲסִירִים בַּכּוֹשָׁרוֹת אַךְ סוֹרְרִים שָׁכְנוּ צְחִיחָה׃	7	God brings the lonely back home and sets captives free, to their delight, but the rebellious must dwell in a parched wasteland.
אֱלֹהִים בְּצֵאתְךָ לִפְנֵי עַמֶּךָ בְּצַעְדְּךָ בִישִׁימוֹן סֶלָה׃	8	O God, when You went out before Your people, when You strode through the wilderness – Selah –
אֶרֶץ רָעָשָׁה ׀ אַף־שָׁמַיִם נָטְפוּ מִפְּנֵי אֱלֹהִים זֶה סִינַי מִפְּנֵי אֱלֹהִים אֱלֹהֵי יִשְׂרָאֵל׃	9	the earth shook; the heavens, too, poured down before God, Sinai itself before God, God of Israel!

גֶּשֶׁם נְדָבוֹת תָּנִיף אֱלֹהִים
נַחֲלָתְךָ וְנִלְאָה אַתָּה כוֹנַנְתָּהּ:

10 You, God, unleashed a lavish rain,
   reviving Your weary heritage.

חַיָּתְךָ יָשְׁבוּ־בָהּ
תָּכִין בְּטוֹבָתְךָ לֶעָנִי אֱלֹהִים:

11 Your own flock settled there;
   in Your goodness, God,
   You provided for the lowly.

אֲדֹנָי יִתֶּן־אֹמֶר
הַמְבַשְּׂרוֹת צָבָא רָב:

12 The LORD made His decree;
   a great host of women spread the news:

מַלְכֵי צְבָאוֹת יִדֹּדוּן יִדֹּדוּן
וּנְוַת־בַּיִת תְּחַלֵּק שָׁלָל:

13 "Kings with their armies are fleeing,
   fleeing,
   while housewives share out the spoil."

אִם־תִּשְׁכְּבוּן בֵּין שְׁפַתָּיִם
כַּנְפֵי יוֹנָה נֶחְפָּה בַכֶּסֶף
וְאֶבְרוֹתֶיהָ בִּירַקְרַק חָרוּץ:

14 Even for those of you
   who lie among the sheepfolds,
   the wings of the dove
   are inlaid with silver,
   her pinions with glittering gold.

בְּפָרֵשׂ שַׁדַּי מְלָכִים בָּהּ
תַּשְׁלֵג בְּצַלְמוֹן:

15 When Shaddai scattered the kings there,
   it was like snow falling on Tzalmon.

הַר־אֱלֹהִים הַר־בָּשָׁן
הַר גַּבְנֻנִּים הַר־בָּשָׁן:

16 O mighty mountain, Mount Bashan,
   O Mount Bashan of many peaks,

לָמָּה ׀ תְּרַצְּדוּן הָרִים גַּבְנֻנִּים
הָהָר חָמַד אֱלֹהִים לְשִׁבְתּוֹ
אַף־יְהוָה יִשְׁכֹּן לָנֶצַח:

17 why do you glare so,
   O many-peaked mountains,
   at the mountain God desires
   for His abode?
   Yes, the LORD will dwell there forever.

רֶכֶב אֱלֹהִים
רִבֹּתַיִם אַלְפֵי שִׁנְאָן
אֲדֹנָי בָם סִינַי בַּקֹּדֶשׁ:

18 God's chariots are many myriads,
   thousands upon thousands;
   the LORD is among them as at Sinai
   in holiness.

עָלִיתָ לַמָּרוֹם ׀ שָׁבִיתָ שֶּׁבִי
לָקַחְתָּ מַתָּנוֹת בָּאָדָם
וְאַף סוֹרְרִים לִשְׁכֹּן ׀ יָהּ
אֱלֹהִים:

19 You ascended the heights
and carried off captives;
You received tributes from people,
even from those rebellious
against the Lord God's dwelling there.

בָּרוּךְ אֲדֹנָי יוֹם ׀ יוֹם
יַעֲמָס־לָנוּ הָאֵל ׀ יְשׁוּעָתֵנוּ
סֶלָה:

20 Blessed be the Lord,
who bears our burdens every day;
God is our salvation – Selah.

הָאֵל ׀ לָנוּ אֵל לְמוֹשָׁעוֹת
וְלֵיהוִֹה אֲדֹנָי לַמָּוֶת תּוֹצָאוֹת:

21 Our God is for us a saving God;
God, the Lord, provides an escape
from death,

אַךְ־אֱלֹהִים יִמְחַץ רֹאשׁ אֹיְבָיו
קָדְקֹד שֵׂעָר מִתְהַלֵּךְ בַּאֲשָׁמָיו:

22 but God will crush the heads
of His enemies,
the hairy scalps of those who walk about
in guilt.

אָמַר אֲדֹנָי
מִבָּשָׁן אָשִׁיב
אָשִׁיב מִמְּצֻלוֹת יָם:

23 The Lord decreed,
"I will bring them back from Bashan;
I will bring them back from the depths
of the sea,

לְמַעַן ׀ תִּמְחַץ רַגְלְךָ בְּדָם
לְשׁוֹן כְּלָבֶיךָ מֵאוֹיְבִים מִנֵּהוּ:

24 so that your feet may wade
through blood,
so that the tongues of your dogs
may take their share of the enemy."

רָאוּ הֲלִיכוֹתֶיךָ אֱלֹהִים
הֲלִיכוֹת אֵלִי מַלְכִּי בַקֹּדֶשׁ:

25 They saw Your processions, God,
the processions of my God,
of my King, into the sanctuary.

קִדְּמוּ שָׁרִים אַחַר נֹגְנִים
בְּתוֹךְ עֲלָמוֹת תּוֹפֵפוֹת:

26 First came the singers;
next came the musicians amidst the girls
playing tambourines.

בְּמַקְהֵלוֹת בָּרְכוּ אֱלֹהִים
אֲדֹנָי מִמְּקוֹר יִשְׂרָאֵל:

27 Bless God in chorus,
the Lord, you of Israel's fountain!

שָׁם בִּנְיָמִן ׀ צָעִיר רֹדֵם
שָׂרֵי יְהוּדָה רִגְמָתָם
שָׂרֵי זְבֻלוּן שָׂרֵי נַפְתָּלִי׃

28 There young Binyamin leads them,
the princes of Yehuda in their throngs,
princes of Zevulun, princes of Naftali.

צִוָּה אֱלֹהֶיךָ עֻזֶּךָ
עוּזָּה אֱלֹהִים
זוּ פָּעַלְתָּ לָּנוּ׃

29 Your God has commanded your might,
the might, God,
that You have shown us!

מֵהֵיכָלֶךָ עַל־יְרוּשָׁלִָם
לְךָ יוֹבִילוּ מְלָכִים שָׁי׃

30 For Your Temple over Jerusalem,
kings will come to You bearing gifts.

גְּעַר חַיַּת קָנֶה
עֲדַת אַבִּירִים ׀ בְּעֶגְלֵי עַמִּים
מִתְרַפֵּס בְּרַצֵּי־כָסֶף
בִּזַּר עַמִּים קְרָבוֹת יֶחְפָּצוּ׃

31 Tame the beast of the marsh,
the herd of fierce bulls,
of feisty young calves, the peoples;
until they come cringing
with pieces of silver,
scatter the peoples who delight in battle.

יֶאֱתָיוּ חַשְׁמַנִּים מִנִּי מִצְרָיִם
כּוּשׁ תָּרִיץ יָדָיו לֵאלֹהִים׃

32 Let the nobles of Egypt come;
let Kush swiftly reach out its hands
to God.

מַמְלְכוֹת הָאָרֶץ שִׁירוּ לֵאלֹהִים
זַמְּרוּ אֲדֹנָי סֶלָה׃

33 Kingdoms of earth, sing to God;
sing praise to the Lord – Selah.

לָרֹכֵב בִּשְׁמֵי שְׁמֵי־קֶדֶם
הֵן יִתֵּן בְּקוֹלוֹ קוֹל עֹז׃

34 To Him who rides
the highest heavens of old,
listen! His voice rings out with might.

תְּנוּ עֹז לֵאלֹהִים
עַל־יִשְׂרָאֵל גַּאֲוָתוֹ
וְעֻזּוֹ בַּשְּׁחָקִים׃

35 Ascribe might to God,
whose majesty is over Israel,
whose might fills the skies.

נוֹרָא אֱלֹהִים ׀ מִמִּקְדָּשֶׁיךָ
אֵל יִשְׂרָאֵל
הוּא נֹתֵן ׀ עֹז וְתַעֲצֻמוֹת לָעָם
בָּרוּךְ אֱלֹהִים׃

36 Your awe, God,
emanates from Your sanctuaries,
It is Israel's God
who gives might and power to the people.
blessed is God!

אהללה שם אלהים בשיר, ויאגדלנו בתודה

I will praise God's name with song; I will glorify Him in thanksgiving

I am drowning. It is futile to hope for rescue.
It is senseless to even try to pray.
Daringly, I say "Don't disappoint those who look up to me.
Don't deny the dreams of those who count on me."
I don't deserve that You hear my prayers.
But they do deserve that You hear theirs.

PSALM 69

לַמְנַצֵּחַ עַל־שׁוֹשַׁנִּים לְדָוִד׃

1 To the lead singer, set to *shoshanim* –
   of David

הוֹשִׁיעֵנִי אֱלֹהִים
כִּי בָאוּ מַיִם עַד־נָפֶשׁ׃

2 Save me, God,
   for the waters have reached my neck;

טָבַעְתִּי ׀ בִּיוֵן מְצוּלָה
וְאֵין מָעֳמָד
בָּאתִי בְמַעֲמַקֵּי־מַיִם
וְשִׁבֹּלֶת שְׁטָפָתְנִי׃

3 I am drowning in the mire of the deep
   with nowhere to stand;
   I have reached the watery depths,
   and the current has swept me away.

יָגַעְתִּי בְקָרְאִי נִחַר גְּרוֹנִי
כָּלוּ עֵינַי מְיַחֵל לֵאלֹהָי׃

4 I am weary from calling out;
   my throat is hoarse;
   my eyes are dim from searching
   for my God.

רַבּוּ ׀ מִשַּׂעֲרוֹת רֹאשִׁי
שֹׂנְאַי חִנָּם
עָצְמוּ מַצְמִיתַי אֹיְבַי שֶׁקֶר
אֲשֶׁר לֹא־גָזַלְתִּי אָז אָשִׁיב׃

5 There are more who hate me
   without cause
   than there are hairs on my head,
   so many treacherous foes
   who long to destroy me.
   Must I return what I have not stolen?

אֱלֹהִים אַתָּה יָדַעְתָּ לְאִוַּלְתִּי
וְאַשְׁמוֹתַי מִמְּךָ לֹא־נִכְחָדוּ׃

6 God, You know my folly;
   my guilt is not hidden from You.

אַל־יֵבֹשׁוּ בִי ׀ קֹוֶיךָ אֲדֹנָי
יְהוִה צְבָאוֹת
אַל־יִכָּלְמוּ בִי מְבַקְשֶׁיךָ
אֱלֹהֵי יִשְׂרָאֵל׃

7 Let not those who hope for You
   be shamed through me,
   Lord God of hosts;
   let not those who seek You
   be disgraced through me, God of Israel.

כִּי־עָלֶיךָ נָשָׂאתִי חֶרְפָּה
כִּסְּתָה כְלִמָּה פָנָי׃

8 For Your sake I bear taunting;
   my face is draped in disgrace.

מוּזָר הָיִיתִי לְאֶחָי
וְנָכְרִי לִבְנֵי אִמִּי׃

9 I have become a stranger to my brothers,
   an alien to my mother's children,

כִּי־קִנְאַת בֵּיתְךָ אֲכָלָתְנִי 10 for fervor for Your House
וְחֶרְפּוֹת חוֹרְפֶּיךָ נָפְלוּ עָלָי: has destroyed me;
the taunts of Your taunters
have fallen on me.

וָאֶבְכֶּה בַצּוֹם נַפְשִׁי 11 When I wept and fasted,
וַתְּהִי לַחֲרָפוֹת לִי: I was taunted for it;

וָאֶתְּנָה לְבוּשִׁי שָׂק 12 when I clothed myself in sackcloth,
וָאֱהִי לָהֶם לְמָשָׁל: I became a cautionary tale for them.

יָשִׂיחוּ בִי יֹשְׁבֵי שָׁעַר 13 Loiterers at the gate gossip about me;
וּנְגִינוֹת שׁוֹתֵי שֵׁכָר: drunkards sing about me,

וַאֲנִי תְפִלָּתִי־לְךָ ׀ יהוה 14 but as for me,
עֵת רָצוֹן may my prayer come to You, LORD,
in a moment of favor.
אֱלֹהִים בְּרָב־חַסְדֶּךָ God, in Your great loyalty,
עֲנֵנִי בֶּאֱמֶת יִשְׁעֶךָ: answer me with Your true salvation.

הַצִּילֵנִי מִטִּיט וְאַל־אֶטְבָּעָה 15 Save me from drowning in the mud;
אִנָּצְלָה מִשֹּׂנְאַי let me be saved from my haters,
וּמִמַּעֲמַקֵּי־מָיִם: from the watery depths.

אַל־תִּשְׁטְפֵנִי ׀ שִׁבֹּלֶת מַיִם 16 Do not let me be swept away
in the current
וְאַל־תִּבְלָעֵנִי מְצוּלָה or swallowed by the deep;
וְאַל־תֶּאְטַר־עָלַי בְּאֵר פִּיהָ: do not let the Pit close its mouth over me.

עֲנֵנִי יהוה כִּי־טוֹב חַסְדֶּךָ 17 Answer me, LORD, in Your good loyalty;
כְּרֹב רַחֲמֶיךָ פְּנֵה אֵלָי: turn to me in Your great compassion.

וְאַל־תַּסְתֵּר פָּנֶיךָ מֵעַבְדֶּךָ 18 Do not hide Your face from Your servant,
כִּי־צַר־לִי מַהֵר עֲנֵנִי: for I am in danger – hurry, answer me!

קָרְבָה אֶל־נַפְשִׁי גְאָלָהּ 19 Draw near to me; redeem me;
לְמַעַן אֹיְבַי פְּדֵנִי: free me from my enemies.

20 You know of how I am taunted,
of my shame and disgrace –
all my foes are before You.

אַתָּה יָדַעְתָּ חֶרְפָּתִי
וּבָשְׁתִּי וּכְלִמָּתִי
נֶגְדְּךָ כָּל־צוֹרְרָי׃

21 Taunts have broken my heart,
and I am deathly ill;
I hope for consolation, but there is none;
for comforters, but find none –

חֶרְפָּה ׀ שָׁבְרָה לִבִּי וָאָנוּשָׁה
וָאֲקַוֶּה לָנוּד וָאַיִן
וְלַמְנַחֲמִים וְלֹא מָצָאתִי׃

22 they gave me poison for my fare
and vinegar to quench my thirst.

וַיִּתְּנוּ בְּבָרוּתִי רֹאשׁ
וְלִצְמָאִי יַשְׁקוּנִי חֹמֶץ׃

23 Let their own table
be a death trap to them,
a snare for their friends.

יְהִי־שֻׁלְחָנָם לִפְנֵיהֶם לְפָח
וְלִשְׁלוֹמִים לְמוֹקֵשׁ׃

24 May their eyes grow too dark to see;
may their loins ever tremble.

תֶּחְשַׁכְנָה עֵינֵיהֶם מֵרְאוֹת
וּמָתְנֵיהֶם תָּמִיד הַמְעַד׃

25 Pour Your wrath upon them;
let Your blazing fury overcome them.

שְׁפָךְ־עֲלֵיהֶם זַעְמֶךָ
וַחֲרוֹן אַפְּךָ יַשִּׂיגֵם׃

26 May their encampment be laid waste,
their tents stand empty,

תְּהִי־טִירָתָם נְשַׁמָּה
בְּאָהֳלֵיהֶם אַל־יְהִי יֹשֵׁב׃

27 for they persecuted those
You struck down
and recounted the pain of Your victims.

כִּי־אַתָּה אֲשֶׁר־הִכִּיתָ רָדָפוּ
וְאֶל־מַכְאוֹב חֲלָלֶיךָ יְסַפֵּרוּ׃

28 Add that offense to their offenses;
never let them share in Your favor.

תְּנָה־עָוֹן עַל־עֲוֹנָם
וְאַל־יָבֹאוּ בְּצִדְקָתֶךָ׃

29 Let them be blotted out
from the book of life,
not ever inscribed among the righteous,

יִמָּחוּ מִסֵּפֶר חַיִּים
וְעִם צַדִּיקִים אַל־יִכָּתֵבוּ׃

30 but as for me,
I am lowly and in pain;
Your salvation, God, will lift me up.

וַאֲנִי עָנִי וְכוֹאֵב
יְשׁוּעָתְךָ אֱלֹהִים תְּשַׂגְּבֵנִי׃

אֲהַלְלָה שֵׁם־אֱלֹהִים בְּשִׁיר וַאֲגַדְּלֶנּוּ בְתוֹדָה:	31	I will praise God's name with song; I will glorify Him in thanksgiving.
וְתִיטַב לַיהוה מִשּׁוֹר פָּר מַקְרִן מַפְרִיס:	32	This will please the LORD more than any ox or any horned and cloven-hooved bull.
רָאוּ עֲנָוִים יִשְׂמָחוּ דֹּרְשֵׁי אֱלֹהִים וִיחִי לְבַבְכֶם:	33	The lowly will see and rejoice; take heart, you who seek God –
כִּי־שֹׁמֵעַ אֶל־אֶבְיוֹנִים יהוה וְאֶת־אֲסִירָיו לֹא בָזָה:	34	for the LORD listens to the needy and does not neglect His captives.
יְהַלְלוּהוּ שָׁמַיִם וָאָרֶץ יַמִּים וְכָל־רֹמֵשׂ בָּם:	35	Let heaven and earth praise Him, the seas and all that stir within them,
כִּי אֱלֹהִים ׀ יוֹשִׁיעַ צִיּוֹן וְיִבְנֶה עָרֵי יְהוּדָה וְיָשְׁבוּ שָׁם וִירֵשׁוּהָ:	36	for God will save Zion and rebuild the towns of Yehuda; they will settle there and take possession.
וְזֶרַע עֲבָדָיו יִנְחָלוּהָ וְאֹהֲבֵי שְׁמוֹ יִשְׁכְּנוּ־בָהּ:	37	The seed of His servants will inherit it, and those who love His name will dwell there.

May all who seek You rejoice and delight in You

People tell me, "You're a man of faith.""Hang in there."
"Be patient." But men of faith can't wait. Faith makes us impatient.
God's salvation comes in the blink of an eye.
Make haste . . . come quickly . . . Now! Now! Now!

PSALM 70

1   לַמְנַצֵּחַ לְדָוִד לְהַזְכִּיר:

To the lead singer – of David, *lehazkir*

2   אֱלֹהִים לְהַצִּילֵנִי
יְהֹוָה לְעֶזְרָתִי חוּשָׁה:

O God, save me;
O LORD, rush to my help –

3   יֵבֹשׁוּ וְיַחְפְּרוּ מְבַקְשֵׁי נַפְשִׁי
יִסֹּגוּ אָחוֹר וְיִכָּלְמוּ חֲפֵצֵי רָעָתִי:

let those who seek my life
be shamed and disgraced;
let those who wish me harm
retreat in humiliation;

4   יָשׁוּבוּ עַל־עֵקֶב בָּשְׁתָּם
הָאֹמְרִים הֶאָח ׀ הֶאָח:

let those who leer "Aha! Aha!"
turn away in shame.

5   יָשִׂישׂוּ וְיִשְׂמְחוּ ׀ בְּךָ
כָּל־מְבַקְשֶׁיךָ
וְיֹאמְרוּ תָמִיד יִגְדַּל אֱלֹהִים
אֹהֲבֵי יְשׁוּעָתֶךָ:

May all who seek You
rejoice and delight in You;
may those who long for Your salvation
always proclaim, "God is great."

6   וַאֲנִי ׀ עָנִי וְאֶבְיוֹן
אֱלֹהִים חוּשָׁה־לִּי
עֶזְרִי וּמְפַלְּטִי אַתָּה
יְהֹוָה אַל־תְּאַחַר:

As for me, I am poor and needy –
God, rush to me;
You are my help and my rescuer;
LORD, do not delay.

My lips will delight in singing praise to You

"What is life all about?" He answered his own question:
"It's all about struggle." He's wrong. It's also about song.
That's the lesson of the psalms:
Deliver me and rescue me...revive me once more! Struggle.
Lyre...harp...lips...tongue! Song. Sing along!

PSALM 71

בְּךָֽ־יהוה חָסִ֑יתִי אַל־אֵב֥וֹשָׁה לְעוֹלָֽם׃	1	In You, Lord, I take refuge; may I never be put to shame.
בְּצִדְקָתְךָ֗ תַּצִּילֵ֥נִי וּֽתְפַלְּטֵ֑נִי הַטֵּֽה־אֵלַ֥י אָ֝זְנְךָ֗ וְהֽוֹשִׁיעֵֽנִי׃	2	Deliver me; rescue me in Your righteousness; lend Your ear to me and save me.
הֱיֵ֤ה לִ֨י ׀ לְצ֥וּר מָע֡וֹן לָב֪וֹא תָּמִ֗יד צִוִּ֥יתָ לְהוֹשִׁיעֵ֑נִי כִּֽי־סַלְעִ֖י וּמְצֽוּדָתִ֣י אָֽתָּה׃	3	Be a rock of refuge where I may always come; command my salvation, for You are my rock and my fortress.
אֱֽלֹהַ֗י פַּ֭לְּטֵנִי מִיַּ֣ד רָשָׁ֑ע מִכַּ֖ף מְעַוֵּ֣ל וְחוֹמֵֽץ׃	4	My God, rescue me from the hands of the wicked, from the grip of the evil and the violent,
כִּֽי־אַתָּ֥ה תִקְוָתִ֑י אֲדֹנָ֥י יֱהֹוִ֗ה מִבְטַחִ֥י מִנְּעוּרָֽי׃	5	for You are my hope, O Lord God, my trust since my youth.
עָלֶ֤יךָ ׀ נִסְמַ֬כְתִּי מִבֶּ֗טֶן מִמְּעֵ֣י אִ֭מִּי אַתָּ֣ה גוֹזִ֑י בְּךָ֖ תְהִלָּתִ֣י תָמִֽיד׃	6	I have relied upon You since conception; from my mother's womb You brought me out; I will praise You always.
כְּ֭מוֹפֵת הָיִ֣יתִי לְרַבִּ֑ים וְ֝אַתָּ֗ה מַחֲסִי־עֹֽז׃	7	I have set an example for many while You have been my mighty refuge;
יִמָּ֣לֵא פִ֭י תְּהִלָּתֶ֑ךָ כׇּל־הַ֝יּ֗וֹם תִּפְאַרְתֶּֽךָ׃	8	may my mouth be filled with Your praise, Your glory, all day long.
אַֽל־תַּ֭שְׁלִיכֵנִי לְעֵ֣ת זִקְנָ֑ה כִּכְל֥וֹת כֹּ֝חִ֗י אַֽל־תַּֽעַזְבֵֽנִי׃	9	Do not cast me away in old age; when my strength fails, do not abandon me,
כִּֽי־אָמְר֣וּ אוֹיְבַ֣י לִ֑י וְשֹׁמְרֵ֥י נַ֝פְשִׁ֗י נוֹעֲצ֥וּ יַחְדָּֽו׃	10	for my enemies say of me, those who stalk me and conspire together,
לֵ֭אמֹר אֱלֹהִ֣ים עֲזָב֑וֹ רִֽדְפ֥וּ וְ֝תִפְשׂ֗וּהוּ כִּי־אֵ֥ין מַצִּֽיל׃	11	"God has abandoned him. Chase him and catch him, for no one will save him."

	אֱלֹהִים אַל־תִּרְחַק מִמֶּנִּי	12 God, do not stray far from me;
חִישָׁה	אֱלֹהַי לְעֶזְרָתִי חוּשָׁה׃	my God, rush to my help.

יֵבֹשׁוּ יִכְלוּ שֹׂטְנֵי נַפְשִׁי 13 Let my accusers be shamed and ruined;
יַעֲטוּ חֶרְפָּה וּכְלִמָּה let those who seek my harm
מְבַקְשֵׁי רָעָתִי׃ be cloaked in disgrace and humiliation.

וַאֲנִי תָּמִיד אֲיַחֵל 14 As for me, I shall always hope
וְהוֹסַפְתִּי עַל־כָּל־תְּהִלָּתֶךָ׃ and praise You ever more and more.

פִּי ׀ יְסַפֵּר צִדְקָתֶךָ 15 My mouth will tell of Your righteousness,
כָּל־הַיּוֹם תְּשׁוּעָתֶךָ Your salvation all day long,
כִּי לֹא יָדַעְתִּי סְפֹרוֹת׃ though it is immeasurable.

אָבוֹא בִּגְבֻרוֹת אֲדֹנָי יֱהֹוִה 16 I will come tell of Your powerful deeds,
אַזְכִּיר צִדְקָתְךָ לְבַדֶּךָ׃ O LORD God;
I will proclaim Your righteousness –
Yours alone.

אֱלֹהִים לִמַּדְתַּנִי מִנְּעוּרָי 17 God, You have taught me since my youth;
וְעַד־הֵנָּה אַגִּיד נִפְלְאוֹתֶיךָ׃ to this day I tell of Your wonders.

וְגַם עַד־זִקְנָה ׀ וְשֵׂיבָה 18 Now that I am old and grey, God,
אֱלֹהִים אַל־תַּעַזְבֵנִי do not abandon me
עַד־אַגִּיד זְרוֹעֲךָ לְדוֹר until I tell the next generation
לְכָל־יָבוֹא גְּבוּרָתֶךָ׃ of Your power,
all those to come of Your power.

וְצִדְקָתְךָ אֱלֹהִים עַד־מָרוֹם 19 Your righteousness, God,
אֲשֶׁר־עָשִׂיתָ גְדֹלוֹת reaches the highest heights,
אֱלֹהִים מִי כָמוֹךָ׃ for You have done great things.
O God, who is like You?

הִרְאִיתָנוּ	אֲשֶׁר הִרְאִיתַנִי ׀	20 You who have shown me
	צָרוֹת רַבּוֹת וְרָעוֹת	great and terrible troubles
תְּחַיֵּינוּ	תָּשׁוּב תְּחַיֵּינִי	will revive me once more;
	וּמִתְּהֹמוֹת הָאָרֶץ	from the depths of the earth You will
תַּעֲלֵנוּ	תָּשׁוּב תַּעֲלֵנִי׃	once more raise me up.

תֶּרֶב ׀ גְּדֻלָּתִי
וְתִסֹּב תְּנַחֲמֵנִי׃

21 You will increase my greatness
and comfort me again,

גַּם־אֲנִי ׀ אוֹדְךָ בִכְלִי־נֶבֶל
אֲמִתְּךָ אֱלֹהָי
אֲזַמְּרָה לְךָ בְכִנּוֹר
קְדוֹשׁ יִשְׂרָאֵל׃

22 then I will praise You with the lyre
for Your faithfulness, my God;
I will sing praises to You with the harp,
O Holy One of Israel.

תְּרַנֵּנָּה שְׂפָתַי כִּי אֲזַמְּרָה־לָּךְ
וְנַפְשִׁי אֲשֶׁר פָּדִיתָ׃

23 My lips will delight
in singing praise to You,
my very being, whom You redeemed.

גַּם־לְשׁוֹנִי כָּל־הַיּוֹם
תֶּהְגֶּה צִדְקָתֶךָ
כִּי־בֹשׁוּ כִי־חָפְרוּ
מְבַקְשֵׁי רָעָתִי׃

24 My tongue, too, will express Your
righteousness all day long,
how those who sought my harm were
shamed and reviled.

May the mountains yield peace for the people, the hills righteousness

We live on the surface. We don't see what God is doing.
Blessed be the Lord. . .who alone does wondrous things!
As the Talmud states, "The beneficiary of the miracle is unaware
of his own miracle." What He did for you saved your life.
But you'll never know.

PSALM 72

לִשְׁלֹמֹה ׀

אֱלֹהִים מִשְׁפָּטֶיךָ לְמֶלֶךְ תֵּן

וְצִדְקָתְךָ לְבֶן־מֶלֶךְ:

1 Of Shlomo

God, grant Your judgment to the king,

Your justice to the king's son

יָדִין עַמְּךָ בְצֶדֶק

וַעֲנִיֶּיךָ בְמִשְׁפָּט:

2 so that he may judge Your people fairly,

Your lowly ones with justice.

יִשְׂאוּ הָרִים שָׁלוֹם לָעָם

וּגְבָעוֹת בִּצְדָקָה:

3 May the mountains yield peace

for the people,

the hills righteousness;

יִשְׁפֹּט ׀ עֲנִיֵּי־עָם

יוֹשִׁיעַ לִבְנֵי אֶבְיוֹן

וִידַכֵּא עוֹשֵׁק:

4 may he bring justice to the lowly people,

save the children of the needy,

and crush the oppressor.

יִירָאוּךָ עִם־שָׁמֶשׁ

וְלִפְנֵי יָרֵחַ דּוֹר דּוֹרִים:

5 May they revere You

as long as the sun shines,

as long as the moon glows,

for generations untold.

יֵרֵד כְּמָטָר עַל־גֵּז

כִּרְבִיבִים זַרְזִיף אָרֶץ:

6 May he be like rain

falling on mown grass,

like showers watering the earth.

יִפְרַח־בְּיָמָיו צַדִּיק

וְרֹב שָׁלוֹם עַד־בְּלִי יָרֵחַ:

7 In his time, may the righteous bloom;

may peace abound

until the moon ceases to be.

וְיֵרְדְּ מִיָּם עַד־יָם

וּמִנָּהָר עַד־אַפְסֵי־אָרֶץ:

8 May he rule from sea to sea,

from the river to the ends of the earth.

לְפָנָיו יִכְרְעוּ צִיִּים

וְאֹיְבָיו עָפָר יְלַחֵכוּ:

9 Let the desert nomads kneel before him;

let his enemies lick the dust;

מַלְכֵי תַרְשִׁישׁ וְאִיִּים

מִנְחָה יָשִׁיבוּ

מַלְכֵי שְׁבָא וּסְבָא

אֶשְׁכָּר יַקְרִיבוּ:

10 let kings of Tarshish and the isles

pay him tribute,

kings of Sheba and Seba offer gifts;

וְיִשְׁתַּחֲווּ־לוֹ כָל־מְלָכִים
כָּל־גּוֹיִם יַעַבְדֽוּהוּ׃

11 let all kings bow down to him,
and let all nations serve him,

כִּי־יַצִּיל אֶבְיוֹן מְשַׁוֵּעַ
וְעָנִי וְאֵין־עֹזֵר לֽוֹ׃

12 for he brings salvation
to the needy who cry out,
to the lowly with none to help them.

יָחֹס עַל־דַּל וְאֶבְיוֹן
וְנַפְשׁוֹת אֶבְיוֹנִים יוֹשִֽׁיעַ׃

13 He pities the poor and the needy
and saves the lives of the needy,

מִתּוֹךְ וּמֵחָמָס יִגְאַל נַפְשָׁם
וְיֵיקַר דָּמָם בְּעֵינָֽיו׃

14 redeeming them from deceit
and violence,
for their blood is precious in his sight.

וִיחִי וְיִתֶּן־לוֹ מִזְּהַב שְׁבָא
וְיִתְפַּלֵּל בַּעֲדוֹ תָמִיד
כָּל־הַיּוֹם יְבָרַכֶֽנְהוּ׃

15 Long may he live!
May he be granted the gold of Sheba;
may they always pray on his behalf,
blessing him all day long.

יְהִי פִסַּת־בַּר ׀ בָּאָרֶץ
בְּרֹאשׁ הָרִים
יִרְעַשׁ כַּלְּבָנוֹן פִּרְיוֹ
וְיָצִיצוּ מֵעִיר כְּעֵשֶׂב הָאָֽרֶץ׃

16 May there be a wealth of grain in the land,
even on the mountaintops;
let its fruit rustle like Lebanon
and the people thrive in the towns
like field grass.

יָנִין

יְהִי שְׁמוֹ ׀ לְעוֹלָם
לִפְנֵי־שֶׁמֶשׁ יִנּוֹן שְׁמוֹ
וְיִתְבָּרְכוּ בוֹ כָּל־גּוֹיִם
יְאַשְּׁרֽוּהוּ׃

17 May his name be forever;
may his name endure as long as the sun;
let all nations be blessed through him
and praise his fortune.

בָּרוּךְ ׀ יהוה אֱלֹהִים
אֱלֹהֵי יִשְׂרָאֵל
עֹשֵׂה נִפְלָאוֹת לְבַדּֽוֹ׃

18 Blessed be the LORD God, God of Israel,
who alone does wonders;

וּבָרוּךְ ׀ שֵׁם כְּבוֹדוֹ לְעוֹלָם
וְיִמָּלֵא כְבוֹדוֹ אֶת־כֹּל־הָאָרֶץ
אָמֵן ׀ וְאָמֵֽן׃

19 blessed be His glorious name forever.
May the whole world be filled
with His glory!
Amen and Amen!

כָּלּוּ תְפִלּוֹת דָּוִד בֶּן־יִשָֽׁי׃

20 Here end the prayers of David,
son of Yishai.

Until I came to God's Sanctuary

We all have our doubts. We wonder:
"The righteous suffer so, and good things happen to bad people."
Asaf struggled with his doubts. He found his answer. Find yours.

PSALM 73

	מִזְמוֹר לְאָסָף	1
	אַךְ טוֹב לְיִשְׂרָאֵל אֱלֹהִים	
	לְבָרֵי לֵבָב:	

1 A psalm of Asaf
God is truly good to Israel,
to those pure of heart;

נטוי
שפכה
וַאֲנִי כִּמְעַט נָטָיוּ רַגְלָי
כְּאַיִן שֻׁפְּכוּ אֲשֻׁרָי:

2 but as for me, my feet nearly strayed,
my steps had all but slipped,

כִּי־קִנֵּאתִי בַּהוֹלְלִים
שְׁלוֹם רְשָׁעִים אֶרְאֶה:

3 for I was envious of the revelers;
I saw the well-being of the wicked,

כִּי אֵין חַרְצֻבּוֹת לְמוֹתָם
וּבָרִיא אוּלָם:

4 how they were free of death's torments
with their sound, healthy forms,

בַּעֲמַל אֱנוֹשׁ אֵינֵמוֹ
וְעִם־אָדָם לֹא יְנֻגָּעוּ:

5 with no part in human misery,
not suffering like other people.

לָכֵן עֲנָקַתְמוֹ גַאֲוָה
יַעֲטָף־שִׁית חָמָס לָמוֹ:

6 Therefore they wear arrogance
like a necklace
and drape themselves in violence;

יָצָא מֵחֵלֶב עֵינֵמוֹ
עָבְרוּ מַשְׂכִּיּוֹת לֵבָב:

7 their eyes bulge out;
their hearts overflow with fancies.

יָמִיקוּ ׀ וִידַבְּרוּ בְרָע עֹשֶׁק
מִמָּרוֹם יְדַבֵּרוּ:

8 They mock and speak with malice;
from on high they plan oppression.

שַׁתּוּ בַשָּׁמַיִם פִּיהֶם
וּלְשׁוֹנָם תִּהֲלַךְ בָּאָרֶץ:

9 Their lips are aimed against the heavens;
their tongues prowl over the earth.

ישׁיב
לָכֵן ׀ יָשׁוּב עַמּוֹ הֲלֹם
וּמֵי מָלֵא יִמָּצוּ לָמוֹ:

10 Thus His people are drawn back to them,
and they lap up their words.

וְאָמְרוּ אֵיכָה יָדַע־אֵל
וְיֵשׁ דֵּעָה בְעֶלְיוֹן:

11 They say, "How could God know?
What knowledge has the Most High?"

הִנֵּה־אֵלֶּה רְשָׁעִים
וְשַׁלְוֵי עוֹלָם הִשְׂגּוּ־חָיִל:

12 Look at these wicked people–
always at ease, amassing wealth.

אַךְ־רִיק זִכִּיתִי לְבָבִי
וָאֶרְחַץ בְּנִקָּיוֹן כַּפָּי:

13 All in vain have I kept my heart pure
and washed my hands in innocence –

וָאֱהִי נָגוּעַ כָּל־הַיּוֹם
וְתוֹכַחְתִּי לַבְּקָרִים:

14 when all day long I suffer from pain,
tormented each morning anew.

אִם־אָמַרְתִּי אֲסַפְּרָה כְמוֹ
הִנֵּה דוֹר בָּנֶיךָ בָגָדְתִּי:

15 Were I to speak out in this way,
I would betray the circle of Your children.

וָאֲחַשְּׁבָה לָדַעַת זֹאת
עָמָל הוּא בְעֵינָי:

היא

16 When I tried to understand this,
it made me miserable

עַד־אָבוֹא אֶל־מִקְדְּשֵׁי־אֵל
אָבִינָה לְאַחֲרִיתָם:

17 until I came to God's Sanctuary
and realized what their end would be.

אַךְ בַּחֲלָקוֹת תָּשִׁית לָמוֹ
הִפַּלְתָּם לְמַשּׁוּאוֹת:

18 You set them on a slippery path
and plunge them into devastation;

אֵיךְ הָיוּ לְשַׁמָּה כְרָגַע
סָפוּ תַמּוּ מִן־בַּלָּהוֹת:

19 how they suddenly come to ruin,
swept away by utter terror,

כַּחֲלוֹם מֵהָקִיץ
אֲדֹנָי בָּעִיר צַלְמָם תִּבְזֶה:

20 like a dream upon waking, O Lord.
Upon rising You despise their image.

כִּי יִתְחַמֵּץ לְבָבִי
וְכִלְיוֹתַי אֶשְׁתּוֹנָן:

21 When my heart was sour and my
conscience pricked,

וַאֲנִי־בַעַר וְלֹא אֵדַע
בְּהֵמוֹת הָיִיתִי עִמָּךְ:

22 I was stupid and ignorant –
like a brute beast before You.

וַאֲנִי תָמִיד עִמָּךְ
אָחַזְתָּ בְּיַד־יְמִינִי:

23 Yet I am always with You;
You hold my right hand.

בַּעֲצָתְךָ תַנְחֵנִי
וְאַחַר כָּבוֹד תִּקָּחֵנִי:

24 You guide me with Your counsel;
You take me toward glory.

מִי־לִי בַשָּׁמָיִם
וְעִמְּךָ לֹא־חָפַצְתִּי בָאָרֶץ:

25 Whom else do I have in heaven?
With You, I desire nothing else on earth.

כָּלָה שְׁאֵרִי וּלְבָבִי
צוּר־לְבָבִי וְחֶלְקִי אֱלֹהִים
לְעוֹלָם:

26 Though my flesh and heart waste away,
God is the rock of my heart
and my portion forever,

כִּי־הִנֵּה רְחֵקֶיךָ יֹאבֵדוּ
הִצְמַתָּה כָּל־זוֹנֶה מִמֶּךָּ:

27 for look – those far from You are lost;
You destroy all those who stray from You,

וַאֲנִי ׀ קִרְבַת אֱלֹהִים לִי טוֹב
שַׁתִּי ׀ בַּאדֹנָי יֱהֹוִה מַחְסִי
לְסַפֵּר כָּל־מַלְאֲכוֹתֶיךָ:

28 but as for me,
God's closeness is good for me.
I have made the Lord God my refuge,
to tell of all Your works.

Mount Zion where You dwell

The enemy's every tactic works for him. Nothing works for me.
It was once very different. I could do no wrong.
You were on my side then. Come back! Please, come back.

PSALM 74

מַשְׂכִּיל לְאָסָף
לָמָה אֱלֹהִים זָנַחְתָּ לָנֶצַח
יֶעְשַׁן אַפְּךָ בְּצֹאן מַרְעִיתֶךָ׃

1 A *maskil* of Asaf
Why, God, have You forsaken us forever?
Your wrath smolders
against the flock You tend.

זְכֹר עֲדָתְךָ ׀ קָנִיתָ קֶּדֶם
גָּאַלְתָּ שֵׁבֶט נַחֲלָתֶךָ
הַר־צִיּוֹן זֶה ׀ שָׁכַנְתָּ בּוֹ׃

2 Remember the congregation
You made Yours long ago,
the tribe You redeemed as Your share,
Mount Zion where You dwell.

הָרִימָה פְעָמֶיךָ לְמַשֻּׁאוֹת נֶצַח
כָּל־הֵרַע אוֹיֵב בַּקֹּדֶשׁ׃

3 Rush over to the endless devastation,
all the evil the enemy has wrought
in the Sanctuary.

שָׁאֲגוּ צֹרְרֶיךָ בְּקֶרֶב מוֹעֲדֶךָ
שָׂמוּ אוֹתֹתָם אֹתוֹת׃

4 Your foes roared out
in Your meeting place,
displaying their own signs as signs.

יִוָּדַע כְּמֵבִיא לְמָעְלָה
בִּסֲבָךְ־עֵץ קַרְדֻּמּוֹת׃

5 They are renowned as wielders of axes
against the tangled branches of trees,

וְעֵת פִּתּוּחֶיהָ יָּחַד
בְּכַשִּׁיל וְכֵילַפּוֹת יַהֲלֹמוּן׃

6 then they smashed all its carvings
with pick and hatchet;

שִׁלְחוּ בָאֵשׁ מִקְדָּשֶׁךָ
לָאָרֶץ חִלְּלוּ מִשְׁכַּן־שְׁמֶךָ׃

7 they burned Your Sanctuary
down to the ground;
they desecrated Your name's dwelling
place.

אָמְרוּ בְלִבָּם נִינָם יָחַד
שָׂרְפוּ כָל־מוֹעֲדֵי־אֵל בָּאָרֶץ׃

8 They said in their hearts,
"We will crush them completely,"
and burned all God's meeting places
in the land.

אוֹתֹתֵינוּ לֹא־רָאִינוּ
אֵין־עוֹד נָבִיא וְלֹא־אִתָּנוּ
יֹדֵעַ עַד־מָה׃

9 No signs appear for us,
no prophets are left,
and none of us know for how long.

עַד־מָתַי אֱלֹהִים יְחָרֶף צָר
יְנָאֵץ אוֹיֵב שִׁמְךָ לָנֶצַח׃

10 For how long, God,
will the foe blaspheme?
Will the enemy revile Your name forever?

חוקך

לָמָּה תָשִׁיב יָדְךָ וִימִינֶךָ
מִקֶּרֶב חֵיקְךָ כַלֵּה:

11 Why do You hold back Your right hand?
Thrust it out from Your bosom!

וֵאלֹהִים מַלְכִּי מִקֶּדֶם
פֹּעֵל יְשׁוּעוֹת בְּקֶרֶב הָאָרֶץ:

12 Yet You, God, are my King of old,
bringing salvation throughout the land.

אַתָּה פוֹרַרְתָּ בְעָזְּךָ יָם
שִׁבַּרְתָּ רָאשֵׁי תַנִּינִים
עַל־הַמָּיִם:

13 In Your might You tore the sea to shreds
and smashed the heads of sea-monsters
on the waters.

אַתָּה רִצַּצְתָּ רָאשֵׁי לִוְיָתָן
תִּתְּנֶנּוּ מַאֲכָל לְעָם לְצִיִּים:

14 You shattered the head of Leviathan
and fed him to the desert-peoples.

אַתָּה בָקַעְתָּ מַעְיָן וָנָחַל
אַתָּה הוֹבַשְׁתָּ נַהֲרוֹת אֵיתָן:

15 You split open spring and stream;
You dried up surging rivers.

לְךָ יוֹם אַף־לְךָ לָיְלָה
אַתָּה הֲכִינוֹתָ מָאוֹר וָשָׁמֶשׁ:

16 Yours is the day; Yours, too, is the night;
You fashioned luminary and sun.

אַתָּה הִצַּבְתָּ כָּל־גְּבוּלוֹת אָרֶץ
קַיִץ וָחֹרֶף אַתָּה יְצַרְתָּם:

17 You set all the boundaries of the earth;
summer and winter – You made them.

זְכָר־זֹאת אוֹיֵב חֵרֵף ׀ יְהוָה
וְעַם־נָבָל נִאֲצוּ שְׁמֶךָ:

18 Remember this, Lord,
when the enemy taunts,
when a brutish people revile Your name.

אַל־תִּתֵּן לְחַיַּת נֶפֶשׁ תּוֹרֶךָ
חַיַּת עֲנִיֶּיךָ אַל־תִּשְׁכַּח לָנֶצַח:

19 Do not give up Your dove
to the wild beasts
or forget Your lowly flock forever.

הַבֵּט לַבְּרִית
כִּי־מָלְאוּ מַחֲשַׁכֵּי־אֶרֶץ
נְאוֹת חָמָס:

20 Look to the covenant –
for the land's dark crevasses
are haunted with violence.

אַל־יָשֹׁב דַּךְ נִכְלָם
עָנִי וְאֶבְיוֹן יְהַלְלוּ שְׁמֶךָ:

21 Do not let the downtrodden
turn away in disgrace;
let the lowly and needy praise Your name.

קוּמָה אֱלֹהִים רִיבָה רִיבֶךָ
זְכֹר חֶרְפָּתְךָ מִנִּי־נָבָל
כָּל־הַיּוֹם:

22 Arise, O God! Defend Your cause;
remember how brutes taunt You
all day long.

אַל־תִּשְׁכַּח קוֹל צֹרְרֶיךָ
שְׁאוֹן קָמֶיךָ עֹלֶה תָמִיד:

23 Do not forget the voice of Your foes,
the ever-rising din of those against You.

I will hack off all the horns of the wicked, while the horns of the righteous

will be raised up

There are times when God considers destroying the world.
One such time was in the days of Noaḥ.
Another such time was at Mount Sinai. No one wanted the Torah;
it was just too cumbersome. God was ready to return the world
to its primeval chaos. The Jewish people accepted the Torah,
willingly and eagerly. I still hold its pillars firm.
And so the world still stands.

PSALM 75

לַמְנַצֵּחַ אַל־תַּשְׁחֵת
מִזְמוֹר לְאָסָף שִׁיר:

1 To the lead singer, *al tashḥet* –
a psalm of Asaf, a song

הוֹדִינוּ לְךָ ׀ אֱלֹהִים
הוֹדִינוּ וְקָרוֹב שְׁמֶךָ
סִפְּרוּ נִפְלְאוֹתֶיךָ:

2 We praise You, God; we praise You,
and Your name is near.
They tell of Your wonders.

כִּי אֶקַּח מוֹעֵד
אֲנִי מֵישָׁרִים אֶשְׁפֹּט:

3 "At the appointed time I set,
I will judge with equity.

נְמֹגִים אֶרֶץ וְכָל־יֹשְׁבֶיהָ
אָנֹכִי תִכַּנְתִּי עַמּוּדֶיהָ סֶּלָה:

4 When the earth and all its dwellers
dissolve,
It is I who hold its pillars firm" – Selah.

אָמַרְתִּי לַהוֹלְלִים אַל־תָּהֹלּוּ
וְלָרְשָׁעִים אַל־תָּרִימוּ קָרֶן:

5 I warn the brazen, "Do not be brazen,"
and the wicked,
"Do not raise your horn –

אַל־תָּרִימוּ לַמָּרוֹם קַרְנְכֶם
תְּדַבְּרוּ בְּצַוָּאר עָתָק:

6 do not raise your horn up high,
preening with a haughty neck,"

כִּי לֹא מִמּוֹצָא וּמִמַּעֲרָב
וְלֹא מִמִּדְבַּר הָרִים:

7 for neither from the east
nor from the west
nor from the wilderness
is anyone raised up.

כִּי־אֱלֹהִים שֹׁפֵט
זֶה יַשְׁפִּיל וְזֶה יָרִים:

8 God alone is the Judge;
it is He who brings down or raises up,

כִּי כוֹס בְּיַד־יהוה
וְיַיִן חָמַר ׀ מָלֵא מֶסֶךְ
וַיַּגֵּר מִזֶּה
אַךְ־שְׁמָרֶיהָ יִמְצוּ יִשְׁתּוּ
כֹּל רִשְׁעֵי־אָרֶץ:

9 for in the Lᴏʀᴅ's hand there is a cup
of foaming wine, laced and brimming;
from this He will pour,
and all the wicked of the earth will drink
and drain it to its very dregs.

וַאֲנִי אַגִּיד לְעֹלָם
אֲזַמְּרָה לֵאלֹהֵי יַעֲקֹב:

10 As for me, I will declare it forever;
I will sing praises to the God of Yaakov.

11 וְכָל־קַרְנֵי רְשָׁעִים אֲגַדֵּעַ
תְּרוֹמַ֫מְנָה קַרְנ֥וֹת צַדִּֽיק:

11 "I will hack off all the horns
of the wicked,
while the horns of the righteous
will be raised up."

His tent is set in Salem, His abode in Zion

What propels man to compose music? Victory motivates him. It matters not whether he triumphs over an enemy from without, or vanquishes the enemy within. Either way, melody ensues.

PSALM 76

לַמְנַצֵּחַ בִּנְגִינֹת	1	To the lead singer,
מִזְמוֹר לְאָסָף שִׁיר׃		accompanied by music–
		a psalm of Asaf, a song
נוֹדָע בִּיהוּדָה אֱלֹהִים	2	God is renowned in Yehuda;
בְּיִשְׂרָאֵל גָּדוֹל שְׁמוֹ׃		in Israel His name is great;
וַיְהִי בְשָׁלֵם סוּכּוֹ	3	His tent is set in Salem,
וּמְעוֹנָתוֹ בְצִיּוֹן׃		His abode in Zion.
שָׁמָּה שִׁבַּר רִשְׁפֵי־קָשֶׁת	4	There He shattered the bow's fiery shafts,
מָגֵן וְחֶרֶב וּמִלְחָמָה סֶלָה׃		the shield and sword
		and weapons of war – Selah.
נָאוֹר אַתָּה	5	Dazzling You were,
אַדִּיר מֵהַרְרֵי־טָרֶף׃		mightier than the mountains of prey.
אֶשְׁתּוֹלְלוּ ׀ אַבִּירֵי לֵב	6	The fiercest of heart were plundered,
נָמוּ שְׁנָתָם		lulled into a trance;
וְלֹא־מָצְאוּ כָל־אַנְשֵׁי־חַיִל		the most powerful of warriors
יְדֵיהֶם׃		could not lift their hands.
מִגַּעֲרָתְךָ אֱלֹהֵי יַעֲקֹב	7	At Your onslaught, God of Yaakov,
נִרְדָּם וְרֶכֶב וָסוּס׃		horse and chariot were stunned.
אַתָּה ׀ נוֹרָא אַתָּה	8	You – O You are fearsome.
וּמִי־יַעֲמֹד לְפָנֶיךָ מֵאָז אַפֶּךָ׃		Who can stand before You
		once Your anger is roused?
מִשָּׁמַיִם הִשְׁמַעְתָּ דִּין	9	From the heavens
אֶרֶץ יָרְאָה וְשָׁקָטָה׃		You sounded Your decree;
		the earth was stilled with fright
בְּקוּם־לַמִּשְׁפָּט אֱלֹהִים	10	when God arose for judgment
לְהוֹשִׁיעַ כָּל־עַנְוֵי־אֶרֶץ סֶלָה׃		to save all the lowly of the earth – Selah.
כִּי־חֲמַת אָדָם תּוֹדֶךָּ	11	Human fury serves only to praise You
שְׁאֵרִית חֵמֹת תַּחְגֹּר׃		when You gird the last of Your fury.

נִדְרוּ וְשַׁלְּמוּ֮ לַיהֹוָ֪ה אֱלֹ֫הֵיכֶ֥ם
כׇּל־סְבִיבָ֑יו יֹבִ֥ילוּ שַׁ֝֗י לַמּוֹרָֽא׃

12 Make vows and fulfill them to the LORD
your God;
all around Him will bring tribute
to the Fearsome One.

יִבְצֹ֭ר ר֣וּחַ נְגִידִ֑ים
נ֝וֹרָ֗א לְמַלְכֵי־אָֽרֶץ׃

13 He humbles the spirits of princes;
He strikes fear in the kings of the earth.

God, Your way is holy. What god is as great as our God?

Despair is crippling. It paralyzes us. It feels total, "no exit."
We have options. We must be strong enough to remember them.
But we are too feeble to hope. We no longer know who we are.
And we have forgotten how to pray.

PSALM 77

יְדִיתוּן

לַמְנַצֵּחַ עַל־יְדוּתוּן
לְאָסָף מִזְמוֹר׃

קוֹלִי אֶל־אֱלֹהִים וְאֶצְעָקָה
קוֹלִי אֶל־אֱלֹהִים וְהַאֲזִין
אֵלָי׃

בְּיוֹם צָרָתִי אֲדֹנָי דָּרָשְׁתִּי
יָדִי ׀ לַיְלָה נִגְּרָה וְלֹא תָפוּג
מֵאֲנָה הִנָּחֵם נַפְשִׁי׃

אֶזְכְּרָה אֱלֹהִים וְאֶהֱמָיָה
אָשִׂיחָה ׀ וְתִתְעַטֵּף רוּחִי
סֶלָה׃

אָחַזְתָּ שְׁמֻרוֹת עֵינָי
נִפְעַמְתִּי וְלֹא אֲדַבֵּר׃

חִשַּׁבְתִּי יָמִים מִקֶּדֶם
שְׁנוֹת עוֹלָמִים׃

אֶזְכְּרָה נְגִינָתִי בַּלָּיְלָה
עִם־לְבָבִי אָשִׂיחָה
וַיְחַפֵּשׂ רוּחִי׃

הַלְעוֹלָמִים יִזְנַח ׀ אֲדֹנָי
וְלֹא־יֹסִיף לִרְצוֹת עוֹד׃

הֶאָפֵס לָנֶצַח חַסְדּוֹ
גָּמַר אֹמֶר לְדֹר וָדֹר׃

הֲשָׁכַח חַנּוֹת אֵל
אִם־קָפַץ בְּאַף רַחֲמָיו סֶלָה׃

וָאֹמַר חַלּוֹתִי הִיא
שְׁנוֹת יְמִין עֶלְיוֹן׃

1 To the lead singer, for *Yedutun* –
a psalm of Asaf

2 My voice cries out to God –
my voice to God that He might hear me.

3 On the day of my distress I seek the
Lord;
at night my hand reaches out unceasingly;
my soul refuses to be comforted.

4 I call God to mind and sigh in longing;
I reflect, and my spirit grows faint –
Selah.

5 You hold my eyelids open;
I am anguished and cannot speak.

6 I think about the olden days,
the years long gone.

7 I recall my contemplation by night –
I reflect within my heart;
I search within my soul.

8 Will the Lord forsake us forever
and never again show favor?

9 Is His loyalty gone forever,
His promise ended for all generations?

10 Has God forgotten to show grace
and in His wrath, curbed His
compassion? – Selah.

11 And I said, "I am grieved
that the Most High's right hand
has changed."

אזכיר	אֶזְכּ֤וֹר מַֽעַלְלֵי־יָ֑הּ 12
	כִּֽי־אֶזְכְּרָ֖ה מִקֶּ֣דֶם פִּלְאֶֽךָ׃

12 I will call to mind the LORD's acts;
    I will recall Your wonders of old.

וְהָגִ֥יתִי בְכָל־פָּעֳלֶ֑ךָ 13
וּֽבַעֲלִילוֹתֶ֥יךָ אָשִֽׂיחָה׃

13 I will contemplate all Your works
    and reflect upon Your acts.

אֱ֭לֹהִים בַּקֹּ֣דֶשׁ דַּרְכֶּ֑ךָ 14
מִי־אֵ֥ל גָּ֝ד֗וֹל כֵּֽאלֹהִֽים׃

14 God, Your way is holy.
    What god is as great as our God?

אַתָּ֣ה הָ֭אֵל עֹ֣שֵׂה פֶ֑לֶא 15
הוֹדַ֖עְתָּ בָעַמִּ֣ים עֻזֶּֽךָ׃

15 You are the God who performs wonders;
    You show Your might to the nations.

גָּאַ֣לְתָּ בִּזְר֣וֹעַ עַמֶּ֑ךָ 16
בְּנֵי־יַעֲקֹ֖ב וְיוֹסֵ֣ף סֶֽלָה׃

16 You redeemed Your people
    with Your own arm,
    the children of Yaakov and Yosef – Selah.

רָ֘א֤וּךָ מַּ֨יִם ׀ אֱֽלֹהִ֗ים 17
רָא֣וּךָ מַּ֣יִם יָחִ֑ילוּ
אַ֝֗ף יִרְגְּז֥וּ תְהֹמֽוֹת׃

17 When the waters saw You, God,
    when the waters saw You, they shivered;
    the very depths shuddered.

זֹ֤רְמוּ מַ֨יִם ׀ עָב֗וֹת 18
ק֭וֹל נָתְנ֣וּ שְׁחָקִ֑ים
אַף־חֲ֝צָצֶ֗יךָ יִתְהַלָּֽכוּ׃

18 The clouds streamed with water;
    the skies sounded with thunder;
    Your bolts, too, flashed.

ק֤וֹל רַעַמְךָ֙ ׀ בַּגַּלְגַּ֗ל 19
הֵאִ֣ירוּ בְרָקִ֣ים תֵּבֵ֑ל
רָגְזָ֖ה וַתִּרְעַ֣שׁ הָאָֽרֶץ׃

19 The sound of Your thunder
    rattled like wheels;
    lightning lit up the world;
    the earth trembled and shook.

ושבילך	בַּיָּ֤ם דַּרְכֶּ֗ךָ 20
	וּֽשְׁבִ֣ילְךָ בְּמַ֣יִם רַבִּ֑ים
	וְ֝עִקְּבוֹתֶ֗יךָ לֹ֣א נֹדָֽעוּ׃

20 You made Your way through the sea,
    Your path through the mighty waters,
    and Your footsteps left no trace.

נָחִ֣יתָ כַצֹּ֣אן עַמֶּ֑ךָ 21
בְּֽיַד־מֹשֶׁ֥ה וְאַהֲרֹֽן׃

21 You led Your people like a flock
    by the hands of Moshe and Aharon.

He guided them with cloud by day, with firelight all through the night

Is He the riddle, or are we?
Which of us is the greater mystery?
Our stubborn ingratitude is our mystery.
Forgiveness is His.

PSALM 78

מַשְׂכִּיל לְאָסָף
הַאֲזִינָה עַמִּי תּוֹרָתִי
הַטּוּ אָזְנְכֶם לְאִמְרֵי־פִי׃

1 A *maskil* of Asaf
Hear my teaching, O my people;
lend Your ear to what I say.

אֶפְתְּחָה בְמָשָׁל פִּי
אַבִּיעָה חִידוֹת מִנִּי־קֶדֶם׃

2 I will open my mouth with a metaphor,
I will disclose an ancient mystery –

אֲשֶׁר שָׁמַעְנוּ וַנֵּדָעֵם
וַאֲבוֹתֵינוּ סִפְּרוּ־לָנוּ׃

3 what we have heard, what we know,
and what our ancestors have told us

לֹא נְכַחֵד ׀ מִבְּנֵיהֶם
לְדוֹר אַחֲרוֹן מְסַפְּרִים
תְּהִלּוֹת יהוה
וֶעֱזוּזוֹ וְנִפְלְאֹתָיו אֲשֶׁר עָשָׂה׃

4 we will not hide from their children;
to the next generation
we will sing the Lord's praises
and the mighty deeds and wonders
He has done.

וַיָּקֶם עֵדוּת ׀ בְּיַעֲקֹב
וְתוֹרָה שָׂם בְּיִשְׂרָאֵל
אֲשֶׁר צִוָּה אֶת־אֲבוֹתֵינוּ
לְהוֹדִיעָם לִבְנֵיהֶם׃

5 He established a decree in Yaakov
and founded the teaching in Israel,
charging our ancestors
to teach it to their children

לְמַעַן יֵדְעוּ ׀ דּוֹר אַחֲרוֹן
בָּנִים יִוָּלֵדוּ
יָקֻמוּ וִיסַפְּרוּ לִבְנֵיהֶם׃

6 so that the next generation
would know it,
the children yet unborn,
and tell it, in turn, to their own children

וְיָשִׂימוּ בֵאלֹהִים כִּסְלָם
וְלֹא יִשְׁכְּחוּ מַעַלְלֵי־אֵל
וּמִצְוֺתָיו יִנְצֹרוּ׃

7 and place their trust in God
and not forget God's acts
but keep His commandments

וְלֹא יִהְיוּ ׀ כַּאֲבוֹתָם
דּוֹר סוֹרֵר וּמֹרֶה
דּוֹר לֹא־הֵכִין לִבּוֹ
וְלֹא־נֶאֶמְנָה אֶת־אֵל רוּחוֹ׃

8 instead of being like their ancestors,
a wayward, rebellious generation,
a generation not firm of heart,
its spirit unfaithful to God.

בְּנֵי־אֶפְרַיִם נוֹשְׁקֵי רוֹמֵי־קָשֶׁת
הָפְכוּ בְּיוֹם קְרָב׃

9 The men of Efrayim,
armed wielders of bows,
turned and fled on the day of battle.

לֹא שָׁמְרוּ בְּרִית אֱלֹהִים
וּבְתוֹרָתוֹ מֵאֲנוּ לָלֶכֶת:

10 They did not keep God's covenant
and refused to follow His teaching;

וַיִּשְׁכְּחוּ עֲלִילוֹתָיו
וְנִפְלְאוֹתָיו אֲשֶׁר הֶרְאָם:

11 they forgot His acts
and the wonders that He showed them;

נֶגֶד אֲבוֹתָם עָשָׂה פֶלֶא
בְּאֶרֶץ מִצְרַיִם שְׂדֵה־צֹעַן:

12 before their ancestors
He worked wonders,
in the land of Egypt,
in the fields of Tzoan:

בָּקַע יָם וַיַּעֲבִירֵם
וַיַּצֶּב־מַיִם כְּמוֹ־נֵד:

13 He split the sea and led them across
and stood the waters like a wall;

וַיַּנְחֵם בֶּעָנָן יוֹמָם
וְכָל־הַלַּיְלָה בְּאוֹר אֵשׁ:

14 He guided them with cloud by day,
with firelight all through the night;

יְבַקַּע צֻרִים בַּמִּדְבָּר
וַיַּשְׁקְ כִּתְהֹמוֹת רַבָּה:

15 He split rocks open in the wilderness
and gave them drink
as from the great deep;

וַיּוֹצִא נוֹזְלִים מִסָּלַע
וַיּוֹרֶד כַּנְּהָרוֹת מָיִם:

16 He brought out streams from stone
and made water run down like rivers.

וַיּוֹסִיפוּ עוֹד לַחֲטֹא־לוֹ
לַמְרוֹת עֶלְיוֹן בַּצִּיָּה:

17 Yet they continued to sin against Him,
to defy the Most High in the desert.

וַיְנַסּוּ־אֵל בִּלְבָבָם
לִשְׁאָל־אֹכֶל לְנַפְשָׁם:

18 They were determined to test God
by demanding food for themselves;

וַיְדַבְּרוּ בֵּאלֹהִים
אָמְרוּ הֲיוּכַל אֵל
לַעֲרֹךְ שֻׁלְחָן בַּמִּדְבָּר:

19 they spoke out against God, saying,
"Can God spread a table
in the wilderness?

הֵן הִכָּה־צוּר ׀ וַיָּזוּבוּ מַיִם
וּנְחָלִים יִשְׁטֹפוּ
הֲגַם־לֶחֶם יוּכַל תֵּת
אִם־יָכִין שְׁאֵר לְעַמּוֹ:

20 Yes, He struck a rock and water flowed
and streams gushed forth,
but can He give us bread as well?
Can He provide meat for His people?"

לָכֵן ׀ שָׁמַע יהוה וַיִּתְעַבָּר וְאֵשׁ נִשְּׂקָה בְיַעֲקֹב וְגַם־אַף עָלָה בְיִשְׂרָאֵל:	21 When the LORD heard this, He grew furious; fire flared out against Yaakov; wrath blazed against Israel,
כִּי לֹא הֶאֱמִינוּ בֵּאלֹהִים וְלֹא בָטְחוּ בִּישׁוּעָתוֹ:	22 for they did not believe in God and did not trust in His salvation,
וַיְצַו שְׁחָקִים מִמָּעַל וְדַלְתֵי שָׁמַיִם פָּתָח:	23 but He commanded the skies above and opened the doors of heaven;
וַיַּמְטֵר עֲלֵיהֶם מָן לֶאֱכֹל וּדְגַן־שָׁמַיִם נָתַן לָמוֹ:	24 He rained down manna upon them for food and gave them the grain of heaven.
לֶחֶם אַבִּירִים אָכַל אִישׁ צֵידָה שָׁלַח לָהֶם לָשֹׂבַע:	25 Each one ate a mighty feast; He sent down abundant fare for them;
יַסַּע קָדִים בַּשָּׁמָיִם וַיְנַהֵג בְּעֻזּוֹ תֵימָן:	26 He stirred up the east wind across the heavens and drove the south wind with His might
וַיַּמְטֵר עֲלֵיהֶם כֶּעָפָר שְׁאֵר וּכְחוֹל יַמִּים עוֹף כָּנָף:	27 and rained down meat on them like dust, winged fowl like ocean sand;
וַיַּפֵּל בְּקֶרֶב מַחֲנֵהוּ סָבִיב לְמִשְׁכְּנֹתָיו:	28 He made them fall inside His camp, all around His dwelling place,
וַיֹּאכְלוּ וַיִּשְׂבְּעוּ מְאֹד וְתַאֲוָתָם יָבִא לָהֶם:	29 so they ate and ate their fill; He brought them what they craved,
לֹא־זָרוּ מִתַּאֲוָתָם עוֹד אָכְלָם בְּפִיהֶם:	30 but before they tired of their cravings, while their food still filled their mouths,
וְאַף אֱלֹהִים ׀ עָלָה בָהֶם וַיַּהֲרֹג בְּמִשְׁמַנֵּיהֶם וּבַחוּרֵי יִשְׂרָאֵל הִכְרִיעַ:	31 God's wrath flared up against them. He killed the strongest ones among them; He brought down the young men of Israel.

בְּכָל־זֹאת חָטְאוּ־עֹ֑וד 32 Despite all this they went on sinning
וְלֹא הֶ֝אֱמִ֗ינוּ בְּנִפְלְאוֹתָֽיו׃ and did not believe in His wonders,

וַיְכַל־בַּהֶ֥בֶל יְמֵיהֶ֑ם 33 so He wasted their days like breath
וּ֝שְׁנוֹתָ֗ם בַּבֶּהָלָֽה׃ and their years in dismay.

אִם־הֲרָגָ֥ם וּדְרָשׁ֑וּהוּ 34 When He killed them,
וְ֝שָׁ֗בוּ וְשִֽׁחֲרוּ־אֵֽל׃ they sought Him out;
they came back
and desperately sought God.

וַֽ֭יִּזְכְּרוּ כִּֽי־אֱלֹהִ֣ים צוּרָ֑ם 35 They remembered that God
וְאֵ֥ל עֶ֝לְיֹ֗ון גֹּאֲלָֽם׃ was their rock,
God Most High their redeemer,

וַיְפַתּ֥וּהוּ בְּפִיהֶ֑ם 36 but they betrayed Him with their lips,
וּ֝בִלְשׁוֹנָ֗ם יְכַזְּבוּ־לֹֽו׃ and with their tongues they lied to Him;

וְ֭לִבָּם לֹא־נָכ֣וֹן עִמֹּ֑ו 37 their hearts were not firmly with Him;
וְלֹ֥א נֶ֝אֶמְנ֗וּ בִּבְרִיתֹֽו׃ they were not faithful to His covenant,

וְה֤וּא רַח֨וּם ׀ 38 but He is merciful;
יְכַפֵּ֥ר עָ֘וֹ֤ן וְֽלֹא־יַשְׁחִ֗ית He forgives offense and does not destroy.
וְ֭הִרְבָּה לְהָשִׁ֣יב אַפֹּ֑ו He suppresses His anger again and again
וְלֹֽא־יָ֝עִיר כָּל־חֲמָתֹֽו׃ and never rouses His full fury.

וַ֭יִּזְכֹּר כִּי־בָשָׂ֣ר הֵ֑מָּה 39 He remembers that they are but flesh,
ר֥וּחַ ה֝וֹלֵ֗ךְ וְלֹ֣א יָשֽׁוּב׃ a passing breath that never returns.

כַּ֭מָּה יַמְר֣וּהוּ בַמִּדְבָּ֑ר 40 How often they defied Him
יַ֝עֲצִיב֗וּהוּ בִּֽישִׁימֹֽון׃ in the wilderness,
aggrieving Him in the wasteland;

וַיָּשׁ֣וּבוּ וַיְנַסּ֣וּ אֵ֑ל 41 they tested God again and again,
וּקְדֹ֖ושׁ יִשְׂרָאֵ֣ל הִתְוֽוּ׃ provoking the Holy One of Israel.

לֹא־זָכְר֥וּ אֶת־יָדֹ֑ו 42 They did not recall His power
יֹ֝֗ום אֲֽשֶׁר־פָּדָ֥ם מִנִּי־צָֽר׃ on the day He redeemed them
from the foe,

אֲשֶׁר־שָׂ֣ם בְּמִצְרַ֣יִם אֹתוֹתָ֑יו
וּמ֝וֹפְתָ֗יו בִּשְׂדֵה־צֹֽעַן׃

43 when He set out His signs in Egypt
and His wonders in the fields of Tzoan.

וַיַּהֲפֹ֣ךְ לְ֭דָם יְאֹרֵיהֶ֑ם
וְ֝נֹזְלֵיהֶ֗ם בַּל־יִשְׁתָּיֽוּן׃

44 He turned their rivers to blood,
their streams undrinkable;

יְשַׁלַּ֬ח בָּהֶ֣ם עָ֭רֹב וַיֹּאכְלֵ֑ם
וּ֝צְפַרְדֵּ֗עַ וַתַּשְׁחִיתֵֽם׃

45 He unleashed swarms to consume them
and frogs to destroy them;

וַיִּתֵּ֣ן לֶחָסִ֣יל יְבוּלָ֑ם
וִ֝יגִיעָ֗ם לָאַרְבֶּֽה׃

46 He gave their crops to blight,
their produce to the locust;

יַהֲרֹ֣ג בַּבָּרָ֣ד גַּפְנָ֑ם
וְ֝שִׁקְמוֹתָ֗ם בַּֽחֲנָמַֽל׃

47 He killed their vines with hail,
their sycamores with frost;

וַיַּסְגֵּ֣ר לַבָּרָ֣ד בְּעִירָ֑ם
וּ֝מִקְנֵיהֶ֗ם לָרְשָׁפִֽים׃

48 He abandoned their livestock to the hail,
their cattle to bolts of lightning;

יְשַׁלַּח־בָּ֨ם ׀ חֲר֬וֹן אַפּ֗וֹ
עֶבְרָ֣ה וָזַ֣עַם וְצָרָ֑ה
מִ֝שְׁלַ֗חַת מַלְאֲכֵ֥י רָעִֽים׃

49 He unleashed against them
His blazing fury,
wrath, rage, and misery,
a legion of destroying angels.

יְפַלֵּ֥ס נָתִ֗יב לְאַ֫פּ֥וֹ
לֹא־חָשַׂ֣ךְ מִמָּ֣וֶת נַפְשָׁ֑ם
וְ֝חַיָּתָ֗ם לַדֶּ֥בֶר הִסְגִּֽיר׃

50 He leveled a path for His fury;
He did not spare their souls from death
but abandoned their lives to the plague.

וַיַּ֣ךְ כָּל־בְּכ֣וֹר בְּמִצְרָ֑יִם
רֵאשִׁ֥ית א֝וֹנִ֗ים בְּאָהֳלֵי־חָֽם׃

51 He struck down every firstborn in Egypt,
the first fruits of manhood
in the tents of Ham,

וַיַּסַּ֣ע כַּצֹּ֣אן עַמּ֑וֹ
וַֽיְנַהֲגֵ֥ם כַּ֝עֵ֗דֶר בַּמִּדְבָּֽר׃

52 then He led His people on like sheep,
guiding them like a flock
through the wilderness.

וַיַּנְחֵ֣ם לָ֭בֶטַח וְלֹ֣א פָחָ֑דוּ
וְאֶת־א֝וֹיְבֵיהֶ֗ם כִּסָּ֥ה הַיָּֽם׃

53 He led them in safety;
they did not fear,
while the sea covered their enemies.

<table>
<tr>
<td>וַיְבִיאֵם אֶל־גְּבוּל קָדְשׁוֹ
הַר־זֶ֗ה קָנְתָ֥ה יְמִינֽוֹ׃</td>
<td>54</td>
<td>He brought them to His holy realm,
to the mountain His right hand had won.</td>
</tr>
<tr>
<td>וַיְגָ֤רֶשׁ מִפְּנֵיהֶ֨ם ׀ גּוֹיִ֗ם
וַֽיַּפִּילֵם בְּחֶ֣בֶל נַחֲלָ֑ה
וַיַּשְׁכֵּ֥ן בְּֽאָהֳלֵיהֶ֗ם
שִׁבְטֵ֥י יִשְׂרָאֵֽל׃</td>
<td>55</td>
<td>He dispossessed nations before them,
allotted them shares of inheritance,
and settled the tribes of Israel
in their tents,</td>
</tr>
<tr>
<td>וַיְנַסּ֣וּ וַ֭יַּמְרוּ אֶת־אֱלֹהִ֣ים עֶלְי֑וֹן
וְ֝עֵדוֹתָ֗יו לֹ֣א שָׁמָֽרוּ׃</td>
<td>56</td>
<td>but they tested and defied God
Most High
and did not keep His decrees.</td>
</tr>
<tr>
<td>וַיִּסֹּ֣גוּ וַ֭יִּבְגְּדוּ כַּאֲבוֹתָ֑ם
נֶ֝הְפְּכ֗וּ כְּקֶ֣שֶׁת רְמִיָּֽה׃</td>
<td>57</td>
<td>They turned back and rebelled
like their ancestors,
treacherous as a faulty bow;</td>
</tr>
<tr>
<td>וַיַּכְעִיס֥וּהוּ בְּבָמוֹתָ֑ם
וּ֝בִפְסִילֵיהֶ֗ם יַקְנִיאֽוּהוּ׃</td>
<td>58</td>
<td>they angered Him with their high shrines
and aroused His jealousy with their idols.</td>
</tr>
<tr>
<td>שָׁמַ֣ע אֱ֭לֹהִים וַֽיִּתְעַבָּ֑ר
וַיִּמְאַ֥ס מְ֝אֹ֗ד בְּיִשְׂרָאֵֽל׃</td>
<td>59</td>
<td>God heard and grew furious
and utterly rejected Israel.</td>
</tr>
<tr>
<td>וַ֭יִּטֹּשׁ מִשְׁכַּ֣ן שִׁל֑וֹ
אֹ֝֗הֶל שִׁכֵּ֥ן בָּאָדָֽם׃</td>
<td>60</td>
<td>He abandoned the sanctuary of Shiloh,
the tent where He dwelled
among humanity.</td>
</tr>
<tr>
<td>וַיִּתֵּ֣ן לַשְּׁבִ֣י עֻזּ֑וֹ
וְֽתִפְאַרְתּ֥וֹ בְיַד־צָֽר׃</td>
<td>61</td>
<td>He let His might fall captive,
His beauty into enemy hands;</td>
</tr>
<tr>
<td>וַיַּסְגֵּ֣ר לַחֶ֣רֶב עַמּ֑וֹ
וּ֝בְנַחֲלָת֗וֹ הִתְעַבָּֽר׃</td>
<td>62</td>
<td>He abandoned His people to the sword,
so furious with His share was He.</td>
</tr>
<tr>
<td>בַּחוּרָ֥יו אָכְלָה־אֵ֑שׁ
וּ֝בְתוּלֹתָ֗יו לֹ֣א הוּלָּֽלוּ׃</td>
<td>63</td>
<td>His young men were consumed by fire;
His maidens had no wedding songs.</td>
</tr>
<tr>
<td>כֹּ֭הֲנָיו בַּחֶ֣רֶב נָפָ֑לוּ
וְ֝אַלְמְנֹתָ֗יו לֹ֣א תִבְכֶּֽינָה׃</td>
<td>64</td>
<td>His priests fell by the sword;
their widows never lamented them,</td>
</tr>
<tr>
<td>וַיִּקַ֖ץ כְּיָשֵׁ֥ן ׀ אֲדֹנָ֑י
כְּ֝גִבּ֗וֹר מִתְרוֹנֵ֥ן מִיָּֽיִן׃</td>
<td>65</td>
<td>then the LORD awoke as if from sleep,
like a warrior shaking off wine,</td>
</tr>
</table>

וַיַּךְ־צָרָיו אָחֹור 66 and beat back His foes,
חֶרְפַּת עֹולָם נָתַן לָמֹו: subjecting them to lasting shame.

וַיִּמְאַס בְּאֹהֶל יֹוסֵף 67 Yet He rejected the tent of Yosef
וּבְשֵׁבֶט אֶפְרַיִם לֹא בָחָר: and did not choose the tribe of Efrayim;

וַיִּבְחַר אֶת־שֵׁבֶט יְהוּדָה 68 He chose the tribe of Yehuda,
אֶת־הַר צִיֹּון אֲשֶׁר אָהֵב: Mount Zion that He loves.

וַיִּבֶן כְּמֹו־רָמִים מִקְדָּשֹׁו 69 He built His sanctuary
כְּאֶרֶץ יְסָדָהּ לְעֹולָם: like the high heavens,
like the earth that He founded forever,

וַיִּבְחַר בְּדָוִד עַבְדֹּו 70 and He chose David, His servant,
וַיִּקָּחֵהוּ מִמִּכְלְאֹת צֹאן: taking him from the sheepfolds.

מֵאַחַר עָלֹות הֱבִיאֹו 71 From among the ewes He brought Him
לִרְעֹות בְּיַעֲקֹב עַמֹּו to tend to Yaakov, His people,
וּבְיִשְׂרָאֵל נַחֲלָתֹו: and Israel, His share.

וַיִּרְעֵם כְּתֹם לְבָבֹו 72 He tended them with a sound heart
וּבִתְבוּנֹות כַּפָּיו יַנְחֵם: and guided them with a skillful hand.

...the nations have invaded Your heritage, defiled Your holy Temple

I met them both on the streets of Brooklyn,
when I was still in my teens. One, a refusenik, knew the dungeons
of the Communist "utopia." Now, his spirit freed,
he gaily led the circle of dancing Torahs. Let the prisoner's sighs
come before You. The other was a ghost of a man.
He was a kazetnik, resurrected from the hell of Auschwitz.
He sang soothing melodies to ease the Sabbath's departure.
With Your strong arm unchain those who stand at the brink
of death.

PSALM 79

מִזְמוֹר לְאָסָף
אֱלֹהִים בָּאוּ גוֹיִם ׀ בְּנַחֲלָתֶךָ
טִמְּאוּ אֶת־הֵיכַל קָדְשֶׁךָ
שָׂמוּ אֶת־יְרוּשָׁלַ͏ִם לְעִיִּים׃

1 A psalm of Asaf
God, the nations have invaded
Your heritage,
defiled Your holy Temple,
and turned Jerusalem into ruins.

נָתְנוּ אֶת־נִבְלַת עֲבָדֶיךָ
מַאֲכָל לְעוֹף הַשָּׁמָיִם
בְּשַׂר חֲסִידֶיךָ לְחַיְתוֹ־אָרֶץ׃

2 They have left Your servants' corpses
as food for the fowl of the heavens,
the flesh of Your devoted ones
for the beasts of the earth.

שָׁפְכוּ דָמָם ׀ כַּמַּיִם
סְבִיבוֹת יְרוּשָׁלַ͏ִם
וְאֵין קוֹבֵר׃

3 They have spilled their blood like water
all around Jerusalem,
with none to bury them.

הָיִינוּ חֶרְפָּה לִשְׁכֵנֵינוּ
לַעַג וָקֶלֶס לִסְבִיבוֹתֵינוּ׃

4 We have become the scorn of our
neighbors,
the laughingstock of those around us.

עַד־מָה יהוה תֶּאֱנַף לָנֶצַח
תִּבְעַר כְּמוֹ־אֵשׁ קִנְאָתֶךָ׃

5 How long, Lord?
Will You show Your anger forever,
Your indignation blazing like fire?

שְׁפֹךְ חֲמָתְךָ ׀ אֶל־הַגּוֹיִם
אֲשֶׁר לֹא־יְדָעוּךָ
וְעַל מַמְלָכוֹת אֲשֶׁר בְּשִׁמְךָ
לֹא קָרָאוּ׃

6 Pour out Your fury
on the nations that do not know You,
on the kingdoms that do not
invoke Your name –

כִּי אָכַל אֶת־יַעֲקֹב
וְאֶת־נָוֵהוּ הֵשַׁמּוּ׃

7 for they have devoured Yaakov
and laid his homeland waste.

אַל־תִּזְכָּר־לָנוּ עֲוֹנֹת רִאשֹׁנִים
מַהֵר יְקַדְּמוּנוּ רַחֲמֶיךָ
כִּי דַלּוֹנוּ מְאֹד׃

8 Do not hold our ancestors' sins
against us;
let Your mercy rush toward us,
for we have sunk so low.

עָזְרֵנוּ ׀ אֱלֹהֵי יִשְׁעֵנוּ
עַל־דְּבַר כְּבוֹד־שְׁמֶךָ
וְהַצִּילֵנוּ וְכַפֵּר עַל־חַטֹּאתֵינוּ
לְמַעַן שְׁמֶךָ׃

9 Help us, God of our salvation,
for Your name's glory;
deliver us and forgive our sins
for the sake of Your name.

לָמֶה ׀ יֹאמְר֪וּ הַגּוֹיִם֮
אַיֵּ֪ה אֱלֹ֫הֵיהֶ֥ם

בגיים

יִוָּדַ֣ע בַּגֹּיִ֣ם לְעֵינֵ֑ינוּ
נִ֝קְמַ֗ת דַּֽם־עֲבָדֶ֥יךָ הַשָּׁפֽוּךְ׃

10 Why should the nations say,
"Where is their God?"
Let the vengeance of Your servants'
spilled blood
be known among the nations
before our own eyes.

תָּ֤בֹ֣א לְפָנֶיךָ֮ אֶנְקַ֪ת אָ֫סִ֥יר
כְּגֹ֥דֶל זְרוֹעֲךָ֑
ה֝וֹתֵ֗ר בְּנֵ֣י תְמוּתָֽה׃

11 Let the captives' groans come before You;
with Your arm's great strength,
preserve those on the brink of death.

וְהָ֘שֵׁ֤ב לִשְׁכֵנֵ֣ינוּ שִׁ֭בְעָתַיִם
אֶל־חֵיקָ֑ם
חֶרְפָּתָ֓ם אֲשֶׁ֖ר חֵרְפ֣וּךָ אֲדֹנָֽי׃

12 Pay back our neighbors sevenfold
with the very scorn they showed You,
LORD,

וַאֲנַ֤חְנוּ עַמְּךָ֨ ׀ וְצֹ֥אן מַרְעִיתֶ֗ךָ
נ֥וֹדֶ֬ה לְּךָ֮ לְע֫וֹלָ֥ם
לְד֥וֹר וָדֹ֑ר נְ֝סַפֵּ֗ר תְּהִלָּתֶֽךָ׃

13 then we, Your people
and the flock You tend,
will give thanks to You forever;
throughout the generations
we will sing Your praise.

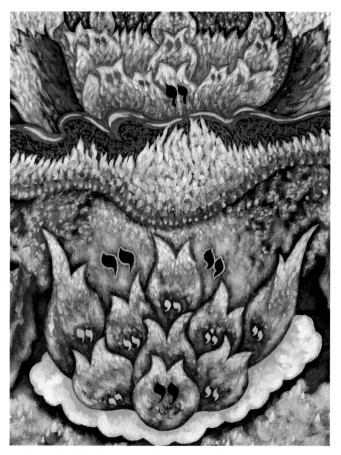

God, bring us back; let Your presence shine, that we may be saved

Where does God sit? Some consider such a question naïve,
others find it blasphemous. Our psalm knows where He sits.
He sits enthroned upon the cherubim. The cherubim face each
other in friendship and love. Where does God sit?
He sits where He can best bless lovers and friends.

PSALM 80

לַמְנַצֵּחַ אֶל־שֹׁשַׁנִּים
עֵדוּת לְאָסָף מִזְמוֹר׃

1 To the lead singer,
   set to *shoshanim edut*, a psalm of Asaf

רֹעֵה יִשְׂרָאֵל ׀ הַאֲזִינָה
נֹהֵג כַּצֹּאן יוֹסֵף
יֹשֵׁב הַכְּרוּבִים הוֹפִיעָה׃

2 Shepherd of Israel, give ear;
   You who lead Yosef like a flock,
   You who are enthroned on the cherubim,
   shine forth.

לִפְנֵי אֶפְרַיִם ׀ וּבִנְיָמִן וּמְנַשֶּׁה
עוֹרְרָה אֶת־גְּבוּרָתֶךָ
וּלְכָה לִישֻׁעָתָה לָּנוּ׃

3 Before Efrayim, Binyamin, and Menashe,
   stir Your strength
   and come to save us.

אֱלֹהִים הֲשִׁיבֵנוּ
וְהָאֵר פָּנֶיךָ וְנִוָּשֵׁעָה׃

4 God, bring us back;
   let Your presence shine,
   that we may be saved.

יְהוָה אֱלֹהִים צְבָאוֹת
עַד־מָתַי עָשַׁנְתָּ בִּתְפִלַּת עַמֶּךָ׃

5 O Lord, God of hosts,
   how long will You fume
   at Your people's prayers?

הֶאֱכַלְתָּם לֶחֶם דִּמְעָה
וַתַּשְׁקֵמוֹ בִּדְמָעוֹת שָׁלִישׁ׃

6 You have fed them tear-soaked bread
   and made them drink tears
   by the bowlful.

תְּשִׂימֵנוּ מָדוֹן לִשְׁכֵנֵינוּ
וְאֹיְבֵינוּ יִלְעֲגוּ־לָמוֹ׃

7 You have set us in strife
   with our neighbors,
   and our enemies mock us.

אֱלֹהִים צְבָאוֹת הֲשִׁיבֵנוּ
וְהָאֵר פָּנֶיךָ וְנִוָּשֵׁעָה׃

8 God of hosts, bring us back;
   let Your presence shine
   so that we may be saved.

גֶּפֶן מִמִּצְרַיִם תַּסִּיעַ
תְּגָרֵשׁ גּוֹיִם וַתִּטָּעֶהָ׃

9 You carried a vine out of Egypt;
   You drove out the nations and planted it.

פִּנִּיתָ לְפָנֶיהָ
וַתַּשְׁרֵשׁ שָׁרָשֶׁיהָ
וַתְּמַלֵּא־אָרֶץ׃

10 You cleared the ground for it;
    it took deep root and filled the land.

כָּסּוּ הָרִים צִלָּהּ
וַעֲנָפֶיהָ אַרְזֵי־אֵל׃

11 The hills were covered by its shade,
mighty cedars by its branches.

תְּשַׁלַּח קְצִירֶהָ עַד־יָם
וְאֶל־נָהָר יֽוֹנְקוֹתֶֽיהָ׃

12 Its boughs reached as far as the sea,
its shoots as far as the river.

לָמָּה פָּרַצְתָּ גְדֵרֶיהָ
וְאָרֽוּהָ כָּל־עֹֽבְרֵי דָֽרֶךְ׃

13 Why have You broken through its walls
so that any passerby can pluck its fruit?

יְכַרְסְמֶנָּה חֲזִיר מִיָּעַר
וְזִיז שָׂדַי יִרְעֶֽנָּה׃

14 The wild forest boars gnaw at it;
the field creatures graze at it.

אֱלֹהִים צְבָאוֹת שֽׁוּב נָא
הַבֵּט מִשָּׁמַיִם וּרְאֵה
וּפְקֹד גֶּפֶן זֹֽאת׃

15 God of hosts, come back;
Look down from heaven and see;
take note of this vine,

וְכַנָּה אֲשֶׁר־נָֽטְעָה יְמִינֶךָ
וְעַל־בֵּן אִמַּצְתָּה לָּֽךְ׃

16 this seedling Your right hand planted,
this shoot You nurtured as Your own –

שְׂרֻפָה בָאֵשׁ כְּסוּחָה
מִגַּעֲרַת פָּנֶיךָ יֹאבֵֽדוּ׃

17 now burnt by fire, chopped down,
destroyed by the blast of Your presence.

תְּהִי־יָֽדְךָ עַל־אִישׁ יְמִינֶךָ
עַל־בֶּן־אָדָם אִמַּצְתָּ לָּֽךְ׃

18 Let Your hand rest on the person
at Your right hand,
the person You nurtured as Your own,

וְלֹא־נָסוֹג מִמֶּֽךָּ
תְּחַיֵּֽנוּ וּבְשִׁמְךָ נִקְרָֽא׃

19 then we will not turn away from You.
Give us life,
and we will invoke Your name.

יהוה אֱלֹהִים צְבָאוֹת הֲשִׁיבֵֽנוּ
הָאֵר פָּנֶיךָ וְנִוָּשֵֽׁעָה׃

20 LORD, God of hosts, bring us back;
let Your presence shine
so that we may be saved.

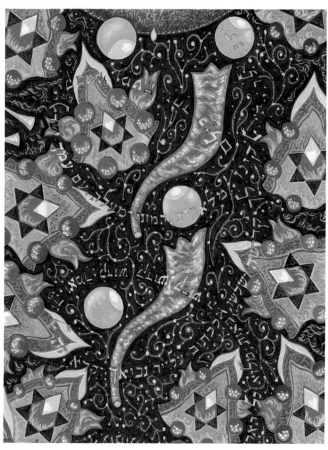

Sound the shofar on the New Moon, on our feast day when the moon is full

I quiver with pangs of guilt, fearful of judgment.
I pluck the strings of the harp and the lyre with joyous abandon.
I shudder at the shofar's demand that I repent. Yet it relieves me of
my sins. Am I hopelessly confused? No. It is Rosh HaShana,
a day of paradox. In spite of God's sure knowledge
that I will sin again, He forgives me, and assures me,
"I'll feed you honey from the rock."

PSALM 81

לַמְנַצֵּ֥חַ ׀ עַל־הַגִּתִּ֗ית לְאָסָֽף׃	1 To the lead singer, on the *gittit* – of Asaf
הַרְנִ֭ינוּ לֵאלֹהִ֣ים עוּזֵּ֑נוּ הָ֝רִ֗יעוּ לֵאלֹהֵ֥י יַעֲקֹֽב׃	2 Sing for joy to God, our might; shout out to the God of Yaakov.
שְׂאוּ־זִ֭מְרָה וּתְנוּ־תֹ֑ף כִּנּ֖וֹר נָעִ֣ים עִם־נָֽבֶל׃	3 Raise a song, beat the drum, and play the sweet harp and lyre.
תִּקְע֣וּ בַחֹ֣דֶשׁ שׁוֹפָ֑ר בַּ֝כֵּ֗סֶה לְי֣וֹם חַגֵּֽנוּ׃	4 Sound the shofar on the New Moon, on our feast day when the moon is full,
כִּ֤י חֹ֣ק לְיִשְׂרָאֵ֣ל ה֑וּא מִ֝שְׁפָּ֗ט לֵאלֹהֵ֥י יַעֲקֹֽב׃	5 for it is a statute for Israel, an ordinance of the God of Yaakov.
עֵד֤וּת ׀ בִּיה�‏וֹסֵ֣ף שָׂמ֗וֹ בְּ֭צֵאתוֹ עַל־אֶ֣רֶץ מִצְרָ֑יִם שְׂפַ֖ת לֹא־יָדַ֣עְתִּי אֶשְׁמָֽע׃	6 He established it as a decree for Yosef when He rose against the land of Egypt, where I heard a language that I did not know.
הֲסִיר֣וֹתִי מִסֵּ֣בֶל שִׁכְמ֑וֹ כַּ֝פָּ֗יו מִדּ֥וּד תַּעֲבֹֽרְנָה׃	7 I relieved his shoulders of the burden; his hands were freed from the builder's basket.
בַּצָּרָ֥ה קָרָ֗אתָ וָאֲחַ֫לְּצֶ֥ךָּ אֶ֭עֶנְךָ בְּסֵ֣תֶר רַ֑עַם אֶבְחָנְךָ֨ עַל־מֵ֖י מְרִיבָ֣ה סֶֽלָה׃	8 In distress you called, and I rescued you; I answered you from the secret place of thunder; I tested you at the waters of Meriva – Selah.
שְׁמַ֣ע עַ֭מִּי וְאָעִ֣ידָה בָּ֑ךְ יִ֝שְׂרָאֵ֗ל אִם־תִּֽשְׁמַֽע־לִֽי׃	9 Hear, My people, and I will warn you, Israel, if you would only listen to Me!
לֹֽא־יִהְיֶ֣ה בְ֭ךָ אֵ֣ל זָ֑ר וְלֹ֥א תִ֝שְׁתַּחֲוֶ֗ה לְאֵ֣ל נֵכָֽר׃	10 Let there be no strange god among you; do not bow to an alien god.
אָנֹכִ֨י ׀ יְה‏וָ֣ה אֱלֹהֶ֗יךָ הַֽמַּעַלְךָ֮ מֵאֶ֢רֶץ מִצְרָ֥יִם הַרְחֶב־פִּ֝֗יךָ וַאֲמַלְאֵֽהוּ׃	11 I am the Lord your God who brought you out of the land of Egypt – open your mouth wide, and I will fill it.

וְלֹא־שָׁמַע עַמִּי לְקוֹלִי
וְיִשְׂרָאֵל לֹא־אָבָה לִי:

12 Yet My people would not heed My voice;
Israel would not submit to Me,

וָאֲשַׁלְּחֵהוּ בִּשְׁרִירוּת לִבָּם
יֵלְכוּ בְּמוֹעֲצוֹתֵיהֶם:

13 so I left them to their stubborn hearts,
letting them follow their own devices.

לוּ עַמִּי שֹׁמֵעַ לִי
יִשְׂרָאֵל בִּדְרָכַי יְהַלֵּכוּ:

14 If only My people would listen to Me,
if Israel would walk in My ways,

כִּמְעַט אוֹיְבֵיהֶם אַכְנִיעַ
וְעַל־צָרֵיהֶם אָשִׁיב יָדִי:

15 I would soon subdue their enemies
and turn My hand against their foes.

מְשַׂנְאֵי יהוה יְכַחֲשׁוּ־לוֹ
וִיהִי עִתָּם לְעוֹלָם:

16 Those who hate the Lᴏʀᴅ would come
cringing before Him;
their doom would last forever.

וַיַּאֲכִילֵהוּ מֵחֵלֶב חִטָּה
וּמִצּוּר דְּבַשׁ אַשְׂבִּיעֶךָ:

17 He would feed Israel
with the finest wheat;
with honey from the rock
I would satisfy you.

Arise, O God; judge the earth, for all the nations are Your possession

I had high hopes. I put my trust in him.
But he was no better than the worst of men.
Now I trust no one, not even myself.
I am disillusioned. Disillusionment is the worst form of despair.

PSALM 82

מִזְמוֹר לְאָסָף 1 A psalm of Asaf
אֱלֹהִים נִצָּב בַּעֲדַת־אֵל God stands in the divine assembly;
בְּקֶרֶב אֱלֹהִים יִשְׁפֹּט: among divine beings
He delivers judgment.

עַד־מָתַי תִּשְׁפְּטוּ־עָוֶל 2 How long will you judge unjustly,
וּפְנֵי רְשָׁעִים תִּשְׂאוּ־סֶלָה: showing favor to the wicked? Selah.

שִׁפְטוּ־דַל וְיָתוֹם 3 Do justice to the weak and the orphaned;
עָנִי וָרָשׁ הַצְדִּיקוּ: vindicate the poor and destitute;

פַּלְּטוּ־דַל וְאֶבְיוֹן 4 rescue the weak and needy;
מִיַּד רְשָׁעִים הַצִּילוּ: save them from the hand of the wicked.

לֹא יָדְעוּ ׀ וְלֹא יָבִינוּ 5 They do not know,
בַּחֲשֵׁכָה יִתְהַלָּכוּ nor do they understand;
יִמּוֹטוּ כָּל־מוֹסְדֵי אָרֶץ: they walk about in darkness
while all the earth's foundations shudder.

אֲנִי־אָמַרְתִּי אֱלֹהִים אַתֶּם 6 I once thought, "You are divine beings;
וּבְנֵי עֶלְיוֹן כֻּלְּכֶם: all of you are children of the Most High,"

אָכֵן כְּאָדָם תְּמוּתוּן 7 but you shall die like mere men;
וּכְאַחַד הַשָּׂרִים תִּפֹּלוּ: you will fall like any prince.

קוּמָה אֱלֹהִים שָׁפְטָה הָאָרֶץ 8 Arise, O God; judge the earth,
כִּי־אַתָּה תִנְחַל בְּכָל־הַגּוֹיִם: for all the nations are Your possession.

Then they will know that Your name, Yours alone, is the LORD, Most High over all the earth

It's an old story. It has happened many times before.
It is the story of seventy wolves against one sheep.
What unites the seventy wolves? What do they hope to gain
from one meager sheep? It is not the sheep alone
that they pursue. It is the Shepherd.

PSALM 83

שִׁיר מִזְמוֹר לְאָסָף׃ 1 A song, a psalm of Asaf

אֱלֹהִים אַל־דֳּמִי־לָךְ 2 God, do not remain silent;
אַל־תֶּחֱרַשׁ וְאַל־תִּשְׁקֹט אֵל׃ be not deaf to me;
be not still, O God,

כִּי־הִנֵּה אוֹיְבֶיךָ יֶהֱמָיוּן 3 for look – Your enemies bustle;
וּמְשַׂנְאֶיךָ נָשְׂאוּ רֹאשׁ׃ Your haters have raised their heads;

עַל־עַמְּךָ יַעֲרִימוּ סוֹד 4 they devise sly schemes
וְיִתְיָעֲצוּ עַל־צְפוּנֶיךָ׃ against Your people;
they conspire against Your sheltered ones.

אָמְרוּ לְכוּ וְנַכְחִידֵם מִגּוֹי 5 They say,
וְלֹא־יִזָּכֵר שֵׁם־יִשְׂרָאֵל עוֹד׃ "Let us go and obliterate them
as a nation,
and Israel's name will be mentioned
no more."

כִּי נוֹעֲצוּ לֵב יַחְדָּו 6 Yes, their hearts conspire as one;
עָלֶיךָ בְּרִית יִכְרֹתוּ׃ they have formed a pact against You:

אׇהֳלֵי אֱדוֹם וְיִשְׁמְעֵאלִים 7 the tents of Edom and the Ishmaelites,
מוֹאָב וְהַגְרִים׃ Moav and the Hagrites,

גְּבָל וְעַמּוֹן וַעֲמָלֵק 8 Geval, Amon, and Amalek,
פְּלֶשֶׁת עִם־יֹשְׁבֵי צוֹר׃ Philistia, and the people of Tyre;

גַּם־אַשּׁוּר נִלְוָה עִמָּם 9 Assyria, too, has joined them,
הָיוּ זְרוֹעַ לִבְנֵי־לוֹט סֶלָה׃ giving aid to the sons of Lot – Selah.

עֲשֵׂה־לָהֶם כְּמִדְיָן 10 Treat them as You did Midyan –
כְּסִיסְרָא כְיָבִין בְּנַחַל קִישׁוֹן׃ and Sisera and Yavin at Kishon Stream,

נִשְׁמְדוּ בְעֵין־דֹּאר 11 who perished at Ein Dor,
הָיוּ דֹּמֶן לָאֲדָמָה׃ who turned into dung for the soil.

שִׁיתֵמוֹ נְדִיבֵמוֹ כְּעֹרֵב וְכִזְאֵב 12 Render their nobles like Orev and Ze'ev,
וּכְזֶבַח וּכְצַלְמֻנָּע כָּל־נְסִיכֵמוֹ׃ all their princes like Zevaḥ and Tzalmuna,

אֲשֶׁר אָמְרוּ נִירֲשָׁה לָּנוּ
אֵת נְאוֹת אֱלֹהִים:

13 who said, "We will seize possession
of God's meadows."

אֱלֹהַי שִׁיתֵמוֹ כַגַּלְגַּל
כְּקַשׁ לִפְנֵי־רוּחַ:

14 My God, make them like thistledown,
like straw before the wind.

כְּאֵשׁ תִּבְעַר־יָעַר
וּכְלֶהָבָה תְּלַהֵט הָרִים:

15 As fire burns up forests,
as flame sets the hills ablaze,

כֵּן תִּרְדְּפֵם בְּסַעֲרֶךָ
וּבְסוּפָתְךָ תְבַהֲלֵם:

16 so shall You chase them with Your storm
and terrify them with Your whirlwind.

מַלֵּא פְנֵיהֶם קָלוֹן
וִיבַקְשׁוּ שִׁמְךָ יהוה:

17 Fill their faces with humiliation
until they seek Your name, LORD.

יֵבֹשׁוּ וְיִבָּהֲלוּ עֲדֵי־עַד
וְיַחְפְּרוּ וְיֹאבֵדוּ:

18 May they ever be shamed and terrified;
let them be reviled; let them perish.

וְיֵדְעוּ כִּי־אַתָּה שִׁמְךָ
יהוה לְבַדֶּךָ
עֶלְיוֹן עַל־כָּל־הָאָרֶץ:

19 Then they will know that Your name,
Yours alone, is the LORD,
Most High over all the earth.

My soul longs and pines for the LORD's courtyards; my heart and my body
sing out to the living God

It is a challenge to remain challenged. After an arduous climb
we relish a plateau. Even Jacob yearned for serenity.
He had climbed enough. But he never knew Zion in her glory.
Those who knew her glory never rest again. They strive for more,
always more. They go from strength to strength.

PSALM 84

לַמְנַצֵּחַ עַל־הַגִּתִּית
לִבְנֵי־קֹרַח מִזְמוֹר:

1 To the lead singer, on the *gittit* –
a psalm of the sons of Koraḥ

מַה־יְדִידוֹת מִשְׁכְּנוֹתֶיךָ
יהוה צְבָאוֹת:

2 How lovely is Your dwelling place,
O Lord of hosts.

נִכְסְפָה וְגַם־כָּלְתָה ׀ נַפְשִׁי
לְחַצְרוֹת יהוה
לִבִּי וּבְשָׂרִי יְרַנְּנוּ אֶל אֵל־חָי:

3 My soul longs and pines
for the Lord's courtyards;
my heart and my body sing out
to the living God.

גַּם־צִפּוֹר ׀ מָצְאָה בַיִת
וּדְרוֹר ׀ קֵן ׀ לָהּ
אֲשֶׁר־שָׁתָה אֶפְרֹחֶיהָ
אֶת־מִזְבְּחוֹתֶיךָ יהוה צְבָאוֹת
מַלְכִּי וֵאלֹהָי:

4 Even the bird makes a home for herself,
the swallow a nest
where she lays her young–
near Your altars, Lord of hosts,
my King and my God.

אַשְׁרֵי יוֹשְׁבֵי בֵיתֶךָ
עוֹד יְהַלְלוּךָ סֶּלָה:

5 Happy are those
who dwell in Your house;
they will ever praise You – Selah.

אַשְׁרֵי אָדָם עוֹז־לוֹ בָךְ
מְסִלּוֹת בִּלְבָבָם:

6 Happy are those
whose strength is in You,
the paths ahead are in their hearts,

עֹבְרֵי ׀ בְּעֵמֶק הַבָּכָא
מַעְיָן יְשִׁיתוּהוּ
גַּם־בְּרָכוֹת יַעְטֶה מוֹרֶה:

7 those who pass through
the Valley of the Baca
make it into a spring
as if the early rain cloaks it with blessing,

יֵלְכוּ מֵחַיִל אֶל־חָיִל
יֵרָאֶה אֶל־אֱלֹהִים בְּצִיּוֹן:

8 so they go from rampart to rampart
and appear before God in Zion.

יהוה אֱלֹהִים צְבָאוֹת
שִׁמְעָה תְפִלָּתִי
הַאֲזִינָה אֱלֹהֵי יַעֲקֹב סֶלָה:

9 O Lord, God of hosts,
listen to my prayer;
Give ear, O God of Yaakov – Selah.

מָגִנֵּנוּ רְאֵה אֱלֹהִים
וְהַבֵּט פְּנֵי מְשִׁיחֶךָ:

10 See our shield, God,
    and look upon the face
        of Your anointed one,

כִּי טוֹב־יוֹם בַּחֲצֵרֶיךָ מֵאָלֶף
בָּחַרְתִּי הִסְתּוֹפֵף בְּבֵית אֱלֹהַי
מִדּוּר בְּאָהֳלֵי־רֶשַׁע:

11 for a single day in Your courtyards
    is better than a thousand elsewhere;
    I would rather remain
        at the threshold of the House of my God
    than dwell in tents of wickedness,

כִּי שֶׁמֶשׁ ׀ וּמָגֵן יהוה אֱלֹהִים
חֵן וְכָבוֹד יִתֵּן יהוה
לֹא יִמְנַע־טוֹב
לַהֹלְכִים בְּתָמִים:

12 for the Lord God is sun and shield;
    the Lord will grant grace and glory;
    He will not withhold good
        from those who walk blamelessly.

יהוה צְבָאוֹת
אַשְׁרֵי אָדָם בֹּטֵחַ בָּךְ:

13 O Lord of hosts,
    happy are those who trust in You.

Truth will sprout up from the earth, and justice will gaze down from heaven

God says, "Return to Me. Change your ways.
Then I'll return to you." We stubbornly respond, "You return to us.
Then we'll change." There is a way for Him to break this ancient
deadlock. He can help us turn to each other, at the same instant.
Turn us, God of our salvation.

PSALM 85

לַמְנַצֵּחַ לִבְנֵי־קֹרַח מִזְמוֹר׃ 1 To the lead singer –
a psalm of the sons of Koraḥ

רָצִיתָ יְהוָה אַרְצֶךָ 2 You showed favor to Your land, LORD;
שַׁבְתָּ שְׁבִית יַעֲקֹב׃ You restored Yaakov's fortune.

שבות

נָשָׂאתָ עֲוֺן עַמֶּךָ 3 You forgave Your people's offense
כִּסִּיתָ כָל־חַטָּאתָם סֶלָה׃ and covered over all their sins – Selah.

אָסַפְתָּ כָל־עֶבְרָתֶךָ 4 You gathered up all Your anger
הֱשִׁיבוֹתָ מֵחֲרוֹן אַפֶּךָ׃ and turned back from Your blazing fury.

שׁוּבֵנוּ אֱלֹהֵי יִשְׁעֵנוּ 5 Bring us back, God of our salvation;
וְהָפֵר כַּעַסְךָ עִמָּנוּ׃ retract Your wrath against us.

הַלְעוֹלָם תֶּאֱנַף־בָּנוּ 6 Will You show Your anger against us
forever,
תִּמְשֹׁךְ אַפְּךָ לְדֹר וָדֹר׃ drawing out Your fury
throughout the generations?

הֲלֹא־אַתָּה תָּשׁוּב תְּחַיֵּינוּ 7 Will You not give us life once more
וְעַמְּךָ יִשְׂמְחוּ־בָךְ׃ so that Your people may rejoice in You?

הַרְאֵנוּ יְהוָה חַסְדֶּךָ 8 Show us Your loyalty, LORD;
וְיֶשְׁעֲךָ תִּתֶּן־לָנוּ׃ grant us Your salvation.

אֶשְׁמְעָה מַה־יְדַבֵּר הָאֵל ׀ 9 I wish to hear what God, the LORD,
יְהוָה will speak
כִּי ׀ יְדַבֵּר שָׁלוֹם אֶל־עַמּוֹ when He speaks of peace for His people
וְאֶל־חֲסִידָיו and devoted ones –
וְאַל־יָשׁוּבוּ לְכִסְלָה׃ may they not turn back to foolishness,

אַךְ קָרוֹב לִירֵאָיו יִשְׁעוֹ 10 for His salvation is close
to those who fear Him –
לִשְׁכֹּן כָּבוֹד בְּאַרְצֵנוּ׃ so that His glory will dwell in our land.

חֶסֶד־וֶאֱמֶת נִפְגָּשׁוּ 11 Loyalty and truth will meet;
צֶדֶק וְשָׁלוֹם נָשָׁקוּ׃ justice and peace will kiss.

אֱמֶת מֵאֶרֶץ תִּצְמָח 12 Truth will sprout up from the earth,
וְצֶדֶק מִשָּׁמַיִם נִשְׁקָף: and justice will gaze down from heaven.

גַּם־יְהוה יִתֵּן הַטּוֹב 13 Yes, the LORD will grant goodness,
וְאַרְצֵנוּ תִּתֵּן יְבוּלָהּ: and our land will yield its fruit.

צֶדֶק לְפָנָיו יְהַלֵּךְ 14 Justice will walk before Him,
וְיָשֵׂם לְדֶרֶךְ פְּעָמָיו: marking a path for His steps.

Bring joy to the soul of Your servant, for to You, Lord, I lift up my soul

If you sin, feel guilty. Feelings of guilt prompt repentance. But feelings of guilt can be destructive. They can leave a person paralyzed, unable to move on. God's greatest gift is forgiveness. He forgives us so that we are free to progress. He teaches us to forgive others. He teaches us to forgive ourselves. Those are hard lessons to learn.

PSALM 86

תְּפִלָּה לְדָוִד	1 A prayer of David
הַטֵּה־יהוה אׇזְנְךָ עֲנֵנִי	Lend Your ear to me, LORD,
כִּי־עָנִי וְאֶבְיוֹן אָנִי׃	and answer me,
	for I am poor and needy.
שׇׁמְרָה נַפְשִׁי כִּי־חָסִיד אָנִי	2 Preserve my life, for I am devoted.
הוֹשַׁע עַבְדְּךָ אַתָּה אֱלֹהַי	You are my God;
הַבּוֹטֵחַ אֵלֶיךָ׃	save Your servant who trusts in You.
חׇנֵּנִי אֲדֹנָי	3 Show me grace, LORD,
כִּי־אֵלֶיךָ אֶקְרָא כׇּל־הַיּוֹם׃	for to You I call all day long.
שַׂמֵּחַ נֶפֶשׁ עַבְדֶּךָ	4 Bring joy to the soul of Your servant,
כִּי־אֵלֶיךָ אֲדֹנָי נַפְשִׁי אֶשָּׂא׃	for to You, LORD, I lift up my soul,
כִּי־אַתָּה אֲדֹנָי טוֹב וְסַלָּח	5 for You, LORD, are good and forgiving,
וְרַב־חֶסֶד לְכׇל־קֹרְאֶיךָ׃	abounding in loyalty to all
	who call to You.
הַאֲזִינָה יהוה תְּפִלָּתִי	6 Give ear, LORD, to my prayer;
וְהַקְשִׁיבָה בְּקוֹל תַּחֲנוּנוֹתָי׃	listen to the sound of my plea.
בְּיוֹם צָרָתִי אֶקְרָאֶךָּ	7 On the day of my distress I call to You,
כִּי תַעֲנֵנִי׃	for You will answer me.
אֵין־כָּמוֹךָ בָאֱלֹהִים ׀ אֲדֹנָי	8 There are none like You, LORD,
וְאֵין כְּמַעֲשֶׂיךָ׃	among the gods,
	and no works like Yours.
כׇּל־גּוֹיִם ׀ אֲשֶׁר עָשִׂיתָ	9 All the nations You have made
יָבוֹאוּ ׀ וְיִשְׁתַּחֲווּ לְפָנֶיךָ אֲדֹנָי	will come and bow before You, LORD,
וִיכַבְּדוּ לִשְׁמֶךָ׃	adding glory to Your name,
כִּי־גָדוֹל אַתָּה וְעֹשֵׂה נִפְלָאוֹת	10 for You are great and work wonders;
אַתָּה אֱלֹהִים לְבַדֶּךָ׃	You alone are God.
הוֹרֵנִי יהוה ׀ דַּרְכֶּךָ	11 Teach me Your way, LORD;
אֲהַלֵּךְ בַּאֲמִתֶּךָ	I will walk in Your truth.
יַחֵד לְבָבִי לְיִרְאָה שְׁמֶךָ׃	Make my heart whole
	to revere Your name.

אוֹדְךָ ׀ אֲדֹנָי אֱלֹהַי בְּכָל־לְבָבִי
וַאֲכַבְּדָה שִׁמְךָ לְעוֹלָם:

12 I will praise You, Lᴏʀᴅ my God,
with all my heart,
and give glory to Your name forever,

כִּי־חַסְדְּךָ גָּדוֹל עָלָי
וְהִצַּלְתָּ נַפְשִׁי מִשְּׁאוֹל תַּחְתִּיָּה:

13 for Your loyalty to me is great;
You have saved my soul
from the depths of Sheol.

אֱלֹהִים ׀ זֵדִים קָמוּ־עָלַי
וַעֲדַת עָרִיצִים בִּקְשׁוּ נַפְשִׁי
וְלֹא שָׂמוּךָ לְנֶגְדָּם:

14 God, the insolent have risen against me;
a cruel mob seeks my life –
they have no regard for You,

וְאַתָּה אֲדֹנָי אֵל־רַחוּם וְחַנּוּן
אֶרֶךְ אַפַּיִם וְרַב־חֶסֶד וֶאֱמֶת:

15 but You, Lᴏʀᴅ, are a compassionate
and gracious God,
slow to anger and abounding in
kindness and truth.

פְּנֵה אֵלַי וְחָנֵּנִי
תְּנָה־עֻזְּךָ לְעַבְדֶּךָ
וְהוֹשִׁיעָה לְבֶן־אֲמָתֶךָ:

16 Turn to me and show me grace;
grant Your might to Your servant;
save the child of Your handmaid.

עֲשֵׂה־עִמִּי אוֹת לְטוֹבָה
וְיִרְאוּ שֹׂנְאַי וְיֵבֹשׁוּ
כִּי־אַתָּה יְהוָה עֲזַרְתַּנִי
וְנִחַמְתָּנִי:

17 Show me a sign of favor
so that my haters will see and be shamed
when You, Lᴏʀᴅ, give me help
and comfort.

The LORD loves the gates of Zion more than all of Yaakov's dwellings

Ancient cities had gates. That's where the wise men sat.
Justice could be found there. God loved those gates.
He loved them more than Jacob's other dwellings.
Today, cities have no gates. So God loves the halls where justice
is studied. I know a city which has those gates. Zion.

PSALM 87

לִבְנֵי־קֹרַח מִזְמוֹר שִׁיר 1 Of the sons of Koraḥ – a psalm, a song
יְסוּדָתוֹ בְּהַרְרֵי־קֹדֶשׁ:   His foundation on the holy mountains –

אֹהֵב יהוה שַׁעֲרֵי צִיּוֹן 2 the Lord loves the gates of Zion
מִכֹּל מִשְׁכְּנוֹת יַעֲקֹב: more than all of Yaakov's dwellings.

נִכְבָּדוֹת מְדֻבָּר בָּךְ 3 Glorious things are said of you,
עִיר הָאֱלֹהִים סֶלָה: O city of God – Selah.

אַזְכִּיר ׀ רַהַב וּבָבֶל לְיֹדְעָי 4 Among those who know me
הִנֵּה פְלֶשֶׁת וְצוֹר עִם־כּוּשׁ   I mention Rahav and Babylon,
זֶה יֻלַּד־שָׁם: Philistia, Tyre, or Kush –
     "This one was born there" –

וּלְצִיּוֹן ׀ יֵאָמַר 5 but of Zion it is said,
אִישׁ וְאִישׁ יֻלַּד־בָּהּ   "One and all were born there,"
וְהוּא יְכוֹנְנֶהָ עֶלְיוֹן: and the Most High Himself
     has established her.

יהוה יִסְפֹּר בִּכְתוֹב עַמִּים 6 The Lord will keep count
זֶה יֻלַּד־שָׁם סֶלָה: in the record of peoples:
     "This one was born there" – Selah.

וְשָׁרִים כְּחֹלְלִים 7 They will dance and sing,
כָּל־מַעְיָנַי בָּךְ:   "All my springs well from you!"

As for me – to You, O Lᴏʀᴅ, I cry out; my prayers greet You each morning

Death is not a mystery. We know a lot about death.
The dead are free from pain and suffering. They are free of
obligation and opportunity. They have no friends.
They are forgotten. No wonder we pray for life. We want
obligations and opportunity. We want friendship, and fear being
forgotten. We'll tolerate the pain and suffering. Life is a mystery.

PSALM 88

שִׁיר מִזְמוֹר לִבְנֵי קֹרַח
לַמְנַצֵּחַ עַל־מָחֲלַת לְעַנּוֹת
מַשְׂכִּיל לְהֵימָן הָאֶזְרָחִי:

1 A song, a psalm of the sons of Koraḥ–
to the lead singer, *maḥalat le'annot*–
a *maskil* of Heiman the Ezrahite

יהוה אֱלֹהֵי יְשׁוּעָתִי
יוֹם־צָעַקְתִּי בַלַּיְלָה נֶגְדֶּךָ:

2 O Lord, God of my salvation,
I cried out by day
and before You by night.

תָּבוֹא לְפָנֶיךָ תְּפִלָּתִי
הַטֵּה אָזְנְךָ לְרִנָּתִי:

3 Let my prayer come before You;
lend Your ear to my plea,

כִּי־שָׂבְעָה בְרָעוֹת נַפְשִׁי
וְחַיַּי לִשְׁאוֹל הִגִּיעוּ:

4 for my soul is glutted with misery;
my life hovers on the brink of Sheol;

נֶחְשַׁבְתִּי עִם־יוֹרְדֵי בוֹר
הָיִיתִי כְּגֶבֶר אֵין־אֱיָל:

5 I am counted among those
down in the Pit.
I am like one drained of vitality,

בַּמֵּתִים חָפְשִׁי
כְּמוֹ חֲלָלִים שֹׁכְבֵי קֶבֶר
אֲשֶׁר לֹא זְכַרְתָּם עוֹד
וְהֵמָּה מִיָּדְךָ נִגְזָרוּ:

6 abandoned among the dead
like corpses lying in the grave
whom You no longer recall,
cut off from Your care.

שַׁתַּנִי בְּבוֹר תַּחְתִּיּוֹת
בְּמַחֲשַׁכִּים בִּמְצֹלוֹת:

7 You have set me in the deepest pit,
in the darkness, in the depths;

עָלַי סָמְכָה חֲמָתֶךָ
וְכָל־מִשְׁבָּרֶיךָ עִנִּיתָ סֶּלָה:

8 Your wrath weighs down upon me
with all Your overwhelming waves.

הִרְחַקְתָּ מְיֻדָּעַי מִמֶּנִּי
שַׁתַּנִי תוֹעֵבוֹת לָמוֹ
כָּלֻא וְלֹא אֵצֵא:

9 You have distanced my friends from me;
You made me a horror to them;
I am trapped with no way out.

עֵינִי דָאֲבָה מִנִּי
עֹנִי קְרָאתִיךָ יהוה בְּכָל־יוֹם
שִׁטַּחְתִּי אֵלֶיךָ כַפָּי:

10 My eyes are sore from suffering;
I call out to You, Lord, each day;
I stretch my hands out to You.

הֲלַמֵּתִים תַּעֲשֶׂה־פֶּלֶא אִם־רְפָאִים יָקוּמוּ ׀ יוֹדוּךָ סֶּלָה:	11 Will You work wonders for the dead? Will the shades rise up and praise You? – Selah.
הַיְסֻפַּר בַּקֶּבֶר חַסְדֶּךָ אֱמוּנָתְךָ בָּאֲבַדּוֹן:	12 Is Your loyalty mentioned in the grave, Your faithfulness in the realm of destruction?
הֲיִוָּדַע בַּחֹשֶׁךְ פִּלְאֶךָ וְצִדְקָתְךָ בְּאֶרֶץ נְשִׁיָּה:	13 Are Your wonders known in the darkness, Your righteousness in the land of oblivion?
וַאֲנִי ׀ אֵלֶיךָ יהוה שִׁוַּעְתִּי וּבַבֹּקֶר תְּפִלָּתִי תְקַדְּמֶךָּ:	14 As for me – to You, O Lᴏʀᴅ, I cry out; my prayers greet You each morning.
לָמָה יהוה תִּזְנַח נַפְשִׁי תַּסְתִּיר פָּנֶיךָ מִמֶּנִּי:	15 Why, O Lᴏʀᴅ, have You forsaken me; why do You hide Your face from me?
עָנִי אֲנִי וְגֹוֵעַ מִנֹּעַר נָשָׂאתִי אֵמֶיךָ אָפוּנָה:	16 Since my youth I have been poor, wasting away, bearing Your terrors wherever I turn.
עָלַי עָבְרוּ חֲרוֹנֶיךָ בִּעוּתֶיךָ צִמְּתוּתֻנִי:	17 Your fury has washed over me; Your agonies devastate me.
סַבּוּנִי כַמַּיִם כָּל־הַיּוֹם הִקִּיפוּ עָלַי יָחַד:	18 They surround me like water all day long, completely encircling me.
הִרְחַקְתָּ מִמֶּנִּי אֹהֵב וָרֵעַ מְיֻדָּעַי מַחְשָׁךְ:	19 You have distanced me from loved one and friend; those who know me are but darkness.

You rule over the surging sea – when its waves mount high, it is You who stills them

God's loving-kindness is forever. But I won't live forever.
The Lord knows the rest of the story. Will I live long enough to see
how it all turns out? If I don't, will my life have been worth living?
I've seen suffering in my time. I wonder, "Will it cease before I
die?" That's why I pray for longevity. I want to be there when the
curtain falls.

PSALM 89

מַשְׂכִּיל לְאֵיתָן הָאֶזְרָחִי׃	1	A *maskil* of Eitan the Ezrahite
חַסְדֵי יהוה עוֹלָם אָשִׁירָה לְדֹר וָדֹר ו אוֹדִיעַ אֱמוּנָתְךָ בְּפִי׃	2	Let me sing of the Lord's loyalty forever; I will spread word of Your faithfulness for all generations,
כִּי־אָמַרְתִּי עוֹלָם חֶסֶד יִבָּנֶה שָׁמַיִם ו תָּכִן אֱמוּנָתְךָ בָהֶם׃	3	for I thought, eternal loyalty has been built, constant as the heavens You established with Your faithfulness –
כָּרַתִּי בְרִית לִבְחִירִי נִשְׁבַּעְתִּי לְדָוִד עַבְדִּי׃	4	"I have formed a covenant with My chosen one; I have sworn to My servant David.
עַד־עוֹלָם אָכִין זַרְעֶךָ וּבָנִיתִי לְדֹר־וָדוֹר כִּסְאֲךָ סֶלָה׃	5	I will establish your seed forever; I have built your throne for all generations" – Selah.
וְיוֹדוּ שָׁמַיִם פִּלְאֲךָ יהוה אַף־אֱמוּנָתְךָ בִּקְהַל קְדֹשִׁים׃	6	The heavens praise Your wonders, Lord, Your faithfulness among the holy assembly,
כִּי מִי בַשַּׁחַק יַעֲרֹךְ לַיהוה יִדְמֶה לַיהוה בִּבְנֵי אֵלִים׃	7	for who in the skies can compare with the Lord? Who is like the Lord among the heavenly beings,
אֵל נַעֲרָץ בְּסוֹד־קְדֹשִׁים רַבָּה וְנוֹרָא עַל־כָּל־סְבִיבָיו׃	8	a God so dreaded in the holy council, fearsome to all around Him?
יהוה ו אֱלֹהֵי צְבָאוֹת מִי־כָמוֹךָ חֲסִין ו יָהּ וֶאֱמוּנָתְךָ סְבִיבוֹתֶיךָ׃	9	O Lord, God of hosts, who is as powerful as You, Lord? Your faithfulness surrounds You.
אַתָּה מוֹשֵׁל בְּגֵאוּת הַיָּם בְּשׂוֹא גַלָּיו אַתָּה תְשַׁבְּחֵם׃	10	You rule over the surging sea – when its waves mount high, it is You who stills them.

אַתָּה דִכִּאתָ כֶחָלָל רָהַב
בִּזְרוֹעַ עֻזְּךָ פִּזַּרְתָּ אוֹיְבֶיךָ:

11 It is You who crushed Rahav to a corpse;
with Your mighty arm
You scattered Your enemies.

לְךָ שָׁמַיִם אַף־לְךָ אָרֶץ
תֵּבֵל וּמְלֹאָהּ אַתָּה יְסַדְתָּם:

12 Yours are the heavens;
Yours, too, is the earth –
You founded the world and all that fills it.

צָפוֹן וְיָמִין אַתָּה בְרָאתָם
תָּבוֹר וְחֶרְמוֹן בְּשִׁמְךָ יְרַנֵּנוּ:

13 The north and the south
were created by You;
Tavor and Ḥermon sing
for joy of Your name.

לְךָ זְרוֹעַ עִם־גְּבוּרָה
תָּעֹז יָדְךָ תָּרוּם יְמִינֶךָ:

14 Yours is an arm endowed with strength;
Your hand is mighty;
Your right hand is raised high.

צֶדֶק וּמִשְׁפָּט מְכוֹן כִּסְאֶךָ
חֶסֶד וֶאֱמֶת יְקַדְּמוּ פָנֶיךָ:

15 Righteousness and justice
form the base of Your throne;
loyalty and truth go before You.

אַשְׁרֵי הָעָם יוֹדְעֵי תְרוּעָה
יהוה בְּאוֹר־פָּנֶיךָ יְהַלֵּכוּן:

16 Happy are the people
who know the joyful shout, Lord;
they walk in the light of Your presence.

בְּשִׁמְךָ יְגִילוּן כָּל־הַיּוֹם
וּבְצִדְקָתְךָ יָרוּמוּ:

17 They rejoice in Your name all day long,
raised up through Your righteousness,

כִּי־תִפְאֶרֶת עֻזָּמוֹ אָתָּה
וּבִרְצוֹנְךָ תָּרוּם קַרְנֵנוּ:

תרים

18 for You are their beauty and might,
and our horn is raised high
by Your favor,

כִּי לַיהוה מָגִנֵּנוּ
וְלִקְדוֹשׁ יִשְׂרָאֵל מַלְכֵּנוּ:

19 for our shield belongs to the Lord,
our king to the Holy One of Israel.

אָז דִּבַּרְתָּ בְחָזוֹן לַחֲסִידֶיךָ
וַתֹּאמֶר שִׁוִּיתִי עֵזֶר עַל־גִּבּוֹר
הֲרִימוֹתִי בָחוּר מֵעָם:

20 Once in a vision
You spoke to Your devoted ones, saying,
"I have granted help for a hero;
I have raised up a chosen one
from the people.

מְצָאתִי דָּוִד עַבְדִּי
בְּשֶׁמֶן קׇדְשִׁי מְשַׁחְתִּיו:

21 I have found David, My servant,
and with My holy oil anointed him

אֲשֶׁר יָדִי תִּכּוֹן עִמּוֹ
אַף־זְרוֹעִי תְאַמְּצֶנּוּ:

22 so that My hand will be ready
to help him,
My arm to give him strength.

לֹא־יַשִּׁא אוֹיֵב בּוֹ
וּבֶן־עַוְלָה לֹא יְעַנֶּנּוּ:

23 No enemy shall harm him,
no wicked one oppress him;

וְכַתּוֹתִי מִפָּנָיו צָרָיו
וּמְשַׂנְאָיו אֶגּוֹף:

24 I will cut down his foes before him
and strike down his haters.

וֶאֱמוּנָתִי וְחַסְדִּי עִמּוֹ
וּבִשְׁמִי תָּרוּם קַרְנוֹ:

25 My faithfulness and loyalty are with him;
his horn will be raised up in My name.

וְשַׂמְתִּי בַיָּם יָדוֹ
וּבַנְּהָרוֹת יְמִינוֹ:

26 I will set his hand upon the sea,
his right hand over the rivers.

הוּא יִקְרָאֵנִי אָבִי אָתָּה
אֵלִי וְצוּר יְשׁוּעָתִי:

27 He will say to me, 'You are my father,
My God, the rock of my salvation,'

אַף־אָנִי בְּכוֹר אֶתְּנֵהוּ
עֶלְיוֹן לְמַלְכֵי־אָרֶץ:

28 and I will make him my firstborn,
most high over kings of the earth.

לְעוֹלָם אֶשְׁמׇר־לוֹ חַסְדִּי
וּבְרִיתִי נֶאֱמֶנֶת לוֹ:

29 I will ever keep My loyalty for him,
my covenant ever faithful to him;

אשמור־

וְשַׂמְתִּי לָעַד זַרְעוֹ
וְכִסְאוֹ כִּימֵי שָׁמָיִם:

30 I will appoint his seed forever,
his throne as lasting as the heavens.

אִם־יַעַזְבוּ בָנָיו תּוֹרָתִי
וּבְמִשְׁפָּטַי לֹא יֵלֵכוּן:

31 But if his children forsake My teaching
and do not follow in My laws,

אִם־חֻקֹּתַי יְחַלֵּלוּ
וּמִצְוֺתַי לֹא יִשְׁמֹרוּ:

32 if they violate My statutes
and do not keep My commandments,

וּפָקַדְתִּי בְשֵׁבֶט פִּשְׁעָם
וּבִנְגָעִים עֲוֺנָם:

33 I will punish their transgressions
with the rod,
their offenses with wounds,

וְחַסְדִּי לֹא־אָפִיר מֵעִמּוֹ 34 but I will never withdraw from him
וְלֹא־אֲשַׁקֵּר בֶּאֱמוּנָתִי: My loyalty,
nor betray My faithfulness;

לֹא־אֲחַלֵּל בְּרִיתִי 35 I will not violate My covenant,
וּמוֹצָא שְׂפָתַי לֹא אֲשַׁנֶּה: nor alter what My lips have uttered.

אַחַת נִשְׁבַּעְתִּי בְקָדְשִׁי 36 I have sworn by My holiness
אִם־לְדָוִד אֲכַזֵּב: once and for all –
I will never be false to David.

זַרְעוֹ לְעוֹלָם יִהְיֶה 37 His seed will continue forever,
וְכִסְאוֹ כַשֶּׁמֶשׁ נֶגְדִּי: His throne before Me like the sun,

כְּיָרֵחַ יִכּוֹן עוֹלָם 38 established forever like the moon,
וְעֵד בַּשַּׁחַק נֶאֱמָן סֶלָה: that faithful witness in the sky" – Selah.

וְאַתָּה זָנַחְתָּ וַתִּמְאָס 39 But You – You have forsaken,
הִתְעַבַּרְתָּ עִם־מְשִׁיחֶךָ: You have spurned,
You grew furious at Your anointed.

נֵאַרְתָּה בְּרִית עַבְדֶּךָ 40 You renounced Your servant's covenant
חִלַּלְתָּ לָאָרֶץ נִזְרוֹ: and defiled his crown in the dust.

פָּרַצְתָּ כָל־גְּדֵרֹתָיו 41 You broke down all his walls,
שַׂמְתָּ מִבְצָרָיו מְחִתָּה: and turned his fortresses to ruins.

שַׁסֻּהוּ כָּל־עֹבְרֵי דָרֶךְ 42 All who pass by plunder him,
הָיָה חֶרְפָּה לִשְׁכֵנָיו: and he has become his neighbors' scorn.

הֲרִימוֹתָ יְמִין צָרָיו 43 You raised the right hand of his foes
הִשְׂמַחְתָּ כָּל־אוֹיְבָיו: and delighted all his enemies.

אַף־תָּשִׁיב צוּר חַרְבּוֹ 44 You even turned back
וְלֹא הֲקֵימֹתוֹ בַּמִּלְחָמָה: the blade of his sword,
and did not bolster him in battle.

הִשְׁבַּתָּ מִטְּהָרוֹ 45 You brought his glory to an end
וְכִסְאוֹ לָאָרֶץ מִגַּרְתָּה: and hurled his throne to the ground.

הִקְצַ֫רְתָּ יְמֵ֥י עֲלוּמָ֑יו
הֶעֱטִ֨יתָ עָלָ֖יו בּוּשָׁ֣ה סֶֽלָה׃

46 You cut short the days of his prime
and cloaked him with shame – Selah.

עַד־מָ֣ה יהוה תִּסָּתֵ֣ר לָנֶ֑צַח
תִּבְעַ֖ר כְּמוֹ־אֵ֣שׁ חֲמָתֶֽךָ׃

47 How long, LORD?
Will You hide Yourself forever,
Your wrath blazing like fire?

זְכׇר־אֲנִ֥י מֶה־חָ֑לֶד
עַל־מַה־שָּׁ֝֗וְא בָּרָ֥אתָ כׇל־בְּנֵי־
אָדָֽם׃

48 Remember how brief my life is –
did You create humanity for naught?

מִ֤י גֶ֣בֶר יִֽחְיֶה וְלֹ֣א יִרְאֶה־מָּ֑וֶת
יְמַלֵּ֨ט נַפְשׁ֖וֹ מִיַּד־שְׁא֣וֹל
סֶֽלָה׃

49 Who can live without seeing death
or save himself from Sheol's grasp? –
Selah.

אַיֵּ֤ה ׀ חֲסָדֶ֖יךָ הָרִֽאשֹׁנִ֥ים ׀ אֲדֹנָ֑י
נִשְׁבַּ֥עְתָּ לְ֝דָוִ֗ד בֶּאֱמוּנָתֶֽךָ׃

50 Where are Your loyalties of old, LORD,
when You faithfully swore to David?

זְכֹ֣ר אֲדֹנָ֮י חֶרְפַּ֢ת עֲבָ֫דֶ֥יךָ
שְׂאֵתִ֥י בְחֵיקִ֑י כׇּל־רַבִּ֥ים
עַמִּֽים׃

51 Remember, LORD,
the taunts Your servants bore,
what I bore from so many people,

אֲשֶׁ֤ר חֵרְפ֖וּ אוֹיְבֶ֥יךָ ׀ יהוה
אֲשֶׁ֥ר חֵ֝רְפ֗וּ עִקְּב֥וֹת מְשִׁיחֶֽךָ׃

52 the taunts of Your enemies, LORD,
who taunted Your anointed at every step.

בָּר֖וּךְ יהוה לְעוֹלָ֑ם
אָ֘מֵ֥ן ׀ וְאָמֵֽן׃

53 Blessed is the LORD forever,
Amen and Amen.

May the LORD our God's sweetness be upon us. Grant us success through our efforts, and may our efforts succeed!

Life is much too short. I've accomplished but a little.
My misdeeds are many. I sense that God is angry with me.
I'd like to repent. Is there enough time? The Sages tell us
that Moshe composed eleven psalms. Our psalm is one of them.
We can expect to hear unique words in our psalm,
words that could not have been expressed by anyone other than Moshe.

PSALM 90

תְּפִלָּה לְמֹשֶׁה אִישׁ־הָאֱלֹהִים
אֲדֹנָי מָעוֹן אַתָּה הָיִיתָ לָּנוּ
בְּדֹר וָדֹר:

1 A prayer of Moshe, the man of God
LORD, You have been our shelter
in every generation.

בְּטֶרֶם ׀ הָרִים יֻלָּדוּ
וַתְּחוֹלֵל אֶרֶץ וְתֵבֵל
וּמֵעוֹלָם עַד־עוֹלָם אַתָּה אֵל:

2 Before the mountains were born,
before You brought forth the earth
and the world,
from eternity to eternity, You are God.

תָּשֵׁב אֱנוֹשׁ עַד־דַּכָּא
וַתֹּאמֶר שׁוּבוּ בְנֵי־אָדָם:

3 You turn mortals back into dust,
saying, "Return, you children of men,"

כִּי אֶלֶף שָׁנִים בְּעֵינֶיךָ
כְּיוֹם אֶתְמוֹל כִּי יַעֲבֹר
וְאַשְׁמוּרָה בַלָּיְלָה:

4 for a thousand years in Your sight
are like yesterday that has passed,
like a brief watch in the night.

זְרַמְתָּם שֵׁנָה יִהְיוּ
בַּבֹּקֶר כֶּחָצִיר יַחֲלֹף:

5 You sweep them away
like a fleeting dream;
in the morning they are
like grass newly grown–

בַּבֹּקֶר יָצִיץ וְחָלָף
לָעֶרֶב יְמוֹלֵל וְיָבֵשׁ:

6 in the morning it sprouts and flourishes;
by evening it withers and dries up,

כִּי־כָלִינוּ בְאַפֶּךָ
וּבַחֲמָתְךָ נִבְהָלְנוּ:

7 for we are consumed by Your anger,
terrified by Your fury.

שַׁתָּ עֲוֹנֹתֵינוּ לְנֶגְדֶּךָ
עֲלֻמֵנוּ לִמְאוֹר פָּנֶיךָ:

8 You have set our iniquities
before Yourself,
our secret sins in the light
of Your presence.

כִּי כָל־יָמֵינוּ פָּנוּ בְעֶבְרָתֶךָ
כִּלִּינוּ שָׁנֵינוּ כְמוֹ־הֶגֶה:

9 All our days pass away in Your wrath;
we spend our years like a sigh.

יְמֵי־שְׁנוֹתֵינוּ בָהֶם שִׁבְעִים שָׁנָה
וְאִם בִּגְבוּרֹת ׀ שְׁמוֹנִים שָׁנָה
וְרָהְבָּם עָמָל וָאָוֶן
כִּי־גָז חִישׁ וַנָּעֻפָה:

10 The span of our life is seventy years–
perhaps eighty, if we are strong –
but the best of them are toil and sorrow,
for they are soon gone, and we fly away.

11 Who can know the force of Your anger?
Your wrath matches the reverence
due to You.

מִי־יוֹדֵעַ עֹז אַפֶּךָ
וּכְיִרְאָתְךָ עֶבְרָתֶךָ:

12 Teach us to count our days rightly,
that our hearts may grow wise.

לִמְנוֹת יָמֵינוּ כֵּן הוֹדַע
וְנָבִא לְבַב חָכְמָה:

13 Relent, O LORD!
How much longer?
Show compassion for Your servants.

שׁוּבָה יהוה עַד־מָתָי
וְהִנָּחֵם עַל־עֲבָדֶיךָ:

14 Nourish us each morning
with Your loving-kindness
so that we may sing and rejoice
all our days.

שַׂבְּעֵנוּ בַבֹּקֶר חַסְדֶּךָ
וּנְרַנְּנָה וְנִשְׂמְחָה בְּכָל־יָמֵינוּ:

15 Repay us with joy for the pain
You inflicted upon us,
for all the years we saw suffering.

שַׂמְּחֵנוּ כִּימוֹת עִנִּיתָנוּ
שְׁנוֹת רָאִינוּ רָעָה:

16 Let Your deeds be seen by Your servants
and Your glory by their children.

יֵרָאֶה אֶל־עֲבָדֶיךָ פָעֳלֶךָ
וַהֲדָרְךָ עַל־בְּנֵיהֶם:

17 May the LORD our God's sweetness
be upon us.
Grant us success through our efforts,
and may our efforts succeed!

וִיהִי נֹעַם אֲדֹנָי אֱלֹהֵינוּ עָלֵינוּ
וּמַעֲשֵׂה יָדֵינוּ כּוֹנְנָה עָלֵינוּ
וּמַעֲשֵׂה יָדֵינוּ כּוֹנְנֵהוּ:

He who lives in the shelter of the Most High dwells in the shadow of Shaddai

I am vulnerable. I am terrified of plagues and pestilence.
I am deathly frightened of lions, and vipers, and snakes.
I am surrounded by ten thousand enemies.
God, please protect me. Be my refuge, my shelter, and my shield.

PSALM 91

יֹשֵׁב בְּסֵתֶר עֶלְיוֹן בְּצֵל שַׁדַּי יִתְלוֹנָן׃	1 He who lives in the shelter of the Most High dwells in the shadow of Shaddai.
אֹמַר לַיהוה מַחְסִי וּמְצוּדָתִי אֱלֹהַי אֶבְטַח־בּוֹ׃	2 I say of the Lord, "My refuge and stronghold, my God in whom I trust,"
כִּי הוּא יַצִּילְךָ מִפַּח יָקוּשׁ מִדֶּבֶר הַוּוֹת׃	3 for He will save you from the fowler's snare, from deadly plague.
בְּאֶבְרָתוֹ ׀ יָסֶךְ לָךְ וְתַחַת־כְּנָפָיו תֶּחְסֶה צִנָּה וְסֹחֵרָה אֲמִתּוֹ׃	4 With His pinions He will cover you; beneath His wings you will find shelter; His loyalty is an encircling shield.
לֹא־תִירָא מִפַּחַד לָיְלָה מֵחֵץ יָעוּף יוֹמָם׃	5 You need not fear terror by night, nor the arrow that flies by day,
מִדֶּבֶר בָּאֹפֶל יַהֲלֹךְ מִקֶּטֶב יָשׁוּד צָהֳרָיִם׃	6 nor the plague that stalks in darkness, nor disease that ravages at noon.
יִפֹּל מִצִּדְּךָ ׀ אֶלֶף וּרְבָבָה מִימִינֶךָ אֵלֶיךָ לֹא יִגָּשׁ׃	7 A thousand may fall beside you, ten thousand at your right hand, but it will not come near you.
רַק בְּעֵינֶיךָ תַבִּיט וְשִׁלֻּמַת רְשָׁעִים תִּרְאֶה׃	8 You will only look with your eyes and see the punishment of the wicked.
כִּי־אַתָּה יהוה מַחְסִי עֶלְיוֹן שַׂמְתָּ מְעוֹנֶךָ׃	9 For you – "the Lord is my Refuge" – you have made the Most High your abode.
לֹא־תְאֻנֶּה אֵלֶיךָ רָעָה וְנֶגַע לֹא־יִקְרַב בְּאָהֳלֶךָ׃	10 No harm will befall you; no sickness will come near your home,
כִּי מַלְאָכָיו יְצַוֶּה־לָּךְ לִשְׁמָרְךָ בְּכָל־דְּרָכֶיךָ׃	11 for He will command His angels about you to guard you in all your ways.

עַל־כַּפַּיִם יִשָּׂאוּנְךָ
פֶּן־תִּגֹּף בָּאֶבֶן רַגְלֶךָ׃

12 They will lift you in their hands
lest your foot stumble on a stone.

עַל־שַׁחַל וָפֶתֶן תִּדְרֹךְ
תִּרְמֹס כְּפִיר וְתַנִּין׃

13 You will tread over lions and vipers;
you will trample on young lions
and snakes.

כִּי בִי חָשַׁק וַאֲפַלְּטֵהוּ
אֲשַׂגְּבֵהוּ כִּי־יָדַע שְׁמִי׃

14 "Because he loves Me, I will rescue him;
I will protect him
because he acknowledges My name.

יִקְרָאֵנִי ׀ וְאֶעֱנֵהוּ
עִמּוֹ־אָנֹכִי בְצָרָה
אֲחַלְּצֵהוּ וַאֲכַבְּדֵהוּ׃

15 When he calls on Me, I will answer him;
I will be with him in distress;
I will rescue him and bring him honor.

אֹרֶךְ יָמִים אַשְׂבִּיעֵהוּ
וְאַרְאֵהוּ בִּישׁוּעָתִי׃

16 With long life I will satisfy him
and show him My salvation."

It is good to thank the LORD, to sing psalms to Your name, Most High

My weekdays are workdays. I have no time to think.
On Shabbat, I have time to think. That is just one of Shabbat's
gifts to me. I think back to that primeval Shabbat. All was perfect
then, but is no longer so. On Shabbat I taste perfection.
Shabbat brings me another gift: belief.
Belief that all will one day be perfect again.

PSALM 92

מִזְמוֹר שִׁיר לְיוֹם הַשַּׁבָּת:	1	A psalm, a song for the Sabbath day
טוֹב לְהֹדוֹת לַיהוה וּלְזַמֵּר לְשִׁמְךָ עֶלְיוֹן:	2	It is good to thank the Lord, to sing psalms to Your name, Most High,
לְהַגִּיד בַּבֹּקֶר חַסְדֶּךָ וֶאֱמוּנָתְךָ בַּלֵּילוֹת:	3	to sing of Your loving-kindness in the morning and Your devotion at night,
עֲלֵי־עָשׂוֹר וַעֲלֵי־נָבֶל עֲלֵי הִגָּיוֹן בְּכִנּוֹר:	4	to the music of the ten-stringed lyre, to the melody of the harp.
כִּי שִׂמַּחְתַּנִי יהוה בְּפָעֳלֶךָ בְּמַעֲשֵׂי יָדֶיךָ אֲרַנֵּן:	5	For Your work delights me, O Lord; I sing for joy at the deeds of Your hands.
מַה־גָּדְלוּ מַעֲשֶׂיךָ יהוה מְאֹד עָמְקוּ מַחְשְׁבֹתֶיךָ:	6	How great are Your deeds, Lord; how profound Your thoughts!
אִישׁ־בַּעַר לֹא יֵדָע וּכְסִיל לֹא־יָבִין אֶת־זֹאת:	7	A boor cannot know this, nor can a fool understand:
בִּפְרֹחַ רְשָׁעִים ׀ כְּמוֹ עֵשֶׂב וַיָּצִיצוּ כָּל־פֹּעֲלֵי אָוֶן לְהִשָּׁמְדָם עֲדֵי־עַד:	8	though the wicked may spring up like grass and all evildoers seem to flourish, they will be destroyed for all eternity,
וְאַתָּה מָרוֹם לְעֹלָם יהוה:	9	but You, Lord, are exalted forever,
כִּי הִנֵּה אֹיְבֶיךָ יהוה כִּי־הִנֵּה אֹיְבֶיךָ יֹאבֵדוּ יִתְפָּרְדוּ כָּל־פֹּעֲלֵי אָוֶן:	10	for Your enemies, O Lord– why, Your enemies will perish; all evildoers will be scattered.
וַתָּרֶם כִּרְאֵים קַרְנִי בַּלֹּתִי בְּשֶׁמֶן רַעֲנָן:	11	You raise up my horn like the wild ox; I am anointed with fresh oil.
וַתַּבֵּט עֵינִי בְּשׁוּרָי בַּקָּמִים עָלַי מְרֵעִים תִּשְׁמַעְנָה אָזְנָי:	12	My eyes will see my enemies' downfall; my ears will hear my wicked attackers' doom.

צַדִּיק כַּתָּמָר יִפְרָח
כְּאֶרֶז בַּלְּבָנוֹן יִשְׂגֶּה:

13 The righteous will flourish
like a palm tree;
they will grow tall
like a cedar in Lebanon.

שְׁתוּלִים בְּבֵית יהוה
בְּחַצְרוֹת אֱלֹהֵינוּ יַפְרִיחוּ:

14 Planted in the Lord's House,
they will blossom in the courtyards
of our God.

עוֹד יְנוּבוּן בְּשֵׂיבָה
דְּשֵׁנִים וְרַעֲנַנִּים יִהְיוּ:

15 Even in old age, they will still bear fruit,
always lush and fresh,

לְהַגִּיד כִּי־יָשָׁר יהוה
צוּרִי וְלֹא־עוֹלָתָה בּוֹ:

עלתה

16 proclaiming that the Lord is upright.
He is my Rock,
in whom there is no wrong.

More powerful than the sounds of many waters, than the mighty waves of the sea,
is the LORD on high

God disguises Himself so well that we often cannot find Him.
He camouflages Himself to look like nature.
Our psalm tells us that He is robed in majesty.
In what costume has He appeared to you?

PSALM 93

יְהֹוָה מָלָךְ גֵּאוּת לָבֵשׁ
לָבֵשׁ יְהֹוָה עֹז הִתְאַזָּר
אַף־תִּכּוֹן תֵּבֵל בַּל־תִּמּוֹט:

1 The Lord reigns, robed in majesty;
the Lord is robed, girded with strength –
the world stands firm;
it will never be shaken.

נָכוֹן כִּסְאֲךָ מֵאָז
מֵעוֹלָם אָתָּה:

2 Your throne has always stood firm;
You are of eternity.

נָשְׂאוּ נְהָרוֹת ׀ יְהֹוָה נָשְׂאוּ
נְהָרוֹת קוֹלָם
יִשְׂאוּ נְהָרוֹת דָּכְיָם:

3 The rivers rise up, O Lord;
the river sounds surge;
the rivers surge and swell and crash.

מִקֹּלוֹת ׀ מַיִם רַבִּים אַדִּירִים
מִשְׁבְּרֵי־יָם
אַדִּיר בַּמָּרוֹם יְהֹוָה:

4 More powerful than the sounds
of many waters,
than the mighty waves of the sea,
is the Lord on high.

עֵדֹתֶיךָ ׀ נֶאֶמְנוּ מְאֹד
לְבֵיתְךָ נַאֲוָה־קֹדֶשׁ
יְהֹוָה לְאֹרֶךְ יָמִים:

5 Your decrees are most faithful;
holiness adorns Your House, Lord,
for evermore.

O God of retribution, LORD – O God of retribution, shine forth!

I see a picture taken during the Holocaust. I cannot get it out of my mind. It is a picture of a torture chamber. There are two words written on the wall. They are written in blood, human blood. "*Yidden, nekama!*""Jews, revenge!" A voice within me shrieks: "God, revenge!"

PSALM 94

אֵל־נְקָמוֹת יהוה	1	O God of retribution, LORD–
אֵל נְקָמוֹת הוֹפִֽיעַ:		O God of retribution, shine forth!
הִנָּשֵׂא שֹׁפֵט הָאָֽרֶץ	2	Rise up, Judge of the earth;
הָשֵׁב גְּמוּל עַל־גֵּאִֽים:		treat the arrogant as they deserve.
עַד־מָתַי רְשָׁעִים ׀ יהוה	3	For how long, LORD,
עַד־מָתַי רְשָׁעִים יַעֲלֹֽזוּ:		for how long shall the wicked triumph?
יַבִּֽיעוּ יְדַבְּרוּ עָתָק	4	They pour out insolent words;
יִֽתְאַמְּרוּ כָּל־פֹּֽעֲלֵי אָֽוֶן:		all the evildoers are full of boasting.
עַמְּךָ יהוה יְדַכְּאוּ	5	They crush Your people, LORD,
וְנַחֲלָתְךָ יְעַנּֽוּ:		and oppress Your own heritage.
אַלְמָנָה וְגֵר יַהֲרֹגוּ	6	They kill the widow and the stranger;
וִיתוֹמִים יְרַצֵּֽחוּ:		they murder the orphaned,
וַיֹּֽאמְרוּ לֹא יִרְאֶה־יָּהּ	7	saying, "The LORD does not see;
וְלֹא־יָבִין אֱלֹהֵי יַעֲקֹֽב:		the God of Yaakov pays no heed."
בִּֽינוּ בֹּֽעֲרִים בָּעָם	8	Take heed, you most brutish people;
וּכְסִילִים מָתַי תַּשְׂכִּֽילוּ:		you fools, when will you grow wise?
הֲנֹטַע אֹזֶן הֲלֹא יִשְׁמָע	9	Will He who implants the ear fail to hear?
אִם־יֹצֵר עַיִן הֲלֹא יַבִּֽיט:		Will He who forms the eye fail to see?
הֲיֹסֵר גּוֹיִם הֲלֹא יוֹכִיחַ	10	Will He who disciplines nations,
הַֽמְלַמֵּד אָדָם דָּֽעַת:		He who teaches man knowledge,
		fail to punish?
יהוה יֹדֵעַ מַחְשְׁבוֹת אָדָם	11	The Lord knows that the thoughts of man
כִּי־הֵמָּה הָֽבֶל:		are but mere fleeting breath.
אַשְׁרֵי ׀ הַגֶּבֶר אֲשֶׁר־תְּיַסְּרֶנּוּ יָּהּ	12	Happy is the person
וּֽמִתּוֹרָתְךָ תְלַמְּדֶֽנּוּ:		whom You discipline, LORD,
		whom You instruct in Your teaching,
לְהַשְׁקִיט לוֹ מִימֵי רָע	13	lending him peace in times of trouble
עַד יִכָּרֶה לָרָשָׁע שָֽׁחַת:		until a pit is dug for the wicked,

כִּי ׀ לֹא־יִטֹּשׁ יהוה עַמּוֹ
וְנַחֲלָתוֹ לֹא יַעֲזֹב:

14 for the LORD will not forsake His people,
nor abandon His heritage.

כִּי־עַד־צֶדֶק יָשׁוּב מִשְׁפָּט
וְאַחֲרָיו כָּל־יִשְׁרֵי־לֵב:

15 Judgment shall again accord with justice,
and all the true-hearted will follow it.

מִי־יָקוּם לִי עִם־מְרֵעִים
מִי־יִתְיַצֵּב לִי עִם־פֹּעֲלֵי אָוֶן:

16 Who will protect me against the wicked?
Who will stand up for me
against evildoers?

לוּלֵי יהוה עֶזְרָתָה לִּי
כִּמְעַט ׀ שָׁכְנָה דוּמָה נַפְשִׁי:

17 Had the LORD not been my help,
I would soon have dwelt
in death's silence.

אִם־אָמַרְתִּי מָטָה רַגְלִי
חַסְדְּךָ יהוה יִסְעָדֵנִי:

18 When I felt my foot was slipping,
Your loving-kindness, LORD,
gave me support.

בְּרֹב שַׂרְעַפַּי בְּקִרְבִּי
תַּנְחוּמֶיךָ יְשַׁעַשְׁעוּ נַפְשִׁי:

19 When my dread rose within me,
Your consolations soothed my soul.

הַיְחָבְרְךָ כִּסֵּא הַוּוֹת
יֹצֵר עָמָל עֲלֵי־חֹק:

20 Can a corrupt throne be allied with You,
a throne that brings misery
through its law?

יָגוֹדּוּ עַל־נֶפֶשׁ צַדִּיק
וְדָם נָקִי יַרְשִׁיעוּ:

21 They join forces against the life
of the righteous
and condemn the innocent to death,

וַיְהִי יהוה לִי לְמִשְׂגָּב
וֵאלֹהַי לְצוּר מַחְסִי:

22 but the LORD is my stronghold;
my God is the rock of my refuge.

וַיָּשֶׁב עֲלֵיהֶם ׀ אֶת־אוֹנָם
וּבְרָעָתָם יַצְמִיתֵם
יַצְמִיתֵם יהוה אֱלֹהֵינוּ:

23 He will return their own evil
back upon them
and with their own corruption
destroy them –
the LORD our God will destroy them.

Come, let us sing for joy to the LORD and shout out to the rock of our salvation

God's salvation comes as quickly as the blink of an eye.
But we can't just stand there and blink.
We must do our part, today.
The Messiah says he'll come today.
The Messiah doesn't lie. Listen to His voice, today.

PSALM 95

לְכוּ נְרַנְּנָה לַיהוָה נָרִיעָה לְצוּר יִשְׁעֵנוּ:	1 Come, let us sing for joy to the LORD and shout out to the rock of our salvation.
נְקַדְּמָה פָנָיו בְּתוֹדָה בִּזְמִרוֹת נָרִיעַ לוֹ:	2 Let us greet Him with thanksgiving and shout out to Him with songs of praise,
כִּי אֵל גָּדוֹל יהוה וּמֶלֶךְ גָּדוֹל עַל־כָּל־אֱלֹהִים:	3 for the LORD is the great God, the great King, above all divine beings.
אֲשֶׁר בְּיָדוֹ מֶחְקְרֵי־אָרֶץ וְתוֹעֲפוֹת הָרִים לוֹ:	4 The depths of the earth are in His hand; the mountain peaks are His;
אֲשֶׁר־לוֹ הַיָּם וְהוּא עָשָׂהוּ וְיַבֶּשֶׁת יָדָיו יָצָרוּ:	5 the sea is His, for He made it; the dry land too, for His hands formed it.
בֹּאוּ נִשְׁתַּחֲוֶה וְנִכְרָעָה נִבְרְכָה לִפְנֵי־יהוה עֹשֵׂנוּ:	6 Come, let us bow in worship and kneel before the LORD our Maker,
כִּי הוּא אֱלֹהֵינוּ וַאֲנַחְנוּ ׀ עַם מַרְעִיתוֹ וְצֹאן יָדוֹ הַיּוֹם אִם־בְּקֹלוֹ תִשְׁמָעוּ:	7 for He is our God, and we are the people of His pasture, the flock He tends – today, if you would heed His voice.
אַל־תַּקְשׁוּ לְבַבְכֶם כִּמְרִיבָה כְּיוֹם מַסָּה בַּמִּדְבָּר:	8 Do not harden your hearts as you did at Meriva, as you did then at Masa in the desert
אֲשֶׁר נִסּוּנִי אֲבוֹתֵיכֶם בְּחָנוּנִי גַּם־רָאוּ פָעֳלִי:	9 when your ancestors tested Me and tried Me though they had seen My deeds.
אַרְבָּעִים שָׁנָה ׀ אָקוּט בְּדוֹר וָאֹמַר עַם תֹּעֵי לֵבָב הֵם וְהֵם לֹא־יָדְעוּ דְרָכָי:	10 For forty years I was riled by that generation. I said, "They are a people whose hearts go astray, and they will not acknowledge My ways,"
אֲשֶׁר־נִשְׁבַּעְתִּי בְאַפִּי אִם־יְבֹאוּן אֶל־מְנוּחָתִי:	11 so I swore in My anger, "They will not enter My place of rest."

שמחו השמים ותגל הארץ

Nachshon 2015

נחשון
ב"ה, חקרון, תשע"ה

Let the heavens rejoice and the earth exult

It is a wonderful vision, a hopeful vision. It is a calming vision.
But it seems such a long way off. It is a vision of peace and of
justice. When true justice is achieved, real peace follows in its
wake. Never has the world known such peace. A song must be
sung, a song for us all. A new song must be sung, one never sung
before. How soon will we sing it?

PSALM 96

<table>
<tr><td>

שִׁירוּ לַיהוה שִׁיר חָדָשׁ
שִׁירוּ לַיהוה כָּל־הָאָרֶץ:
</td><td>1</td><td>

Sing to the LORD a new song;
sing to the LORD, all the earth;
</td></tr>
<tr><td>

שִׁירוּ לַיהוה בָּרְכוּ שְׁמוֹ
בַּשְּׂרוּ מִיּוֹם־לְיוֹם יְשׁוּעָתוֹ:
</td><td>2</td><td>

sing to the LORD, bless His name;
proclaim His salvation day by day.
</td></tr>
<tr><td>

סַפְּרוּ בַגּוֹיִם כְּבוֹדוֹ
בְּכָל־הָעַמִּים נִפְלְאוֹתָיו:
</td><td>3</td><td>

Declare His glory among the nations,
His wonders among all peoples,
</td></tr>
<tr><td>

כִּי גָדוֹל יהוה וּמְהֻלָּל מְאֹד
נוֹרָא הוּא עַל־כָּל־אֱלֹהִים:
</td><td>4</td><td>

for the LORD is great, of highest praise,
to be held in awe above all divine beings,
</td></tr>
<tr><td>

כִּי ׀ כָּל־אֱלֹהֵי הָעַמִּים אֱלִילִים
וַיהוה שָׁמַיִם עָשָׂה:
</td><td>5</td><td>

for all the gods of the peoples
are mere idols–
it was the LORD who made the heavens.
</td></tr>
<tr><td>

הוֹד־וְהָדָר לְפָנָיו
עֹז וְתִפְאֶרֶת בְּמִקְדָּשׁוֹ:
</td><td>6</td><td>

Majesty and splendor are before Him;
strength and beauty fill His sanctuary.
</td></tr>
<tr><td>

הָבוּ לַיהוה מִשְׁפְּחוֹת עַמִּים
הָבוּ לַיהוה כָּבוֹד וָעֹז:
</td><td>7</td><td>

Render to the LORD,
O families of the peoples,
render to the LORD glory and might.
</td></tr>
<tr><td>

הָבוּ לַיהוה כְּבוֹד שְׁמוֹ
שְׂאוּ־מִנְחָה וּבֹאוּ לְחַצְרוֹתָיו:
</td><td>8</td><td>

Render to the LORD
the glory due His name;
bring an offering,
and come into His courts.
</td></tr>
<tr><td>

הִשְׁתַּחֲווּ לַיהוה בְּהַדְרַת־קֹדֶשׁ
חִילוּ מִפָּנָיו כָּל־הָאָרֶץ:
</td><td>9</td><td>

Bow to the LORD
in the splendor of holiness;
tremble before Him, all the earth.
</td></tr>
<tr><td>

אִמְרוּ בַגּוֹיִם ׀ יהוה מָלָךְ
אַף־תִּכּוֹן תֵּבֵל בַּל־תִּמּוֹט
יָדִין עַמִּים בְּמֵישָׁרִים:
</td><td>10</td><td>

Say among the nations,
"The LORD is King."
The world stands firm;
it will never be shaken.
He will judge the peoples with equity.
</td></tr>
<tr><td>

יִשְׂמְחוּ הַשָּׁמַיִם וְתָגֵל הָאָרֶץ
יִרְעַם הַיָּם וּמְלֹאוֹ:
</td><td>11</td><td>

Let the heavens rejoice
and the earth exult;
let the sea roar, and all that fills it;
</td></tr>
</table>

יַעֲלֹז שָׂדַי וְכָל־אֲשֶׁר־בֹּו
אָז יְרַנְּנוּ כָּל־עֲצֵי־יָעַר׃

12 let the fields revel, and all they contain,
then all the trees of the forest
will sing for joy

לִפְנֵי יהוה ׀ כִּי בָא
כִּי בָא לִשְׁפֹּט הָאָרֶץ
יִשְׁפֹּט־תֵּבֵל בְּצֶדֶק
וְעַמִּים בֶּאֱמוּנָתוֹ׃

13 before the Lord, for He is coming;
He is coming to judge the earth.
He will judge the world with justice
and the peoples with His faithfulness.

Light is sown for the righteous, and joy for the upright of heart

I need this psalm. I am in deep and dark despair.
There is tragedy in the world, and great evil. Where is hope?
This psalm is a message of hope. It was written for people like
me. It brings us joy. It assures us that we have our priorities
straight. It helps us know where we stand.
It lights up the darkness.

PSALM 97

יְהוָה מָלָךְ תָּגֵל הָאָרֶץ 1
יִשְׂמְחוּ אִיִּים רַבִּים:

עָנָן וַעֲרָפֶל סְבִיבָיו צֶדֶק 2
וּמִשְׁפָּט מְכוֹן כִּסְאוֹ:

אֵשׁ לְפָנָיו תֵּלֵךְ 3
וּתְלַהֵט סָבִיב צָרָיו:

הֵאִירוּ בְרָקָיו תֵּבֵל 4
רָאֲתָה וַתָּחֵל הָאָרֶץ:

הָרִים כַּדּוֹנַג נָמַסּוּ מִלִּפְנֵי יְהוָה 5
מִלִּפְנֵי אֲדוֹן כָּל־הָאָרֶץ:

הִגִּידוּ הַשָּׁמַיִם צִדְקוֹ 6
וְרָאוּ כָל־הָעַמִּים כְּבוֹדוֹ:

יֵבֹשׁוּ ׀ כָּל־עֹבְדֵי פֶסֶל 7
הַמִּתְהַלְלִים בָּאֱלִילִים
הִשְׁתַּחֲווּ־לוֹ כָּל־אֱלֹהִים:

שָׁמְעָה וַתִּשְׂמַח ׀ צִיּוֹן 8
וַתָּגֵלְנָה בְּנוֹת יְהוּדָה
לְמַעַן מִשְׁפָּטֶיךָ יְהוָה:

כִּי־אַתָּה יְהוָה עֶלְיוֹן 9
עַל־כָּל־הָאָרֶץ
מְאֹד נַעֲלֵיתָ עַל־כָּל־אֱלֹהִים:

אֹהֲבֵי יְהוָה שִׂנְאוּ רָע 10
שֹׁמֵר נַפְשׁוֹת חֲסִידָיו
מִיַּד רְשָׁעִים יַצִּילֵם:

1 The LORD is king; let the earth exult;
  let the many islands rejoice.

2 Clouds and deep mist surround Him;
  righteousness and justice form the base
  of His throne.

3 Fire blazes before Him,
  burning His enemies on every side.

4 His lightning lights up the world;
  the earth sees and trembles.

5 Mountains melt like wax before the Lord,
  before the Master of all the earth.

6 The heavens proclaim His righteousness,
  and all the peoples see His glory.

7 All who worship images
  and boast of idols are put to shame;
  all divine beings bow down to Him.

8 Zion hears and rejoices;
  let the towns of Yehuda be glad
  because of Your judgments, LORD,

9 for You, LORD, are supreme
  over all the earth;
  You are exalted far above all
  heavenly powers.

10 O lovers of the LORD, hate evil,
   for He protects the lives
   of his devoted ones,
   delivering them
   from the hand of the wicked.

אוֹר זָרֻעַ לַצַּדִּיק 11 Light is sown for the righteous,
וּלְיִשְׁרֵי־לֵב שִׂמְחָה: and joy for the upright of heart.

שִׂמְחוּ צַדִּיקִים בַּיהוָה 12 Rejoice in the Lord, righteous ones;
וְהוֹדוּ לְזֵכֶר קָדְשׁוֹ: give thanks to His holy name.

With trumpets and the sound of the shofar; shout for joy before the LORD, the King!

God works wonders. When Israel triumphs and celebrates,
that's a wonder. When other nations celebrate too, that's a
wonder of wonders. That's an occasion for a new song.
Everyone will sing it, the rivers will applaud, the hills will rejoice.
God will then judge the world with righteousness.
Will the singing continue? If it does, that's a wondrous wonder.

PSALM 98

מִזְמוֹר
שִׁירוּ לַיהוָֹה ׀ שִׁיר חָדָשׁ
כִּי־נִפְלָאוֹת עָשָׂה
הוֹשִׁיעָה־לּוֹ יְמִינוֹ וּזְרוֹעַ קָדְשׁוֹ׃

1 A psalm
Sing a new song to the LORD,
for He has done wondrous things;
His right hand and His holy arm
have brought about victory.

הוֹדִיעַ יְהוָֹה יְשׁוּעָתוֹ
לְעֵינֵי הַגּוֹיִם גִּלָּה צִדְקָתוֹ׃

2 The Lord has made His salvation known,
displaying His righteousness
before the eyes of the nations.

זָכַר חַסְדּוֹ ׀ וֶאֱמוּנָתוֹ
לְבֵית יִשְׂרָאֵל
רָאוּ כָל־אַפְסֵי־אָרֶץ
אֵת יְשׁוּעַת אֱלֹהֵינוּ׃

3 He has remembered His loving-kindness
and loyalty to the house of Israel;
all the ends of the earth have seen
the victory of our God.

הָרִיעוּ לַיהוָֹה כָּל־הָאָרֶץ
פִּצְחוּ וְרַנְּנוּ וְזַמֵּרוּ׃

4 Shout for joy to the LORD, all the earth;
burst into song; sing with joy;
make music.

זַמְּרוּ לַיהוָֹה בְּכִנּוֹר
בְּכִנּוֹר וְקוֹל זִמְרָה׃

5 Make music to the LORD on the harp;
sing along with the harp

בַּחֲצֹצְרוֹת וְקוֹל שׁוֹפָר
הָרִיעוּ לִפְנֵי ׀ הַמֶּלֶךְ יְהוָֹה׃

6 with trumpets and the sound
of the shofar;
shout for joy before the LORD, the King!

יִרְעַם הַיָּם וּמְלֹאוֹ
תֵּבֵל וְיֹשְׁבֵי בָהּ׃

7 Let the sea roar, and all that fills it,
the world and all who live in it.

נְהָרוֹת יִמְחֲאוּ־כָף
יַחַד הָרִים יְרַנֵּנוּ׃

8 Let the rivers clap their hands
and the mountains sing together for joy

לִפְנֵי־יְהוָֹה
כִּי בָא לִשְׁפֹּט הָאָרֶץ
יִשְׁפֹּט־תֵּבֵל בְּצֶדֶק
וְעַמִּים בְּמֵישָׁרִים׃

9 before the LORD,
for He is coming to judge the earth.
He will judge the world with justice
and the peoples with equity.

Moshe and Aharon of His priests, Shmuel of those who called on His name

It is Friday evening and the sun is setting. I prepare for Shabbat by singing songs of David. Are we glad, and cannot be shaken? Or do we tremble and quake? Is this one of the Lord's many mysteries? Or is it our choice? This week, this Shabbat, let the world neither tremble nor quake. Let the earth be glad.

PSALM 99

<table>
<tr>
<td>

יְהוָה מָלָךְ יִרְגְּזוּ עַמִּים
יֹשֵׁב כְּרוּבִים תָּנוּט הָאָֽרֶץ׃

</td>
<td>1</td>
<td>

The Lord reigns–
let the peoples tremble;
He sits enthroned on the cherubim–
let the earth quake.

</td>
</tr>
<tr>
<td>

יְהוָה בְּצִיּוֹן גָּדוֹל
וְרָם הוּא עַל־כָּל־הָעַמִּֽים׃

</td>
<td>2</td>
<td>

Great is the Lord in Zion;
He is exalted over all the peoples.

</td>
</tr>
<tr>
<td>

יוֹדוּ שִׁמְךָ גָּדוֹל וְנוֹרָא
קָדוֹשׁ הֽוּא׃

</td>
<td>3</td>
<td>

Let them praise
Your great and awesome name.
He is holy!

</td>
</tr>
<tr>
<td>

וְעֹז מֶלֶךְ מִשְׁפָּט אָהֵב
אַתָּה כּוֹנַנְתָּ מֵישָׁרִים
מִשְׁפָּט וּצְדָקָה בְּיַעֲקֹב ׀
אַתָּה עָשִֽׂיתָ׃

</td>
<td>4</td>
<td>

O mighty King who loves justice,
You have established equity;
Justice and righteousness in Yaakov
is Your doing.

</td>
</tr>
<tr>
<td>

רוֹמְמוּ יְהוָה אֱלֹהֵינוּ
וְהִשְׁתַּחֲווּ לַהֲדֹם רַגְלָיו
קָדוֹשׁ הֽוּא׃

</td>
<td>5</td>
<td>

Exalt the Lord our God
and bow at His footstool.
He is holy!

</td>
</tr>
<tr>
<td>

מֹשֶׁה וְאַהֲרֹן ׀ בְּכֹהֲנָיו
וּשְׁמוּאֵל בְּקֹרְאֵי שְׁמוֹ
קֹרִאים אֶל־יְהוָה וְהוּא יַעֲנֵֽם׃

</td>
<td>6</td>
<td>

Moshe and Aharon of His priests,
Shmuel of those who called
on His name –
they called on the Lord,
and He answered them.

</td>
</tr>
<tr>
<td>

בְּעַמּוּד עָנָן יְדַבֵּר אֲלֵיהֶם
שָׁמְרוּ עֵדֹתָיו וְחֹק נָתַן־לָֽמוֹ׃

</td>
<td>7</td>
<td>

He spoke to them in a pillar of cloud;
they observed His decrees
and the statutes He gave them.

</td>
</tr>
<tr>
<td>

יְהוָה אֱלֹהֵינוּ אַתָּה עֲנִיתָם
אֵל נֹשֵׂא הָיִיתָ לָהֶם
וְנֹקֵם עַל־עֲלִילוֹתָֽם׃

</td>
<td>8</td>
<td>

Lord our God, You answered them.
You were for them a forgiving God
though You punished their misdeeds.

</td>
</tr>
<tr>
<td>

רוֹמְמוּ יְהוָה אֱלֹהֵינוּ
וְהִשְׁתַּחֲווּ לְהַר קָדְשׁוֹ
כִּי־קָדוֹשׁ יְהוָה אֱלֹהֵֽינוּ׃

</td>
<td>9</td>
<td>

Exalt the Lord our God
and bow at His holy mountain,
for the Lord our God is holy.

</td>
</tr>
</table>

A psalm of thanksgiving. Shout out to the LORD, all the earth!

Gratitude can't be expressed in solitude.
Sure, it is a very spiritual feeling.
It makes you feel close to God. But it also makes you shout for joy.
It makes you sing and dance. It makes you want to tell your story.

PSALM 100

מִזְמוֹר לְתוֹדָה	1	A psalm of thanksgiving
הָרִיעוּ לַיהוֹה כָּל־הָאָרֶץ:		Shout out to the LORD, all the earth!
עִבְדוּ אֶת־יהוה בְּשִׂמְחָה	2	Serve the LORD with joy;
בֹּאוּ לְפָנָיו בִּרְנָנָה:		come before Him in glad song.
דְּעוּ כִּי־יהוה הוּא אֱלֹהִים	3	Know that the LORD is God;
וְלֹא הוּא עָשָׂנוּ וְלוֹ אֲנַחְנוּ		He made us, and we are His;
עַמּוֹ וְצֹאן מַרְעִיתוֹ:		we are His people, the flock He tends.
בֹּאוּ שְׁעָרָיו ׀ בְּתוֹדָה	4	Enter His gates with thanksgiving,
חֲצֵרֹתָיו בִּתְהִלָּה		His courts with praise;
הוֹדוּ לוֹ בָּרְכוּ שְׁמוֹ:		thank Him and bless His name,
כִּי־טוֹב יהוה לְעוֹלָם חַסְדּוֹ	5	for the LORD is good;
וְעַד־דֹּר וָדֹר אֱמוּנָתוֹ:		His loving-kindness is forever,
		His faithfulness for all generations.

My eyes are on the faithful ones of the land to have them dwell with me.

Those whose ways are blameless, they will serve me

I earn a living helping others.
I spend my work day doing charity, achieving justice.
My colleagues share my goals and we work together.
Thank You, God, for assigning me this job, my job.

PSALM 101

לְדָוִד מִזְמוֹר 1 Of David – a psalm
חֶסֶד־וּמִשְׁפָּט אָשִׁירָה I will sing of loyalty and justice;
לְךָ יהוה אֲזַמֵּרָה: to You, Lord, I will sing praise.

אַשְׂכִּילָה ׀ בְּדֶרֶךְ תָּמִים 2 I contemplate the way of the blameless –
מָתַי תָּבוֹא אֵלַי when shall I reach it?
אֶתְהַלֵּךְ בְּתָם־לְבָבִי בְּקֶרֶב I walk about with a blameless heart
בֵּיתִי: within my own home.

לֹא־אָשִׁית ׀ לְנֶגֶד עֵינַי 3 I will not set any depravity
דְּבַר־בְּלִיָּעַל before my eyes.
עֲשֹׂה־סֵטִים שָׂנֵאתִי I despise shifty dealing–
לֹא יִדְבַּק בִּי: such things will not cling to me.

לֵבָב עִקֵּשׁ יָסוּר מִמֶּנִּי 4 Perverse hearts will keep away from me;
רָע לֹא אֵדָע: I will have nothing to do with evil.

מְלָשְׁנִי בַסֵּתֶר ׀ רֵעֵהוּ 5 Those who slander their fellows in secret
אוֹתוֹ אַצְמִית I will destroy:
גְּבַהּ־עֵינַיִם וּרְחַב לֵבָב those of haughty eyes and proud hearts
אֹתוֹ לֹא אוּכָל: I cannot bear.

עֵינַי ׀ בְּנֶאֶמְנֵי־אֶרֶץ 6 My eyes are on the faithful ones
לָשֶׁבֶת עִמָּדִי of the land
הֹלֵךְ בְּדֶרֶךְ תָּמִים to have them dwell with me.
הוּא יְשָׁרְתֵנִי: Those whose ways are blameless,
they will serve me.

לֹא־יֵשֵׁב ׀ בְּקֶרֶב בֵּיתִי 7 There shall not dwell within my house
עֹשֵׂה רְמִיָּה anyone who practices deceit;
דֹּבֵר שְׁקָרִים No one who speaks lies
לֹא־יִכּוֹן לְנֶגֶד עֵינָי: shall endure before my eyes.

לַבְּקָרִים אַצְמִית 8 Morning after morning
כָּל־רִשְׁעֵי־אָרֶץ I destroy all the wicked of the land,
לְהַכְרִית מֵעִיר־יהוה ridding the Lord's city
כָּל־פֹּעֲלֵי אָוֶן: of all evildoers.

Nachshon

Rise up and have mercy on Zion; the time has come to grant her grace;
the hour has arrived

God, don't file away my prayer in some folder.
Give it Your special attention.
For me, these prayers are urgent.
I have nowhere else to turn.
Hear my prayers, and may they bear fruit.

PSALM 102

תְּפִלָּה לְעָנִי כִי־יַעֲטֹף
וְלִפְנֵי יְהֹוָה יִשְׁפֹּךְ שִׂיחוֹ:

1 A prayer for the lowly
when they grow overwhelmed
and pour out their lament
before the Lord:

יְהֹוָה שִׁמְעָה תְפִלָּתִי
וְשַׁוְעָתִי אֵלֶיךָ תָבוֹא:

2 O Lord, listen to my prayer;
let my cry reach You.

אַל־תַּסְתֵּר פָּנֶיךָ ׀ מִמֶּנִּי
בְּיוֹם צַר לִי
הַטֵּה־אֵלַי אָזְנֶךָ
בְּיוֹם אֶקְרָא מַהֵר עֲנֵנִי:

3 Do not hide Your face from me
on the day of my distress;
lend Your ear to me
on the day that I call –
hurry, answer me! –

כִּי־כָלוּ בְעָשָׁן יָמָי
וְעַצְמוֹתַי כְּמוֹקֵד נִחָרוּ:

4 for my days dissipate like smoke;
my bones are scorched as in a furnace;

הוּכָּה כָעֵשֶׂב וַיִּבַשׁ לִבִּי
כִּי־שָׁכַחְתִּי מֵאֲכֹל לַחְמִי:

5 my heart is trampled
and withered like grass;
I neglect to eat my food.

מִקּוֹל אַנְחָתִי
דָּבְקָה עַצְמִי לִבְשָׂרִי:

6 From the noise of my groans,
my bones cleave to my flesh.

דָּמִיתִי לִקְאַת מִדְבָּר
הָיִיתִי כְּכוֹס חֳרָבוֹת:

7 I have become like a desert owl,
like an owl among ruins;

שָׁקַדְתִּי וָאֶהְיֶה
כְּצִפּוֹר בּוֹדֵד עַל־גָּג:

8 I lie awake;
I have become like a lonely bird
upon a rooftop.

כָּל־הַיּוֹם חֵרְפוּנִי אוֹיְבָי
מְהוֹלָלַי בִּי נִשְׁבָּעוּ:

9 All day long my enemies taunt me;
my revilers use my name as a curse,

כִּי־אֵפֶר כַּלֶּחֶם אָכָלְתִּי
וְשִׁקֻּוַי בִּבְכִי מָסָכְתִּי:

10 for I eat ashes for bread
and mingle my drink with tears

מִפְּנֵי־זַעַמְךָ וְקִצְפֶּךָ
כִּי נְשָׂאתַנִי וַתַּשְׁלִיכֵנִי:

11 because of Your fury and wrath,
because You raised me up
and flung me down.

יָמַי כְּצֵל נָטוּי
וַאֲנִי כָּעֵשֶׂב אִיבָשׁ:

12 My days are like lengthening shadows,
and I wither away like grass,

וְאַתָּה יהוה לְעוֹלָם תֵּשֵׁב
וְזִכְרְךָ לְדֹר וָדֹר:

13 but You, Lord, are enthroned forever;
Your name endures for all generations.

אַתָּה תָקוּם תְּרַחֵם צִיּוֹן
כִּי־עֵת לְחֶנְנָהּ כִּי־בָא מוֹעֵד:

14 Rise up and have mercy on Zion;
the time has come to grant her grace;
the hour has arrived,

כִּי־רָצוּ עֲבָדֶיךָ אֶת־אֲבָנֶיהָ
וְאֶת־עֲפָרָהּ יְחֹנֵנוּ:

15 for Your servants love her very stones;
they even cherish her dust.

וְיִירְאוּ גוֹיִם אֶת־שֵׁם יהוה
וְכָל־מַלְכֵי הָאָרֶץ אֶת־כְּבוֹדֶךָ:

16 Then the nations will fear
the name of the Lord,
all the kings of the earth Your glory –

כִּי־בָנָה יהוה צִיּוֹן
נִרְאָה בִּכְבוֹדוֹ:

17 when the Lord rebuilds Zion
and appears in His glory.

פָּנָה אֶל־תְּפִלַּת הָעַרְעָר
וְלֹא־בָזָה אֶת־תְּפִלָּתָם:

18 He turns to the prayer of the destitute
and does not show contempt
for their prayers.

תִּכָּתֶב זֹאת לְדוֹר אַחֲרוֹן
וְעַם נִבְרָא יְהַלֶּל־יָהּ:

19 May this be inscribed
for a generation to come,
that people yet unborn
will praise the Lord,

כִּי־הִשְׁקִיף מִמְּרוֹם קָדְשׁוֹ
יהוה מִשָּׁמַיִם ׀
אֶל־אֶרֶץ הִבִּיט:

20 for the Lord gazes down
from His holy heights;
He looks down from heaven to earth

לִשְׁמֹעַ אֶנְקַת אָסִיר
לְפַתֵּחַ בְּנֵי תְמוּתָה:

21 to hear the groans of captives,
to free those doomed to death

לְסַפֵּר בְּצִיּוֹן שֵׁם יהוה
וּתְהִלָּתוֹ בִּירוּשָׁלָ͏ִם:

22 so that the Lord's name may be
proclaimed in Zion
and in Jerusalem His praise

בְּהִקָּבֵץ עַמִּים יַחְדָּו
וּמַמְלָכוֹת לַעֲבֹד אֶת־יהוה:

23 when peoples gather together,
as well as kingdoms, to serve the Lord.

כֹּחוֹ

עִנָּה בַדֶּרֶךְ כֹּחִי
קִצַּר יָמָי:

24 He has sapped my strength in midcourse
and shortened my days.

אֹמַר אֵלִי אַל־תַּעֲלֵנִי בַּחֲצִי יָמָי
בְּדוֹר דּוֹרִים שְׁנוֹתֶיךָ:

25 I say, "O my God, do not take me away
when only half my days are done –
You whose years span the generations."

לְפָנִים הָאָרֶץ יָסַדְתָּ
וּמַעֲשֵׂה יָדֶיךָ שָׁמָיִם:

26 You founded the earth long ago;
the heavens are Your handiwork.

הֵמָּה ׀ יֹאבֵדוּ וְאַתָּה תַעֲמֹד
וְכֻלָּם כַּבֶּגֶד יִבְלוּ
כַּלְּבוּשׁ תַּחֲלִיפֵם וְיַחֲלֹפוּ:

27 When they are long gone,
You will still stand;
they will all wear out like a garment;
You change them like clothing,
and they fade away,

וְאַתָּה־הוּא
וּשְׁנוֹתֶיךָ לֹא יִתָּמּוּ:

28 but You are always the same –
Your years never end.

בְּנֵי־עֲבָדֶיךָ יִשְׁכּוֹנוּ
וְזַרְעָם לְפָנֶיךָ יִכּוֹן:

29 May Your servants' children dwell
in peace
and their own seed be established
in Your presence.

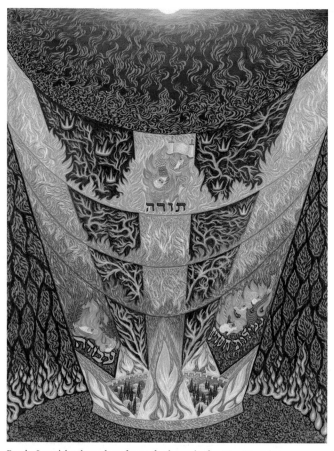

But the Lᴏʀᴅ's loyalty endures forever for those who fear Him, His righteousness for their children's children

We pass through five worlds. In each, the soul sings God's praises; in each, a different song. In the womb it sings a song of anticipation. When it is born it sings exuberant songs. Songs of hope help it cope with life's twists and turns. It departs the body, and returns to God to sing in His presence. When the world is perfect, it will sing once again. In each world the soul sings a different song.

PSALM 103

לְדָוִד ׀ בָּרְכִי נַפְשִׁי אֶת־יהוה וְכָל־קְרָבַי אֶת־שֵׁם קָדְשׁוֹ:	1 Of David. Bless the LORD, my soul, His holy name with all my being;
בָּרְכִי נַפְשִׁי אֶת־יהוה וְאַל־תִּשְׁכְּחִי כָּל־גְּמוּלָיו:	2 bless the LORD, my soul; forget none of His benefits—
הַסֹּלֵחַ לְכָל־עֲוֺנֵכִי הָרֹפֵא לְכָל־תַּחֲלֻאָיְכִי:	3 He forgives all your sins, He heals all your ills,
הַגּוֹאֵל מִשַּׁחַת חַיָּיְכִי הַמְעַטְּרֵכִי חֶסֶד וְרַחֲמִים:	4 He redeems your life from the pit, He crowns you with love and compassion,
הַמַּשְׂבִּיעַ בַּטּוֹב עֶדְיֵךְ תִּתְחַדֵּשׁ כַּנֶּשֶׁר נְעוּרָיְכִי:	5 and He sates you with good in your prime so that your youth is renewed like the eagle's.
עֹשֵׂה צְדָקוֹת יהוה וּמִשְׁפָּטִים לְכָל־עֲשׁוּקִים:	6 The LORD executes righteousness and brings justice to all the oppressed.
יוֹדִיעַ דְּרָכָיו לְמֹשֶׁה לִבְנֵי יִשְׂרָאֵל עֲלִילוֹתָיו:	7 He revealed His ways to Moshe, His deeds to the people of Israel.
רַחוּם וְחַנּוּן יהוה אֶרֶךְ אַפַּיִם וְרַב־חָסֶד:	8 The Lord is compassionate and gracious, slow to anger, abounding in kindness.
לֹא־לָנֶצַח יָרִיב וְלֹא לְעוֹלָם יִטּוֹר:	9 He does not contend for long or bear a grudge forever;
לֹא כַחֲטָאֵינוּ עָשָׂה לָנוּ וְלֹא כַעֲוֺנֹתֵינוּ גָּמַל עָלֵינוּ:	10 He has not treated us according to our sins or repaid us according to our misdeeds,
כִּי כִגְבֹהַּ שָׁמַיִם עַל־הָאָרֶץ גָּבַר חַסְדּוֹ עַל־יְרֵאָיו:	11 for as high as the heavens reach above the earth is the strength of His love for those who fear Him;

כְּרְחֹק מִזְרָח מִמַּעֲרָב הִרְחִיק מִמֶּנּוּ אֶת־פְּשָׁעֵינוּ:	12 as far as the east is from the west He has distanced our transgressions from us.
כְּרַחֵם אָב עַל־בָּנִים רִחַם יְהוָה עַל־יְרֵאָיו:	13 As a father has compassion on his children, so the LORD has compassion on those who fear Him,
כִּי־הוּא יָדַע יִצְרֵנוּ זָכוּר כִּי־עָפָר אֲנָחְנוּ:	14 for He knows how we are formed; He remembers that we are dust.
אֱנוֹשׁ כֶּחָצִיר יָמָיו כְּצִיץ הַשָּׂדֶה כֵּן יָצִיץ:	15 Like grass are the days of mortals, who spring up like wildflowers;
כִּי רוּחַ עָבְרָה־בּוֹ וְאֵינֶנּוּ וְלֹא־יַכִּירֶנּוּ עוֹד מְקוֹמוֹ:	16 with a mere gust of wind they are gone, leaving no trace behind them,
וְחֶסֶד יְהוָה ׀ מֵעוֹלָם וְעַד־ עוֹלָם עַל־יְרֵאָיו וְצִדְקָתוֹ לִבְנֵי בָנִים:	17 but the LORD's loyalty endures forever for those who fear Him, His righteousness for their children's children,
לְשֹׁמְרֵי בְרִיתוֹ וּלְזֹכְרֵי פִקֻּדָיו לַעֲשׂוֹתָם:	18 for those who keep His covenant and remember to obey His laws.
יְהוָה בַּשָּׁמַיִם הֵכִין כִּסְאוֹ וּמַלְכוּתוֹ בַּכֹּל מָשָׁלָה:	19 The LORD has established His throne in heaven; His kingdom rules over all.
בָּרְכוּ יְהוָה מַלְאָכָיו גִּבֹּרֵי כֹחַ עֹשֵׂי דְבָרוֹ לִשְׁמֹעַ בְּקוֹל דְּבָרוֹ:	20 Bless the LORD, you His angels, those mighty in power who do His bidding, who obey His word.
בָּרְכוּ יְהוָה כָּל־צְבָאָיו מְשָׁרְתָיו עֹשֵׂי רְצוֹנוֹ:	21 Bless the LORD, all you His host, you ministers who do His will;
בָּרְכוּ יְהוָה ׀ כָּל־מַעֲשָׂיו בְּכָל־מְקֹמוֹת מֶמְשַׁלְתּוֹ בָּרְכִי נַפְשִׁי אֶת־יְהוָה:	22 bless the LORD and all His works in every part of His dominion. Bless the LORD, my soul.

May the glory of the Lord last forever; may the Lord rejoice in His works

I was just a city boy. City boys think they know everything, but they don't. They know Man's world, but not the world where the "grass grows" and "the trees are well watered." That's God's world. He showed His world to me. Now I'm not just a city boy. I am His world's boy.

PSALM 104

בָּרֲכִי נַפְשִׁי אֶת־יהוה 1
יהוה אֱלֹהַי גָּדַלְתָּ מְּאֹד
הוֹד וְהָדָר לָבָשְׁתָּ:

Bless the Lord, my soul.
O Lord my God,
You are exceedingly great,
clothed in majesty and splendor;

עֹטֶה־אוֹר כַּשַּׂלְמָה 2
נוֹטֶה שָׁמַיִם כַּיְרִיעָה:

cloaked in a robe of light,
You have spread out the heavens
like a tent.

הַמְקָרֶה בַמַּיִם עֲלִיּוֹתָיו 3
הַשָּׂם־עָבִים רְכוּבוֹ
הַמְהַלֵּךְ עַל־כַּנְפֵי־רוּחַ:

He roofs His upper chambers with water;
He harnesses the clouds as His chariot
and rides on wings of wind.

עֹשֶׂה מַלְאָכָיו רוּחוֹת 4
מְשָׁרְתָיו אֵשׁ לֹהֵט:

He makes the winds His messengers,
flames of fire His ministers.

יָסַד־אֶרֶץ עַל־מְכוֹנֶיהָ 5
בַּל־תִּמּוֹט עוֹלָם וָעֶד:

He has fixed the earth on its foundations
so that it will never be shaken.

תְּהוֹם כַּלְּבוּשׁ כִּסִּיתוֹ 6
עַל־הָרִים יַעַמְדוּ־מָיִם:

You covered it with the deep like a cloak;
the waters stood above the mountains.

מִן־גַּעֲרָתְךָ יְנוּסוּן 7
מִן־קוֹל רַעַמְךָ יֵחָפֵזוּן:

At Your onslaught they fled;
at the sound of Your thunder
they rushed away,

יַעֲלוּ הָרִים יֵרְדוּ בְקָעוֹת 8
אֶל־מְקוֹם זֶה ׀ יָסַדְתָּ לָהֶם:

flowing over the hills,
streaming down into the valleys
to the place You determined for them.

גְּבוּל־שַׂמְתָּ בַּל־יַעֲבֹרוּן 9
בַּל־יְשֻׁבוּן לְכַסּוֹת הָאָרֶץ:

You set a boundary they were not to pass
so that they would never cover the earth
again.

הַמְשַׁלֵּחַ מַעְיָנִים בַּנְּחָלִים 10
בֵּין הָרִים יְהַלֵּכוּן:

He makes springs flow in the valleys;
they make their way between the hills,

יַשְׁקוּ כָּל־חַיְתוֹ שָׂדָי 11
יִשְׁבְּרוּ פְרָאִים צְמָאָם:

watering all the beasts of the field;
the wild donkeys quench their thirst.

עֲלֵיהֶם עוֹף־הַשָּׁמַיִם יִשְׁכּוֹן
מִבֵּין עֳפָאיִם יִתְּנוּ־קוֹל:

12 The birds of the sky roost above them,
singing among the foliage.

מַשְׁקֶה הָרִים מֵעֲלִיּוֹתָיו
מִפְּרִי מַעֲשֶׂיךָ תִּשְׂבַּע הָאָרֶץ:

13 He waters the mountains
from His upper chambers;
the earth is sated
with the fruit of Your work.

מַצְמִיחַ חָצִיר ׀ לַבְּהֵמָה
וְעֵשֶׂב לַעֲבֹדַת הָאָדָם
לְהוֹצִיא לֶחֶם מִן־הָאָרֶץ:

14 He makes grass grow for the cattle
and plants for human use
to bring forth food from the earth,

וְיַיִן ׀ יְשַׂמַּח לְבַב־אֱנוֹשׁ
לְהַצְהִיל פָּנִים מִשָּׁמֶן
וְלֶחֶם לְבַב־אֱנוֹשׁ יִסְעָד:

15 wine to cheer people's hearts,
oil to make their faces shine,
bread to sustain people's hearts.

יִשְׂבְּעוּ עֲצֵי יהוה
אַרְזֵי לְבָנוֹן אֲשֶׁר נָטָע:

16 The trees of the LORD drink their fill,
the cedars of Lebanon that He planted.

אֲשֶׁר־שָׁם צִפֳּרִים יְקַנֵּנוּ
חֲסִידָה בְּרוֹשִׁים בֵּיתָהּ:

17 There birds build their nests;
the stork makes its home in the cypresses.

הָרִים הַגְּבֹהִים לַיְּעֵלִים
סְלָעִים מַחְסֶה לַשְׁפַנִּים:

18 High hills are for the wild goats;
rocky crags are shelter for the hyraxes.

עָשָׂה יָרֵחַ לְמוֹעֲדִים
שֶׁמֶשׁ יָדַע מְבוֹאוֹ:

19 He made the moon to mark the seasons;
the sun knows when to set.

תָּשֶׁת־חֹשֶׁךְ וִיהִי לָיְלָה
בּוֹ־תִרְמֹשׂ כָּל־חַיְתוֹ־יָעַר:

20 You cast darkness, night falls,
and all the forest creatures stir.

הַכְּפִירִים שֹׁאֲגִים לַטָּרֶף
וּלְבַקֵּשׁ מֵאֵל אָכְלָם:

21 The young lions roar for prey;
they seek their food from God.

תִּזְרַח הַשֶּׁמֶשׁ יֵאָסֵפוּן
וְאֶל־מְעוֹנֹתָם יִרְבָּצוּן:

22 When the sun rises, they slink away
and settle down in their lairs.

יֵצֵא אָדָם לְפָעֳלוֹ 23 People go out to their work,
וְלַעֲבֹדָתוֹ עֲדֵי־עָרֶב: to their labor until evening.

מָה־רַבּוּ מַעֲשֶׂיךָ ׀ יְהֹוָה 24 How many are Your works, LORD;
כֻּלָּם בְּחָכְמָה עָשִׂיתָ You made them all in wisdom;
מָלְאָה הָאָרֶץ קִנְיָנֶךָ: the earth is full of Your creations.

זֶה ׀ הַיָּם גָּדוֹל וּרְחַב יָדָיִם 25 There is the vast, immeasurable sea
שָׁם־רֶמֶשׂ וְאֵין מִסְפָּר teeming with countless creatures,
חַיּוֹת קְטַנּוֹת עִם־גְּדֹלוֹת: living things great and small.

שָׁם אֳנִיּוֹת יְהַלֵּכוּן 26 There ships sail;
לִוְיָתָן זֶה־יָצַרְתָּ לְשַׂחֶק־בּוֹ: You created that Leviathan
for Your own pleasure.

כֻּלָּם אֵלֶיךָ יְשַׂבֵּרוּן 27 All of them look to You in hope,
לָתֵת אָכְלָם בְּעִתּוֹ: to give them their food when it is due.

תִּתֵּן לָהֶם יִלְקֹטוּן 28 They gather up what You give them;
תִּפְתַּח יָדְךָ יִשְׂבְּעוּן טוֹב: when You open Your hand,
they are sated with good.

תַּסְתִּיר פָּנֶיךָ יִבָּהֵלוּן 29 When You hide Your face,
תֹּסֵף רוּחָם יִגְוָעוּן they grow terrified.
וְאֶל־עֲפָרָם יְשׁוּבוּן: When You take away their breath,
they die and return to dust.

תְּשַׁלַּח רוּחֲךָ יִבָּרֵאוּן 30 When You emit Your breath,
וּתְחַדֵּשׁ פְּנֵי אֲדָמָה: they are created,
bringing new life to the face of the earth.

יְהִי כְבוֹד יְהֹוָה לְעוֹלָם 31 May the glory of the LORD last forever;
יִשְׂמַח יְהֹוָה בְּמַעֲשָׂיו: may the LORD rejoice in His works.

הַמַּבִּיט לָאָרֶץ וַתִּרְעָד 32 When He looks at the earth, it trembles;
יִגַּע בֶּהָרִים וְיֶעֱשָׁנוּ: when He touches the mountains,
they smoke.

אָשִׁירָה לַיהוָה בְּחַיָּי
אֲזַמְּרָה לֵאלֹהַי בְּעוֹדִי:

33 I will sing to the Lord all my life;
I will sing to my God as long as I live.

יֶעֱרַב עָלָיו שִׂיחִי
אָנֹכִי אֶשְׂמַח בַּיהוָה:

34 May my reflections delight Him;
I will rejoice in the Lord.

יִתַּמּוּ חַטָּאִים ׀ מִן־הָאָרֶץ
וּרְשָׁעִים ׀ עוֹד אֵינָם
בָּרְכִי נַפְשִׁי אֶת־יהוה
הַלְלוּיָהּ:

35 May sinners vanish from the earth
and the wicked be no more.
Bless the Lord, my soul.
Halleluya!

He brought His people out in joy, His chosen ones in glad song

History repeats itself. We must learn its many lessons.
The story of our forefathers is our story. It began with God's
promise to Avraham. Avraham was just the beginning.
Yosef's trials added suspense to the story. Slavery ensued. Finally,
the climax: Exodus and Redemption. But the story didn't end
there. The story continues.

PSALM 105

הוֹדוּ לַיהוה קִרְאוּ בִשְׁמוֹ
הוֹדִיעוּ בָעַמִּים עֲלִילוֹתָיו:

1 Give thanks to the Lord;
call on His name;
proclaim His acts among the peoples.

שִׁירוּ־לוֹ זַמְּרוּ־לוֹ
שִׂיחוּ בְּכָל־נִפְלְאוֹתָיו:

2 Sing to Him; make music to Him;
tell of all His wonders.

הִתְהַלְלוּ בְּשֵׁם קָדְשׁוֹ
יִשְׂמַח לֵב ׀ מְבַקְשֵׁי יהוה:

3 Glory in His holy name;
let the hearts of the Lord's seekers
rejoice.

דִּרְשׁוּ יהוה וְעֻזּוֹ
בַּקְּשׁוּ פָנָיו תָּמִיד:

4 Long for the Lord and His might;
seek out His presence always.

זִכְרוּ נִפְלְאוֹתָיו אֲשֶׁר־עָשָׂה
מֹפְתָיו וּמִשְׁפְּטֵי־פִיו:

5 Recall the wonders He has done,
the marvels and judgments
He has pronounced,

זֶרַע אַבְרָהָם עַבְדּוֹ
בְּנֵי יַעֲקֹב בְּחִירָיו:

6 O seed of Avraham His servant,
O children of Yaakov, His chosen ones.

הוּא יהוה אֱלֹהֵינוּ
בְּכָל־הָאָרֶץ מִשְׁפָּטָיו:

7 He is the Lord, our God;
His judgments are throughout the land.

זָכַר לְעוֹלָם בְּרִיתוֹ
דָּבָר צִוָּה לְאֶלֶף דּוֹר:

8 He remembers His covenant forever,
His word of command
for a thousand generations –

אֲשֶׁר כָּרַת אֶת־אַבְרָהָם
וּשְׁבוּעָתוֹ לְיִשְׂחָק:

9 which He formed with Avraham,
swore to Yishak,

וַיַּעֲמִידֶהָ לְיַעֲקֹב לְחֹק
לְיִשְׂרָאֵל בְּרִית עוֹלָם:

10 and established with Yaakov as a statute,
as an eternal covenant for Israel –

לֵאמֹר לְךָ אֶתֵּן
אֶת־אֶרֶץ־כְּנָעַן
חֶבֶל נַחֲלַתְכֶם:

11 saying, "To you I will give
the land of Canaan
as your share of inheritance" –

בִּהְיוֹתָם מְתֵי מִסְפָּר
כִּמְעַט וְגָרִים בָּהּ:

12 when you were few in number,
scarce, strangers there,

וַיִּתְהַלְּכוּ מִגּוֹי אֶל־גּוֹי 13 wandering from nation to nation,
מִמַּמְלָכָה אֶל־עַם אַחֵר: from one kingdom to another people.

לֹא־הִנִּיחַ אָדָם לְעָשְׁקָם 14 Yet He let no one oppress them
וַיּוֹכַח עֲלֵיהֶם מְלָכִים: and rebuked kings for their sake, saying,

אַל־תִּגְּעוּ בִמְשִׁיחָי 15 "Touch not My anointed ones,
וְלִנְבִיאַי אַל־תָּרֵעוּ: and do My prophets no harm."

וַיִּקְרָא רָעָב עַל־הָאָרֶץ 16 He summoned famine to the land
כָּל־מַטֵּה־לֶחֶם שָׁבָר: and cut off all supply of bread,

שָׁלַח לִפְנֵיהֶם אִישׁ 17 but He sent a man before them –
לְעֶבֶד נִמְכַּר יוֹסֵף: Yosef, sold into slavery.

רַגְלָיו

עִנּוּ בַכֶּבֶל רַגְלוֹ 18 They pressed his feet into fetters,
בַּרְזֶל בָּאָה נַפְשׁוֹ: and an iron collar closed around his neck;

עַד־עֵת בֹּא־דְבָרוֹ 19 until his words came to pass,
אִמְרַת יהוה צְרָפָתְהוּ: the Lord's decree purged him.

שָׁלַח מֶלֶךְ וַיַּתִּירֵהוּ 20 The king sent and set him free;
מֹשֵׁל עַמִּים וַיְפַתְּחֵהוּ: the ruler of peoples released him.

שָׂמוֹ אָדוֹן לְבֵיתוֹ 21 He made him master of his house,
וּמֹשֵׁל בְּכָל־קִנְיָנוֹ: ruler over all he owned

לֶאְסֹר שָׂרָיו בְּנַפְשׁוֹ 22 with the power to imprison princes
וּזְקֵנָיו יְחַכֵּם: at will
so that he could teach his elders wisdom.

וַיָּבֹא יִשְׂרָאֵל מִצְרָיִם 23 Then Israel came to Egypt,
וְיַעֲקֹב גָּר בְּאֶרֶץ־חָם: and Yaakov settled in the land of Ham.

וַיֶּפֶר אֶת־עַמּוֹ מְאֹד 24 He made His people most fruitful,
וַיַּעֲצִמֵהוּ מִצָּרָיו: more numerous than their enemies.

הָפַךְ לִבָּם לִשְׂנֹא עַמּוֹ 25 He changed their hearts
לְהִתְנַכֵּל בַּעֲבָדָיו: to hate His people,
to conspire against His servants.

שָׁלַח מֹשֶׁה עַבְדּוֹ	26	He sent His servant Moshe
אַהֲרֹן אֲשֶׁר בָּחַר־בּוֹ:		and Aharon, whom He had chosen,
שָׂמוּ־בָם דִּבְרֵי אֹתוֹתָיו	27	and they performed His signs
וּמֹפְתִים בְּאֶרֶץ חָם:		among them,
		wonders in the land of Ham.
שָׁלַח חֹשֶׁךְ וַיַּחְשִׁךְ	28	He sent darkness; it grew dark,
וְלֹא־מָרוּ אֶת־דְּבָרוֹ:		yet they still rebelled against His word.
הָפַךְ אֶת־מֵימֵיהֶם לְדָם	29	He turned their water into blood;
וַיָּמֶת אֶת־דְּגָתָם:		He killed their fish;
שָׁרַץ אַרְצָם צְפַרְדְּעִים	30	their land teemed with frogs,
בְּחַדְרֵי מַלְכֵיהֶם:		even in their royal chambers.
אָמַר וַיָּבֹא עָרֹב	31	He gave the word, and swarms came,
כִּנִּים בְּכָל־גְּבוּלָם:		and lice throughout their borders.
נָתַן גִּשְׁמֵיהֶם בָּרָד	32	He made their rain into hail,
אֵשׁ לֶהָבוֹת בְּאַרְצָם:		with flames of fire throughout their land.
וַיַּךְ גַּפְנָם וּתְאֵנָתָם	33	He struck down their vines and figs
וַיְשַׁבֵּר עֵץ גְּבוּלָם:		and shattered the trees
		throughout their borders.
אָמַר וַיָּבֹא אַרְבֶּה	34	He gave the word, and the locusts came,
וְיֶלֶק וְאֵין מִסְפָּר:		grasshoppers without number;
וַיֹּאכַל כָּל־עֵשֶׂב בְּאַרְצָם	35	they devoured all the grass in their land
וַיֹּאכַל פְּרִי אַדְמָתָם:		and devoured the fruits of their soil.
וַיַּךְ כָּל־בְּכוֹר בְּאַרְצָם	36	He struck down every firstborn
רֵאשִׁית לְכָל־אוֹנָם:		in their land,
		all the first fruits of their manhood,
וַיּוֹצִיאֵם בְּכֶסֶף וְזָהָב	37	then He brought them out
וְאֵין בִּשְׁבָטָיו כּוֹשֵׁל:		with silver and gold,
		and none among His tribes did falter.

דברי

שָׂמַח מִצְרַיִם בְּצֵאתָם 38 Egypt rejoiced when they went out,
כִּי־נָפַל פַּחְדָּם עֲלֵיהֶם: for their terror had fallen upon them.

פָּרַשׂ עָנָן לְמָסָךְ 39 He spread out a cloud as a screen
וְאֵשׁ לְהָאִיר לָיְלָה: and fire to light up the night.

שָׁאַל וַיָּבֵא שְׂלָו 40 They asked, and He provided quail;
וְלֶחֶם שָׁמַיִם יַשְׂבִּיעֵם: He sated them with heavenly bread.

פָּתַח צוּר וַיָּזוּבוּ מָיִם 41 He opened up a rock,
הָלְכוּ בַּצִּיּוֹת נָהָר: and water flowed out,
running like a river in the parched land,

כִּי־זָכַר אֶת־דְּבַר קָדְשׁוֹ 42 for He remembered His holy word
אֶת־אַבְרָהָם עַבְדּוֹ: to Avraham, His servant.

וַיּוֹצֵא עַמּוֹ בְשָׂשׂוֹן 43 He brought His people out in joy,
בְּרִנָּה אֶת־בְּחִירָיו: His chosen ones in glad song.

וַיִּתֵּן לָהֶם אַרְצוֹת גּוֹיִם 44 He gave them the lands of the nations;
וַעֲמַל לְאֻמִּים יִירָשׁוּ: they took possession
of the wealth of peoples

בַּעֲבוּר ׀ יִשְׁמְרוּ חֻקָּיו 45 so that they might keep His statutes
וְתוֹרֹתָיו יִנְצֹרוּ and observe His teachings.
הַלְלוּיָהּ: Halleluya!

Save us, LORD our God, and gather us from the nations so that we may give thanks to Your holy name and glory in Your praise

We sin. He forgives us. We take that for granted.
After all, He is a forgiving God. We sin again, and again.
He still forgives us. Who can declare all the praise due to Him?

PSALM 106

הַלְלוּיָהּ ׀
הוֹדוּ לַיהוָה כִּי־טוֹב
כִּי לְעוֹלָם חַסְדּוֹ׃

1 Halleluya!
Thank the LORD for He is good;
His loving-kindness is forever.

מִי יְמַלֵּל גְּבוּרוֹת יהוה
יַשְׁמִיעַ כָּל־תְּהִלָּתוֹ׃

2 Who can articulate
the LORD's mighty acts;
who can express all His praise?

אַשְׁרֵי שֹׁמְרֵי מִשְׁפָּט
עֹשֵׂה צְדָקָה בְכָל־עֵת׃

3 Happy are those who keep justice,
who do what is right at all times.

זָכְרֵנִי יהוה בִּרְצוֹן עַמֶּךָ
פָּקְדֵנִי בִּישׁוּעָתֶךָ׃

4 Remember me, LORD,
when You show Your people favor;
keep me in mind for Your salvation,

לִרְאוֹת ׀ בְּטוֹבַת בְּחִירֶיךָ
לִשְׂמֹחַ בְּשִׂמְחַת גּוֹיֶךָ
לְהִתְהַלֵּל עִם־נַחֲלָתֶךָ׃

5 that I may share in the good
of Your chosen ones,
rejoice in the joy of Your own nation,
and glory in Your heritage.

חָטָאנוּ עִם־אֲבוֹתֵינוּ
הֶעֱוִינוּ הִרְשָׁעְנוּ׃

6 We have sinned like our ancestors;
we have offended; we have done evil.

אֲבוֹתֵינוּ בְמִצְרַיִם ׀
לֹא־הִשְׂכִּילוּ נִפְלְאוֹתֶיךָ
לֹא זָכְרוּ אֶת־רֹב חֲסָדֶיךָ
וַיַּמְרוּ עַל־יָם בְּיַם־סוּף׃

7 Our ancestors in Egypt
did not appreciate Your wonders,
did not recall Your great loyalty –
they were defiant at the sea,
at the Sea of Reeds,

וַיּוֹשִׁיעֵם לְמַעַן שְׁמוֹ
לְהוֹדִיעַ אֶת־גְּבוּרָתוֹ׃

8 yet He saved them
for the sake of His name,
to make known His mighty deeds.

וַיִּגְעַר בְּיַם־סוּף וַיֶּחֱרָב
וַיּוֹלִיכֵם בַּתְּהֹמוֹת כַּמִּדְבָּר׃

9 He blasted the Sea of Reeds,
and it dried up;
He led them through the deep
as through wilderness.

וַיּוֹשִׁיעֵם מִיַּד שׂוֹנֵא
וַיִּגְאָלֵם מִיַּד אוֹיֵב׃

10 He saved them from the hands of haters
and redeemed them
from the hands of enemies.

וַיְכַסּוּ־מַיִם צָרֵיהֶם אֶחָד מֵהֶם לֹא נוֹתָר:	11	The waters covered their foes; not one of them remained.
וַיַּאֲמִינוּ בִדְבָרָיו יָשִׁירוּ תְּהִלָּתוֹ:	12	They had faith in His words and sang His praises,
מִהֲרוּ שָׁכְחוּ מַעֲשָׂיו לֹא־חִכּוּ לַעֲצָתוֹ:	13	but they soon forgot what He had done and would not await His counsel.
וַיִּתְאַוּוּ תַאֲוָה בַּמִּדְבָּר וַיְנַסּוּ־אֵל בִּישִׁימוֹן:	14	They were seized with craving in the wilderness and tested God in the wasteland.
וַיִּתֵּן לָהֶם שֶׁאֱלָתָם וַיְשַׁלַּח רָזוֹן בְּנַפְשָׁם:	15	He granted what they asked for but made them waste away.
וַיְקַנְאוּ לְמֹשֶׁה בַּמַּחֲנֶה לְאַהֲרֹן קְדוֹשׁ יְהוָה:	16	They grew envious of Moshe in the camp, of Aharon, the LORD's holy one.
תִּפְתַּח־אֶרֶץ וַתִּבְלַע דָּתָן וַתְּכַס עַל־עֲדַת אֲבִירָם:	17	The earth opened up and swallowed Datan and closed over Aviram's mob,
וַתִּבְעַר־אֵשׁ בַּעֲדָתָם לֶהָבָה תְּלַהֵט רְשָׁעִים:	18	then fire burned up their mob; flame set the wicked ones ablaze.
יַעֲשׂוּ־עֵגֶל בְּחֹרֵב וַיִּשְׁתַּחֲווּ לְמַסֵּכָה:	19	They made a calf at Ḥorev and bowed to a molten image,
וַיָּמִירוּ אֶת־כְּבוֹדָם בְּתַבְנִית שׁוֹר אֹכֵל עֵשֶׂב:	20	exchanging their Glory for a figure of a grass-eating ox.
שָׁכְחוּ אֵל מוֹשִׁיעָם עֹשֶׂה גְדֹלוֹת בְּמִצְרָיִם:	21	They forgot God their Savior, who had done great things in Egypt,
נִפְלָאוֹת בְּאֶרֶץ חָם נוֹרָאוֹת עַל־יַם־סוּף:	22	wonders in the land of Ham, awesome deeds at the Sea of Reeds.

וַיֹּאמֶר לְהַשְׁמִידָם
לוּלֵי מֹשֶׁה בְחִירוֹ
עָמַד בַּפֶּרֶץ לְפָנָיו
לְהָשִׁיב חֲמָתוֹ מֵהַשְׁחִית:

23 He would have wiped them out
were it not for Moshe, His chosen one,
who stood in the breach before Him
to hold back His wrath
from destroying them.

וַיִּמְאֲסוּ בְּאֶרֶץ חֶמְדָּה
לֹא־הֶאֱמִינוּ לִדְבָרוֹ:

24 They spurned the most desirable land
and did not have faith in His promise.

וַיֵּרָגְנוּ בְאׇהֳלֵיהֶם
לֹא שָׁמְעוּ בְּקוֹל יהוה:

25 They grumbled in their tents
and would not heed the Lord's voice,

וַיִּשָּׂא יָדוֹ לָהֶם
לְהַפִּיל אוֹתָם בַּמִּדְבָּר:

26 so He raised His hand against them
to cast them down in the wilderness,

וּלְהַפִּיל זַרְעָם בַּגּוֹיִם
וּלְזָרוֹתָם בָּאֲרָצוֹת:

27 cast their seed among the nations,
and scattered them throughout the lands.

וַיִּצָּמְדוּ לְבַעַל פְּעוֹר
וַיֹּאכְלוּ זִבְחֵי מֵתִים:

28 They embraced Baal Peor
and ate sacrifices of the dead.

וַיַּכְעִיסוּ בְּמַעַלְלֵיהֶם
וַתִּפְרׇץ־בָּם מַגֵּפָה:

29 Their practices provoked Him,
and a plague broke out among them,

וַיַּעֲמֹד פִּינְחָס וַיְפַלֵּל
וַתֵּעָצַר הַמַּגֵּפָה:

30 then Phineas took a stand
and intervened,
and the plague ceased.

וַתֵּחָשֶׁב לוֹ לִצְדָקָה
לְדֹר וָדֹר עַד־עוֹלָם:

31 This was counted to his merit
for all generations forever.

וַיַּקְצִיפוּ עַל־מֵי מְרִיבָה
וַיֵּרַע לְמֹשֶׁה בַּעֲבוּרָם:

32 They moved Him to fury
at the waters of Meriva,
and Moshe suffered because of them

כִּי־הִמְרוּ אֶת־רוּחוֹ
וַיְבַטֵּא בִּשְׂפָתָיו:

33 when they defied his spirit,
and he spoke rash words.

לֹא־הִשְׁמִידוּ אֶת־הָעַמִּים
אֲשֶׁר אָמַר יהוה לָהֶם:

34 They did not destroy the peoples
that the Lord bade them to destroy;

וַיִּתְעָרְב֥וּ בַגּוֹיִ֑ם 35 they mingled with the nations
וַֽ֝יִּלְמְד֗וּ מַֽעֲשֵׂיהֶֽם׃ and learned their ways.

וַיַּעַבְד֥וּ אֶת־עֲצַבֵּיהֶ֑ם 36 They served their idols,
וַיִּהְי֖וּ לָהֶ֣ם לְמוֹקֵֽשׁ׃ which became a snare for them;

וַיִּזְבְּח֣וּ אֶת־בְּ֭נֵיהֶם וְאֶת־ 37 they sacrificed their sons
בְּנֽוֹתֵיהֶ֗ם לַשֵּׁדִֽים׃ and their daughters to demons.

וַיִּֽשְׁפְּכ֨וּ דָ֪ם נָקִ֡י 38 They spilled innocent blood,
דַּם־בְּנֵ֘יהֶ֤ם וּֽבְנוֹתֵיהֶ֗ם the blood of their sons and daughters;
אֲשֶׁ֣ר זִ֭בְּחוּ לַעֲצַבֵּ֣י כְנָ֑עַן they sacrificed to the idols of Canaan,
וַתֶּחֱנַ֥ף הָ֝אָ֗רֶץ בַּדָּמִֽים׃ and the land grew polluted with blood.

וַיִּטְמְא֥וּ בְמַעֲשֵׂיהֶ֑ם 39 They defiled with their deeds,
וַ֝יִּזְנ֗וּ בְּמַֽעַלְלֵיהֶֽם׃ and strayed with their practices;

וַיִּֽחַר־אַ֣ף יְהוָ֣ה בְּעַמּ֑וֹ 40 The LORD's fury blazed against His
וַ֝יְתָעֵ֗ב אֶת־נַחֲלָתֽוֹ׃ people,
and He abhorred His share,

וַֽיִּתְּנֵ֥ם בְּיַד־גּוֹיִ֑ם 41 so He handed them over to the nations,
וַֽיִּמְשְׁל֥וּ בָ֝הֶ֗ם שֹׂנְאֵיהֶֽם׃ and their haters ruled over them.

וַיִּלְחָצ֥וּם אוֹיְבֵיהֶ֑ם 42 Their enemies oppressed them,
וַ֝יִּכָּנְע֗וּ תַּ֣חַת יָדָֽם׃ and they were brought low
by their power.

פְּעָמִ֥ים רַבּ֗וֹת יַצִּ֫ילֵ֥ם 43 Many times He saved them,
וְ֭הֵמָּה יַמְר֣וּ בַעֲצָתָ֑ם but they were defiant in their schemes
וַ֝יָּמֹ֗כּוּ בַּעֲוֺנָֽם׃ and sank low in their guilt,

וַ֭יַּרְא בַּצַּ֣ר לָהֶ֑ם 44 yet He saw their torment
בְּ֝שָׁמְע֗וֹ אֶת־רִנָּתָֽם׃ when He heard their cry.

וַיִּזְכֹּ֣ר לָהֶ֣ם בְּרִית֑וֹ 45 He remembered His covenant
וַ֝יִּנָּחֵ֗ם כְּרֹ֣ב חֲסָדָֽיו׃ for their sake,
and He relented in His great loyalty.

וַיִּתֵּ֣ן אוֹתָ֣ם לְרַחֲמִ֑ים
לִ֝פְנֵ֗י כָּל־שׁוֹבֵיהֶֽם׃

46 He stirred compassion for them
in the hearts of all their captors.

הוֹשִׁיעֵ֨נוּ ׀ יְה֘וָ֤ה אֱלֹהֵ֗ינוּ
וְקַבְּצֵנוּ֮ מִֽן־הַגּ֫וֹיִ֥ם
לְ֭הֹדוֹת לְשֵׁ֣ם קָדְשֶׁ֑ךָ
לְ֝הִשְׁתַּבֵּ֗חַ בִּתְהִלָּתֶֽךָ׃

47 Save us, Lord our God,
and gather us from the nations
so that we may give thanks
to Your holy name
and glory in Your praise.

בָּר֤וּךְ יְהוָ֨ה ׀ אֱלֹהֵ֥י יִשְׂרָאֵ֗ל
מִן־הָעוֹלָ֨ם ׀ וְעַ֬ד הָעוֹלָ֗ם
וְאָמַ֖ר כָּל־הָעָ֥ם אָמֵ֗ן
הַֽלְלוּ־יָֽהּ׃

48 Blessed is the Lord, God of Israel,
forever and ever,
and let all the people say "Amen."
Halleluya!

הודו לה' כי טוב

לי לעולם וחסדו:

Thank the LORD for He is good; His loving-kindness is forever

I spend my week wandering in the wilderness.
The path to safety eludes me. Nausea denies me every pleasure.
I am tossed about by the waves of circumstance.
Shabbat draws near, and the path slowly emerges from its shroud.
With Shabbat comes freedom, healing, and a safe harbor.

PSALM 107

הוֹדוּ לַיהוה כִּי־טוֹב 1 Thank the Lord for He is good;
כִּי לְעוֹלָם חַסְדּוֹ:   His loving-kindness is forever;

יֹאמְרוּ גְּאוּלֵי יהוה 2 let the Lord's redeemed say this –
אֲשֶׁר גְּאָלָם מִיַּד־צָר: those He redeemed
     from the enemy's hand,

וּמֵאֲרָצוֹת קִבְּצָם 3 those He gathered from the lands,
מִמִּזְרָח וּמִמַּעֲרָב מִצָּפוֹן וּמִיָּם: from east and west,
     from north and south.

תָּעוּ בַמִּדְבָּר בִּישִׁימוֹן דָּרֶךְ 4 Some lost their way in desert wastelands,
עִיר מוֹשָׁב לֹא מָצָאוּ:   finding no inhabited towns.

רְעֵבִים גַּם־צְמֵאִים 5 Hungry and thirsty,
נַפְשָׁם בָּהֶם תִּתְעַטָּף: their will to live grew faint.

וַיִּצְעֲקוּ אֶל־יהוה בַּצַּר לָהֶם 6 They cried out to the Lord
מִמְּצוּקוֹתֵיהֶם יַצִּילֵם: in their torment;
     He rescued them from their distress;

וַיַּדְרִיכֵם בְּדֶרֶךְ יְשָׁרָה 7 He led them by a straight path
לָלֶכֶת אֶל־עִיר מוֹשָׁב: to a town where they could settle.

יוֹדוּ לַיהוה חַסְדּוֹ 8 Let them thank the Lord
וְנִפְלְאוֹתָיו לִבְנֵי אָדָם: for His loving-kindness,
     for His wondrous deeds for humanity,

כִּי־הִשְׂבִּיעַ נֶפֶשׁ שֹׁקֵקָה 9 for He quenches thirsty souls
וְנֶפֶשׁ רְעֵבָה מִלֵּא־טוֹב: and fills up hungry souls with goodness.

יֹשְׁבֵי חֹשֶׁךְ וְצַלְמָוֶת 10 Some sat in darkness and death-shadow,
אֲסִירֵי עֳנִי וּבַרְזֶל: bound in cruel iron chains,

כִּי־הִמְרוּ אִמְרֵי־אֵל 11 for they had defied God's words
וַעֲצַת עֶלְיוֹן נָאָצוּ:   and reviled the counsel of the Most High.

וַיַּכְנַע בֶּעָמָל לִבָּם 12 He humbled their hearts with toil;
כָּשְׁלוּ וְאֵין עֹזֵר: they stumbled, with none to help.

וַיִּזְעֲק֣וּ אֶל־יהוה בַּצַּ֣ר לָהֶ֑ם
מִֽמְּצֻ֥קוֹתֵיהֶ֗ם יוֹשִׁיעֵֽם׃

13 They cried out to the LORD
in their torment;
He saved them from their distress.

יֽוֹצִיאֵ֭ם מֵחֹ֣שֶׁךְ וְצַלְמָ֑וֶת
וּמֽוֹסְרֽוֹתֵיהֶ֣ם יְנַתֵּֽק׃

14 He brought them out
from darkness and death-shadow
and broke apart their bonds.

יוֹד֣וּ לַיהוה חַסְדּ֑וֹ
וְ֝נִפְלְאוֹתָ֗יו לִבְנֵ֥י אָדָֽם׃

15 Let them thank the LORD
for His loving-kindness,
for His wondrous deeds for humanity,

כִּֽי־שִׁ֭בַּר דַּלְת֣וֹת נְחֹ֑שֶׁת
וּבְרִיחֵ֖י בַרְזֶ֣ל גִּדֵּֽעַ׃

16 for He shattered gates of bronze
and cut their iron bars.

אֱ֭וִלִים מִדֶּ֣רֶךְ פִּשְׁעָ֑ם
וּֽמֵעֲוֺ֣נֹתֵיהֶ֗ם יִתְעַנּֽוּ׃

17 Some were fools of sinful ways,
suffering because of their iniquities.

כׇּל־אֹ֭כֶל תְּתַעֵ֣ב נַפְשָׁ֑ם
וַ֝יַּגִּ֗יעוּ עַד־שַׁ֥עֲרֵי מָֽוֶת׃

18 They found all food repulsive
and came close to the gates of death.

וַיִּזְעֲק֣וּ אֶל־יהוה בַּצַּ֣ר לָהֶ֑ם
מִֽמְּצֻ֥קוֹתֵיהֶ֗ם יוֹשִׁיעֵֽם׃

19 They cried out to the LORD
in their torment;
He saved them from their distress.

יִשְׁלַ֣ח דְּ֭בָרוֹ וְיִרְפָּאֵ֑ם
וִ֝ימַלֵּ֗ט מִשְּׁחִיתוֹתָֽם׃

20 He sent His word and healed them
and rescued them from their destruction.

יוֹד֣וּ לַיהוה חַסְדּ֑וֹ
וְ֝נִפְלְאוֹתָ֗יו לִבְנֵ֥י אָדָֽם׃

21 Let them thank the LORD
for His loving-kindness,
for His wondrous deeds for humanity;

וְ֭יִזְבְּחוּ זִבְחֵ֣י תוֹדָ֑ה
וִיסַפְּר֖וּ מַעֲשָׂ֣יו בְּרִנָּֽה׃ ‹

22 let them sacrifice thanksgiving offerings
and tell of His deeds with joy.

יוֹרְדֵ֣י הַ֭יָּם בׇּאֳנִיּ֑וֹת
עֹשֵׂ֥י מְ֝לָאכָ֗ה בְּמַ֣יִם
רַבִּֽים׃ ‹

23 Those who go down to the sea in ships,
sailing across the mighty waters –

הֵ֣מָּה רָ֭אוּ מַעֲשֵׂ֣י יהוה
וְ֝נִפְלְאוֹתָ֗יו בִּמְצוּלָֽה׃ ‹

24 they have seen the works of the LORD,
His wondrous deeds in the deep.

וַיֹּאמֶר וַיַּעֲמֵד רוּחַ סְעָרָה	25 He spoke and stirred up a tempest
וַתְּרוֹמֵם גַּלָּיו: ‎	that lifted up the waves;
יַעֲלוּ שָׁמַיִם יֵרְדוּ תְהוֹמוֹת	26 they rose to the heavens and
נַפְשָׁם בְּרָעָה תִתְמוֹגָג: ‎	plunged down to the depths,
	their souls melted in misery.
יָחוֹגּוּ וְיָנוּעוּ כַּשִּׁכּוֹר	27 They reeled and staggered like drunkards;
וְכָל־חָכְמָתָם תִּתְבַּלָּע: ‎	all their skill was to no avail.
וַיִּצְעֲקוּ אֶל־יהוה בַּצַּר לָהֶם	28 They cried out to the Lord
וּמִמְּצוּקֹתֵיהֶם יוֹצִיאֵם:	in their torment;
	He brought them out from their distress.
יָקֵם סְעָרָה לִדְמָמָה	29 He stilled the storm to a whisper,
וַיֶּחֱשׁוּ גַּלֵּיהֶם:	and the waves of the sea grew calm.
וַיִּשְׂמְחוּ כִי־יִשְׁתֹּקוּ	30 They rejoiced when all was quiet,
וַיַּנְחֵם אֶל־מְחוֹז חֶפְצָם:	then He guided them
	to their desired harbor.
יוֹדוּ לַיהוה חַסְדּוֹ	31 Let them thank the Lord
וְנִפְלְאוֹתָיו לִבְנֵי אָדָם:	for His loving-kindness,
	for His wondrous deeds for humanity.
וִירֹמְמוּהוּ בִּקְהַל־עָם	32 Let them exalt Him before the assembly
וּבְמוֹשַׁב זְקֵנִים יְהַלְלוּהוּ:	and praise Him in the council
	of the elders.
יָשֵׂם נְהָרוֹת לְמִדְבָּר	33 He turns rivers into desert land,
וּמֹצָאֵי מַיִם לְצִמָּאוֹן:	springs of water into parched ground,
אֶרֶץ פְּרִי לִמְלֵחָה	34 fruitful land into salt-sown waste
מֵרָעַת יוֹשְׁבֵי בָהּ:	because of the corruption of its people.
יָשֵׂם מִדְבָּר לַאֲגַם־מַיִם	35 He turns desert land into pools of water,
וְאֶרֶץ צִיָּה לְמֹצָאֵי מָיִם:	wasteland into flowing springs;
וַיּוֹשֶׁב שָׁם רְעֵבִים	36 He brings the hungry to live there,
וַיְכוֹנְנוּ עִיר מוֹשָׁב:	to build a town in which to live.

וַיִּזְרְע֣וּ שָׂ֭דוֹת וַיִּטְּע֣וּ כְרָמִ֑ים
וַ֝יַּעֲשׂ֗וּ פְּרִ֣י תְבוּאָֽה׃

37 They sow fields and plant vineyards
that yield a fruitful harvest;

וַיְבָרֲכֵ֣ם וַיִּרְבּ֣וּ מְאֹ֑ד
וּ֝בְהֶמְתָּ֗ם לֹ֣א יַמְעִֽיט׃

38 He blesses them, and they flourish;
He does not let their herds decrease,

וַיִּמְעֲט֥וּ וַיָּשֹׁ֑חוּ
מֵעֹ֖צֶר רָעָ֣ה וְיָגֽוֹן׃ ﬠ

39 but they shrink and languish
under tyranny, cruelty, and sorrow.

שֹׁפֵ֣ךְ בּ֭וּז עַל־נְדִיבִ֑ים
וַ֝יַּתְעֵ֗ם בְּתֹ֣הוּ לֹא־דָֽרֶךְ׃

40 He pours contempt on nobles
and leads them astray into pathless chaos.

וַיְשַׂגֵּ֣ב אֶבְי֣וֹן מֵע֑וֹנִי
וַיָּ֥שֶׂם כַּ֝צֹּ֗אן מִשְׁפָּחֽוֹת׃

41 He lifts the destitute from poverty
and increases their families like flocks.

יִרְא֣וּ יְשָׁרִ֣ים וְיִשְׂמָ֑חוּ
וְכָל־עַ֝וְלָ֗ה קָ֣פְצָה פִּֽיהָ׃

42 The upright see and rejoice,
while all wicked mouths are silenced.

מִי־חָכָ֥ם וְיִשְׁמָר־אֵ֑לֶּה
וְ֝יִתְבּֽוֹנְנ֗וּ חַֽסְדֵ֥י יְהוָֽה׃

43 Let the wise keep all this in mind;
let them reflect
on the LORD's loving-kindness.

My heart is sound, God; my heart is sound – I will sing and chant praises from my very soul

We cannot brazenly knock on God's door and expect Him to answer. We must first prepare ourselves. I do what David did. He summoned his harp and lyre. His music empowered him to pray. My music can't compare to his, so I just hum a tune. That gives me the confidence to knock on God's door.

PSALM 108

שִׁיר מִזְמוֹר לְדָוִד:	1 A song – a psalm of David
נָכוֹן לִבִּי אֱלֹהִים אָשִׁירָה וַאֲזַמְּרָה אַף־כְּבוֹדִי:	2 My heart is sound, God; my heart is sound – I will sing and chant praises from my very soul.
עוּרָה הַנֵּבֶל וְכִנּוֹר אָעִירָה שָּׁחַר:	3 Stir, harp and lyre! I will stir the dawn.
אוֹדְךָ בָעַמִּים ׀ יהוה וַאֲזַמֶּרְךָ בַּלְאֻמִּים:	4 I will praise You among the peoples, Lord; I will chant Your praise among the nations,
כִּי־גָדֹל מֵעַל־שָׁמַיִם חַסְדֶּךָ וְעַד־שְׁחָקִים אֲמִתֶּךָ:	5 for Your loyalty is higher than the heavens; Your truth reaches the skies.
רוּמָה עַל־שָׁמַיִם אֱלֹהִים וְעַל כָּל־הָאָרֶץ כְּבוֹדֶךָ:	6 Rise up, God, over the heavens; unleash Your glory over all the earth
לְמַעַן יֵחָלְצוּן יְדִידֶיךָ הוֹשִׁיעָה יְמִינְךָ וַעֲנֵנִי: ועננו	7 so that Your dear ones may be rescued; let Your right hand bring victory – answer me!
אֱלֹהִים ׀ דִּבֶּר בְּקָדְשׁוֹ אֶעְלֹזָה אֲחַלְּקָה שְׁכֶם וְעֵמֶק סֻכּוֹת אֲמַדֵּד:	8 God promised in His sanctuary that I would triumph: I will divide up Shekhem and measure out the Valley of Sukot;
לִי גִלְעָד ׀ לִי מְנַשֶּׁה וְאֶפְרַיִם מָעוֹז רֹאשִׁי יְהוּדָה מְחֹקְקִי:	9 Gilad and Menashe will be mine; Efrayim will be my chief stronghold, Yehuda my scepter.
מוֹאָב ׀ סִיר רַחְצִי עַל־אֱדוֹם אַשְׁלִיךְ נַעֲלִי עֲלֵי־פְלֶשֶׁת אֶתְרוֹעָע:	10 Moav will be my washbasin; at Edom I will fling my shoe; I will crow over Philistia,

מִי יֹבִלֵנִי עִיר מִבְצָר
מִי נָחַנִי עַד־אֱדֽוֹם:

11 but who will bring me
to the fortified cities?
Who will lead me to Edom?

הֲלֹא־אֱלֹהִים זְנַחְתָּנוּ
וְלֹא־תֵצֵא אֱלֹהִים
בְּצִבְאֹתֵֽינוּ:

12 Have You not forsaken us, God?
God, You no longer march out
with our forces.

הָֽבָה־לָּנוּ עֶזְרָת מִצָּר
וְשָׁוְא תְּשׁוּעַת אָדָֽם:

13 Come to our aid against the enemy,
for human help is worthless.

בֵּֽאלֹהִים נַעֲשֶׂה־חָֽיִל
וְהוּא יָבוּס צָרֵֽינוּ:

14 With God, we will triumph valiantly,
and He will trample our enemies.

I pray for them

Why do they hate me? I love them. I love Him.
Do they hate me because I love Him? Can they not tolerate my
love for Him? Is it Him they really hate? Or is it my love for them
that they despise? These questions have no answer.
They necessitated the invention of a new term: "anti-Semitism."

PSALM 109

לַמְנַצֵּחַ לְדָוִד מִזְמוֹר אֱלֹהֵי תְהִלָּתִי אַל־תֶּחֱרַשׁ:	1	To the lead singer, of David – a psalm God of my praise, do not remain silent,
כִּי פִי רָשָׁע וּפִי־מִרְמָה עָלַי פָּתָחוּ דִּבְּרוּ אִתִּי לְשׁוֹן שָׁקֶר:	2	for wicked mouths, deceitful mouths have opened against me. They speak to me with lying tongues;
וְדִבְרֵי שִׂנְאָה סְבָבוּנִי וַיִּלָּחֲמוּנִי חִנָּם:	3	they surround me with words of hatred, attacking me without cause.
תַּחַת־אַהֲבָתִי יִשְׂטְנוּנִי וַאֲנִי תְפִלָּה:	4	In return for my love they accuse me, yet I pray for them.
וַיָּשִׂימוּ עָלַי רָעָה תַּחַת טוֹבָה וְשִׂנְאָה תַּחַת אַהֲבָתִי:	5	They repay me with evil for good, with hatred for my love.
הַפְקֵד עָלָיו רָשָׁע וְשָׂטָן יַעֲמֹד עַל־יְמִינוֹ:	6	"Station a wicked person over him; let an adversary stand on his right.
בְּהִשָּׁפְטוֹ יֵצֵא רָשָׁע וּתְפִלָּתוֹ תִּהְיֶה לַחֲטָאָה:	7	When he is tried, let him be found guilty; may his prayer count as offense.
יִהְיוּ־יָמָיו מְעַטִּים פְּקֻדָּתוֹ יִקַּח אַחֵר:	8	May his days be few; may another seize his post.
יִהְיוּ־בָנָיו יְתוֹמִים וְאִשְׁתּוֹ אַלְמָנָה:	9	May his children become orphans, his wife a widow;
וְנוֹעַ יָנוּעוּ בָנָיו וְשִׁאֵלוּ וְדָרְשׁוּ מֵחָרְבוֹתֵיהֶם:	10	may his children wander and beg, foraging far from their ruined homes.
יְנַקֵּשׁ נוֹשֶׁה לְכָל־אֲשֶׁר־לוֹ וְיָבֹזּוּ זָרִים יְגִיעוֹ:	11	May a usurer seize all he owns and strangers plunder his wealth.
אַל־יְהִי־לוֹ מֹשֵׁךְ חָסֶד וְאַל־יְהִי חוֹנֵן לִיתוֹמָיו:	12	May no one show him any kindness and no one pity his orphans.
יְהִי־אַחֲרִיתוֹ לְהַכְרִית בְּדוֹר אַחֵר יִמַּח שְׁמָם:	13	May his posterity be cut off, their name erased by the next generation.

יִזָּכֵ֤ר ׀ עֲוֺ֣ן אֲ֭בֹתָיו אֶל־יְהֹוָ֑ה וְחַטַּ֥את אִ֝מּ֗וֹ אַל־תִּמָּֽח׃	14 May the LORD recall his fathers' offense, and may his mother's sin never be erased;
יִהְי֣וּ נֶגֶד־יְהֹוָ֣ה תָּמִ֑יד וְיַכְרֵ֖ת מֵאֶ֣רֶץ זִכְרָֽם׃	15 may these ever be before the LORD until He cuts off their name from the earth,
יַ֗עַן אֲשֶׁ֤ר ׀ לֹ֥א זָכַר֮ עֲשׂ֢וֹת חָ֥֫סֶד וַיִּרְדֹּ֡ף אִישׁ־עָנִ֣י וְ֭אֶבְיוֹן וְנִכְאֵ֨ה לֵבָ֬ב לְמוֹתֵֽת׃	16 for he was never mindful of showing kindness but drove the poor, the needy, the heart-sore to death.
וַיֶּאֱהַ֣ב קְ֭לָלָה וַתְּבוֹאֵ֑הוּ וְֽלֹא־חָפֵ֥ץ בִּ֝בְרָכָ֗ה וַתִּרְחַ֥ק מִמֶּֽנּוּ׃	17 He loved to curse – may curses come upon him – and showed no desire for blessing – may it keep far away from him;
וַיִּלְבַּ֥שׁ קְלָלָ֗ה כְּמַ֫דּ֥וֹ וַתָּבֹ֣א כַמַּ֣יִם בְּקִרְבּ֑וֹ וְ֝כַשֶּׁ֗מֶן בְּעַצְמוֹתָֽיו׃	18 he donned cursing as his attire – may it seep inside him like water, like oil within his bones.
תְּהִי־ל֭וֹ כְּבֶ֣גֶד יַעְטֶ֑ה וּ֝לְמֵ֗זַח תָּמִ֥יד יַחְגְּרֶֽהָ׃	19 May it cloak him like a garment, always clasped around him like a belt."
זֹ֤את ׀ פְּעֻלַּ֣ת שֹׂ֭טְנַי מֵאֵ֣ת יְהֹוָ֑ה וְהַדֹּבְרִ֥ים רָ֝֗ע עַל־נַפְשִֽׁי׃	20 May this be the due of my accusers from the LORD, of those who speak evil against me,
וְאַתָּ֤ה ׀ יֱהֹוִ֣ה אֲ֭דֹנָי עֲשֵׂה־אִ֭תִּי לְמַ֣עַן שְׁמֶ֑ךָ כִּי־ט֥וֹב חַ֝סְדְּךָ֗ הַצִּילֵֽנִי׃	21 and may You, God my LORD, deal with me in keeping with Your name; save me in Your good loyalty,
כִּֽי־עָנִ֣י וְאֶבְי֣וֹן אָנֹ֑כִי וְ֝לִבִּ֗י חָלַ֥ל בְּקִרְבִּֽי׃	22 for I am but poor and needy, and my heart is pierced within me.
כְּצֵל־כִּנְטוֹת֥וֹ נֶהֱלָ֑כְתִּי נִ֝נְעַ֗רְתִּי כָּֽאַרְבֶּֽה׃	23 I fade away like a lengthening shadow; I am shaken off like a locust.
בִּ֭רְכַּי כָּשְׁל֣וּ מִצּ֑וֹם וּ֝בְשָׂרִ֗י כָּחַ֥שׁ מִשָּֽׁמֶן׃	24 My knees give way from fasting; my flesh is gaunt and lean.

וַאֲנִי ׀ הָיִ֣יתִי חֶרְפָּ֣ה לָהֶ֑ם   25 As for me, I have become their scorn;
יִ֝רְא֗וּנִי יְנִיע֥וּן רֹאשָֽׁם: when they see me, they shake their heads.

עׇ֭זְרֵנִי יְהֹוָ֣ה אֱלֹהָ֑י   26 Help me, LORD my God;
ה֖וֹשִׁיעֵ֣נִי כְחַסְדֶּֽךָ:   save me in keeping with Your loyalty,

וְֽ֭יֵדְעוּ כִּי־יָ֣דְךָ זֹּ֑את   27 and they will know that this is Your hand,
אַתָּ֖ה יְהֹוָ֣ה עֲשִׂיתָֽהּ:   that You, O LORD, have done this,

יְקַלְלוּ־הֵ֨מָּה֙ וְאַתָּ֣ה תְבָרֵ֔ךְ   28 so let them curse, but You will bless;
קָ֤מוּ ׀ וַיֵּבֹ֗שׁוּ וְֽעַבְדְּךָ֥ יִשְׂמָֽח: they will rise and be shamed
                                         while Your servant will rejoice.

יִלְבְּשׁ֣וּ שׂוֹטְנַ֣י כְּלִמָּ֑ה   29 My accusers will don disgrace;
וְיַעֲט֖וּ כַמְעִ֣יל בׇּשְׁתָּֽם: their shame will cloak them like a robe

א֘וֹדֶ֤ה יְהֹוָ֣ה מְאֹ֣ד בְּפִ֑י   30 while my mouth will declare great thanks
                                         to the LORD;
וּבְת֖וֹךְ רַבִּ֣ים אֲהַֽלְלֶֽנּוּ:   I will praise Him in the midst
                                         of the crowd,

כִּֽי־יַ֭עֲמֹד לִימִ֣ין אֶבְי֑וֹן   31 for He stands at the right hand
לְ֝הוֹשִׁ֗יעַ מִשֹּׁפְטֵ֥י נַפְשֽׁוֹ:   of the needy
                                         to save their lives from their condemners.

In sacred splendor adored from birth, yours is the dew-bloom of youth

The Sages paint a bloody scene. Revenge against millennia of evil
is not a pretty sight. God the Judge will wear His royal robe.
It will be stained with the blood of every martyr ever.
Rivers of their blood will flow. A bird will try to drink from one
such river, but will lift his head in flight.

PSALM 110

He will be repelled by the river's raging waves.
The rivers will not quench the poor bird's thirst.

לְדָוִד מִזְמֽוֹר
נְאֻם יהוה ׀ לַאדֹנִי שֵׁב לִימִינִי
עַד־אָשִׁית אֹיְבֶיךָ
הֲדֹם לְרַגְלֶֽיךָ׃

1 Of David – a psalm
The LORD has spoken to my lord:
"Sit at My right hand
until I make your enemies
a stool for your feet."

מַטֵּֽה־עֻזְּךָ יִשְׁלַח יהוה מִצִּיּוֹן
רְדֵה בְּקֶרֶב אֹיְבֶֽיךָ׃

2 Your mighty scepter
the LORD has sent forth from Zion;
dominate your enemies.

עַמְּךָ נְדָבֹת בְּיוֹם חֵילֶךָ
בְּהַדְרֵי־קֹדֶשׁ מֵרֶחֶם מִשְׁחָר
לְךָ טַל יַלְדֻתֶֽיךָ׃

3 Your people offer themselves willingly
on your day of battle.
In sacred splendor adored from birth,
yours is the dew-bloom of youth.

נִשְׁבַּע יהוה ׀ וְלֹא יִנָּחֵם
אַתָּה־כֹהֵן לְעוֹלָם
עַל־דִּבְרָתִי מַלְכִּי־צֶֽדֶק׃

4 The LORD has sworn
and will never retract:
"You are a priest forever
by My decree, a rightful king."

אֲדֹנָי עַל־יְמִֽינְךָ
מָחַץ בְּיוֹם־אַפּוֹ מְלָכִֽים׃

5 The LORD is at your right hand,
He who crushes kings
on the day of His wrath.

יָדִין בַּגּוֹיִם מָלֵא גְוִיּוֹת
מָחַץ רֹאשׁ עַל־אֶרֶץ רַבָּֽה׃

6 He executes judgment upon the nations –
so many corpses! –
crushing heads far and wide.

מִנַּחַל בַּדֶּרֶךְ יִשְׁתֶּה
עַל־כֵּן יָרִים רֹֽאשׁ׃

7 He will drink from wayside streams
and thus hold his head high.

Majestic and splendid are His deeds; His righteousness stands forever

Help me begin my search for wisdom. This world is vast and wonderful. Can I ever understand it? It is the Creator's world. Can I ever understand Him? I stand in awe of Him and revere the world He created. I must preserve that awe and never lose that reverence. They are my first steps on the path to wisdom.

PSALM 111

הַלְלוּיָהּ ׀ אוֹדֶה יהוה בְּכָל־לֵבָב בְּסוֹד יְשָׁרִים וְעֵדָה:	1 Halleluya! I will praise the LORD with all my heart in the gathered assembly of the upright.
גְּדֹלִים מַעֲשֵׂי יהוה דְּרוּשִׁים לְכָל־חֶפְצֵיהֶם:	2 Great are the LORD's works, sought by all who delight in them.
הוֹד־וְהָדָר פָּעֳלוֹ וְצִדְקָתוֹ עֹמֶדֶת לָעַד:	3 Majestic and splendid are His deeds; His righteousness stands forever.
זֵכֶר עָשָׂה לְנִפְלְאֹתָיו חַנּוּן וְרַחוּם יהוה:	4 He has won fame for His wonders; the LORD is gracious and compassionate.
טֶרֶף נָתַן לִירֵאָיו יִזְכֹּר לְעוֹלָם בְּרִיתוֹ:	5 He provides food for those who fear Him and forever remembers His covenant.
כֹּחַ מַעֲשָׂיו הִגִּיד לְעַמּוֹ לָתֵת לָהֶם נַחֲלַת גּוֹיִם:	6 He has revealed His powerful deeds to His people by granting them their share of the nations.
מַעֲשֵׂי יָדָיו אֱמֶת וּמִשְׁפָּט נֶאֱמָנִים כָּל־פִּקּוּדָיו:	7 Truth and justice are His handiwork; all His decrees are faithful,
סְמוּכִים לָעַד לְעוֹלָם עֲשׂוּיִם בֶּאֱמֶת וְיָשָׁר:	8 steady for all eternity, formed in truth and right.
פְּדוּת ׀ שָׁלַח לְעַמּוֹ צִוָּה־לְעוֹלָם בְּרִיתוֹ קָדוֹשׁ וְנוֹרָא שְׁמוֹ:	9 He sent freedom to His people, ordaining His covenant forever; holy and awesome is His name.
רֵאשִׁית חָכְמָה ׀ יִרְאַת יהוה שֵׂכֶל טוֹב לְכָל־עֹשֵׂיהֶם תְּהִלָּתוֹ עֹמֶדֶת לָעַד:	10 Wisdom begins with fear of the LORD; good sense is gained by all who practice it; His praise stands forever.

Even in the darkness light glows for the upright; they are gracious, compassionate, and just

A *mensch* is always fair, even when the tide turns against him.
He is always considerate, even when he is teased and taunted.
Success does not blind him to the needs of others.
He helps the poor even when he himself is in need.

PSALM 112

הַלְלוּיָהּ ׀ 1 Halleluya!
אַשְׁרֵי־אִישׁ יָרֵא אֶת־יְהוָה Happy are those who fear the LORD,
בְּמִצְוֺתָיו חָפֵץ מְאֹד׃ who deeply delight in His
commandments.

גִּבּוֹר בָּאָרֶץ יִהְיֶה זַרְעוֹ 2 Their seed will be powerful in the land,
דּוֹר יְשָׁרִים יְבֹרָךְ׃ a blessed upright generation.

הוֹן־וָעֹשֶׁר בְּבֵיתוֹ 3 Wealth and riches fill their homes;
וְצִדְקָתוֹ עֹמֶדֶת לָעַד׃ their righteousness stands forever.

זָרַח בַּחֹשֶׁךְ אוֹר לַיְשָׁרִים 4 Even in the darkness
חַנּוּן וְרַחוּם וְצַדִּיק׃ light glows for the upright;
they are gracious, compassionate,
and just.

טוֹב־אִישׁ חוֹנֵן וּמַלְוֶה 5 All is well for those who lend graciously,
יְכַלְכֵּל דְּבָרָיו בְּמִשְׁפָּט׃ who conduct their affairs with justice,

כִּי־לְעוֹלָם לֹא־יִמּוֹט 6 for they will never be shaken;
לְזֵכֶר עוֹלָם יִהְיֶה צַדִּיק׃ the righteous are remembered forever.

מִשְּׁמוּעָה רָעָה לֹא יִירָא 7 They will fear no evil tidings;
נָכוֹן לִבּוֹ בָּטֻחַ בַּיהוָה׃ their hearts are firm;
they trust in the LORD.

סָמוּךְ לִבּוֹ לֹא יִירָא 8 Their hearts are steady;
עַד אֲשֶׁר־יִרְאֶה בְצָרָיו׃ they shall not fear;
in the end they will witness
the fall of their foes.

פִּזַּר ׀ נָתַן לָאֶבְיוֹנִים 9 They give freely to the needy;
צִדְקָתוֹ עֹמֶדֶת לָעַד their righteousness stands forever;
קַרְנוֹ תָּרוּם בְּכָבוֹד׃ their horn will be raised up in glory.

רָשָׁע יִרְאֶה ׀ וְכָעָס 10 The wicked shall see and grow furious,
שִׁנָּיו יַחֲרֹק וְנָמָס gnash their teeth, and shrink away;
תַּאֲוַת רְשָׁעִים תֹּאבֵד׃ the desire of the wicked shall perish.

Sing praise, servants of the Lᴏʀᴅ; praise the name of the Lᴏʀᴅ

She desperately wants a child, but cannot conceive.
Her tragedy is in a league of its own.
Ask her, and she'll tell you that no pain can compare with hers.
Should she conceive, she'll tell you,
no joy will compare with hers.

PSALM 113

הַלְלוּיָהּ ׀
הַלְלוּ עַבְדֵי יהוה
הַלְלוּ אֶת־שֵׁם יהוה:

1 Halleluya!
Sing praise, servants of the Lord;
praise the name of the Lord.

יְהִי שֵׁם יהוה מְבֹרָךְ
מֵעַתָּה וְעַד־עוֹלָם:

2 Blessed be the name of the Lord,
now and for evermore.

מִמִּזְרַח־שֶׁמֶשׁ עַד־מְבוֹאוֹ
מְהֻלָּל שֵׁם יהוה:

3 From sunrise to sunset
may the Lord's name be praised.

רָם עַל־כָּל־גּוֹיִם ׀ יהוה
עַל הַשָּׁמַיִם כְּבוֹדוֹ:

4 The Lord is exalted above all nations;
His glory soars above the heavens.

מִי כַּיהוה אֱלֹהֵינוּ
הַמַּגְבִּיהִי לָשָׁבֶת:

5 Who is like the Lord our God,
who sits enthroned so high

הַמַּשְׁפִּילִי לִרְאוֹת
בַּשָּׁמַיִם וּבָאָרֶץ:

6 yet looks down so low
to see the heavens and the earth?

מְקִימִי מֵעָפָר דָּל
מֵאַשְׁפֹּת יָרִים אֶבְיוֹן:

7 He lifts the poor from the dust,
raises the needy from the refuse heap,

לְהוֹשִׁיבִי עִם־נְדִיבִים
עִם נְדִיבֵי עַמּוֹ:

8 and seats them beside nobility,
beside the nobles of His people.

מוֹשִׁיבִי ׀ עֲקֶרֶת הַבַּיִת
אֵם־הַבָּנִים שְׂמֵחָה
הַלְלוּיָהּ:

9 He settles the childless woman
in her home
as a joyous mother of children.
Halleluya!

When Israel came out of Egypt, the House of Yaakov from a people of foreign tongue

"Earthshaking" is a powerful word. It is a word that we misuse.
When we are surprised we say we heard "earthshaking" news.
But "earthshaking" means so much more than "surprising."
"Earthshaking" means that objects which never moved before
are now shaking. "Earthshaking" means that they are shaking
with fear. "Earthshaking" means that the entire earth is shaking.
"Earthshaking" means unprecedented. Our exodus from Egypt
was an "earthshaking" event.

PSALM 114

בְּצֵאת יִשְׂרָאֵל מִמִּצְרָיִם 1 When Israel came out of Egypt,
בֵּית יַעֲקֹב מֵעַם לֹעֵז: the House of Yaakov from a people of
foreign tongue,

הָיְתָה יְהוּדָה לְקָדְשׁוֹ 2 Yehuda became His sanctuary,
יִשְׂרָאֵל מַמְשְׁלוֹתָיו: Israel His dominion.

הַיָּם רָאָה וַיָּנֹס 3 The sea saw and fled;
הַיַּרְדֵּן יִסֹּב לְאָחוֹר: the Jordan turned back.

הֶהָרִים רָקְדוּ כְאֵילִים 4 The mountains skipped like rams,
גְּבָעוֹת כִּבְנֵי־צֹאן: the hills like lambs.

מַה־לְּךָ הַיָּם כִּי תָנוּס 5 What happened, sea, that you fled?
הַיַּרְדֵּן תִּסֹּב לְאָחוֹר: Jordan, why did you turn back?

הֶהָרִים תִּרְקְדוּ כְאֵילִים 6 Why, mountains, did you skip like rams,
גְּבָעוֹת כִּבְנֵי־צֹאן: you hills like lambs?

מִלִּפְנֵי אָדוֹן חוּלִי אָרֶץ 7 Tremble, O earth, in the Lord's presence,
מִלִּפְנֵי אֱלוֹהַּ יַעֲקֹב: in the presence of the God of Yaakov –

הַהֹפְכִי הַצּוּר אֲגַם־מָיִם 8 He turned the rock into a pool of water,
חַלָּמִישׁ לְמַעְיְנוֹ־מָיִם: the flint into a flowing spring.

ברוכים אתם לה' עושה שמים וארץ :

May you be blessed by the LORD, Maker of heaven and earth

Are we entitled to pray?
Do we deserve His answer to our prayers? We deserve very little.
We ask that He answer us for His own sake.
If alive, we can at least try to do His will.
Dead, we can do nothing for Him.

PSALM 115

לֹא לָנוּ יהוה לֹא לָנוּ כִּי־לְשִׁמְךָ תֵּן כָּבוֹד עַל־חַסְדְּךָ עַל־אֲמִתֶּךָ׃	1 Not to us, LORD, not to us, but to Your name give glory for Your love, for Your faithfulness.
לָמָּה יֹאמְרוּ הַגּוֹיִם אַיֵּה־נָא אֱלֹהֵיהֶם׃	2 Why should the nations say, "Where, now, is their God?"
וֵאלֹהֵינוּ בַשָּׁמָיִם כֹּל אֲשֶׁר־חָפֵץ עָשָׂה׃	3 Our God is in heaven; He does as He pleases.
עֲצַבֵּיהֶם כֶּסֶף וְזָהָב מַעֲשֵׂה יְדֵי אָדָם׃	4 Their idols are silver and gold, made by human hands.
פֶּה־לָהֶם וְלֹא יְדַבֵּרוּ עֵינַיִם לָהֶם וְלֹא יִרְאוּ׃	5 They have mouths but cannot speak, eyes but cannot see;
אָזְנַיִם לָהֶם וְלֹא יִשְׁמָעוּ אַף לָהֶם וְלֹא יְרִיחוּן׃	6 they have ears but cannot hear, noses but cannot smell;
יְדֵיהֶם ׀ וְלֹא יְמִישׁוּן רַגְלֵיהֶם וְלֹא יְהַלֵּכוּ לֹא־יֶהְגּוּ בִּגְרוֹנָם׃	7 they have hands but cannot feel, feet but cannot walk; no sound comes from their throat.
כְּמוֹהֶם יִהְיוּ עֹשֵׂיהֶם כֹּל אֲשֶׁר־בֹּטֵחַ בָּהֶם׃	8 Their makers will become like them; so will all who trust in them.
יִשְׂרָאֵל בְּטַח בַּיהוה עֶזְרָם וּמָגִנָּם הוּא׃	9 Israel, trust in the LORD– He is their help and their shield.
בֵּית אַהֲרֹן בִּטְחוּ בַיהוה עֶזְרָם וּמָגִנָּם הוּא׃	10 House of Aharon, trust in the LORD– He is their help and their shield.
יִרְאֵי יהוה בִּטְחוּ בַיהוה עֶזְרָם וּמָגִנָּם הוּא׃	11 You who fear the Lord, trust in the Lord – He is their help and their shield.

יהוה זְכָרָנוּ יְבָרֵךְ 12 The Lord remembers us
יְבָרֵךְ אֶת־בֵּית יִשְׂרָאֵל and will bless us –
יְבָרֵךְ אֶת־בֵּית אַהֲרֹן: He will bless the house of Israel;
He will bless the house of Aharon;

יְבָרֵךְ יִרְאֵי יהוה 13 He will bless those who fear the Lord,
הַקְּטַנִּים עִם־הַגְּדֹלִים: small and great alike.

יֹסֵף יהוה עֲלֵיכֶם 14 May the Lord grant you increase,
עֲלֵיכֶם וְעַל־בְּנֵיכֶם: you and your children.

בְּרוּכִים אַתֶּם לַיהוה 15 May you be blessed by the Lord,
עֹשֵׂה שָׁמַיִם וָאָרֶץ: Maker of heaven and earth.

הַשָּׁמַיִם שָׁמַיִם לַיהוה 16 The heavens are the Lord's,
וְהָאָרֶץ נָתַן לִבְנֵי־אָדָם: but He has granted the earth to mankind.

לֹא הַמֵּתִים יְהַלְלוּ־יָהּ 17 It is not the dead who praise the Lord,
וְלֹא כָּל־יֹרְדֵי דוּמָה: nor any of those
who descend into silence,

וַאֲנַחְנוּ ׀ נְבָרֵךְ יָהּ 18 but we who will bless the Lord
מֵעַתָּה וְעַד־עוֹלָם now and forever.
הַלְלוּיָהּ: Halleluya!

I will raise the cup of salvation and call on the name of the LORD

My life has been a turbulent one. But I have found peace.
I have known failure and defeat. But now I am on the right track.
I was suspicious and distrustful.
But faithful friends now surround me. Thank you, God.

PSALM 116

אֲהַבְתִּי כִּי־יִשְׁמַע ׀ יְהֹוָה אֶת־קוֹלִי תַּחֲנוּנָי:	1	I love the LORD for He hears my voice, my pleas;
כִּי־הִטָּה אׇזְנוֹ לִי וּבְיָמַי אֶקְרָא:	2	He turns His ear to me whenever I call.
אֲפָפוּנִי ׀ חֶבְלֵי־מָוֶת וּמְצָרֵי שְׁאוֹל מְצָאוּנִי צָרָה וְיָגוֹן אֶמְצָא:	3	The bonds of death encompassed me; the pangs of the grave came upon me; I was overcome by trouble and sorrow,
וּבְשֵׁם־יְהֹוָה אֶקְרָא אָנָּה יְהֹוָה מַלְּטָה נַפְשִׁי:	4	then I called on the name of the LORD: "LORD, I pray, save my life."
חַנּוּן יְהֹוָה וְצַדִּיק וֵאלֹהֵינוּ מְרַחֵם:	5	Gracious is the LORD, and righteous; our God is full of compassion.
שֹׁמֵר פְּתָאיִם יְהֹוָה דַּלּוֹתִי וְלִי יְהוֹשִׁיעַ:	6	The LORD protects the simple-hearted; when I was brought low, He saved me.
שׁוּבִי נַפְשִׁי לִמְנוּחָיְכִי כִּי־יְהֹוָה גָּמַל עָלָיְכִי:	7	Be at peace once more, my soul, for the LORD has been good to you,
כִּי חִלַּצְתָּ נַפְשִׁי מִמָּוֶת אֶת־עֵינִי מִן־דִּמְעָה אֶת־רַגְלִי מִדֶּחִי:	8	for You have rescued me from death, my eyes from weeping, my feet from stumbling.
אֶתְהַלֵּךְ לִפְנֵי יְהֹוָה בְּאַרְצוֹת הַחַיִּים:	9	I shall walk in the LORD's presence in the land of the living.
הֶאֱמַנְתִּי כִּי אֲדַבֵּר אֲנִי עָנִיתִי מְאֹד:	10	I had faith even when I said, "I suffer terribly,"
אֲנִי אָמַרְתִּי בְחׇפְזִי כׇּל־הָאָדָם כֹּזֵב:	11	even when I said rashly, "All people are liars."
מָה־אָשִׁיב לַיהֹוָה כׇּל־תַּגְמוּלוֹהִי עָלָי:	12	How can I repay the LORD for all His goodness to me?

כּוֹס־יְשׁוּעוֹת אֶשָּׂא
וּבְשֵׁם יְהוָה אֶקְרָא:

13 I will raise the cup of salvation
and call on the name of the LORD;

נְדָרַי לַיהוָה אֲשַׁלֵּם
נֶגְדָה־נָּא לְכָל־עַמּוֹ:

14 I will fulfill my vows to the LORD
in the presence of all His people.

יָקָר בְּעֵינֵי יְהוָה
הַמָּוְתָה לַחֲסִידָיו:

15 The LORD grieves at the death
of His devoted ones.

אָנָּה יְהוָה כִּי־אֲנִי עַבְדֶּךָ
אֲנִי־עַבְדְּךָ בֶּן־אֲמָתֶךָ
פִּתַּחְתָּ לְמוֹסֵרָי:

16 Please, O LORD, I am Your servant—
I am Your servant,
the child of Your handmaid;
You set me free from my chains.

לְךָ־אֶזְבַּח זֶבַח תּוֹדָה
וּבְשֵׁם יְהוָה אֶקְרָא:

17 To You I will bring
a thanksgiving-offering
and call on the LORD by name.

נְדָרַי לַיהוָה אֲשַׁלֵּם
נֶגְדָה־נָּא לְכָל־עַמּוֹ:

18 I will fulfill my vows to the LORD
in the presence of all His people,

בְּחַצְרוֹת ׀ בֵּית יְהוָה
בְּתוֹכֵכִי יְרוּשָׁלִָם
הַלְלוּיָהּ:

19 in the courts of the House of the LORD,
in your midst, Jerusalem.
Halleluya!

The LORD's truth is everlasting. Halleluya!

The story of my people is the story of a sheep among seventy wolves. One day that story will end happily. We will then sing God's praises. So will the seventy wolves.

PSALM 117

הַלְלוּ אֶת־יהוה כָּל־גּוֹיִם 1 Praise the LORD, all nations,
שַׁבְּחוּהוּ כָּל־הָאֻמִּים: laud Him, all you peoples,

כִּי גָבַר עָלֵינוּ ׀ חַסְדּוֹ 2 for His loving-kindness overwhelms us,
וֶאֱמֶת־יהוה לְעוֹלָם and the LORD's truth is everlasting.
הַלְלוּיָהּ: Halleluya!

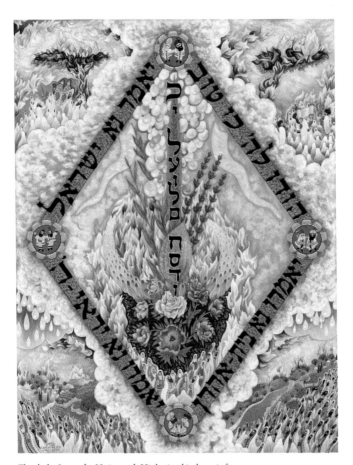

Thank the LORD for He is good; His loving-kindness is forever

I had no exit. I was rejected, scorned, and pitied. There was no one to trust. I surprised myself. I trusted God. He surprised me.

PSALM 118

הוֹדוּ לַיהֹוָה כִּי־טוֹב כִּי לְעוֹלָם חַסְדּוֹ:	1 Thank the LORD for He is good; His loving-kindness is forever.
יֹאמַר־נָא יִשְׂרָאֵל כִּי לְעוֹלָם חַסְדּוֹ:	2 Let Israel say, "His loving-kindness is forever."
יֹאמְרוּ־נָא בֵית־אַהֲרֹן כִּי לְעוֹלָם חַסְדּוֹ:	3 Let the house of Aharon say, "His loving-kindness is forever."
יֹאמְרוּ־נָא יִרְאֵי יְהֹוָה כִּי לְעוֹלָם חַסְדּוֹ:	4 Let those who fear the LORD say, "His loving-kindness is forever."
מִן־הַמֵּצַר קָרָאתִי יָּהּ עָנָנִי בַמֶּרְחָב יָהּ:	5 In my distress I called on the LORD; the LORD answered me and set me free.
יְהֹוָה לִי לֹא אִירָא מַה־יַּעֲשֶׂה לִי אָדָם:	6 The LORD is with me; I have no fear. What can man do to me?
יְהֹוָה לִי בְּעֹזְרָי וַאֲנִי אֶרְאֶה בְשֹׂנְאָי:	7 The LORD is with me; He is my helper – I will see the downfall of my enemies.
טוֹב לַחֲסוֹת בַּיהֹוָה מִבְּטֹחַ בָּאָדָם:	8 It is better to take refuge in the LORD than to trust in man.
טוֹב לַחֲסוֹת בַּיהֹוָה מִבְּטֹחַ בִּנְדִיבִים:	9 It is better to take refuge in the LORD than to trust in nobles.
כָּל־גּוֹיִם סְבָבוּנִי בְּשֵׁם יְהֹוָה כִּי אֲמִילַם:	10 The nations all surrounded me, but in the LORD's name I drove them off.
סַבּוּנִי גַם־סְבָבוּנִי בְּשֵׁם יְהֹוָה כִּי אֲמִילַם:	11 They surrounded me on every side, but in the LORD's name I drove them off.
סַבּוּנִי כִדְבֹרִים דֹּעֲכוּ כְּאֵשׁ קוֹצִים בְּשֵׁם יְהֹוָה כִּי אֲמִילַם:	12 They surrounded me like bees, but they burned like a fire of thorns – in the LORD's name I drove them off.
דָּחֹה דְחִיתַנִי לִנְפֹּל וַיהֹוָה עֲזָרָנִי:	13 You pressed me so hard I nearly fell, but the LORD came to my aid.

עָזִּי וְזִמְרָת יָהּ
וַיְהִי־לִי לִישׁוּעָה׃

14 The Lord is my strength and song–
and now my salvation.

קוֹל ׀ רִנָּה וִישׁוּעָה
בְּאׇהֳלֵי צַדִּיקִים
יְמִין יְהוָֹה עֹשָׂה חָיִל׃

15 Sounds of song and salvation
resound in the tents of the righteous:
"The Lord's right hand
has done mighty deeds;

יְמִין יְהוָֹה רוֹמֵמָה
יְמִין יְהוָֹה עֹשָׂה חָיִל׃

16 the Lord's right hand is lifted high;
the Lord's right hand has done
mighty deeds."

לֹא־אָמוּת כִּי־אֶחְיֶה
וַאֲסַפֵּר מַעֲשֵׂי יָהּ׃

17 I will not die but live,
and I will tell of the Lord's deeds.

יַסֹּר יִסְּרַנִּי יָּהּ
וְלַמָּוֶת לֹא נְתָנָנִי׃

18 The Lord has chastened me severely,
but He has not given me over to death.

פִּתְחוּ־לִי שַׁעֲרֵי־צֶדֶק
אָבֹא־בָם אוֹדֶה יָהּ׃

19 Open for me the gates of righteousness
that I may enter them and thank the
Lord.

זֶה־הַשַּׁעַר לַיהוָֹה
צַדִּיקִים יָבֹאוּ בוֹ׃

20 This is the gateway to the Lord;
through it, the righteous shall enter.

אוֹדְךָ כִּי עֲנִיתָנִי
וַתְּהִי־לִי לִישׁוּעָה׃

21 I will thank You for You answered me
and became my salvation.

אֶבֶן מָאֲסוּ הַבּוֹנִים
הָיְתָה לְרֹאשׁ פִּנָּה׃

22 The stone the builders rejected
has become the main cornerstone.

מֵאֵת יְהוָֹה הָיְתָה זֹּאת
הִיא נִפְלָאת בְּעֵינֵינוּ׃

23 This was from the Lord;
it is wondrous in our eyes.

זֶה־הַיּוֹם עָשָׂה יְהוָֹה
נָגִילָה וְנִשְׂמְחָה בוֹ׃

24 This is the day the Lord has made;
let us rejoice and be glad in it.

אָנָּא יְהוָֹה הוֹשִׁיעָה נָּא
אָנָּא יְהוָֹה הַצְלִיחָה נָּא׃

25 Lord, please save us;
Lord, please grant us success.

26 Blessed is the one who comes
in the name of the LORD;
we bless you from the House of the Lord.

בָּרוּךְ הַבָּא בְּשֵׁם יהוה
בֵּרַכְנוּכֶם מִבֵּית יהוה:

27 The LORD is God; He has given us light.
Bind the festival offering with thick cords
to the horns of the altar!

אֵל ׀ יהוה וַיָּאֶר לָנוּ
אִסְרוּ־חַג בַּעֲבֹתִים
עַד־קַרְנוֹת הַמִּזְבֵּחַ:

28 You are my God, and I will thank You;
You are my God, and I will exalt You.

אֵלִי אַתָּה וְאוֹדֶךָּ
אֱלֹהַי אֲרוֹמְמֶךָּ:

29 Thank the LORD for He is good;
His loving-kindness is forever.

הוֹדוּ לַיהוה כִּי־טוֹב
כִּי לְעוֹלָם חַסְדּוֹ:

Happy are those whose way is blameless, who walk in the LORD's teaching

Have you tasted worldly pleasures? I have.
Why then do you study Torah day and night?
It gives me the greatest pleasure of all.

PSALM 119

א — ALEF

אַשְׁרֵי תְמִימֵי־דֶרֶךְ
הַהֹלְכִים בְּתוֹרַת יהוה:

1 Happy are those whose way is blameless,
who walk in the LORD's teaching.

אַשְׁרֵי נֹצְרֵי עֵדֹתָיו
בְּכָל־לֵב יִדְרְשׁוּהוּ:

2 Happy are those who keep His decrees,
who seek Him with all their heart,

אַף לֹא־פָעֲלוּ עַוְלָה
בִּדְרָכָיו הָלָכוּ:

3 who have done no wrong
and walk in His ways.

אַתָּה צִוִּיתָה פִקֻּדֶיךָ
לִשְׁמֹר מְאֹד:

4 You have commanded that Your decrees
be carefully upheld.

אַחֲלַי יִכֹּנוּ דְרָכָי
לִשְׁמֹר חֻקֶּיךָ:

5 If only my ways were firm
in upholding Your statutes,

אָז לֹא־אֵבוֹשׁ בְּהַבִּיטִי
אֶל־כָּל־מִצְוֹתֶיךָ:

6 then I would not be ashamed
when I behold all Your commandments.

אוֹדְךָ בְּיֹשֶׁר לֵבָב בְּלָמְדִי
מִשְׁפְּטֵי צִדְקֶךָ:

7 I thank You with a sincere heart
as I learn Your just laws.

אֶת־חֻקֶּיךָ אֶשְׁמֹר
אַל־תַּעַזְבֵנִי עַד־מְאֹד:

8 I will uphold Your statutes;
do not utterly forsake me.

ב — BET

בַּמֶּה יְזַכֶּה־נַּעַר אֶת־אָרְחוֹ
לִשְׁמֹר כִּדְבָרֶךָ:

9 How can youths keep their paths pure? –
by upholding Your word.

בְּכָל־לִבִּי דְרַשְׁתִּיךָ
אַל־תַּשְׁגֵּנִי מִמִּצְוֹתֶיךָ:

10 I sought You out with all my heart;
let me not stray from Your
commandments.

בְּלִבִּי צָפַנְתִּי אִמְרָתֶךָ
לְמַעַן לֹא אֶחֱטָא־לָךְ:

11 I keep Your promise hidden in my heart
so that I will not sin against You.

בָּרוּךְ אַתָּה יהוה
לַמְּדֵנִי חֻקֶּיךָ:

12 Blessed are You, LORD;
teach me Your statutes.

בִּשְׂפָתַי סִפַּרְתִּי
כֹּל מִשְׁפְּטֵי־פִֽיךָ:

13 My own lips recount
all the laws of Your mouth.

בְּדֶרֶךְ עֵדְוֺתֶיךָ שַׂשְׂתִּי
כְּעַל כָּל־הֽוֹן:

14 I rejoice in following Your decrees
as if in great wealth.

בְּפִקּוּדֶיךָ אָשִׂיחָה
וְאַבִּיטָה אֹרְחֹתֶֽיךָ:

15 I reflect on Your precepts
and behold Your paths.

בְּחֻקֹּתֶיךָ אֶשְׁתַּעֲשָׁע
לֹא אֶשְׁכַּח דְּבָרֶֽךָ:

16 I delight in Your statutes;
I will never forget Your word.

ג

GIMEL

גְּמֹל עַל־עַבְדְּךָ אֶחְיֶה
וְאֶשְׁמְרָה דְבָרֶֽךָ:

17 Be good to Your servant
so that I may live to uphold Your word.

גַּל־עֵינַי וְאַבִּיטָה
נִפְלָאוֹת מִתּוֹרָתֶֽךָ:

18 Uncover my eyes so that I may behold
the wonders of Your teaching.

גֵּר אָנֹכִי בָאָרֶץ
אַל־תַּסְתֵּר מִמֶּנִּי מִצְוֺתֶֽיךָ:

19 I am but a stranger on earth –
do not hide Your commandments
from me.

גָּרְסָה נַפְשִׁי לְתַאֲבָה
אֶל־מִשְׁפָּטֶיךָ בְכָל־עֵֽת:

20 My soul is shattered with longing
at all times for Your laws.

גָּעַרְתָּ זֵדִים אֲרוּרִים
הַשֹּׁגִים מִמִּצְוֺתֶֽיךָ:

21 You blast the cursed, the insolent
who stray from Your commandments.

גַּל מֵעָלַי חֶרְפָּה וָבוּז
כִּי עֵדֹתֶיךָ נָצָֽרְתִּי:

22 Divest me of scorn and contempt,
for I keep Your decrees.

גַּם יָשְׁבוּ שָׂרִים בִּי נִדְבָּרוּ
עַבְדְּךָ יָשִׂיחַ בְּחֻקֶּֽיךָ:

23 Even when princes sit to scheme
against me,
Your servant reflects upon Your statutes.

גַּם־עֵדֹתֶיךָ שַׁעֲשֻׁעָי
אַנְשֵׁי עֲצָתִֽי:

24 Yes, Your statutes are my delight;
they are my advisors.

ד	DALET

דָּבְקָה לֶעָפָר נַפְשִׁי 25 My soul clings to the dust;
חַיֵּנִי כִּדְבָרֶךָ:   give me life by Your word.

דְּרָכַי סִפַּרְתִּי וַתַּעֲנֵנִי 26 I recounted my ways,
לַמְּדֵנִי חֻקֶּיךָ:   and You answered me;
                                              teach me Your statutes.

דֶּרֶךְ־פִּקּוּדֶיךָ הֲבִינֵנִי 27 Grant me insight to follow Your precepts,
וְאָשִׂיחָה בְּנִפְלְאוֹתֶיךָ:   and I will reflect upon Your wonders.

דָּלְפָה נַפְשִׁי מִתּוּגָה 28 My soul weeps with grief;
קַיְּמֵנִי כִּדְבָרֶךָ:   sustain me by Your word.

דֶּרֶךְ־שֶׁקֶר הָסֵר מִמֶּנִּי 29 Remove from me ways of falsehood,
וְתוֹרָתְךָ חָנֵּנִי: and grace me with Your teaching.

דֶּרֶךְ־אֱמוּנָה בָחָרְתִּי 30 I have chosen ways of truth;
מִשְׁפָּטֶיךָ שִׁוִּיתִי: I have set Your laws before me.

דָּבַקְתִּי בְעֵדְוֺתֶיךָ 31 I cling to Your decrees;
יהוה אַל־תְּבִישֵׁנִי: LORD, let me not be shamed.

דֶּרֶךְ־מִצְוֺתֶיךָ אָרוּץ 32 I rush to follow Your commandments,
כִּי תַרְחִיב לִבִּי: for You broaden my heart.

ה	HEH

הוֹרֵנִי יהוה דֶּרֶךְ חֻקֶּיךָ 33 Teach me the ways of Your statutes,
וְאֶצְּרֶנָּה עֵקֶב: LORD,
                                                 and I will keep to them to the end.

הֲבִינֵנִי וְאֶצְּרָה תוֹרָתֶךָ 34 Grant me insight to keep Your teaching,
וְאֶשְׁמְרֶנָּה בְכָל־לֵב: and I will uphold it with all my heart.

הַדְרִיכֵנִי בִּנְתִיב מִצְוֺתֶיךָ 35 Guide me along the path of Your
כִּי־בוֹ חָפָצְתִּי: commandments,
                                                    for that is my desire.

הַט־לִבִּי אֶל־עֵדְוֹתֶיךָ 36 Turn my heart to Your decrees
וְאַל אֶל־בָּצַע: and not to gain.

הַעֲבֵר עֵינַי מֵרְאוֹת שָׁוְא 37 Divert my eyes from false visions;
בִּדְרָכֶךָ חַיֵּנִי: give me life through Your ways.

הָקֵם לְעַבְדְּךָ אִמְרָתֶךָ 38 Fulfill for Your servant Your promise,
אֲשֶׁר לְיִרְאָתֶךָ: which is for those who fear You.

הַעֲבֵר חֶרְפָּתִי אֲשֶׁר יָגֹרְתִּי 39 Remove the taunts I dread,
כִּי מִשְׁפָּטֶיךָ טוֹבִים: for Your laws are good.

הִנֵּה תָּאַבְתִּי לְפִקֻּדֶיךָ 40 See how I long for Your precepts;
בְּצִדְקָתְךָ חַיֵּנִי: in Your righteousness give me life.

ו VAV

וִיבֹאֻנִי חֲסָדֶךָ יהוה 41 Let Your loyalty come to me, LORD,
תְּשׁוּעָתְךָ כְּאִמְרָתֶךָ: Your salvation, as You promised.

וְאֶעֱנֶה חֹרְפִי דָבָר 42 I will have a retort
כִּי־בָטַחְתִּי בִּדְבָרֶךָ: for those who taunt me,
for I trust in Your word.

וְאַל־תַּצֵּל מִפִּי דְבַר־אֱמֶת 43 Do not utterly strip the truth
עַד־מְאֹד from my mouth,
כִּי לְמִשְׁפָּטֶךָ יִחָלְתִּי: for in Your laws I place my hope.

וְאֶשְׁמְרָה תוֹרָתְךָ תָמִיד 44 I will always uphold Your teaching,
לְעוֹלָם וָעֶד: forever and ever.

וְאֶתְהַלְּכָה בָרְחָבָה 45 I will walk about freely,
כִּי פִקֻּדֶיךָ דָרָשְׁתִּי: for I seek out Your precepts.

וַאֲדַבְּרָה בְעֵדֹתֶיךָ נֶגֶד מְלָכִים 46 I speak of Your decrees
וְלֹא אֵבוֹשׁ: in the presence of kings
without shame.

וְאֶשְׁתַּעֲשַׁע בְּמִצְוֺתֶ֫יךָ
אֲשֶׁר אָהָֽבְתִּי׃

47 I delight in Your commandments,
which I love.

וְאֶשָּׂא־כַפַּ֗י אֶל־מִצְוֺתֶ֫יךָ
אֲשֶׁר אָהָ֑בְתִּי
וְאָשִׂ֥יחָה בְחֻקֶּֽיךָ׃

48 I reach out my hands to Your commandments,
which I love,
and reflect upon Your statutes.

ז   ZAYIN

זְכֹר־דָּבָ֥ר לְעַבְדֶּ֑ךָ
עַ֝֗ל אֲשֶׁ֥ר יִֽחַלְתָּֽנִי׃

49 Recall to Your servant Your word,
by which You have given me hope;

זֹ֣את נֶחָֽמָתִ֣י בְעָנְיִ֑י
כִּ֖י אִמְרָתְךָ֣ חִיָּֽתְנִי׃

50 it is my comfort in my suffering
that Your promise gives me life.

זֵ֭דִים הֱלִיצֻ֣נִי עַד־מְאֹ֑ד
מִ֝תּֽוֹרָֽתְךָ֗ לֹ֣א נָטִֽיתִי׃

51 The insolent mock me bitterly,
but I do not turn away
from Your teaching.

זָכַ֣רְתִּי מִשְׁפָּטֶ֣יךָ מֵעוֹלָ֓ם ׀ יְהֹוָ֗ה
וָֽאֶתְנֶחָֽם׃

52 I call to mind Your eternal judgments,
LORD,
and I am comforted.

זַלְעָפָ֣ה אֲ֭חָזַתְנִי מֵרְשָׁעִ֑ים
עֹ֝זְבֵ֗י תּֽוֹרָתֶֽךָ׃

53 Scorching rage at the wicked grips me,
at those who abandon Your teaching.

זְ֭מִרוֹת הָֽיוּ־לִ֥י חֻקֶּ֗יךָ
בְּבֵ֣ית מְגוּרָֽי׃

54 Your laws are music to me
wherever I dwell.

זָכַ֣רְתִּי בַלַּ֣יְלָה שִׁמְךָ֣ יְהֹוָ֑ה
וָֽ֝אֶשְׁמְרָ֗ה תּוֹרָתֶֽךָ׃

55 At night I recall Your name, LORD,
and I uphold Your teaching;

זֹ֥את הָֽיְתָה־לִּ֑י
כִּ֖י פִקֻּדֶ֣יךָ נָצָֽרְתִּי׃

56 it is my very own,
for I keep Your precepts.

ח   ḤET

חֶלְקִ֖י יְהֹוָ֥ה אָמַ֗רְתִּי
לִשְׁמֹ֥ר דְּבָרֶֽיךָ׃

57 The LORD is my share;
I promised to uphold Your word.

חִלִּיתִי פָנֶיךָ בְכָל־לֵב 58 I implore You with all my heart:
חָנֵּנִי כְּאִמְרָתֶךָ׃ show me grace as You promised.

חִשַּׁבְתִּי דְרָכָי 59 I have considered my ways,
וָאָשִׁיבָה רַגְלַי אֶל־עֵדֹתֶיךָ׃ and my feet have turned back
to Your decrees.

חַשְׁתִּי וְלֹא הִתְמַהְמָהְתִּי 60 I rush – and never delay –
לִשְׁמֹר מִצְוֹתֶיךָ׃ to uphold Your commandments.

חֶבְלֵי רְשָׁעִים עִוְּדֻנִי 61 The ropes of the wicked ensnare me,
תּוֹרָתְךָ לֹא שָׁכָחְתִּי׃ but I do not forget Your teaching.

חֲצוֹת־לַיְלָה אָקוּם לְהוֹדוֹת לָךְ 62 At midnight I rise to give thanks to You
עַל מִשְׁפְּטֵי צִדְקֶךָ׃ for Your just laws.

חָבֵר אָנִי לְכָל־אֲשֶׁר יְרֵאוּךָ 63 I am a friend to all who fear You,
וּלְשֹׁמְרֵי פִּקּוּדֶיךָ׃ to those who uphold Your precepts.

חַסְדְּךָ יהוה מָלְאָה הָאָרֶץ 64 Your loyalty, Lord, fills the earth;
חֻקֶּיךָ לַמְּדֵנִי׃ teach me Your statutes.

ט TET

טוֹב עָשִׂיתָ עִם־עַבְדְּךָ 65 You have shown Your servant favor
יהוה כִּדְבָרֶךָ׃ according to Your word, Lord.

טוּב טַעַם וָדַעַת לַמְּדֵנִי 66 Teach me good sense and knowledge,
כִּי בְמִצְוֹתֶיךָ הֶאֱמָנְתִּי׃ for I believe in Your commandments.

טֶרֶם אֶעֱנֶה אֲנִי שֹׁגֵג 67 Before my suffering I went astray,
וְעַתָּה אִמְרָתְךָ שָׁמָרְתִּי׃ but now I uphold Your promise.

טוֹב־אַתָּה וּמֵטִיב 68 You are good and do good;
לַמְּדֵנִי חֻקֶּיךָ׃ teach me Your statutes.

טָפְלוּ עָלַי שֶׁקֶר זֵדִים 69 Though the insolent falsely accuse me,
אֲנִי בְּכָל־לֵב ׀ אֶצֹּר פִּקּוּדֶיךָ׃ I will keep Your precepts
with all my heart.

טָפַשׁ כַּחֵלֶב לִבָּם
אֲנִי תּוֹרָתְךָ שִׁעֲשָׁעְתִּי:

70 Their hearts are thick like fat,
whereas I delight in Your teaching.

טוֹב־לִי כִי־עֻנֵּיתִי
לְמַעַן אֶלְמַד חֻקֶּיךָ:

71 My suffering was good for me
so that I might learn Your statutes.

טוֹב־לִי תוֹרַת־פִּיךָ
מֵאַלְפֵי זָהָב וָכָסֶף:

72 For me,
the teaching of Your mouth is better
than thousands of pieces
of gold and silver.

׳

YOD

יָדֶיךָ עָשׂוּנִי וַיְכוֹנְנוּנִי
הֲבִינֵנִי וְאֶלְמְדָה מִצְוֹתֶיךָ:

73 Your hands formed me and firmed me;
grant me insight,
and I will learn Your commandments.

יְרֵאֶיךָ יִרְאוּנִי וְיִשְׂמָחוּ
כִּי לִדְבָרְךָ יִחָלְתִּי:

74 Let those who fear You see me
and rejoice,
for in Your word I place my hope.

יָדַעְתִּי יְהוָה כִּי־צֶדֶק מִשְׁפָּטֶיךָ
וֶאֱמוּנָה עִנִּיתָנִי:

75 I know, Lord, that Your laws are just
and that You made me suffer
in faithfulness.

יְהִי־נָא חַסְדְּךָ לְנַחֲמֵנִי
כְּאִמְרָתְךָ לְעַבְדֶּךָ:

76 Now may Your loyalty comfort me
as You promised Your servant.

יְבֹאוּנִי רַחֲמֶיךָ וְאֶחְיֶה
כִּי־תוֹרָתְךָ שַׁעֲשֻׁעָי:

77 Let Your mercy come to me
that I may live,
for Your teaching is my delight.

יֵבֹשׁוּ זֵדִים כִּי־שֶׁקֶר עִוְּתוּנִי
אֲנִי אָשִׂיחַ בְּפִקּוּדֶיךָ:

78 Let the insolent be ashamed
for wronging me without cause
as I reflect upon Your precepts.

יָשׁוּבוּ לִי יְרֵאֶיךָ
וְיֹדְעֵי עֵדֹתֶיךָ:

וידעו

79 May those who fear You
come back to me,
those who know Your decrees.

יְהִי־לִבִּי תָמִים בְּחֻקֶּיךָ
לְמַעַן לֹא אֵבוֹשׁ:

80 May my heart be soundly committed
to Your laws
so that I will never be ashamed.

כ KAF

כָּלְתָה לִתְשׁוּעָתְךָ נַפְשִׁי
לִדְבָרְךָ יִחָלְתִּי:

81 My soul pines for Your salvation;
in Your word I place my hope.

כָּלוּ עֵינַי לְאִמְרָתֶךָ
לֵאמֹר מָתַי תְּנַחֲמֵנִי:

82 My eyes pine for Your promise,
saying, "Oh, when will You comfort me?"

כִּי־הָיִיתִי כְּנֹאד בְּקִיטוֹר
חֻקֶּיךָ לֹא שָׁכָחְתִּי:

83 Though I am like a wine-skin
shriveled in smoke,
Your statutes I have not forgotten.

כַּמָּה יְמֵי־עַבְדֶּךָ
מָתַי תַּעֲשֶׂה בְרֹדְפַי מִשְׁפָּט:

84 How many days does Your servant
have left?
When will You execute judgment
on my pursuers?

כָּרוּ־לִי זֵדִים שִׁיחוֹת
אֲשֶׁר לֹא כְתוֹרָתֶךָ:

85 The insolent have dug pits for me
in defiance of Your teaching.

כָּל־מִצְוֹתֶיךָ אֱמוּנָה
שֶׁקֶר רְדָפוּנִי עָזְרֵנִי:

86 All Your commandments are faithful,
but men pursue me without cause –
help me!

כִּמְעַט כִּלּוּנִי בָאָרֶץ
וַאֲנִי לֹא־עָזַבְתִּי פִקֻּדֶיךָ:

87 They almost swept me off the earth,
but I never abandoned Your precepts.

כְּחַסְדְּךָ חַיֵּנִי וְאֶשְׁמְרָה
עֵדוּת פִּיךָ:

88 In keeping with Your loyalty,
give me life,
and I will uphold Your mouth's decrees.

ל LAMED

לְעוֹלָם יהוה דְּבָרְךָ
נִצָּב בַּשָּׁמָיִם:

89 Forever, LORD,
Your word endures in the heavens;

90 Your faithfulness endures
    throughout the generations;
    You made the earth firm, and it stands.

לְדֹר וָדֹר אֱמוּנָתֶךָ
כּוֹנַנְתָּ אֶרֶץ וַתַּעֲמֹד:

91 By Your laws they stand today,
    for all are Your servants.

לְמִשְׁפָּטֶיךָ עָמְדוּ הַיּוֹם
כִּי הַכֹּל עֲבָדֶיךָ:

92 Were Your teaching not my delight,
    I would have perished in suffering.

לוּלֵי תוֹרָתְךָ שַׁעֲשֻׁעָי
אָז אָבַדְתִּי בְעָנְיִי:

93 I will never forget Your precepts,
    for through them You give me life.

לְעוֹלָם לֹא־אֶשְׁכַּח פִּקּוּדֶיךָ
כִּי־בָם חִיִּיתָנִי:

94 I am Yours – save me,
    for I seek out Your precepts.

לְךָ־אֲנִי הוֹשִׁיעֵנִי
כִּי פִקּוּדֶיךָ דָרָשְׁתִּי:

95 The wicked hoped to destroy me,
    but I contemplate Your decrees.

לִי קִוּוּ רְשָׁעִים לְאַבְּדֵנִי
עֵדֹתֶיךָ אֶתְבּוֹנָן:

96 I have seen that everything,
    however perfect, has a limit,
    but Your commandments are boundless.

לְכָל־תִּכְלָה רָאִיתִי קֵץ
רְחָבָה מִצְוָתְךָ מְאֹד:

MEM

מ

97 How I love Your teaching!
    All day long I reflect upon it.

מָה־אָהַבְתִּי תוֹרָתֶךָ
כָּל־הַיּוֹם הִיא שִׂיחָתִי:

98 Your commandments make me wiser
    than my enemies,
    for they are mine forever.

מֵאֹיְבַי תְּחַכְּמֵנִי מִצְוֹתֶךָ
כִּי לְעוֹלָם הִיא־לִי:

99 I have gained understanding
    from all my teachers,
    for I reflect upon Your decrees.

מִכָּל־מְלַמְּדַי הִשְׂכַּלְתִּי
כִּי עֵדְוֹתֶיךָ שִׂיחָה לִי:

100 I have attained more insight
    than some elders,
    for I keep Your precepts.

מִזְּקֵנִים אֶתְבּוֹנָן
כִּי פִקּוּדֶיךָ נָצָרְתִּי:

מִכָּל־אֹרַח רָע כָּלִאתִי רַגְלָי 101 I hold my feet back
לְמַעַן אֶשְׁמֹר דְּבָרֶךָ: from every evil path
so that I may uphold Your word.

מִמִּשְׁפָּטֶיךָ לֹא־סָרְתִּי 102 I have not turned away
כִּי־אַתָּה הוֹרֵתָנִי: from Your laws,
for You Yourself have taught me.

מַה־נִּמְלְצוּ לְחִכִּי אִמְרָתֶךָ 103 How sweet Your promise is
מִדְּבַשׁ לְפִי: to my palate,
sweeter than honey to my mouth.

מִפִּקּוּדֶיךָ אֶתְבּוֹנָן 104 I gain insight from Your precepts,
עַל־כֵּן שָׂנֵאתִי ׀ so I despise all paths of falsehood.
כָּל־אֹרַח שָׁקֶר:

נ NUN

נֵר־לְרַגְלִי דְבָרֶךָ 105 Your word is a lamp for my feet,
וְאוֹר לִנְתִיבָתִי: a light for my path.

נִשְׁבַּעְתִּי וָאֲקַיֵּמָה 106 I have sworn –
לִשְׁמֹר מִשְׁפְּטֵי צִדְקֶךָ: and I will keep my word –
to uphold Your just laws.

נַעֲנֵיתִי עַד־מְאֹד 107 I have suffered gravely;
יְהֹוָה חַיֵּנִי כִדְבָרֶךָ: Lord, give me life
in keeping with Your word.

נִדְבוֹת פִּי רְצֵה־נָא יְהֹוָה 108 Accept, Lord, what my mouth offers,
וּמִשְׁפָּטֶיךָ לַמְּדֵנִי: and teach me Your laws.

נַפְשִׁי בְכַפִּי תָמִיד 109 My life is constantly in danger,
וְתוֹרָתְךָ לֹא שָׁכָחְתִּי: but I do not forget Your teaching.

נָתְנוּ רְשָׁעִים פַּח לִי 110 The wicked have set a trap for me,
וּמִפִּקּוּדֶיךָ לֹא תָעִיתִי: yet I do not stray from Your precepts.

נָחַלְתִּי עֵדְוֹתֶיךָ לְעוֹלָם 111 Your decrees are my everlasting share,
כִּי־שְׂשׂוֹן לִבִּי הֵמָּה: for they are the joy of my heart.

נָטִיתִי לִבִּי לַעֲשׂוֹת חֻקֶּיךָ
לְעוֹלָם עֵקֶב:

112 I have set my heart
on fulfilling Your statutes
forever, to the end.

ס   **SAMEKH**

סֵעֲפִים שָׂנֵאתִי
וְתוֹרָתְךָ אָהָבְתִּי:

113 Hypocrisy I despise,
and Your teaching I love.

סִתְרִי וּמָגִנִּי אָתָּה
לִדְבָרְךָ יִחָלְתִּי:

114 You are my shelter and shield;
in Your word I place my hope.

סוּרוּ מִמֶּנִּי מְרֵעִים
וְאֶצְּרָה מִצְוֺת אֱלֹהָי:

115 Turn away from me, evil ones,
so that I may keep the commandments
of my God.

סָמְכֵנִי כְאִמְרָתְךָ וְאֶחְיֶה
וְאַל־תְּבִישֵׁנִי מִשִּׂבְרִי:

116 Sustain me as You promised,
and I will live;
do not crush my hopes.

סְעָדֵנִי וְאִוָּשֵׁעָה
וְאֶשְׁעָה בְחֻקֶּיךָ תָמִיד:

117 Care for me, and I will be saved;
I will ever heed Your statutes.

סָלִיתָ כָּל־שׁוֹגִים מֵחֻקֶּיךָ
כִּי־שֶׁקֶר תַּרְמִיתָם:

118 You reject all who stray
from Your statutes,
for their deception is only false.

סִגִים הִשְׁבַּתָּ כָל־רִשְׁעֵי־אָרֶץ
לָכֵן אָהַבְתִּי עֵדֹתֶיךָ:

119 You discard like dross
all the wicked of the land,
so I love Your decrees.

סָמַר מִפַּחְדְּךָ בְשָׂרִי
וּמִמִּשְׁפָּטֶיךָ יָרֵאתִי:

120 My flesh creeps from dread of You,
and Your laws I fear.

ע   **AYIN**

עָשִׂיתִי מִשְׁפָּט וָצֶדֶק
בַּל־תַּנִּיחֵנִי לְעֹשְׁקָי:

121 I have done what is just and right;
do not abandon me to my oppressors.

עֲרֹב עַבְדְּךָ לְטוֹב
אַל־יַעַשְׁקֻנִי זֵדִים:

122 Secure the good of Your servant;
let me not be oppressed by the insolent.

עֵינַי כָּלוּ לִישׁוּעָתֶךָ
וּלְאִמְרַת צִדְקֶךָ:

123 My eyes pine for Your salvation,
for Your righteous promise.

עֲשֵׂה עִם־עַבְדְּךָ כְחַסְדֶּךָ
וְחֻקֶּיךָ לַמְּדֵנִי:

124 Deal loyally with Your servant,
and teach me Your statutes.

עַבְדְּךָ־אָנִי הֲבִינֵנִי
וְאֵדְעָה עֵדֹתֶיךָ:

125 I am Your servant – grant me insight
so that I may know Your decrees.

עֵת לַעֲשׂוֹת לַיהוה
הֵפֵרוּ תּוֹרָתֶךָ:

126 It is time for the LORD to act–
they have violated Your teaching!

עַל־כֵּן אָהַבְתִּי מִצְוֹתֶיךָ
מִזָּהָב וּמִפָּז:

127 Yes, I love Your commandments
more than gold, more than finest gold.

עַל־כֵּן ׀ כָּל־פִּקּוּדֵי כֹל יִשָּׁרְתִּי
כָּל־אֹרַח שֶׁקֶר שָׂנֵאתִי:

128 Yes, I keep in line
with all Your precepts,
and I despise all paths of falsehood.

פ

PEH

פְּלָאוֹת עֵדְוֹתֶיךָ
עַל־כֵּן נְצָרָתַם נַפְשִׁי:

129 Wondrous are Your decrees,
so I keep them.

פֵּתַח־דְּבָרֶיךָ יָאִיר
מֵבִין פְּתָיִים:

130 Your words shine light as they unfold,
granting insight to the simple.

פִּי־פָעַרְתִּי וָאֶשְׁאָפָה
כִּי לְמִצְוֹתֶיךָ יָאָבְתִּי:

131 My lips part to draw deep breath,
for I crave Your commandments.

פְּנֵה־אֵלַי וְחָנֵּנִי כְּמִשְׁפָּט
לְאֹהֲבֵי שְׁמֶךָ:

132 Turn to me and show me grace
as You always do
for those who love Your name.

פְּעָמַי הָכֵן בְּאִמְרָתֶךָ
וְאַל־תַּשְׁלֶט־בִּי כָל־אָוֶן:

133 Firm up my footsteps
with Your promise,
and let no evil rule over me.

פְּדֵנִי מֵעֹשֶׁק אָדָם
וְאֶשְׁמְרָה פִּקּוּדֶיךָ:

134 Free me from human oppression,
and I will uphold Your precepts.

פָּנֶיךָ הָאֵר בְּעַבְדֶּךָ 135 Shine Your face upon Your servant,
וְלַמְּדֵנִי אֶת־חֻקֶּיךָ: and teach me Your statutes.

פַּלְגֵי־מַיִם יָרְדוּ עֵינָי 136 Streams of water flow down
עַל לֹא־שָׁמְרוּ תוֹרָתֶךָ: from my eyes
because they do not uphold
Your teaching.

צ **TZADI**

צַדִּיק אַתָּה יהוה 137 You are righteous, Lord,
וְיָשָׁר מִשְׁפָּטֶיךָ: and Your laws are upright.

צִוִּיתָ צֶדֶק עֵדֹתֶיךָ 138 You impose Your decrees with justice,
וֶאֱמוּנָה מְאֹד: in deep faithfulness.

צִמְּתַתְנִי קִנְאָתִי 139 My fervor consumes me,
כִּי־שָׁכְחוּ דְבָרֶיךָ צָרָי: for my foes have forgotten Your words.

צְרוּפָה אִמְרָתְךָ מְאֹד 140 Your promise is deeply pure,
וְעַבְדְּךָ אֲהֵבָהּ: and Your servant loves it.

צָעִיר אָנֹכִי וְנִבְזֶה 141 I am trivial and scorned,
פִּקֻּדֶיךָ לֹא שָׁכָחְתִּי: but I never forget Your precepts.

צִדְקָתְךָ צֶדֶק לְעוֹלָם 142 Your righteousness is ever just,
וְתוֹרָתְךָ אֱמֶת: and Your teaching is truth.

צַר־וּמָצוֹק מְצָאוּנִי 143 Danger and despair have found me,
מִצְוֺתֶיךָ שַׁעֲשֻׁעָי: but Your commandments
are my delight.

צֶדֶק עֵדְוֺתֶיךָ לְעוֹלָם 144 Your decrees are ever just;
הֲבִינֵנִי וְאֶחְיֶה: grant me insight, and I will live.

ק **KOF**

קָרָאתִי בְכָל־לֵב עֲנֵנִי יהוה 145 I call with all my heart –
חֻקֶּיךָ אֶצֹּרָה: answer me, O Lord,
so that I may keep Your statutes.

קְרָאתִיךָ הוֹשִׁיעֵנִי
וְאֶשְׁמְרָה עֵדֹתֶיךָ:
146 I call out to You to save me
so that I may uphold Your decrees.

קִדַּמְתִּי בַנֶּשֶׁף וָאֲשַׁוֵּעָה
לִדְבָרְךָ יִחָלְתִּי:
147 I greet the dawn and cry out;
in Your word I place my hope.

לדבריך

קִדְּמוּ עֵינַי אַשְׁמֻרוֹת
לָשִׂיחַ בְּאִמְרָתֶךָ:
148 My eyes greet every watch of the night,
reflecting upon Your promise.

קוֹלִי שִׁמְעָה כְחַסְדֶּךָ
יהוה כְּמִשְׁפָּטֶךָ חַיֵּנִי:
149 Hear my voice through Your loyalty;
Lord, through Your laws
You give me life.

קָרְבוּ רֹדְפֵי זִמָּה
מִתּוֹרָתְךָ רָחָקוּ:
150 Pursuers of filth draw near –
far away from Your teaching.

קָרוֹב אַתָּה יהוה
וְכָל־מִצְוֺתֶיךָ אֱמֶת:
151 You draw close, Lord,
and all Your commandments are truth.

קֶדֶם יָדַעְתִּי מֵעֵדֹתֶיךָ
כִּי לְעוֹלָם יְסַדְתָּם:
152 I have long known of Your decrees,
for You established them forever.

ר

RESH

רְאֵה־עָנְיִי וְחַלְּצֵנִי
כִּי־תוֹרָתְךָ לֹא שָׁכָחְתִּי:
153 See my suffering and rescue me,
for I have never forgotten
Your teaching.

רִיבָה רִיבִי וּגְאָלֵנִי
לְאִמְרָתְךָ חַיֵּנִי:
154 Contend on my behalf and redeem me;
give me life through Your promise.

רָחוֹק מֵרְשָׁעִים יְשׁוּעָה
כִּי־חֻקֶּיךָ לֹא דָרָשׁוּ:
155 Salvation is far from the wicked,
for they do not seek out Your statutes.

רַחֲמֶיךָ רַבִּים ו יהוה
כְּמִשְׁפָּטֶיךָ חַיֵּנִי:
156 Your mercy is abundant, Lord;
give me life through Your laws.

רַבִּים רֹדְפַי וְצָרָי
מֵעֵדְוֺתֶיךָ לֹא נָטִיתִי:
157 Though my pursuers and foes are many,
I have not strayed from Your decrees.

רָאִיתִי בֹגְדִים וָאֶתְקוֹטָטָה
אֲשֶׁר אִמְרָתְךָ לֹא שָׁמָרוּ:

158 When I see traitors I am disgusted –
those who do not uphold
Your promise.

רְאֵה כִּי־פִקּוּדֶיךָ אָהָבְתִּי
יהוה כְּחַסְדְּךָ חַיֵּנִי:

159 See how I love Your precepts, LORD;
in keeping with Your loyalty
give me life.

רֹאשׁ־דְּבָרְךָ אֱמֶת
וּלְעוֹלָם כָּל־מִשְׁפַּט צִדְקֶךָ:

160 The essence of Your word is truth;
all Your just laws last forever.

שׁ

SHIN

שָׂרִים רְדָפוּנִי חִנָּם
וּמִדְּבָרְךָ פָּחַד לִבִּי:

וּמדבריך

161 Princes pursue me without cause,
but it is Your word
that my heart dreads.

שָׂשׂ אָנֹכִי עַל־אִמְרָתֶךָ
כְּמוֹצֵא שָׁלָל רָב:

162 I rejoice over Your promise
like one who finds great wealth.

שֶׁקֶר שָׂנֵאתִי וַאֲתַעֵבָה
תּוֹרָתְךָ אָהָבְתִּי:

163 I despise and abhor falsehood;
Your teaching I love.

שֶׁבַע בַּיּוֹם הִלַּלְתִּיךָ
עַל מִשְׁפְּטֵי צִדְקֶךָ:

164 Seven times a day I praise You
for Your just laws.

שָׁלוֹם רָב לְאֹהֲבֵי תוֹרָתֶךָ
וְאֵין־לָמוֹ מִכְשׁוֹל:

165 Lovers of Your teaching
enjoy great peace;
no obstacles hold them back.

שִׂבַּרְתִּי לִישׁוּעָתְךָ יהוה
וּמִצְוֹתֶיךָ עָשִׂיתִי:

166 I hope for Your salvation, LORD,
and I fulfill Your commandments.

שָׁמְרָה נַפְשִׁי עֵדֹתֶיךָ
וָאֹהֲבֵם מְאֹד:

167 I uphold Your decrees
and love them dearly.

שָׁמַרְתִּי פִקּוּדֶיךָ וְעֵדֹתֶיךָ
כִּי כָל־דְּרָכַי נֶגְדֶּךָ:

168 I uphold Your precepts and decrees,
for all my ways are before You.

ת TAV

תִּקְרַב רִנָּתִי לְפָנֶיךָ יהוה 169 Let my plea reach You, Lord;
כִּדְבָרְךָ הֲבִינֵנִי: grant me insight
in accordance with Your word.

תָּבוֹא תְחִנָּתִי לְפָנֶיךָ 170 Let my supplication come before You;
כְּאִמְרָתְךָ הַצִּילֵנִי: deliver me as You promised.

תַּבַּעְנָה שְׂפָתַי תְּהִלָּה 171 My lips shall stream with praise,
כִּי תְלַמְּדֵנִי חֻקֶּיךָ: for You teach me Your statutes.

תַּעַן לְשׁוֹנִי אִמְרָתֶךָ 172 My tongue shall sing of Your promise,
כִּי כָל־מִצְוֺתֶיךָ צֶּדֶק: for all Your commandments are just.

תְּהִי־יָדְךָ לְעָזְרֵנִי 173 Let Your hand be my help,
כִּי פִקּוּדֶיךָ בָחָרְתִּי: for I have chosen Your precepts.

תָּאַבְתִּי לִישׁוּעָתְךָ יהוה 174 I crave Your salvation, Lord,
וְתוֹרָתְךָ שַׁעֲשֻׁעָי: and in Your teaching I delight.

תְּחִי־נַפְשִׁי וּתְהַלְלֶךָּ 175 Let me live so that I can praise You,
וּמִשְׁפָּטֶךָ יַעְזְרֻנִי: and may Your laws help me.

תָּעִיתִי כְּשֶׂה אֹבֵד בַּקֵּשׁ עַבְדֶּךָ 176 I have strayed like a lost sheep –
כִּי מִצְוֺתֶיךָ לֹא שָׁכָחְתִּי: come and seek Your servant,
for I have never forgotten
Your commandments.

I have lived too long among those who hate peace.

This is my world: lies, malicious gossip, and slander.
Everyone schemes and plots against me. I'm not paranoid.
This is my reality. It is foolish to be honest,
and futile to seek peace.

PSALM 120

שִׁיר הַמַּעֲלוֹת
אֶל־יהוה בַּצָּרָתָה לִּי
קָרָאתִי וַיַּעֲנֵנִי׃

1 A song of ascents
I called to the LORD in my distress,
and He answered me.

יהוה הַצִּילָה נַפְשִׁי
מִשְּׂפַת־שֶׁקֶר
מִלָּשׁוֹן רְמִיָּה׃

2 "LORD, save me from lying lips,
from a deceitful tongue."

מַה־יִּתֵּן לְךָ וּמַה־יֹּסִיף לָךְ
לָשׁוֹן רְמִיָּה׃

3 What will be done to you,
and what will you gain,
O deceitful tongue? –

חִצֵּי גִבּוֹר שְׁנוּנִים
עִם גַּחֲלֵי רְתָמִים׃

4 only a warrior's sharp arrows
and hot broom-wood coals.

אוֹיָה־לִי כִּי־גַרְתִּי מֶשֶׁךְ
שָׁכַנְתִּי עִם־אָהֳלֵי קֵדָר׃

5 Woe to me that I dwell in Meshekh,
that I live among the tents of Kedar.

רַבַּת שָׁכְנָה־לָּהּ נַפְשִׁי
עִם שׂוֹנֵא שָׁלוֹם׃

6 I have lived too long
among those who hate peace.

אֲנִי־שָׁלוֹם וְכִי אֲדַבֵּר
הֵמָּה לַמִּלְחָמָה׃

7 I am for peace,
but whenever I speak of it,
they are for war.

I lift my eyes up to the hills; where will my help come from?

I am without hope, utterly alone. I have no answers for my problems. I've looked everywhere for some ray of light. I can't afford to fail again. Who will help me?

PSALM 121

שִׁיר לַמַּעֲלוֹת
אֶשָּׂא עֵינַי אֶל־הֶהָרִים
מֵאַיִן יָבֹא עֶזְרִי:

1 A song of ascents
I lift my eyes up to the hills;
where will my help come from?

עֶזְרִי מֵעִם יהוה
עֹשֵׂה שָׁמַיִם וָאָרֶץ:

2 My help comes from the LORD,
Maker of heaven and earth.

אַל־יִתֵּן לַמּוֹט רַגְלֶךָ
אַל־יָנוּם שֹׁמְרֶךָ:

3 He will not let your foot slip;
He who guards you does not slumber.

הִנֵּה לֹא־יָנוּם וְלֹא יִישָׁן
שׁוֹמֵר יִשְׂרָאֵל:

4 Behold – the Guardian of Israel
neither slumbers nor sleeps.

יהוה שֹׁמְרֶךָ
יהוה צִלְּךָ עַל־יַד יְמִינֶךָ:

5 The LORD is your guardian;
the Lord is your shade at your right hand.

יוֹמָם הַשֶּׁמֶשׁ לֹא־יַכֶּכָּה
וְיָרֵחַ בַּלָּיְלָה:

6 The sun will not strike you by day,
nor the moon by night.

יהוה יִשְׁמָרְךָ מִכָּל־רָע
יִשְׁמֹר אֶת־נַפְשֶׁךָ:

7 The LORD will guard you from all harm;
He will guard your life.

יהוה יִשְׁמָר־צֵאתְךָ וּבוֹאֶךָ
מֵעַתָּה וְעַד־עוֹלָם:

8 The LORD will guard your going
and coming,
now and for evermore.

Our feet stood within your gates, Jerusalem

When I really need a spiritual boost, I think of Jerusalem.
I recall her glorious past.
I imagine her eternal future.
I envision her citizens together at last. I pray for her peace.

PSALM 122

שִׁיר הַמַּעֲלוֹת לְדָוִד 1 A song of ascents – of David
שָׂמַחְתִּי בְּאֹמְרִים לִי I rejoiced when they said to me,
בֵּית יהוה נֵלֵךְ: "Let us go to the House of the LORD."

עֹמְדוֹת הָיוּ רַגְלֵינוּ 2 Our feet stood
בִּשְׁעָרַיִךְ יְרוּשָׁלָ͏ִם: within your gates, Jerusalem:

יְרוּשָׁלַ͏ִם הַבְּנוּיָה 3 Jerusalem,
כְּעִיר שֶׁחֻבְּרָה־לָּהּ יַחְדָּו: built as a city joined together.

שֶׁשָּׁם עָלוּ שְׁבָטִים שִׁבְטֵי־יָהּ 4 There the tribes went up,
עֵדוּת לְיִשְׂרָאֵל the tribes of the LORD,
לְהֹדוֹת לְשֵׁם יהוה: as a decree to Israel,
to give thanks to the LORD's name,

כִּי שָׁמָּה ׀ יָשְׁבוּ 5 for there the thrones of justice were set,
כִסְאוֹת לְמִשְׁפָּט the thrones of the House of David.
כִּסְאוֹת לְבֵית דָּוִד:

שַׁאֲלוּ שְׁלוֹם יְרוּשָׁלָ͏ִם 6 Pray for the peace of Jerusalem:
יִשְׁלָיוּ אֹהֲבָיִךְ: "May those who love you prosper.

יְהִי־שָׁלוֹם בְּחֵילֵךְ 7 May there be peace within your ramparts,
שַׁלְוָה בְּאַרְמְנוֹתָיִךְ: tranquility in your citadels."

לְמַעַן אַחַי וְרֵעָי 8 For the sake of my brothers
אֲדַבְּרָה־נָּא שָׁלוֹם בָּךְ: and my friends,
I shall say, "Peace be within you."

לְמַעַן בֵּית־יהוה אֱלֹהֵינוּ 9 For the sake of the House of the LORD
אֲבַקְשָׁה טוֹב לָךְ: our God,
I shall seek your good.

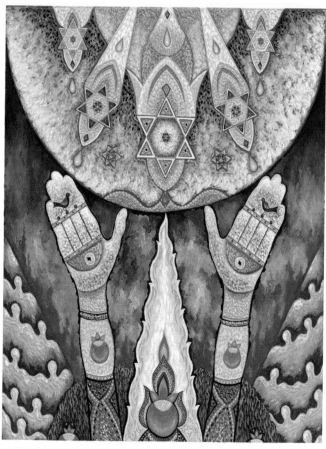

To You, enthroned in heaven, I lift my eyes

I am mocked and teased at every turn.
I don't know what's worse,
the names they call me or their supercilious smiles.
I have had enough.

PSALM 123

שִׁיר הַמַּעֲלוֹת
אֵלֶיךָ נָשָׂאתִי אֶת־עֵינַי
הַיֹּשְׁבִי בַּשָּׁמָיִם:

1 A song of ascents
To You, enthroned in heaven,
I lift my eyes.

הִנֵּה כְעֵינֵי עֲבָדִים
אֶל־יַד אֲדוֹנֵיהֶם
כְּעֵינֵי שִׁפְחָה אֶל־יַד גְּבִרְתָּהּ
כֵּן עֵינֵינוּ אֶל־יהוה אֱלֹהֵינוּ
עַד שֶׁיְּחָנֵּנוּ:

2 As the eyes of slaves turn
to their master's hand,
as the eyes of a slave-girl
to her mistress's hand,
so our eyes turn to the LORD our God,
awaiting His favor.

חָנֵּנוּ יהוה חָנֵּנוּ
כִּי־רַב שָׂבַעְנוּ בוּז:

3 Show us favor, LORD, show us favor,
for we have suffered more than enough
contempt.

רַבַּת שָׂבְעָה־לָּהּ נַפְשֵׁנוּ
הַלַּעַג הַשַּׁאֲנַנִּים
הַבּוּז לִגְאֵי יוֹנִים:

לגאיונים

4 Too long have we suffered
the scorn of the complacent,
the contempt of the arrogant.

Over us would have swept the raging waters

I never thought I'd make it. The odds were against me.
My friends and family gave up hope.
But I am here to tell the tale. Thank God.

PSALM 124

שִׁיר הַמַּעֲלוֹת לְדָוִד
לוּלֵי יהוה שֶׁהָיָה לָנוּ
יֹאמַר־נָא יִשְׂרָאֵל:

1 A song of ascents – of David
Had the LORD not been on our side –
let Israel say it –

לוּלֵי יהוה שֶׁהָיָה לָנוּ
בְּקוּם עָלֵינוּ אָדָם:

2 had the LORD not been on our side
when men rose up against us,

אֲזַי חַיִּים בְּלָעוּנוּ
בַּחֲרוֹת אַפָּם בָּנוּ:

3 they would have swallowed us alive
when their anger raged against us.

אֲזַי הַמַּיִם שְׁטָפוּנוּ
נַחְלָה עָבַר עַל־נַפְשֵׁנוּ:

4 The waters would have engulfed us;
the torrent would have swept over us;

אֲזַי עָבַר עַל־נַפְשֵׁנוּ
הַמַּיִם הַזֵּידוֹנִים:

5 over us would have swept
the raging waters.

בָּרוּךְ יהוה
שֶׁלֹּא נְתָנָנוּ טֶרֶף לְשִׁנֵּיהֶם:

6 Blessed be the LORD,
who did not leave us as prey
for their teeth.

נַפְשֵׁנוּ כְּצִפּוֹר
נִמְלְטָה מִפַּח יוֹקְשִׁים
הַפַּח נִשְׁבָּר וַאֲנַחְנוּ נִמְלָטְנוּ:

7 We escaped like a bird
from the fowler's snare –
the snare broke, and we escaped.

עֶזְרֵנוּ בְּשֵׁם יהוה
עֹשֵׂה שָׁמַיִם וָאָרֶץ:

8 Our help is in the name of the LORD,
Maker of heaven and earth.

As hills surround Jerusalem

They say nice people finish last. But that doesn't tempt me
to change my ways. I'll stay with the nice people.
Our time will come. We'll finish first.

PSALM 125

שִׁיר הַֽמַּעֲלֹ֫ות
הַבֹּטְחִ֥ים בַּיהוָ֑ה
כְּהַר־צִיּ֥וֹן
לֹא־יִ֝מּ֗וֹט לְעוֹלָ֥ם יֵשֵֽׁב׃

1 A song of ascents
Those who trust in the LORD
are like Mount Zion,
which cannot be shaken,
which stands firm forever.

יְרֽוּשָׁלִַ֗ם הָרִים֮ סָבִ֪יב לָ֥֫הּ
וַ֭יהוָה סָבִ֣יב לְעַמּ֑וֹ
מֵ֝עַתָּ֗ה וְעַד־עוֹלָֽם׃

2 As hills surround Jerusalem,
so the LORD surrounds His people,
now and forever.

כִּ֤י לֹ֪א יָנ֡וּחַ שֵׁ֤בֶט הָרֶ֗שַׁע
עַל֮ גּוֹרַ֪ל הַֽצַּדִּ֫יקִ֥ים
לְמַ֡עַן לֹא־יִשְׁלְח֖וּ הַצַּדִּיקִ֥ים ׀
בְּעַוְלָ֣תָה יְדֵיהֶֽם׃

3 The scepter of the wicked shall not rest
on the land allotted to the righteous,
so the righteous shall not set their hand
to wrongdoing.

הֵיטִ֣יבָה יְ֭הוָה לַטּוֹבִ֑ים
וְ֝לִֽישָׁרִ֗ים בְּלִבּוֹתָֽם׃

4 Do good, LORD, to those who are good,
to those who are upright in heart.

וְהַמַּטִּ֤ים עֲקַלְקַלּוֹתָ֗ם
יוֹלִיכֵ֣ם יְהוָה֮ אֶת־פֹּעֲלֵ֪י הָ֫אָ֥וֶן
שָׁ֝ל֗וֹם עַל־יִשְׂרָאֵֽל׃

5 As for those who turn aside
to crooked ways,
may the LORD make them wander
the ways of evildoers.
Peace be on Israel!

When the LORD brought back the exiles of Zion, we were like dreamers

It was all worth it. We suffered. We cried.
But look at us now.
We laugh and sing with joy.

PSALM 126

שִׁיר הַמַּעֲלוֹת
בְּשׁוּב יהוה אֶת־שִׁיבַת צִיּוֹן
הָיִינוּ כְּחֹלְמִים:

אָז יִמָּלֵא שְׂחוֹק פִּינוּ
וּלְשׁוֹנֵנוּ רִנָּה
אָז יֹאמְרוּ בַגּוֹיִם
הִגְדִּיל יהוה לַעֲשׂוֹת עִם־אֵלֶּה:

הִגְדִּיל יהוה לַעֲשׂוֹת עִמָּנוּ
הָיִינוּ שְׂמֵחִים:

שׁוּבָה יהוה אֶת־שְׁבִיתֵנוּ   שבותנו
כַּאֲפִיקִים בַּנֶּגֶב:

הַזֹּרְעִים בְּדִמְעָה
בְּרִנָּה יִקְצֹרוּ:

הָלוֹךְ יֵלֵךְ ׀ וּבָכֹה
נֹשֵׂא מֶשֶׁךְ־הַזָּרַע
בֹּא־יָבֹא בְרִנָּה נֹשֵׂא אֲלֻמֹּתָיו:

1 A song of ascents
When the Lord brought back
the exiles of Zion,
we were like dreamers –

2 then were our mouths filled
with laughter,
our tongues with songs of joy;
then was it said among the nations,
"The Lord has done great things
for them."

3 The Lord has done great things for us,
and we rejoiced.

4 Bring back our exiles, Lord,
like streams in the Negev.

5 May those who sowed in tears
reap in joy;

6 may those who go out weeping,
carrying a sack of seed,
come back in glad song,
carrying their sheaves.

A song of ascents – of Shlomo. Unless the LORD builds the house, its builders labor in vain

I've worked long hours. I've built a house.
I've been involved in my community.
I've raised a family. I've known success.
But it wasn't my doing. I had His help.

PSALM 127

שִׁיר הַמַּעֲלוֹת לִשְׁלֹמֹה
אִם־יהוה ׀ לֹא־יִבְנֶה בַיִת
שָׁוְא ׀ עָמְלוּ בוֹנָיו בּוֹ
אִם־יהוה לֹא־יִשְׁמָר־עִיר
שָׁוְא ׀ שָׁקַד שׁוֹמֵר:

1 A song of ascents – of Shlomo
Unless the Lᴏʀᴅ builds the house,
its builders labor in vain.
Unless the Lᴏʀᴅ guards the city,
the guard keeps watch in vain.

שָׁוְא לָכֶם ׀ מַשְׁכִּימֵי קוּם
מְאַחֲרֵי־שֶׁבֶת
אֹכְלֵי לֶחֶם הָעֲצָבִים
כֵּן יִתֵּן לִידִידוֹ שֵׁנָא:

2 In vain do you rise early
and stay up late,
you who eat hard-earned bread –
He provides for His loved ones
while they sleep.

הִנֵּה נַחֲלַת יהוה בָּנִים
שָׂכָר פְּרִי הַבָּטֶן:

3 Children are a gift from the Lᴏʀᴅ,
the fruit of the womb His reward.

כְּחִצִּים בְּיַד־גִּבּוֹר
כֵּן בְּנֵי הַנְּעוּרִים:

4 Like arrows in a warrior's hand
are the children of one's youth.

אַשְׁרֵי הַגֶּבֶר אֲשֶׁר מִלֵּא
אֶת־אַשְׁפָּתוֹ מֵהֶם
לֹא־יֵבֹשׁוּ
כִּי־יְדַבְּרוּ אֶת־אוֹיְבִים בַּשָּׁעַר:

5 Happy are those
who fill their quivers with them;
they shall not be put to shame
when they contend with the enemy
at the gate.

May the LORD bless you from Zion; may you see Jerusalem thrive all the days of your life

I am truly blessed. I work hard, but productively.
I love my spouse. I am proud of my children.
If Jerusalem was at peace, all would be perfect.

PSALM 128

שִׁיר הַמַּעֲלוֹת

אַשְׁרֵי כָּל־יְרֵא יהוה

הַהֹלֵךְ בִּדְרָכָיו:

יְגִיעַ כַּפֶּיךָ כִּי תֹאכֵל

אַשְׁרֶיךָ וְטוֹב לָךְ:

אֶשְׁתְּךָ ׀ כְּגֶפֶן פֹּרִיָּה

בְּיַרְכְּתֵי בֵיתֶךָ

בָּנֶיךָ כִּשְׁתִלֵי זֵיתִים

סָבִיב לְשֻׁלְחָנֶךָ:

הִנֵּה כִי־כֵן יְבֹרַךְ גָּבֶר

יְרֵא יהוה:

יְבָרֶכְךָ יהוה מִצִּיּוֹן

וּרְאֵה בְּטוּב יְרוּשָׁלָ͏ִם

כֹּל יְמֵי חַיֶּיךָ:

וּרְאֵה־בָנִים לְבָנֶיךָ

שָׁלוֹם עַל־יִשְׂרָאֵל:

1 A song of ascents
   Happy are all who fear the LORD,
   who walk in His ways.

2 You shall eat the fruit of your labor;
   You shall be happy and thriving.

3 Your wife shall be like a fruitful vine
   within your home,
   your children like olive saplings
   around your table;

4 thus shall one who fears the LORD
   be blessed.

5 May the LORD bless you from Zion;
   may you see Jerusalem thrive
   all the days of your life;

6 may you live to see
   your children's children.
   Peace be on Israel!

We bless you in the name of the Lᴏʀᴅ

They hate us because of our nationality. They've hated us from the very beginning. They've tried to exterminate us. Had they had their way, none of us would be here now.

PSALM 129

שִׁיר הַֽמַּעֲלוֹת
רַבַּת צְרָרוּנִי מִנְּעוּרַי
יֹאמַר־נָא יִשְׂרָאֵל׃

1 A song of ascents
I have suffered so much torment
since my youth–
let Israel say it –

רַבַּת צְרָרוּנִי מִנְּעוּרָי
גַּם לֹא־יָכְלוּ לִי׃

2 I have suffered so much torment
since my youth,
but my tormentors have never
overcome me.

עַל־גַּבִּי חָרְשׁוּ חֹרְשִׁים
הֶאֱרִיכוּ לְמַעֲנִיתָם׃

למענותם

3 Plowmen plowed across my back,
making long furrows,

יְהוָה צַדִּיק
קִצֵּץ עֲבוֹת רְשָׁעִים׃

4 but the LORD is just;
He has cut the bonds of the wicked.

יֵבֹשׁוּ וְיִסֹּגוּ אָחוֹר
כֹּל שֹׂנְאֵי צִיּוֹן׃

5 Let all who hate Zion
be driven back in shame;

יִהְיוּ כַּחֲצִיר גַּגּוֹת
שֶׁקַּדְמַת שָׁלַף יָבֵשׁ׃

6 let them be like weeds on rooftops
that wither before they are pulled up,

שֶׁלֹּא מִלֵּא כַפּוֹ קוֹצֵר
וְחִצְנוֹ מְעַמֵּר׃

7 that will never fill a reaper's hand
or yield an armful
for the gatherer of sheaves.

וְלֹא אָמְרוּ ׀ הָעֹבְרִים
בִּרְכַּת־יהוה אֲלֵיכֶם
בֵּרַכְנוּ אֶתְכֶם בְּשֵׁם יהוה׃

8 No passersby will say to them:
"The LORD's blessing be upon you;
we bless you in the name of the LORD."

From the depths I have called out to You, O Lord

I am in deep trouble.
My depth will release me from the depths. Deep faith,
deep sincerity, and deep humility will elevate me once again.
I must descend in order to ascend.
I must not pray from upon a chair. I must pray from here.

PSALM 130

שִׁיר הַמַּעֲלוֹת 1 A song of ascents
מִמַּעֲמַקִּים קְרָאתִיךָ יהוה: From the depths I have called out to You,
O Lord.

אֲדֹנָי שִׁמְעָה בְקוֹלִי 2 Lord, hear my voice;
תִּהְיֶינָה אָזְנֶיךָ קַשֻּׁבוֹת let Your ears be attuned
לְקוֹל תַּחֲנוּנָי: to the sound of my plea.

אִם־עֲוֺנוֹת תִּשְׁמָר־יָהּ 3 If You, Lord, keep account of sins,
אֲדֹנָי מִי יַעֲמֹד: O Lord, who could stand?

כִּי־עִמְּךָ הַסְּלִיחָה 4 But with You there is forgiveness;
לְמַעַן תִּוָּרֵא: therefore You may be revered.

קִוִּיתִי יהוה 5 I wait for the Lord –
קִוְּתָה נַפְשִׁי my soul waits –
וְלִדְבָרוֹ הוֹחָלְתִּי: in His word I put my hope.

נַפְשִׁי לַאדֹנָי 6 My soul waits for the Lord
מִשֹּׁמְרִים לַבֹּקֶר more than watchmen for the morning,
שֹׁמְרִים לַבֹּקֶר: more than watchmen for the morning.

יַחֵל יִשְׂרָאֵל אֶל־יהוה 7 Israel, put your hope in the Lord,
כִּי־עִם־יהוה הַחֶסֶד for loving-kindness is the Lord's,
וְהַרְבֵּה עִמּוֹ פְדוּת: and great is His power to redeem.

וְהוּא יִפְדֶּה אֶת־יִשְׂרָאֵל 8 It is He who will redeem Israel
מִכֹּל עֲוֺנוֹתָיו: from all their sins.

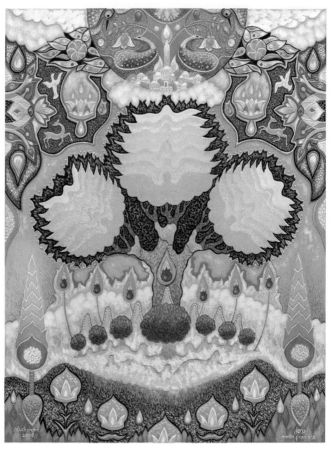

I do not concern myself with great affairs or things beyond me

I am a charitable person. Yet I refuse to help someone who can help himself. Send me someone who is truly helpless. I won't turn him away empty-handed. It is the same way with God. If you want Him to answer your prayers, you should convince Him that you're truly helpless. You are helpless, you know. You are as helpless as a just-weaned child.

PSALM 131

שִׁיר הַמַּעֲלוֹת לְדָוִד
יהוה ׀ לֹא־גָבַהּ לִבִּי
וְלֹא־רָמוּ עֵינַי
וְלֹא־הִלַּכְתִּי ׀ בִּגְדֹלוֹת
וּבְנִפְלָאוֹת מִמֶּנִּי:

אִם־לֹא שִׁוִּיתִי ׀ וְדוֹמַמְתִּי נַפְשִׁי
כְּגָמֻל עֲלֵי אִמּוֹ
כַּגָּמֻל עָלַי נַפְשִׁי:

יַחֵל יִשְׂרָאֵל אֶל־יהוה
מֵעַתָּה וְעַד־עוֹלָם:

1 A song of ascents – of David
Lord – my heart is not proud,
my eyes not raised too high.
I do not concern myself with great affairs
or things beyond me,

2 but I have made my soul calm and quiet
like a soothed child against his mother;
like a soothed child is my soul within me.

3 Israel, put your hope in the Lord,
now and for evermore.

Your priests are robed in righteousness; Your devoted ones sing for joy

There's the external and there's the internal. God's Temple must have both. External does not mean pompous gilded glitter. It means exemplary behavior, priests robed in righteousness. Internal does not mean plans and schemes. It means music and melody, joyous and eternal. Righteousness and song — together, that's the Temple.

PSALM 132

שִׁיר הַמַּעֲלוֹת
זְכוֹר־יהוה לְדָוִד
אֵת כָּל־עֻנּוֹתוֹ:

1 A song of ascents
Lord, remember David
and all his suffering.

אֲשֶׁר נִשְׁבַּע לַיהוה
נָדַר לַאֲבִיר יַעֲקֹב:

2 He swore an oath to the Lord
and made a vow
to the Mighty One of Yaakov:

אִם־אָבֹא בְּאֹהֶל בֵּיתִי
אִם־אֶעֱלֶה עַל־עֶרֶשׂ יְצוּעָי:

3 "I will not enter my house
or go to bed,

אִם־אֶתֵּן שְׁנַת לְעֵינָי
לְעַפְעַפַּי תְּנוּמָה:

4 I will not let my eyes sleep
or let my eyelids close,

עַד־אֶמְצָא מָקוֹם לַיהוה
מִשְׁכָּנוֹת לַאֲבִיר יַעֲקֹב:

5 until I find a place for the Lord,
a dwelling for the Mighty One of Yaakov."

הִנֵּה־שְׁמַעֲנוּהָ בְאֶפְרָתָה
מְצָאנוּהָ בִּשְׂדֵי־יָעַר:

6 We heard of it in Efrat;
we found it in the fields of Yaar.

נָבוֹאָה לְמִשְׁכְּנוֹתָיו
נִשְׁתַּחֲוֶה לַהֲדֹם רַגְלָיו:

7 Let us enter His dwelling;
let us worship at His footstool.

קוּמָה יהוה לִמְנוּחָתֶךָ
אַתָּה וַאֲרוֹן עֻזֶּךָ:

8 Advance, Lord, to Your resting place,
You and Your mighty Ark.

כֹּהֲנֶיךָ יִלְבְּשׁוּ־צֶדֶק
וַחֲסִידֶיךָ יְרַנֵּנוּ:

9 Your priests are robed in righteousness;
Your devoted ones sing for joy.

בַּעֲבוּר דָּוִד עַבְדֶּךָ
אַל־תָּשֵׁב פְּנֵי מְשִׁיחֶךָ:

10 For the sake of Your servant David,
do not reject Your anointed one.

נִשְׁבַּע־יהוה לְדָוִד
אֱמֶת לֹא־יָשׁוּב מִמֶּנָּה
מִפְּרִי בִטְנְךָ אָשִׁית לְכִסֵּא־לָךְ:

11 The Lord swore to David a firm oath
that He will not revoke:
"One of your own descendants
I will set upon your throne.

אִם־יִשְׁמְר֬וּ בָנֶ֙יךָ ׀ בְּרִיתִי֮
וְעֵדֹתִ֥י ז֗וֹ אֲלַ֫מְּדֵ֥ם
גַּם־בְּנֵיהֶ֥ם עֲדֵי־עַ֑ד
יֵ֝שְׁב֗וּ לְכִסֵּא־לָֽךְ׃

כִּֽי־בָחַ֣ר יְהֹוָ֣ה בְּצִיּ֑וֹן
אִ֝וָּ֗הּ לְמוֹשָׁ֥ב לֽוֹ׃

זֹאת־מְנוּחָתִ֥י עֲדֵי־עַ֑ד
פֹּֽה־אֵ֝שֵׁ֗ב כִּ֣י אִוִּתִֽיהָ׃

צֵ֭ידָהּ בָּרֵ֣ךְ אֲבָרֵ֑ךְ
אֶ֝בְיוֹנֶ֗יהָ אַשְׂבִּ֥יעַֽ לָֽחֶם׃

וְ֭כֹהֲנֶיהָ אַלְבִּ֣ישׁ יֶ֑שַׁע
וַ֝חֲסִידֶ֗יהָ רַנֵּ֥ן יְרַנֵּֽנוּ׃

שָׁ֤ם אַצְמִ֣יחַ קֶ֣רֶן לְדָוִ֑ד
עָרַ֥כְתִּי נֵ֝֗ר לִמְשִׁיחִֽי׃

א֭וֹיְבָיו אַלְבִּ֣ישׁ בֹּ֑שֶׁת
וְ֝עָלָ֗יו יָצִ֥יץ נִזְרֽוֹ׃

12 If your children keep My covenant
and My decrees that I teach them,
then their children, too, for evermore
shall sit upon your throne,"

13 for the LORD has chosen Zion;
He desired it for His home:

14 "This is My resting place for all time;
here I will dwell, for that is My desire.

15 I will amply bless its store of food;
its poor I will sate with bread.

16 I will clothe its priests with salvation;
its devoted ones shall sing for joy.

17 There I will make David's horn flourish;
I will prepare a lamp
for My anointed one.

18 I will clothe his enemies with shame,
but on him will rest a shining crown."

Like the dew of Ḥermon that flows down the mountains of Zion

All good things come from Zion.
Torah and blessing come from Zion.
Beauty and sustenance come from Zion.
Greatness, redemption, and life itself come from Zion.
What is Zion's secret?

PSALM 133

שִׁיר הַמַּעֲלוֹת לְדָוִד 1 A song of ascents – of David
הִנֵּה מַה־טּוֹב וּמַה־נָּעִים How good and pleasant it is
שֶׁבֶת אַחִים גַּם־יָחַד: when brothers dwell together –

כַּשֶּׁמֶן הַטּוֹב ׀ עַל־הָרֹאשׁ 2 like fragrant oil on the head
יֹרֵד עַל־הַזָּקָן flowing down onto the beard,
זְקַן־אַהֲרֹן שֶׁיֹּרֵד Aharon's beard that flows down
עַל־פִּי מִדּוֹתָיו: over the collar of his robes,

כְּטַל־חֶרְמוֹן 3 like the dew of Hermon
שֶׁיֹּרֵד עַל־הַרְרֵי צִיּוֹן that flows down the mountains of Zion.
כִּי שָׁם ׀ צִוָּה יהוה אֶת־הַבְּרָכָה There the Lord bestows His blessing,
חַיִּים עַד־הָעוֹלָם: life for evermore.

Lift up your hands toward the Sanctuary and bless the Lord

I have known night. As a child, its dark shadows frightened me.
Later, it became my symbol for the dark moments of history.
Eventually, I learned that night is an opportunity.
God is closest to us then. It is the best time to study Torah.
It is the best time to pray. It is when He Himself prays.

PSALM 134

שִׁיר הַמַּעֲלוֹת 1 A song of ascents
הִנֵּה ׀ בָּרְכוּ אֶת־יהוה Come bless the LORD,
כָּל־עַבְדֵי יהוה all you servants of the LORD,
הָעֹמְדִים בְּבֵית־יהוה you who nightly stand
בַּלֵּילוֹת: in the House of the LORD.

שְׂאוּ־יְדֵכֶם קֹדֶשׁ 2 Lift up your hands toward the Sanctuary
וּבָרְכוּ אֶת־יהוה: and bless the LORD.

יְבָרֶכְךָ יהוה מִצִּיּוֹן 3 May the LORD –
עֹשֵׂה שָׁמַיִם וָאָרֶץ: Maker of heaven and earth–
bless you from Zion!

Blessed is the LORD from Zion, He who dwells in Jerusalem. Halleluya!

My God is special, incomparable. He controls nature.
He protects His people.
He protects me. I sing His praises.
All His people join me in praising Him.

PSALM 135

הַלְלוּיָהּ ׀
הַלְלוּ אֶת־שֵׁם יהוה
הַלְלוּ עַבְדֵי יהוה׃

1 Halleluya!
Praise the name of the LORD;
praise Him, you servants of the LORD

שֶׁעֹמְדִים בְּבֵית יהוה
בְּחַצְרוֹת בֵּית אֱלֹהֵינוּ׃

2 who stand in the LORD's House,
in the courtyards
of the House of our God.

הַלְלוּיָהּ כִּי־טוֹב יהוה
זַמְּרוּ לִשְׁמוֹ כִּי נָעִים׃

3 Praise the LORD,
for the LORD is good;
Sing praises to His name,
for it is lovely,

כִּי־יַעֲקֹב בָּחַר לוֹ יָהּ
יִשְׂרָאֵל לִסְגֻלָּתוֹ׃

4 for the LORD has chosen Yaakov
as His own,
Israel as his treasure,

כִּי אֲנִי יָדַעְתִּי כִּי־גָדוֹל יהוה
וַאֲדֹנֵינוּ מִכָּל־אֱלֹהִים׃

5 for I know that the LORD is great,
that our LORD is above all gods.

כֹּל אֲשֶׁר־חָפֵץ יהוה עָשָׂה
בַּשָּׁמַיִם וּבָאָרֶץ
בַּיַּמִּים וְכָל־תְּהֹמוֹת׃

6 Whatever pleases the LORD, He does
in heaven and on earth,
in the seas and all the depths.

מַעֲלֶה נְשִׂאִים מִקְצֵה הָאָרֶץ
בְּרָקִים לַמָּטָר עָשָׂה
מוֹצֵא־רוּחַ מֵאוֹצְרוֹתָיו׃

7 He raises clouds from the ends
of the earth;
He makes lightning bolts with the rain;
He brings out the wind
from His storehouses.

שֶׁהִכָּה בְּכוֹרֵי מִצְרָיִם
מֵאָדָם עַד־בְּהֵמָה׃

8 He struck down the firstborn of Egypt,
humans and animals alike.

שָׁלַח ׀ אוֹתֹת וּמֹפְתִים
בְּתוֹכֵכִי מִצְרָיִם
בְּפַרְעֹה וּבְכָל־עֲבָדָיו׃

9 He sent signs and wonders
into your midst, Egypt –
against Pharaoh and all his servants.

שֶׁהִכָּה גּוֹיִם רַבִּים
וְהָרַג מְלָכִים עֲצוּמִים׃

10 He struck down many nations
and slew mighty kings:

לְסִיחוֹן ׀ מֶלֶךְ הָאֱמֹרִי 11
וּלְעוֹג מֶלֶךְ הַבָּשָׁן
וּלְכֹל מַמְלְכוֹת כְּנָעַן:

וְנָתַן אַרְצָם נַחֲלָה 12
נַחֲלָה לְיִשְׂרָאֵל עַמּוֹ:

יהוה שִׁמְךָ לְעוֹלָם 13
יהוה זִכְרְךָ לְדֹר־וָדֹר:

כִּי־יָדִין יהוה עַמּוֹ 14
וְעַל־עֲבָדָיו יִתְנֶחָם:

עֲצַבֵּי הַגּוֹיִם כֶּסֶף וְזָהָב 15
מַעֲשֵׂה יְדֵי אָדָם:

פֶּה־לָהֶם וְלֹא יְדַבֵּרוּ 16
עֵינַיִם לָהֶם וְלֹא יִרְאוּ:

אָזְנַיִם לָהֶם וְלֹא יַאֲזִינוּ 17
אַף אֵין־יֶשׁ־רוּחַ בְּפִיהֶם:

כְּמוֹהֶם יִהְיוּ עֹשֵׂיהֶם 18
כֹּל אֲשֶׁר־בֹּטֵחַ בָּהֶם:

בֵּית יִשְׂרָאֵל בָּרְכוּ אֶת־יהוה 19
בֵּית אַהֲרֹן בָּרְכוּ אֶת־יהוה:

בֵּית הַלֵּוִי בָּרְכוּ אֶת־יהוה 20
יִרְאֵי יהוה בָּרְכוּ אֶת־יהוה:

בָּרוּךְ יהוה ׀ מִצִּיּוֹן 21
שֹׁכֵן יְרוּשָׁלָ͏ִם
הַלְלוּיָהּ:

11 Sihon, king of the Amorites,
Og, king of Bashan,
and all the kingdoms of Canaan,

12 and He gave their land as a heritage,
a heritage for His people Israel.

13 Your name, LORD, endures forever;
Your renown, LORD, for all generations.

14 For the LORD will vindicate His people,
bring solace to His servants.

15 The idols of the nations
are silver and gold,
made by human hands.

16 They have mouths but cannot speak;
eyes but cannot see.

17 They have ears but cannot hear;
there is no breath in their mouths.

18 Their makers will become like them;
so will all who trust in them.

19 House of Israel – bless the LORD!
House of Aharon – bless the LORD!

20 House of Levi – bless the LORD!
You who fear the LORD – bless the
LORD!

21 Blessed is the LORD from Zion,
He who dwells in Jerusalem.
Halleluya!

The One who alone works great wonders – His loving-kindness is forever

Danger surrounds us. We are in the dark, oblivious. We'll never
know what could have gone wrong. Even the person for whom a
miracle has occurred has no clue that he owes his life to a miracle.
We don't even see what our vision equips us to see. We see only
what we want to see. God alone sees the whole picture.

PSALM 136

הוֹדוּ לַיהוה כִּי־טוֹב	1	Thank the Lᴏʀᴅ for He is good –
כִּי לְעוֹלָם חַסְדּוֹ:		His loving-kindness is forever.
הוֹדוּ לֵאלֹהֵי הָאֱלֹהִים	2	Thank the God of gods –
כִּי לְעוֹלָם חַסְדּוֹ:		His loving-kindness is forever.
הוֹדוּ לַאֲדֹנֵי הָאֲדֹנִים	3	Thank the Lᴏʀᴅ of lords –
כִּי לְעוֹלָם חַסְדּוֹ:		His loving-kindness is forever;
לְעֹשֵׂה נִפְלָאוֹת גְּדֹלוֹת לְבַדּוֹ	4	the One who alone works great wonders –
כִּי לְעוֹלָם חַסְדּוֹ:		His loving-kindness is forever;
לְעֹשֵׂה הַשָּׁמַיִם בִּתְבוּנָה	5	who made the heavens with wisdom –
כִּי לְעוֹלָם חַסְדּוֹ:		His loving-kindness is forever;
לְרֹקַע הָאָרֶץ עַל־הַמָּיִם	6	who spread the earth upon the waters –
כִּי לְעוֹלָם חַסְדּוֹ:		His loving-kindness is forever;
לְעֹשֵׂה אוֹרִים גְּדֹלִים	7	who made the great lights –
כִּי לְעוֹלָם חַסְדּוֹ:		His loving-kindness is forever;
אֶת־הַשֶּׁמֶשׁ לְמֶמְשֶׁלֶת בַּיּוֹם	8	the sun to rule by day –
כִּי לְעוֹלָם חַסְדּוֹ:		His loving-kindness is forever;
אֶת־הַיָּרֵחַ וְכוֹכָבִים לְמֶמְשְׁלוֹת בַּלָּיְלָה	9	the moon and the stars to rule by night –
כִּי לְעוֹלָם חַסְדּוֹ:		His loving-kindness is forever;
לְמַכֵּה מִצְרַיִם בִּבְכוֹרֵיהֶם	10	who struck Egypt through their firstborn –
כִּי לְעוֹלָם חַסְדּוֹ:		His loving-kindness is forever;
וַיּוֹצֵא יִשְׂרָאֵל מִתּוֹכָם	11	and brought out Israel from their midst –
כִּי לְעוֹלָם חַסְדּוֹ:		His loving-kindness is forever;
בְּיָד חֲזָקָה וּבִזְרוֹעַ נְטוּיָה	12	with a strong hand and outstretched arm –
כִּי לְעוֹלָם חַסְדּוֹ:		His loving-kindness is forever;
לְגֹזֵר יַם־סוּף לִגְזָרִים	13	who split apart the Sea of Reeds –
כִּי לְעוֹלָם חַסְדּוֹ:		His loving-kindness is forever;

וְהֶעֱבִיר יִשְׂרָאֵל בְּתוֹכוֹ	14	and made Israel pass through it –
כִּי לְעוֹלָם חַסְדּוֹ:		His loving-kindness is forever;
וְנִעֵר פַּרְעֹה וְחֵילוֹ בְיַם־סוּף	15	and hurled Pharaoh and his army into the Sea of Reeds –
כִּי לְעוֹלָם חַסְדּוֹ:		His loving-kindness is forever;
לְמוֹלִיךְ עַמּוֹ בַּמִּדְבָּר	16	who led His people through the wilderness –
כִּי לְעוֹלָם חַסְדּוֹ:		His loving-kindness is forever;
לְמַכֵּה מְלָכִים גְּדֹלִים	17	who struck down great kings –
כִּי לְעוֹלָם חַסְדּוֹ:		His loving-kindness is forever;
וַיַּהֲרֹג מְלָכִים אַדִּירִים	18	and slew mighty kings –
כִּי לְעוֹלָם חַסְדּוֹ:		His loving-kindness is forever;
לְסִיחוֹן מֶלֶךְ הָאֱמֹרִי	19	Siḥon, king of the Amorites –
כִּי לְעוֹלָם חַסְדּוֹ:		His loving-kindness is forever;
וּלְעוֹג מֶלֶךְ הַבָּשָׁן	20	and Og, king of Bashan –
כִּי לְעוֹלָם חַסְדּוֹ:		His loving-kindness is forever;
וְנָתַן אַרְצָם לְנַחֲלָה	21	and gave their land as a heritage –
כִּי לְעוֹלָם חַסְדּוֹ:		His loving-kindness is forever;
נַחֲלָה לְיִשְׂרָאֵל עַבְדּוֹ	22	a heritage for His servant Israel –
כִּי לְעוֹלָם חַסְדּוֹ:		His loving-kindness is forever;
שֶׁבְּשִׁפְלֵנוּ זָכַר לָנוּ	23	who remembered us in our lowly state –
כִּי לְעוֹלָם חַסְדּוֹ:		His loving-kindness is forever;
וַיִּפְרְקֵנוּ מִצָּרֵינוּ	24	and rescued us from our tormentors –
כִּי לְעוֹלָם חַסְדּוֹ:		His loving-kindness is forever;
נֹתֵן לֶחֶם לְכָל־בָּשָׂר	25	who gives food to all flesh –
כִּי לְעוֹלָם חַסְדּוֹ:		His loving-kindness is forever.
הוֹדוּ לְאֵל הַשָּׁמָיִם	26	Give thanks to the God of heaven –
כִּי לְעוֹלָם חַסְדּוֹ:		His loving-kindness is forever.

If I do not set Jerusalem above my highest joy

I am homeless. Zion was my home. I am hopeless.
Zion was my hope. Songs cannot be coaxed from
a homeless harp. Hopeless hearts cannot be forced to sing.
I will never forget my home. Remembrance is my only hope.
Revenge is my bitter wish.

PSALM 137

עַל־נַהֲר֣וֹת ׀ בָּבֶ֗ל
שָׁ֣ם יָ֭שַׁבְנוּ גַּם־בָּכִ֑ינוּ
בְּ֝זׇכְרֵ֗נוּ אֶת־צִיּֽוֹן׃

1 By the rivers of Babylon,
   there we sat and wept as we
   remembered Zion.

עַֽל־עֲרָבִ֥ים בְּתוֹכָ֑הּ
תָּ֝לִ֗ינוּ כִּנֹּרוֹתֵֽינוּ׃

2 There on the willow trees
   we hung up our harps,

כִּ֤י שָׁ֨ם ׀ שְׁאֵל֣וּנוּ שׁוֹבֵ֗ינוּ
דִּבְרֵי־שִׁ֖יר וְתוֹלָלֵ֣ינוּ שִׂמְחָ֑ה
שִׁ֥ירוּ לָ֝֗נוּ מִשִּׁ֥יר צִיּֽוֹן׃

3 for there our captors asked us for songs,
   our tormentors for amusement:
   "Sing us one of the songs of Zion!"

אֵ֗יךְ נָשִׁ֥יר אֶת־שִׁיר־יְהֹוָ֑ה
עַ֝֗ל אַדְמַ֥ת נֵכָֽר׃

4 How can we sing the LORD's song
   on foreign soil?

אִֽם־אֶשְׁכָּחֵ֥ךְ יְֽרוּשָׁלָ֗͏ִם
תִּשְׁכַּ֥ח יְמִינִֽי׃

5 If I forget you, O Jerusalem,
   may my right hand forget its skill.

תִּדְבַּ֥ק־לְשׁוֹנִ֨י ׀ לְחִכִּי֮
אִם־לֹ֢א אֶ֫זְכְּרֵ֥כִי
אִם־לֹ֣א אַ֭עֲלֶה אֶת־יְרוּשָׁלַ֑͏ִם
עַ֝֗ל רֹ֣אשׁ שִׂמְחָתִֽי׃

6 May my tongue cling
   to the roof of my mouth
   if I do not remember you,
   if I do not set Jerusalem
   above my highest joy.

זְכֹ֤ר יְהֹוָ֨ה ׀ לִבְנֵ֬י אֱד֗וֹם
אֵת֮ י֤וֹם יְֽרוּשָׁלָ֥͏ִם
הָ֭אֹ֣מְרִים עָ֤רוּ ׀ עָ֑רוּ
עַ֝֗ד הַיְס֥וֹד בָּֽהּ׃

7 Remember, LORD,
   what the Edomites did
   on the day Jerusalem fell.
   They said, "Tear it down; tear it down
   to its very foundations!"

בַּת־בָּבֶ֗ל הַשְּׁד֫וּדָ֥ה
אַשְׁרֵ֥י שֶׁיְשַׁלֶּם־לָ֑ךְ
אֶת־גְּ֝מוּלֵ֗ךְ שֶׁגָּמַ֥לְתְּ לָֽנוּ׃

8 Daughter of Babylon,
   doomed to destruction,
   happy are those who pay you back
   for what you have done to us;

אַשְׁרֵ֤י ׀ שֶׁיֹּאחֵ֓ז
וְנִפֵּ֬ץ אֶֽת־עֹ֝לָלַ֗יִךְ אֶל־הַסָּֽלַע׃

9 happy are those who seize your infants
   and dash them against the rocks.

I thank You with all my heart; before the divine beings I sing Your praise

Some of us feel unexceptional. Others regard themselves as being superior. They are convinced that the Superior is closest to them. They believe that He takes no notice of those who feel unexceptional. But they are in for a surprise. The Almighty is different. He is superior, but distant from those who regard themselves as being superior. He is in fact superior, but He is closest to those who feel unexceptional.

PSALM 138

לְדָוִד ׀
אוֹדְךָ בְכָל־לִבִּי
נֶגֶד אֱלֹהִים אֲזַמְּרֶךָּ׃

1 Of David
I thank You with all my heart;
before the divine beings
I sing Your praise.

אֶשְׁתַּחֲוֶה אֶל־הֵיכַל קָדְשְׁךָ
וְאוֹדֶה אֶת־שְׁמֶךָ
עַל־חַסְדְּךָ וְעַל־אֲמִתֶּךָ
כִּי־הִגְדַּלְתָּ עַל־כָּל־שִׁמְךָ
אִמְרָתֶךָ׃

2 I bow down toward Your holy sanctuary
and give thanks to Your name
for Your loyalty and truth,
for You have exalted Your name
and Your word above all.

בְּיוֹם קָרָאתִי וַתַּעֲנֵנִי
תַּרְהִבֵנִי בְנַפְשִׁי עֹז׃

3 On the day I called You answered me;
You made my soul swell with might.

יוֹדוּךָ יהוה כָּל־מַלְכֵי־אָרֶץ
כִּי שָׁמְעוּ אִמְרֵי־פִיךָ׃

4 All kings of the earth will thank You,
LORD,
for they have heard the words
of Your mouth,

וְיָשִׁירוּ בְּדַרְכֵי יהוה
כִּי־גָדוֹל כְּבוֹד יהוה׃

5 and they will sing of the LORD's ways,
for great is the glory of the LORD.

כִּי־רָם יהוה וְשָׁפָל יִרְאֶה
וְגָבֹהַּ מִמֶּרְחָק יְיֵדָע׃

6 For the LORD is high up,
yet He sees the lowly;
aloft, He discerns them from afar.

אִם־אֵלֵךְ ׀ בְּקֶרֶב צָרָה תְּחַיֵּנִי
עַל אַף אֹיְבַי תִּשְׁלַח יָדֶךָ
וְתוֹשִׁיעֵנִי יְמִינֶךָ׃

7 Though I walk among foes,
You preserve my life;
You thrust out Your hand
against my enemies' wrath,
and Your right hand saves me.

יהוה יִגְמֹר בַּעֲדִי
יהוה חַסְדְּךָ לְעוֹלָם
מַעֲשֵׂי יָדֶיךָ אַל־תֶּרֶף׃

8 The LORD will fulfill His purpose for me;
Your loyalty, LORD, is forever;
never forsake Your handiwork.

If I climb to heaven, You are there; if I make my bed in the underworld, there You are

I know myself well, but You know me better. You were there from
the very beginning. I spent nine months in my mother's womb.
Each day I developed a bit more. After many days
I was fully formed. Then, in an instant, I was born.
I recall none of those many days, but I thank You for them all.
I thank You for giving me myself.

PSALM 139

לַמְנַצֵּחַ לְדָוִד מִזְמוֹר יְהוָה חֲקַרְתַּנִי וַתֵּדָע:	1	To the lead singer, of David – a psalm O Lord, You have searched me, and You know –
אַתָּה יָדַעְתָּ שִׁבְתִּי וְקוּמִי בַּנְתָּה לְרֵעִי מֵרָחוֹק:	2	You know when I sit and when I rise; You understand my thoughts from afar.
אָרְחִי וְרִבְעִי זֵרִיתָ וְכָל־דְּרָכַי הִסְכַּנְתָּה:	3	You trace my going out and lying down; You are familiar with all my ways.
כִּי אֵין מִלָּה בִּלְשׁוֹנִי הֵן יְהוָה יָדַעְתָּ כֻלָּהּ:	4	Even before a word is on my tongue, You, Lord, know it all.
אָחוֹר וָקֶדֶם צַרְתָּנִי וַתָּשֶׁת עָלַי כַּפֶּכָה:	5	You keep close guard behind and before me; You have laid Your hand upon me.
פְּלִיאָה דַעַת מִמֶּנִּי נִשְׂגְּבָה לֹא־אוּכַל לָהּ:	6	Knowledge so wonderful is beyond me, so high that it is above my reach.
אָנָה אֵלֵךְ מֵרוּחֶךָ וְאָנָה מִפָּנֶיךָ אֶבְרָח:	7	Where can I escape from Your spirit? Where can I flee from Your presence?
אִם־אֶסַּק שָׁמַיִם שָׁם אָתָּה וְאַצִּיעָה שְּׁאוֹל הִנֶּךָ:	8	If I climb to heaven, You are there; if I make my bed in the underworld, there You are.
אֶשָּׂא כַנְפֵי־שָׁחַר אֶשְׁכְּנָה בְּאַחֲרִית יָם:	9	If I rise on the wings of the dawn, if I settle on the far side of the sea,
גַּם־שָׁם יָדְךָ תַנְחֵנִי וְתֹאחֲזֵנִי יְמִינֶךָ:	10	even there Your hand will guide me; Your right hand will hold me fast.
וָאֹמַר אַךְ־חֹשֶׁךְ יְשׁוּפֵנִי וְלַיְלָה אוֹר בַּעֲדֵנִי:	11	Were I to say, "Surely the darkness will hide me and light become night around me,"
גַּם־חֹשֶׁךְ לֹא־יַחְשִׁיךְ מִמֶּךָּ וְלַיְלָה כַּיּוֹם יָאִיר כַּחֲשֵׁיכָה כָּאוֹרָה:	12	to You the darkness would not be dark; night is light as day; to You dark and light are one,

פְּלִאָה

כִּֽי־אַ֭תָּה קָנִ֣יתָ כִלְיֹתָ֑י
תְּ֝סֻכֵּ֗נִי בְּבֶ֣טֶן אִמִּֽי׃

13 for You created my innermost being;
You knit me together
in my mother's womb.

אֽוֹדְךָ֗ עַ֤ל כִּ֥י נ֨וֹרָא֗וֹת נִפְלֵ֥יתִי
נִפְלָאִ֥ים מַעֲשֶׂ֑יךָ
וְ֝נַפְשִׁ֗י יֹדַ֥עַת מְאֹֽד׃

14 I praise You because I am awesomely,
wondrously made;
wonderful are Your works;
I know that full well.

לֹא־נִכְחַ֥ד עָצְמִ֗י מִ֫מֶּ֥ךָּ
אֲשֶׁר־עֻשֵּׂ֥יתִי בַסֵּ֑תֶר
רֻ֝קַּ֗מְתִּי בְּֽתַחְתִּיּ֥וֹת אָֽרֶץ׃

15 My frame was not hidden from You
when I was formed in a secret place,
woven in the depths of the earth.

גׇּלְמִ֤י ׀ רָ֘א֤וּ עֵינֶ֗יךָ
וְעַֽל־סִפְרְךָ֮ כֻּלָּ֢ם יִכָּ֫תֵ֥בוּ
יָמִ֥ים יֻצָּ֑רוּ ולא אֶחָ֥ד בָּהֶֽם׃

16 Your eyes saw my unformed substance;
in Your book it was all inscribed
when each part would be formed
before any of them came to be.

וְלִ֗י מַה־יָּקְר֣וּ רֵעֶ֣יךָ אֵ֑ל
מֶ֥ה עָ֝צְמ֗וּ רָאשֵׁיהֶֽם׃

17 How precious to me
are Your thoughts, God;
how vast in number they are.

אֶ֭סְפְּרֵם מֵח֣וֹל יִרְבּ֑וּן
הֱ֝קִיצֹ֗תִי וְעוֹדִ֥י עִמָּֽךְ׃

18 Were I to count them,
they would outnumber the grains
of the sand,
and when I wake again,
I am still with You!

אִם־תִּקְטֹ֖ל אֱל֥וֹהַּ ׀ רָשָׁ֑ע
וְאַנְשֵׁ֥י דָ֝מִ֗ים ס֣וּרוּ מֶֽנִּי׃

19 God, if only You would slay the wicked –
away from me, you men of blood!

אֲשֶׁ֣ר יֹ֭אמְרוּךָ לִמְזִמָּ֑ה
נָשֻׂ֖א לַשָּׁ֣וְא עָרֶֽיךָ׃

20 They speak of You with evil intent;
Your adversaries misuse Your name.

הֲלֽוֹא־מְשַׂנְאֶ֖יךָ יְהֹוָ֥ה ׀ אֶשְׂנָ֑א
וּ֝בִתְקוֹמְמֶ֗יךָ אֶתְקוֹטָֽט׃

21 Do I not hate those who hate You, Lord,
and loathe those who rise up against You?

תַּכְלִ֣ית שִׂנְאָ֣ה שְׂנֵאתִ֑ים
לְ֝אֹיְבִ֗ים הָ֣יוּ לִֽי׃

22 I have nothing but hatred for them;
I count them my enemies.

חָקְרֵנִי אֵל וְדַע לְבָבִי 23 Search me, God, and know my heart;
בְּחָנֵנִי וְדַע שַׂרְעַפָּי: test me and know my innermost
thoughts.

וּרְאֵה אִם־דֶּרֶךְ־עֹצֶב בִּי 24 See if there is any grievous way
וּנְחֵנִי בְּדֶרֶךְ עוֹלָם: within me,
and lead me in the everlasting way.

Yes, the righteous will give thanks to Your name; the upright will dwell in Your presence

It is the schemer whom I really fear. He is deceitful,
and I cannot trust his gestures. He pretends that we are friends.
He is treacherous. How can I protect myself from such an enemy?
That's where God comes in. He'll signal me: "Beware."
Then I'll know how to defend myself.

PSALM 140

לַמְנַצֵּחַ מִזְמוֹר לְדָוִד:

1 To the lead singer – a psalm of David

חַלְּצֵנִי יהוה מֵאָדָם רָע
מֵאִישׁ חֲמָסִים תִּנְצְרֵנִי:

2 Rescue me, Lord, from evil people;
keep me from violent people

אֲשֶׁר חָשְׁבוּ רָעוֹת בְּלֵב
כָּל־יוֹם יָגוּרוּ מִלְחָמוֹת:

3 who plot evil in their hearts,
who incite war day after day.

שָׁנְנוּ לְשׁוֹנָם כְּמוֹ־נָחָשׁ
חֲמַת עַכְשׁוּב
תַּחַת שְׂפָתֵימוֹ סֶלָה:

4 Their tongues are sharpened
like a serpent's;
spider venom is beneath their lips –
Selah.

שָׁמְרֵנִי יהוה ׀ מִידֵי רָשָׁע
מֵאִישׁ חֲמָסִים תִּנְצְרֵנִי
אֲשֶׁר חָשְׁבוּ לִדְחוֹת פְּעָמָי:

5 Watch over me, Lord;
keep me from the grasp of the wicked;
from violent people
who plot to trip me up.

טָמְנוּ־גֵאִים ׀ פַּח לִי וַחֲבָלִים
פָּרְשׂוּ רֶשֶׁת לְיַד־מַעְגָּל
מֹקְשִׁים שָׁתוּ־לִי סֶלָה:

6 The haughty have laid a trap for me;
they spread out a net of ropes by my path;
they have set snares for me – Selah.

אָמַרְתִּי לַיהוה אֵלִי אָתָּה
הַאֲזִינָה יהוה קוֹל תַּחֲנוּנָי:

7 I said to the Lord, "You are my God;
give ear, Lord, to the sound of my plea."

יהוה אֲדֹנָי עֹז יְשׁוּעָתִי
סַכֹּתָה לְרֹאשִׁי בְּיוֹם נָשֶׁק:

8 O God, Lord, my saving might,
shield my head when weapons clash.

אַל־תִּתֵּן יהוה מַאֲוַיֵּי רָשָׁע
זְמָמוֹ אַל־תָּפֵק יָרוּמוּ סֶלָה:

9 O Lord, do not grant the desires
of the wicked;
do not let them fulfill their schemes
lest they exalt themselves – Selah.

רֹאשׁ מְסִבָּי
עֲמַל שְׂפָתֵימוֹ יְכַסֵּמוֹ:

יכסומו

10 May the heads of those surrounding me
be overwhelmed by their own
treacherous lips.

יִמּוֹטוּ עֲלֵיהֶם גֶּחָלִים
בָּאֵשׁ יַפִּלֵם
בְּמַהֲמֹרוֹת בַּל־יָקוּמוּ:

ימיטו

11 May fiery coals rain down on them;
may He cast them into the fire,
into chasms, never to rise.

אִישׁ לָשׁוֹן בַּל־יִכּוֹן בָּאָרֶץ
אִישׁ־חָמָס רָע
יְצוּדֶנּוּ לְמַדְחֵפֹת:

12 Let no slanderer stand firm in the land;
may evil hound the violent,
blow upon blow.

יָדַעְתִּי כִּי־יַעֲשֶׂה יְהוה דִּין עָנִי
מִשְׁפַּט אֶבְיֹנִים:

13 I know that the LORD will uphold
justice for the lowly,
the cause of the needy.

אַךְ צַדִּיקִים יוֹדוּ לִשְׁמֶךָ
יֵשְׁבוּ יְשָׁרִים אֶת־פָּנֶיךָ:

14 Yes, the righteous will give thanks
to Your name;
the upright will dwell in Your presence.

Accept my prayer like incense before You, my lifted hands like the evening offering

Before I pray I must pray.
I must pray that I find the words to express my thoughts.
I must pray that my thoughts be pure.
I must avoid bitterness and cynicism.
I must not surrender to despair.

PSALM 141

מִזְמוֹר לְדָוִד 1 A psalm of David
יהוה קְרָאתִיךָ חוּשָׁה לִּי I call to You, LORD – rush to me;
הַאֲזִינָה קוֹלִי בְּקָרְאִי־לָךְ: give ear to my voice when I call You.

תִּכּוֹן תְּפִלָּתִי קְטֹרֶת לְפָנֶיךָ 2 Accept my prayer like incense before You,
מַשְׂאַת כַּפַּי מִנְחַת־עָרֶב: my lifted hands like the evening offering.

שִׁיתָה יהוה שָׁמְרָה לְפִי 3 Set a guard, LORD, over my mouth,
נִצְּרָה עַל־דַּל שְׂפָתָי: a keeper at the door of my lips;

אַל־תַּט־לִבִּי לְדָבָר רָע 4 do not let my heart turn to anything evil
לְהִתְעוֹלֵל עֲלִלוֹת בְּרֶשַׁע or deal in deeds of wickedness
אֶת־אִישִׁים פֹּעֲלֵי־אָוֶן with evildoers–
וּבַל־אֶלְחַם בְּמַנְעַמֵּיהֶם: let me not feast on their decadence.

יֶהְלְמֵנִי צַדִּיק חֶסֶד 5 Let the righteous strike me,
וְיוֹכִיחֵנִי שֶׁמֶן רֹאשׁ in loyalty reproach me.
אַל־יָנִי רֹאשִׁי Let not fine oil distract my head,
כִּי־עוֹד וּתְפִלָּתִי בְּרָעוֹתֵיהֶם: but set my prayers ever against
their evil deeds.

נִשְׁמְטוּ בִידֵי־סֶלַע שֹׁפְטֵיהֶם 6 May their judges be felled by a rock
וְשָׁמְעוּ אֲמָרַי כִּי נָעֵמוּ: so that they will listen to my words,
for they are sweet.

כְּמוֹ פֹלֵחַ וּבֹקֵעַ בָּאָרֶץ 7 As a person plows
נִפְזְרוּ עֲצָמֵינוּ לְפִי שְׁאוֹל: and breaks up the earth,
so our bones are scattered
at the mouth of Sheol,

כִּי אֵלֶיךָ יהוה אֲדֹנָי עֵינָי 8 for my eyes are on You, God my LORD;
בְּכָה חָסִיתִי אַל־תְּעַר נַפְשִׁי: in you I take refuge –
do not let my life ebb away.

שָׁמְרֵנִי מִידֵי פַח יָקְשׁוּ לִי 9 Guard me from the snare
וּמֹקְשׁוֹת פֹּעֲלֵי אָוֶן: they laid for me,
from the traps of evildoers.

יִפְּלוּ בְמַכְמֹרָיו רְשָׁעִים 10 May the wicked fall into their own nets
יַחַד אָנֹכִי עַד־אֶעֱבוֹר: while I alone move on.

While he was in the cave – a prayer

I am overwhelmed by my troubles. They are too much for me to bear. I turn to You, for only You can help me. But as I turn to You I am overwhelmed by You. You are the Almighty, Creator of the Universe. I must first acknowledge that. First, I pour out my speech before Him. Then, I tell Him of my distress.

PSALM 142

מַשְׂכִּיל לְדָוִד	1	A *maskil* of David
בִּהְיוֹתוֹ בַמְּעָרָה תְפִלָּה:		while he was in the cave – a prayer
קוֹלִי אֶל־יהוה אֶזְעָק	2	My voice cries to the Lord;
קוֹלִי אֶל־יהוה אֶתְחַנָּן:		my voice pleads with the Lord.
אֶשְׁפֹּךְ לְפָנָיו שִׂיחִי	3	I will pour out my lament before Him,
צָרָתִי לְפָנָיו אַגִּיד:		tell my troubles to Him
בְּהִתְעַטֵּף עָלַי ׀ רוּחִי	4	when my spirit grows faint within me.
וְאַתָּה יָדַעְתָּ נְתִיבָתִי		You know my path –
בְּאֹרַח־זוּ אֲהַלֵּךְ		along the way I walk
טָמְנוּ פַח לִי:		they have laid a trap for me.
הַבֵּיט יָמִין ׀ וּרְאֵה	5	Look to the right and witness –
וְאֵין־לִי מַכִּיר		I have not one friend;
אָבַד מָנוֹס מִמֶּנִּי		I have nowhere to flee;
אֵין דּוֹרֵשׁ לְנַפְשִׁי:		no one cares for me.
זָעַקְתִּי אֵלֶיךָ יהוה	6	I cry out to You, Lord –
אָמַרְתִּי אַתָּה מַחְסִי		I say, "You are my refuge,
חֶלְקִי בְּאֶרֶץ הַחַיִּים:		my share in the land of the living."
הַקְשִׁיבָה ׀ אֶל־רִנָּתִי	7	Listen to my plea,
כִּי־דַלּוֹתִי מְאֹד		for I have sunk so low;
הַצִּילֵנִי מֵרֹדְפַי		save me from my pursuers,
כִּי אָמְצוּ מִמֶּנִּי:		for they are too strong for me.
הוֹצִיאָה מִמַּסְגֵּר ׀ נַפְשִׁי	8	Set me free
לְהוֹדוֹת אֶת־שְׁמֶךָ		from this confinement
בִּי יַכְתִּרוּ צַדִּיקִים		so that I may give thanks to Your name;
כִּי תִגְמֹל עָלָי:		the righteous will gather around me
		when You are good to me.

I spread out my hands to You; my soul thirsts for You like a weary land – Selah

Sometimes I am so sure of myself that I say to God, "judge me."
After all, compared to my enemies I am righteous. At other times,
I realize that it is foolhardy of me to ask to be judged.
We all have our faults. Thankfully, He overlooks them.

PSALM 143

מִזְמוֹר לְדָוִד
יהוה ׀ שְׁמַע תְּפִלָּתִי
הַאֲזִינָה אֶל־תַּחֲנוּנַי
בֶּאֱמֻנָתְךָ עֲנֵנִי בְּצִדְקָתֶךָ:

1 A psalm of David
LORD, hear my prayer;
give ear to my pleas;
in Your faithfulness answer me,
in Your righteousness.

וְאַל־תָּבוֹא בְמִשְׁפָּט
אֶת־עַבְדֶּךָ
כִּי לֹא־יִצְדַּק לְפָנֶיךָ כָל־חָי:

2 Do not visit judgment on Your servant,
for no living thing
can be justified before You,

כִּי רָדַף אוֹיֵב ׀ נַפְשִׁי
דִּכָּא לָאָרֶץ חַיָּתִי
הוֹשִׁיבַנִי בְמַחֲשַׁכִּים
כְּמֵתֵי עוֹלָם:

3 for the enemy hunted me down,
trampled my life to the ground,
forced me to dwell in darkness
like those long dead,

וַתִּתְעַטֵּף עָלַי רוּחִי
בְּתוֹכִי יִשְׁתּוֹמֵם לִבִּי:

4 so my spirit is faint within me;
my heart is stunned inside me.

זָכַרְתִּי יָמִים ׀ מִקֶּדֶם
הָגִיתִי בְכָל־פָּעֳלֶךָ
בְּמַעֲשֵׂה יָדֶיךָ אֲשׂוֹחֵחַ:

5 I recall days of old;
I contemplate all Your works;
I reflect upon Your handiwork.

פֵּרַשְׂתִּי יָדַי אֵלֶיךָ
נַפְשִׁי ׀ כְּאֶרֶץ־עֲיֵפָה לְךָ
סֶלָה:

6 I spread out my hands to You;
my soul thirsts for You like a weary land –
Selah.

מַהֵר עֲנֵנִי ׀ יהוה כָּלְתָה רוּחִי
אַל־תַּסְתֵּר פָּנֶיךָ מִמֶּנִּי
וְנִמְשַׁלְתִּי עִם־יֹרְדֵי בוֹר:

7 Swiftly answer me, LORD;
my spirit pines away.
Do not hide Your face from me,
or I shall be like those
who plummet to the Pit.

הַשְׁמִיעֵנִי בַבֹּקֶר ׀ חַסְדֶּךָ
כִּי־בְךָ בָטָחְתִּי
הוֹדִיעֵנִי דֶּרֶךְ־זוּ אֵלֵךְ
כִּי־אֵלֶיךָ נָשָׂאתִי נַפְשִׁי:

8 Let me hear Your loyalty in the morning,
for in You I trust;
let me know the way to go,
for to You I lift up my life.

הַצִּילֵנִי מֵאֹיְבַי ׀ יהוה
אֵלֶיךָ כִסִּתִי:

9 Deliver me from my enemies, LORD;
in You I take cover.

לַמְּדֵנִי ׀ לַעֲשׂוֹת רְצוֹנֶךָ
כִּי־אַתָּה אֱלוֹהָי
רוּחֲךָ טוֹבָה
תַּנְחֵנִי בְּאֶרֶץ מִישׁוֹר:

10 Teach me to do Your will,
for You are my God;
Your good spirit
will guide me along level ground.

לְמַעַן־שִׁמְךָ יהוה תְּחַיֵּנִי
בְּצִדְקָתְךָ ׀
תוֹצִיא מִצָּרָה נַפְשִׁי:

11 For the sake of Your name, LORD,
let me live;
in Your righteousness
bring me out of danger,

וּבְחַסְדְּךָ תַּצְמִית אֹיְבָי
וְהַאֲבַדְתָּ כָּל־צֹרְרֵי נַפְשִׁי
כִּי אֲנִי עַבְדֶּךָ:

12 and in Your loyalty
destroy my enemies;
make all my mortal foes perish,
for I am Your servant.

To You, God, I will sing a new song; to You I will play music on a ten-stringed harp

I fight many battles in my life. Dare I ask Him to help me?
He is wondrous, but I wonder: Does He care? I silently sing to
Him. Does He hear my song? I am happy. How do I thank Him?

PSALM 144

לְדָוִד ׀ בָּרוּךְ יהוה ׀ צוּרִי
הַמְלַמֵּד יָדַי לַקְרָב
אֶצְבְּעוֹתַי לַמִּלְחָמָה:

1 Of David. Blessed is the Lord, my Rock,
who trains my hands for war,
my fingers for battle.

חַסְדִּי וּמְצוּדָתִי
מִשְׂגַּבִּי וּמְפַלְטִי לִי
מָגִנִּי וּבוֹ חָסִיתִי
הָרוֹדֵד עַמִּי תַחְתָּי:

2 He is my benefactor, my fortress,
my stronghold, and my refuge,
my shield in whom I trust,
He who subdues nations under me.

יהוה מָה־אָדָם וַתֵּדָעֵהוּ
בֶּן־אֱנוֹשׁ וַתְּחַשְּׁבֵהוּ:

3 Lord, what is humanity
that You care for it;
what are mortals that You think of them?

אָדָם לַהֶבֶל דָּמָה
יָמָיו כְּצֵל עוֹבֵר:

4 Humanity is no more than a breath,
its days like a fleeting shadow.

יהוה הַט־שָׁמֶיךָ וְתֵרֵד
גַּע בֶּהָרִים וְיֶעֱשָׁנוּ:

5 Lord, bend Your heavens
and come down;
touch the mountains
so that they pour forth smoke;

בְּרוֹק בָּרָק וּתְפִיצֵם
שְׁלַח חִצֶּיךָ וּתְהֻמֵּם:

6 flash forth lightning and scatter them;
shoot Your arrows and panic them.

שְׁלַח יָדֶיךָ מִמָּרוֹם
פְּצֵנִי וְהַצִּילֵנִי מִמַּיִם רַבִּים
מִיַּד בְּנֵי נֵכָר:

7 Reach out Your hand from on high;
deliver me and rescue me
from the mighty waters,
from the hands of foreigners

אֲשֶׁר פִּיהֶם דִּבֶּר־שָׁוְא
וִימִינָם יְמִין שָׁקֶר:

8 whose every word is worthless,
whose right hands are raised in falsehood.

אֱלֹהִים שִׁיר חָדָשׁ אָשִׁירָה לָּךְ
בְּנֵבֶל עָשׂוֹר אֲזַמְּרָה־לָּךְ:

9 To You, God, I will sing a new song;
to You I will play music
on a ten-stringed harp.

הַנּוֹתֵן תְּשׁוּעָה לַמְּלָכִים
הַפּוֹצֶה אֶת־דָּוִד עַבְדּוֹ
מֵחֶרֶב רָעָה:

10 He who gives salvation to kings,
who saves His servant David
from the cruel sword,

פַּצֵּנִי וְהַצִּילֵנִי מִיַּד בְּנֵי־נֵכָר
אֲשֶׁר פִּיהֶם דִּבֶּר־שָׁוְא
וִימִינָם יְמִין שָׁקֶר:

11 may He deliver me and rescue me
   from the hands of foreigners
   whose every word is worthless,
   whose right hands are raised in falsehood.

אֲשֶׁר בָּנֵינוּ ׀ כִּנְטִעִים
מְגֻדָּלִים בִּנְעוּרֵיהֶם
בְּנוֹתֵינוּ כְזָוִיֹּת
מְחֻטָּבוֹת תַּבְנִית הֵיכָל:

12 Then our sons will be like saplings,
   well nurtured in their youth;
   our daughters will be like sculpted pillars,
   fit to adorn a palace;

מְזָוֵינוּ מְלֵאִים
מְפִיקִים מִזַּן אֶל זַן
צֹאונֵנוּ מַאֲלִיפוֹת
מְרֻבָּבוֹת בְּחוּצוֹתֵינוּ:

13 our barns will be filled
   with every kind of provision;
   our sheep will increase by thousands,
   even tens of thousands, in our fields;

אַלּוּפֵינוּ מְסֻבָּלִים
אֵין פֶּרֶץ וְאֵין יוֹצֵאת
וְאֵין צְוָחָה בִּרְחֹבֹתֵינוּ:

14 our oxen will draw heavy loads.
   There will be no breach in the walls,
   no going into captivity,
   no cries of distress in our streets.

אַשְׁרֵי הָעָם שֶׁכָּכָה לּוֹ
אַשְׁרֵי הָעָם שֶׁיהוה אֱלֹהָיו:

15 Happy are the people for whom this is so;
   happy are the people
   whose God is the LORD.

Great is the LORD, of highest praise; His greatness is unfathomable

When He is so close that I can speak to Him directly,
I call Him "You." Every day I will bless You.
When You overwhelm me with Your splendor and might,
I call You "Him." His compassion extends to all His works.

PSALM 145

תְּהִלָּה לְדָוִד
אֲרוֹמִמְךָ אֱלוֹהַי הַמֶּלֶךְ
וַאֲבָרְכָה שִׁמְךָ לְעוֹלָם וָעֶד:

בְּכָל־יוֹם אֲבָרְכֶךָּ
וַאֲהַלְלָה שִׁמְךָ לְעוֹלָם וָעֶד:

גָּדוֹל יהוה וּמְהֻלָּל מְאֹד
וְלִגְדֻלָּתוֹ אֵין חֵקֶר:

דּוֹר לְדוֹר יְשַׁבַּח מַעֲשֶׂיךָ
וּגְבוּרֹתֶיךָ יַגִּידוּ:

הֲדַר כְּבוֹד הוֹדֶךָ
וְדִבְרֵי נִפְלְאֹתֶיךָ אָשִׂיחָה:

וֶעֱזוּז נוֹרְאֹתֶיךָ יֹאמֵרוּ
וּגְדוּלָּתְךָ אֲסַפְּרֶנָּה:

זֵכֶר רַב־טוּבְךָ יַבִּיעוּ
וְצִדְקָתְךָ יְרַנֵּנוּ:

חַנּוּן וְרַחוּם יהוה
אֶרֶךְ אַפַּיִם וּגְדָל־חָסֶד:

טוֹב־יהוה לַכֹּל
וְרַחֲמָיו עַל־כָּל־מַעֲשָׂיו:

יוֹדוּךָ יהוה כָּל־מַעֲשֶׂיךָ
וַחֲסִידֶיךָ יְבָרְכוּכָה:

כְּבוֹד מַלְכוּתְךָ יֹאמֵרוּ
וּגְבוּרָתְךָ יְדַבֵּרוּ:

וגדלותיך

1 A song of praise of David
  I will exalt You, my God, the King,
  and bless Your name
  for ever and all time.

2 Every day I will bless You
  and praise Your name
  for ever and all time.

3 Great is the LORD, of highest praise;
  His greatness is unfathomable.

4 One generation will praise Your works
  to the next
  and tell of Your mighty deeds.

5 On the glorious splendor of Your majesty
  and on the acts of Your wonders,
  I will reflect.

6 They shall talk of the power
  of Your awesome deeds,
  and I will tell of Your greatness.

7 They shall celebrate the fame
  of Your great goodness
  and sing with joy of Your righteousness.

8 The LORD is gracious and
  compassionate,
  slow to anger and great in kindness.

9 The LORD is good to all,
  and His compassion extends
  to all His works.

10 All Your works shall thank You, LORD,
  and Your devoted ones shall bless You.

11 They shall talk of the glory
  of Your kingship
  and speak of Your might,

לְהוֹדִיעַ ׀ לִבְנֵי הָאָדָם גְּבוּרֹתָיו
וּכְבוֹד הֲדַר מַלְכוּתוֹ:

12 revealing to humanity His mighty deeds
and the glorious majesty of His kingship.

מַלְכוּתְךָ מַלְכוּת כָּל־עֹלָמִים
וּמֶמְשַׁלְתְּךָ בְּכָל־דּוֹר וָדֹר:

13 Your kingdom is an everlasting kingdom,
and Your reign is for all generations.

סוֹמֵךְ יהוה לְכָל־הַנֹּפְלִים
וְזוֹקֵף לְכָל־הַכְּפוּפִים:

14 The Lord supports all who fall
and raises all who are bowed down.

עֵינֵי־כֹל אֵלֶיךָ יְשַׂבֵּרוּ
וְאַתָּה נוֹתֵן־לָהֶם
אֶת־אָכְלָם בְּעִתּוֹ:

15 All raise their eyes to You in hope,
and You give them their food in due time.

פּוֹתֵחַ אֶת־יָדֶךָ
וּמַשְׂבִּיעַ לְכָל־חַי רָצוֹן:

16 You open Your hand
and satisfy the needs of every living thing.

צַדִּיק יהוה בְּכָל־דְּרָכָיו
וְחָסִיד בְּכָל־מַעֲשָׂיו:

17 The Lord is righteous in all His ways
and devoted in all He does.

קָרוֹב יהוה לְכָל־קֹרְאָיו
לְכֹל אֲשֶׁר יִקְרָאֻהוּ בֶאֱמֶת:

18 The Lord is close to all who call on Him,
to all who truly call on Him.

רְצוֹן־יְרֵאָיו יַעֲשֶׂה
וְאֶת־שַׁוְעָתָם יִשְׁמַע
וְיוֹשִׁיעֵם:

19 He fulfills the will of those
who revere Him;
He hears their cry and saves them.

שׁוֹמֵר יהוה אֶת־כָּל־אֹהֲבָיו
וְאֵת כָּל־הָרְשָׁעִים יַשְׁמִיד:

20 The Lord guards all who love Him,
but all the wicked He will destroy.

תְּהִלַּת יהוה יְדַבֶּר פִּי
וִיבָרֵךְ כָּל־בָּשָׂר שֵׁם קָדְשׁוֹ
לְעוֹלָם וָעֶד:

21 My mouth shall speak the praise
of the Lord,
and all creatures shall bless His holy
name for ever and all time.

The LORD shall reign forever– He is your God, Zion, for all generations. Halleluya!

Will God redeem us? Yes, but He will use His emissaries to do so. Sure, we are not to put our trust in mortal men. But they are the ones God will send to help us. I don't pray that my doctor should heal me. I pray that God give my doctor the skills to do so. I can't be sure that my soldier will shoot straight. But I can pray to God that he won't miss.

PSALM 146

הַלְלוּיָהּ
הַלְלִי נַפְשִׁי אֶת־יהוה:

1 Halleluya!
Praise the Lord, my soul.

אֲהַלְלָה יהוה בְּחַיָּי
אֲזַמְּרָה לֵאלֹהַי בְּעוֹדִי:

2 I will praise the Lord all my life;
I will sing to my God as long as I live.

אַל־תִּבְטְחוּ בִנְדִיבִים
בְּבֶן־אָדָם ׀ שֶׁאֵין לוֹ תְשׁוּעָה:

3 Put not your trust in nobles,
in mortal man who cannot save.

תֵּצֵא רוּחוֹ יָשֻׁב לְאַדְמָתוֹ
בַּיּוֹם הַהוּא אָבְדוּ עֶשְׁתֹּנֹתָיו:

4 His breath expires;
he returns to the earth;
on that day his plans come to an end.

אַשְׁרֵי שֶׁאֵל יַעֲקֹב בְּעֶזְרוֹ
שִׂבְרוֹ עַל־יהוה אֱלֹהָיו:

5 Happy are those whose help
is the God of Yaakov,
whose hope is in the Lord their God,

עֹשֶׂה ׀ שָׁמַיִם וָאָרֶץ
אֶת־הַיָּם וְאֶת־כָּל־אֲשֶׁר־בָּם
הַשֹּׁמֵר אֱמֶת לְעוֹלָם:

6 who made heaven and earth,
the seas and all they contain –
He who keeps faith forever.

עֹשֶׂה מִשְׁפָּט ׀ לָעֲשׁוּקִים
נֹתֵן לֶחֶם לָרְעֵבִים
יהוה מַתִּיר אֲסוּרִים:

7 He secures justice for the oppressed;
He gives food to the hungry;
the Lord sets captives free.

יהוה ׀ פֹּקֵחַ עִוְרִים
יהוה זֹקֵף כְּפוּפִים
יהוה אֹהֵב צַדִּיקִים:

8 The Lord gives sight to the blind;
the Lord raises those bowed down;
the Lord loves the righteous.

יהוה ׀ שֹׁמֵר אֶת־גֵּרִים
יָתוֹם וְאַלְמָנָה יְעוֹדֵד
וְדֶרֶךְ רְשָׁעִים יְעַוֵּת:

9 The Lord protects the stranger;
He gives courage
to the orphan and widow
and thwarts the way of the wicked.

יִמְלֹךְ יהוה ׀ לְעוֹלָם
אֱלֹהַיִךְ צִיּוֹן לְדֹר וָדֹר
הַלְלוּיָהּ:

10 The Lord shall reign forever–
He is your God, Zion, for all generations.
Halleluya!

The LORD rebuilds Jerusalem; He gathers the scattered exiles of Israel

At times like this, His cosmic greatness does not inspire me.
It helps me to hear that He is rebuilding Jerusalem. It helps more
to hear that He blesses her with peace. It helps most of all to
know that He heals the brokenhearted, and that He gives courage
to the needy. I am brokenhearted, and so is Jerusalem.
I need courage, and so does she.

PSALM 147

הַלְלוּיָהּ ׀	1	Halleluya!
כִּי־טוֹב זַמְּרָה אֱלֹהֵינוּ		How good it is to make music
כִּי־נָעִים נָאוָה תְהִלָּה׃		to our God;
		how sweet it is to sing glorious praise.
בּוֹנֵה יְרוּשָׁלַ͏ִם יהוה	2	The LORD rebuilds Jerusalem;
נִדְחֵי יִשְׂרָאֵל יְכַנֵּס׃		He gathers the scattered exiles of Israel.
הָרֹפֵא לִשְׁבוּרֵי לֵב	3	He heals the brokenhearted
וּמְחַבֵּשׁ לְעַצְּבוֹתָם׃		and binds up their wounds.
מוֹנֶה מִסְפָּר לַכּוֹכָבִים	4	He counts the number of the stars,
לְכֻלָּם שֵׁמוֹת יִקְרָא׃		calling each by name.
גָּדוֹל אֲדוֹנֵינוּ וְרַב־כֹּחַ	5	Great is our LORD and mighty in power;
לִתְבוּנָתוֹ אֵין מִסְפָּר׃		His understanding has no limit.
מְעוֹדֵד עֲנָוִים יהוה	6	The LORD gives courage to the humble
מַשְׁפִּיל רְשָׁעִים עֲדֵי־אָרֶץ׃		but casts the wicked to the ground.
עֱנוּ לַיהוה בְּתוֹדָה	7	Sing to the LORD in thanks;
זַמְּרוּ לֵאלֹהֵינוּ בְכִנּוֹר׃		make music to our God on the harp.
הַמְכַסֶּה שָׁמַיִם ׀ בְּעָבִים	8	He covers the sky with clouds;
הַמֵּכִין לָאָרֶץ מָטָר		He provides the earth with rain
הַמַּצְמִיחַ הָרִים חָצִיר׃		and makes grass grow on the hills.
נוֹתֵן לִבְהֵמָה לַחְמָהּ	9	He gives food to the beasts,
לִבְנֵי עֹרֵב אֲשֶׁר יִקְרָאוּ׃		to young ravens when they cry.
לֹא בִגְבוּרַת הַסּוּס יֶחְפָּץ	10	He does not take delight
לֹא־בְשׁוֹקֵי הָאִישׁ יִרְצֶה׃		in the strength of horses
		or pleasure in the fleetness of man.
רוֹצֶה יהוה אֶת־יְרֵאָיו	11	The LORD takes pleasure
אֶת־הַמְיַחֲלִים לְחַסְדּוֹ׃		in those who fear Him,
		who put their hope in His loyalty.

שַׁבְּחִי יְרוּשָׁלַ͏ִם אֶת־יְהֹוָה הַלְלִי אֱלֹהַיִךְ צִיּוֹן:	12 Praise the Lᴏʀᴅ, Jerusalem; sing to your God, Zion! –
כִּי־חִזַּק בְּרִיחֵי שְׁעָרָיִךְ בֵּרַךְ בָּנַיִךְ בְּקִרְבֵּךְ:	13 for He has strengthened the bars of your gates and blessed your children in your midst.
הַשָּׂם־גְּבוּלֵךְ שָׁלוֹם חֵלֶב חִטִּים יַשְׂבִּיעֵךְ:	14 He has brought peace to your borders and satisfied you with the finest wheat.
הַשֹּׁלֵחַ אִמְרָתוֹ אָרֶץ עַד־מְהֵרָה יָרוּץ דְּבָרוֹ:	15 He sends His commandment to earth; swiftly runs His word.
הַנֹּתֵן שֶׁלֶג כַּצָּמֶר כְּפוֹר כָּאֵפֶר יְפַזֵּר:	16 He spreads snow like fleece, sprinkles frost like ashes,
מַשְׁלִיךְ קַרְחוֹ כְפִתִּים לִפְנֵי קָרָתוֹ מִי יַעֲמֹד:	17 scatters hail like crumbs. Who can withstand His cold?
יִשְׁלַח דְּבָרוֹ וְיַמְסֵם יַשֵּׁב רוּחוֹ יִזְּלוּ־מָיִם:	18 He sends His word and melts them; He stirs up His wind, and the waters flow.
מַגִּיד דְּבָרָו לְיַעֲקֹב חֻקָּיו וּמִשְׁפָּטָיו לְיִשְׂרָאֵל:	19 He has declared His words to Yaakov, His statutes and laws to Israel.
לֹא עָשָׂה כֵן ׀ לְכָל־גּוֹי וּמִשְׁפָּטִים בַּל־יְדָעוּם הַלְלוּיָהּ:	20 He has done this for no other nation; such laws they do not know. Halleluya!

He has raised the horn of His people, glory for all His devoted ones, for the children of Israel, the people close to Him. Halleluya!

I often wonder how the world will end. Will it end with a bang? Or will it end with a whimper? We're all in for a surprise. Nature's wonders will not end at all. He established them forever. Persecution will end, and war, and intolerance. Class distinctions will end. That's how this world will end. A new world will begin.

PSALM 148

הַלְלוּיָהּ ׀	1 Halleluya!
הַלְלוּ אֶת־יהוה מִן־הַשָּׁמַיִם	Praise the LORD from the heavens;
הַלְלוּהוּ בַּמְּרוֹמִים׃	praise Him in the heights.
הַלְלוּהוּ כָל־מַלְאָכָיו	2 Praise Him, all His angels;
הַלְלוּהוּ כָּל־צְבָאָו׃	praise Him, all His hosts.
הַלְלוּהוּ שֶׁמֶשׁ וְיָרֵחַ	3 Praise Him, sun and moon;
הַלְלוּהוּ כָּל־כּוֹכְבֵי אוֹר׃	praise Him, all shining stars.
הַלְלוּהוּ שְׁמֵי הַשָּׁמָיִם	4 Praise Him, highest heavens
וְהַמַּיִם אֲשֶׁר ׀ מֵעַל הַשָּׁמָיִם׃	and the waters above the heavens.
יְהַלְלוּ אֶת־שֵׁם יהוה	5 Let them praise the name of the LORD,
כִּי הוּא צִוָּה וְנִבְרָאוּ׃	for He commanded,
	and they were created.
וַיַּעֲמִידֵם לָעַד לְעוֹלָם	6 He established them forever and all time,
חָק־נָתַן וְלֹא יַעֲבוֹר׃	issuing a decree that will never change.
הַלְלוּ אֶת־יהוה מִן־הָאָרֶץ	7 Praise the LORD from the earth:
תַּנִּינִים וְכָל־תְּהֹמוֹת׃	sea monsters and all the deep seas;
אֵשׁ וּבָרָד שֶׁלֶג וְקִיטוֹר	8 fire and hail, snow, and mist,
רוּחַ סְעָרָה עֹשָׂה דְבָרוֹ׃	storm winds that obey His word;
הֶהָרִים וְכָל־גְּבָעוֹת	9 mountains and all hills,
עֵץ פְּרִי וְכָל־אֲרָזִים׃	fruit trees and all cedars;
הַחַיָּה וְכָל־בְּהֵמָה	10 wild animals and all cattle,
רֶמֶשׂ וְצִפּוֹר כָּנָף׃	creeping things and winged birds;
מַלְכֵי־אֶרֶץ וְכָל־לְאֻמִּים	11 kings of the earth and all nations,
שָׂרִים וְכָל־שֹׁפְטֵי אָרֶץ׃	princes and all judges on earth;
בַּחוּרִים וְגַם־בְּתוּלוֹת	12 youths and maidens alike,
זְקֵנִים עִם־נְעָרִים׃	old and young together.

יְהַלְלוּ ׀ אֶת־שֵׁם יהוה 13 Let them praise the name of the Lord,
כִּי־נִשְׂגָּב שְׁמוֹ לְבַדּוֹ   for His name alone is sublime;
הוֹדוֹ עַל־אֶרֶץ וְשָׁמָיִם: His majesty is above earth and heaven.

וַיָּרֶם קֶרֶן ׀ לְעַמּוֹ 14 He has raised the horn of His people,
תְּהִלָּה לְכָל־חֲסִידָיו   glory for all His devoted ones,
לִבְנֵי יִשְׂרָאֵל עַם קְרֹבוֹ   for the children of Israel,
הַלְלוּיָהּ:   the people close to Him.
                         Halleluya!

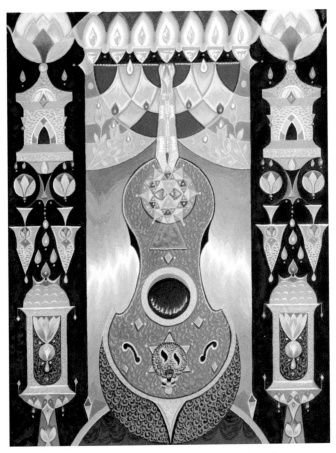

Sing to the LORD a new song, His praise in the assembly of the devoted

As our body ages so does our spirit.
The spirit we fashioned when we were young remains with us.
But the soul becomes new when it sings a new song.
Our souls urge us to compose new songs.
New times demand new songs. New songs create new times.

PSALM 149

הַלְלוּיָהּ ׀ שִׁירוּ לַיהוה שִׁיר חָדָשׁ תְּהִלָּתוֹ בִּקְהַל חֲסִידִים:	1 Halleluya! Sing to the LORD a new song, His praise in the assembly of the devoted.
יִשְׂמַח יִשְׂרָאֵל בְּעֹשָׂיו בְּנֵי־צִיּוֹן יָגִילוּ בְמַלְכָּם:	2 Let Israel rejoice in its Maker; let the children of Zion exult in their King.
יְהַלְלוּ שְׁמוֹ בְמָחוֹל בְּתֹף וְכִנּוֹר יְזַמְּרוּ־לוֹ:	3 Let them praise His name with dancing, sing praises to Him with timbrel and harp,
כִּי־רוֹצֶה יהוה בְּעַמּוֹ יְפָאֵר עֲנָוִים בִּישׁוּעָה:	4 for the LORD delights in His people; He adorns the humble with salvation.
יַעְלְזוּ חֲסִידִים בְּכָבוֹד יְרַנְּנוּ עַל־מִשְׁכְּבוֹתָם:	5 Let the devoted revel in glory; let them sing for joy on their beds.
רוֹמְמוֹת אֵל בִּגְרוֹנָם וְחֶרֶב פִּיפִיּוֹת בְּיָדָם:	6 Let high praises of God be in their throats and two-edged swords in their hands
לַעֲשׂוֹת נְקָמָה בַּגּוֹיִם תּוֹכֵחֹת בַּלְאֻמִּים:	7 to impose retribution on the nations, punishment on the peoples,
לֶאְסֹר מַלְכֵיהֶם בְּזִקִּים וְנִכְבְּדֵיהֶם בְּכַבְלֵי בַרְזֶל:	8 binding their kings with chains, their nobles with iron fetters,
לַעֲשׂוֹת בָּהֶם ׀ מִשְׁפָּט כָּתוּב הָדָר הוּא לְכָל־חֲסִידָיו הַלְלוּיָהּ:	9 carrying out the judgment written against them. This is the glory of all His devoted ones. Halleluya!

Let all that breathe praise the LORD. Halleluya!

Can you imagine how King David felt when he finally finished his book? Remember how you felt when you finished a long and arduous task? Ancient Perek Shira, "Chapter of Song," tells us the rest of the story. David turned to the Holy One, blessed be He. "Has any other living creature ever praised You with such songs?" He then met a frog who said: "David, don't gloat. I've composed many more songs than you and have attached three thousand fables to each."

PSALM 150

הַלְלוּ־יָהּ ׀	1	Halleluya!
הַלְלוּ־אֵל בְּקָדְשׁוֹ		Praise God in His Sanctuary;
הַלְלוּהוּ בִּרְקִיעַ עֻזּוֹ׃		praise Him in His powerful skies.
הַלְלוּהוּ בִגְבוּרֹתָיו	2	Praise Him for His mighty deeds;
הַלְלוּהוּ כְּרֹב גֻּדְלוֹ׃		praise Him for His surpassing greatness.
הַלְלוּהוּ בְּתֵקַע שׁוֹפָר	3	Praise Him with blasts of the shofar;
הַלְלוּהוּ בְּנֵבֶל וְכִנּוֹר׃		praise Him with the harp and lyre.
הַלְלוּהוּ בְּתֹף וּמָחוֹל	4	Praise Him with timbrel and dance;
הַלְלוּהוּ בְּמִנִּים וְעוּגָב׃		praise Him with strings and flute.
הַלְלוּהוּ בְצִלְצְלֵי־שָׁמַע	5	Praise Him with clashing cymbals;
הַלְלוּהוּ בְּצִלְצְלֵי תְרוּעָה׃		praise Him with resounding cymbals.
כֹּל הַנְּשָׁמָה תְּהַלֵּל יָהּ	6	Let all that breathe praise the LORD.
הַלְלוּ־יָהּ׃		Halleluya!

Koren Publishers Jerusalem